Oracle SOA BPEL Process Manager 11gR1 – A Hands-on Tutorial

Your step-by-step, hands-on guide to Oracle SOA BPEL PM 11gR1

Ravi Saraswathi

Jaswant Singh

[PACKT] enterprise 88
PUBLISHING
professional expertise distilled

BIRMINGHAM - MUMBAI

Oracle SOA BPEL Process Manager 11gR1 – A Hands-on Tutorial

First published: June 2013

Production Reference: 1130613

Published by Packt Publishing Ltd.
Livery Place
35 Livery Street
Birmingham B3 2PB, UK.

ISBN 978-1-84968-898-7

www.packtpub.com

Cover Image by Karl Moore (karl@karlmoore.co.uk)

Credits

Authors
Ravi Saraswathi

Jaswant Singh

Reviewers
Mehmet Demir

Hartmut Gräfenstein

Viral Kamdar

Antony Reynolds

Shanthi Viswanathan

Acquisition Editor
Antony Lowe

Lead Technical Editor
Neeshma Ramakrishnan

Technical Editors
Nitee Shetty

Dennis John

Project Coordinator
Amey Sawant

Proofreaders
Linda Morris

Kelly Hutchinson

Indexer
Monica Ajmera Mehta

Graphics
Ronak Dhruv

Abhinash Sahu

Valentina Dsilva

Production Coordinator
Shantanu Zagade

Cover Work
Shantanu Zagade

About the Authors

Ravi Saraswathi is an IT executive with more than 20 years of global professional experience. Ravi has expertise in aligning business and IT, SOA implementation, IT strategy, cloud infrastructure design, IT operations, security, architecture, and performance tuning. For over a decade now, Ravi has been successfully delivering large-scale technical projects and solutions. He is an expert in open source and vendor-based middleware products. From his experience, he gained a solid understanding of the tools and technologies needed to create large-scale web-based software and services.

Ravi currently heads the middleware engineering group for a highly-reputed Fortune 500 financial company. Ravi has spoken in several international conferences such as Apache, WebLogic conferences, and Java user group meetings. His professional focus is on technical management, SOA, middleware architecture, and infrastructure design.

Ravi holds a Masters in Technology Management from George Mason University and is a Bachelor of Engineering in Electronics and Communication Engineering from Karnataka University. Ravi holds a CIO University Certificate from Federal CIO University, General Services Administration, United States. He has extensive experience in architecting and designing solutions using various Oracle Fusion and open source middleware products.

Ravi is an aspiring leader and entrepreneur. He has founded a successful IT professional consulting company. He has trained many associates in Fusion Middleware 11*g* to gain the skills for developing and designing solutions using Oracle SOA Suite and Service Bus. He actively contributes to the online community for open source and commercial middleware products, SOA, cloud, BPM, and infrastructure architecture technologies.

Ravi holds various IT certifications such as TOGAF, Java, ITIL, Oracle, and WebLogic. His interests include open source containers, Java, infrastructure architecture, troubleshooting methodologies, and software design. Ravi blogs at www.ravisaraswathi.com.

Acknowledgement

This book would not have been possible without my wife Priya, who supported me on all those weekends and managed my work and life together. I would like to thank my children, Pritika and Vishnu, my mother Saraswathiamma, and my brother Reji for supporting my efforts in writing this book. I also thank my co-author and dear friend, Jaswant Singh for his contribution, support, and confidence throughout the writing process.

Jaswant Singh brings over 16 years of experience as an Executive Information Technologist with multiple industry verticals. Jaswant presently assists Fortune 1000 CXOs in creating, implementing, and managing technology strategy and roadmaps to gain efficiencies over existing capabilities and build new capabilities economically. As a CTO, he has co-founded *Suchna!*, a web portal linking people worldwide.

Jaswant has expertise in Service Oriented Architecture (SOA), cloud computing, big data, middleware technologies, and web architectures. He is also an expert in Business Continuity & Disaster Recovery (BCDR), Data Center migration and consolidation, and web applications security. He is known for building and leveraging cross-functional working relationships, mentoring, and problem solving for large global multi-organization environments across Asia Pacific, Europe, and North America.

Jaswant has been a recognized industry leader on emerging technologies at various professional trade conferences, companies, and educational institutes. He has been bestowed upon with various awards for outstanding performance, top talent, technological innovations, and technical publications. Jaswant blogs at `http://techblog.baghel.com`.

Jaswant received his CIO Certification from Federal CIO University, General Services Administration, United States. He received his M.S. degree in Technology Management from School of Management, George Mason University, and his M.S. degree in Mathematics with specialization in Operations Research and Statistics from Department of Mathematics, Indian Institute of Technology, Bombay. He served as the President of a cultural student body at the Indian Institute of Technology, Bombay.

I would like to thank my wife Mita for putting up with my writing sessions over weekends and late nights. I would also like to express deep gratitude towards my parents Ms. Kamla Devi and Mr. Jagram Singh for putting up with scaling down the summer outings.

I would also like to thank all of the mentors and mentees that I've had over the years. Last but not least, I would like to pay my sincere thanks to my dear friend and co-author Mr. Ravi Saraswathi.

About the Reviewers

Mehmet Demir is a TOGAF-certified enterprise architect with 15+ years of experience in designing systems for large companies. He has hands-on experience in developing and implementing SOA-based solutions using Oracle Fusion Middleware, WebCenter Portal, WebCenter Content, BEA WebLogic/AquaLogic product technologies, and Oracle Identity Access Management Suite. As an Oracle-certified SOA Architect, IBM-certified SOA Designer, BEA-certified Architect, and an Oracle WebCenter 11g-certified Implementation Specialist, Mehmet focuses on developing high-quality solutions using best practices.

He is currently working for EPAM Canada as an Enterprise Architect delivering high-value IT solutions to many of Canada's most prominent companies such as CIBC, Home Hardware, and Bell TV. Prior to EPAM, Mehmet worked for BEA Systems where he had been a principle member of the Canadian consulting team.

In addition to his technical capabilities, Mehmet has an MBA from Schulich School of Business and is a certified Project Manager with a PMI PMP designation.

Mehmet can be contacted at `http://ca.linkedin.com/in/demirmehmet`.

I would like to thank my beautiful wife Emily and my sweet daughter Lara for their support.

Viral Kamdar is a Principal Solution Architect for Oracle Identity Management products. He has a degree in Computer Science and over 12 years of experience working on enterprise applications using J2EE, SOA, and other middleware technologies.

Currently he is employed with Oracle Corporation in a specialized solution architecture team called the *A-team*. As a part of this team, he gets involved in solving complex customer problems, design discussions, and architecture reviews of fusion middleware products.

I would like to thank my wife for motivating me to review this book.

Antony Reynolds has worked in the IT industry for more than 25 years. First, getting a job to maintain yield calculations for a zinc smelter while still an undergraduate. After graduating from the University of Bristol with a degree in Mathematics and Computer Science, he worked first for a software house named IPL in Bath, England, before joining the travel reservations system named Galileo as a development team lead. Galileo gave him the opportunity to work in Colorado and Illinois where he developed a love for the Rockies and Chicago-style deep pan pizza.

Since joining Oracle in 1998, he has worked in sales consulting and support. He currently works as a sales consultant helping customers across North America realize the benefits of standards-based integration and SOA. While at Oracle, he has co-authored the following books:

- *Oracle SOA Suite 10g Developer's Guide, Packt Publishing*
- *Oracle SOA Suite 11gR1 Developer's Guide, Packt Publishing*
- *Oracle SOA Suite 11g Developer's Cookbook, Packt Publishing*

Antony lives in Colorado with his wife and four children who make sure that he is gainfully employed playing games, watching movies, and acting as an auxiliary taxi service. Antony is a slow but steady runner and can often be seen jogging up and down the trails in the shadow of the Rocky Mountains.

Shanthi Viswanathan is a freelance consultant helping clients with architecture, development, implementation, high availability, performance tuning, and capacity planning of Oracle Fusion Middleware products. She trains and mentors clients and assists in jumpstarting projects. She is currently on assignment with Canon, Europe as a Strategy Architect. Shanthi also teaches at Seton Hall University in New Jersey.

www.PacktPub.com

Support files, eBooks, discount offers and more

You might want to visit www.PacktPub.com for support files and downloads related to your book.

Did you know that Packt offers eBook versions of every book published, with PDF and ePub files available? You can upgrade to the eBook version at www.PacktPub.com and as a print book customer, you are entitled to a discount on the eBook copy. Get in touch with us at service@packtpub.com for more details.

At www.PacktPub.com, you can also read a collection of free technical articles, sign up for a range of free newsletters and receive exclusive discounts and offers on Packt books and eBooks.

http://PacktLib.PacktPub.com

Do you need instant solutions to your IT questions? PacktLib is Packt's online digital book library. Here, you can access, read and search across Packt's entire library of books.

Why Subscribe?

- Fully searchable across every book published by Packt
- Copy and paste, print and bookmark content
- On demand and accessible via web browser

Free Access for Packt account holders

If you have an account with Packt at www.PacktPub.com, you can use this to access PacktLib today and view nine entirely free books. Simply use your login credentials for immediate access.

Instant Updates on New Packt Books

Get notified! Find out when new books are published by following @PacktEnterprise on Twitter, or the *Packt Enterprise* Facebook page.

I would like to dedicate this book to my late father N.K Unnithan. You are deeply missed.

— Ravi Saraswathi

I would like to dedicate this book to our families.

— Jaswant Singh

Table of Contents

Preface	**1**
Chapter 1: Creating Basic BPEL Processes	**7**
Evolution of web applications	7
Evolution of integration technologies	8
An introduction to BPEL	8
Installing and configuring BPEL Process Manager	13
Step 1 – install Oracle JDeveloper	14
Installing SOA extensions	17
Step 2 – download and install Oracle Database	20
Step 3 – install Oracle SOA Suite	28
Creating an SOA Suite domain	32
Creating sample BPEL business processes	41
Deploying BPEL business processes	47
Testing and managing BPEL business process instances	53
Summary	55
Chapter 2: Configuring BPEL Processes	**57**
Understanding the BPEL language framework	57
BPEL activities	58
Creating basic activities in BPEL	59
Activities	62
Basic activities	64
Structured activities	67
Fault and error handling	68
Synchronous versus asynchronous processes	69
Selecting the timeout value for synchronous processes	72
BPEL correlation	74
Creating a Correlation set	74
Associating the Correlation set	76

Creating property aliases	**76**
Adapters	**77**
Database Adapter	79
File Adapter	80
JMS Adapter	81
Web Service Adapter	81
Implementing human workflow with Human Task components	84
Summary	**86**
Chapter 3: Invoking a BPEL Process	**87**
Communicating between BPEL to/from Java	**87**
Invoking a BPEL process from Java	88
Invoking a service from a BPEL process	**89**
Partner Link	90
Writing Java code within BPEL activities	92
Invoking Java from BPEL	**92**
Configuring BPEL timeouts	**93**
Setting the JTA Transaction Timeout aka Global Transaction Timeout parameters	93
Changing the SyncMaxWaitTime parameter	94
Transaction settings	96
BPEL EJB's transaction timeout	96
Timeout for Asynchronous BPELs	98
Summary	**101**
Chapter 4: Orchestrating BPEL Services	**103**
Orchestration	**106**
Designing orchestration	**107**
Flow	109
Switch	112
Custom XPath functions	116
Creating custom XPath functions	117
Custom XPath function class	118
Registering with SOA Suite	118
Registering with JDeveloper	119
Scope	119
BPEL variables	**122**
Human Task	**126**
Worklist application	126
Creating human tasks	127
Standalone Human Task – expose as a service	127
Human Task – part of a BPEL process	128

Business Rules engine **131**
Adding business rules as part of a BPEL process 132
Creating business rules 134
Facts and Bucketsets 135
Summary **137**
Chapter 5: Test and Troubleshoot SOA Composites **139**
Testing SOA composites from the EM **140**
Testing a composite from JDeveloper **142**
Viewing instances and messages on JDeveloper **143**
Creating a test suite **144**
Initiating the Test 146
Emulating inbound messages 146
Emulating outbound messages 147
The Dehydration Store **149**
Options for purging the Dehydration Store 150
Troubleshooting **151**
BPEL Process Manager logging **153**
Domain logs 154
Access.log 154
The admin/managed server log 156
The logging level 158
The audit level 160
Monitoring 164
The MBean browser **167**
Summary **168**
Chapter 6: Architect and Design Services Using BPEL **169**
Services architecture and design guidelines **169**
Services-based application design **170**
SOA Suite 171
Enterprise Service Bus (ESB) 171
Use case of the service bus 172
Interaction design patterns **174**
Synchronous request and response 174
Asynchronous request and response 175
One request and multiple responses 176
One request, a mandatory response, and an optional response 176
One-way message 177
Event-Driven Architecture (EDA) **177**
Request-driven interaction 178
Event-driven interaction 178

Human tasks   **179**
Summary   **181**

**Chapter 7: Performance Tuning – Systems Running
BPEL Processes**   **183**
   The Java Virtual Machine   **184**
     Garbage collection process   184
       Young generation   185
       Tenured generation   185
       Permanent generation   186
     Garbage collection tuning   186
       Choosing the garbage collection algorithm   187
     Garbage collection tool – JVisualVM   188
   SOA Suite   **190**
     SOA infra application   190
     The WebLogic console   190
     The enterprise manager   191
     Dynamic Monitoring Service (DMS)   192
     The B2B console   192
     The System MBeans browser   194
     SOA Suite tuning   195
   Load balancers   **200**
   Operating system   **201**
     File descriptors   201
     Adaptors   202
   Database   **202**
     Dehydration store   203
     Init.Ora   203
     Automatic Workload Repository   203
   Summary   **205**

**Chapter 8: Integrating the BPEL Process Manager with
Service Bus, Registry, and SOA Deployment**   **207**
   The SOA composite application architecture   **207**
   Oracle Registry   **210**
     Service Registry install   213
     Publish services to registry   214
     Consume services from registry   216
   Service bus   **218**
   SOA Suite deployment   **221**
   Summary   **226**

Chapter 9: Securing a BPEL Process — 227

Securing a BPEL process — 228
Enterprise Security Gateway — 229
Oracle Web Service Manager (OWSM) — 230
OWSM security implementation use cases — 232
  Attaching security policies using the OWSM console — 233
  Attaching security policies using JDeveloper — 235
  WS-Security — 236
OWSM implementation – an example — 239
  Configuring a secured service provider with username tokens — 239
  Configuring a service client for calling a secured web service — 241
Oracle security products — 242
  Oracle Identity Manager — 243
  Oracle Entitlement Server — 244
Network Firewall with Intrusion Prevention System — 246
Web Application Firewall — 247
Data security in Transit and at Rest — 247
Summary — 248

Chapter 10: Architecting High Availability for Business Services — 249

SOA environment — 250
Cluster architecture — 251
Load balancer(s) — 253
Compute resource(s) — 253
  Web server(s) – clustering for scalability and availability — 253
  WebLogic application server(s) and Oracle SOA Suite server(s) – clustering
  for scalability and availability — 254
  Database clustering — 255
Backup and recovery strategy — 257
Data center(s) — 257
Deployment architecture options — 258
  Multi data center deployment — 260
Oracle Service Bus — 262
Summary — 262

Chapter 11: The Future of Process Modeling — 263

Commercial off-the-shelf (COTS) — 264
The evolution of business process modeling — 265
Business Process Management (BPM) — 266
Oracle BPM Suite and BPA Suite — 268
Modeling the process – BPMN — 270
BPM Studio — 270
Summary — 274

Chapter 12: Troubleshooting Techniques — 275

JVM issues — 276
  JVM troubleshooting tools — 277
  Linux troubleshooting commands — 278
Application issues — 282
Database issues — 284
CPU spikes — 284
Load balancing issues — 285
SSL issues — 286
Network issues — 286
User activity issues — 287
  Verifying the server health — 287
Extending to a domain — 290
  Oracle troubleshooting tools — 291
    Oracle Remote Diagnostics Agent — 291
  WebLogic Diagnostic Framework — 292
Summary — 294
Index — 295

Preface

For implementing business process agility using Oracle SOA BPEL Process Manager, most books cover few of the following domains:

- Designing and architecting SOA composite applications
- Developing SOA composite applications using BPEL
- Testing and debugging SOA composite applications
- Installing, configuring, deploying, securing, and administering SOA composite applications

In this book, we have combined these domains to deliver the complete handbook. It provides our readers an understanding of what goes outside of their direct responsibilities. This horizontal understanding improves the collaboration among the cross functional groups that would result in increased team productivity.

This book is a comprehensive hands-on industry-leading-practice guide to deliver real-world SOA composite applications using the Oracle SOA Suite BPEL Process Manager platform. The content is 90 percent hands-on instructions with 10 percent of details. You will find an overview of technical fundamentals, step-by-step tutorials, and industry leading practices implementing SOA composite applications.

What this book covers

This book will teach you how to design, develop, test, deploy, secure, and administer an SOA composite application.

Chapter 1, Creating Basic BPEL Processes, provides an understanding of the concept and evolution of Business Process Execution Language (BPEL) and also provides step-by-step instructions for downloading, installing, and configuring Oracle SOA Suite BPEL Processer Manager Platform and JDeveloper.

Chapter 2, Configuring BPEL Processes, teaches about the BPEL language and helps you create basic and complex BPEL processes using JDeveloper and Oracle SOA Suite BPEL Process Manager Platform.

Chapter 3, Invoking a BPEL Process, teaches from examples how to invoke BPEL processes from any Java client or web services and vice versa. It also teaches how to configure transaction timeout for BPEL services.

Chapter 4, Orchestrating BPEL Services, provides step-by-step instructions for designing, creating, and configuring BPEL orchestration, adaptors, business rules, and human workflow. Some of the advanced BPEL orchestration techniques are covered as well.

Chapter 5, Test and Troubleshoot SOA Composites, teaches with examples how to create test suites for BPEL services, how to debug and troubleshoot Oracle SOA Suite Platform and BPEL processes. It also covers dehydration store purge strategies, SOA composites monitoring, SOA Suite logging, and audit configurations.

Chapter 6, Architect and Design Services Using BPEL, covers Oracle SOA Suite components and their use cases, interactions, BPEL design patterns, request- and event- driven architecture. It provides step-by-step instructions for integrating BPEL Process Manager with Oracle Service Bus along with instructions on achieving loose coupling using Oracle Enterprise Service Bus.

Chapter 7, Performance Tuning – Systems Running BPEL Processes, covers performance tuning of SOA composite applications for optimal performance and scalability. The industry leading practices for the Oracle SOA Suite platform components, WebLogic server platform, JVM, operating systems, and load balancers are also included.

Chapter 8, Integrating the BPEL Process Manager with Service Bus, Registry, and SOA Deployment, introduces the design of SOA composite application, use cases of Oracle Service Bus (OSB) and Oracle Registry (OSR) along with ways to create and consume services from Registry and Service Bus. The chapter also takes a look at the deployment of an SOA composite application using JDeveloper and Oracle Enterprise Manager's console.

Chapter 9, Securing a BPEL Process, introduces various options to design and implement a security solution for securing a BPEL process. This chapter provides the available security options and industry leading practices to implement authentication, authorization, data security in transit, and denial-of-service attacks for SOA composite applications. The usage of Oracle Web Service Manager (OWSM) for securing web services are described in detail.

Chapter 10, Architecting High Availability for Business Services, explains the systems architecture options for achieving high availability for SOA composite application's design and deployment. This chapter delves deeper into deployment architecture options – cluster architecture for achieving high scalability and availability of composite applications.

Chapter 11, The Future of Process Modeling, explains the evolution of Process Modeling and what to expect in the near future from various stakeholders in this domain. Also covered are the basics of Oracle BPM Suite (Business Process Management), BPA Suite (Business Process Analysis), along with BPMN (Business Process Model and Notation). It also explains how to use JDeveloper to design and develop process models using BPMN.

Chapter 12, Troubleshooting Techniques, covers possible issues during deployment and runtime with SOA Suite BPEL Process Manager and their troubleshooting techniques. The key takeaway is that knowing all the possible reasons for an issue and then going through the process of elimination to identify the root cause of the issue. The art and science lies in ranking the possible reasons and selecting which one to eliminate first for an issue at hand.

What you need for this book
- Oracle SOA Suite 11*g* Release 11*g*R1 (11.1.1.7.0)
- BPEL Process Manager
- Oracle Business Rules
- Oracle Web service Manager (OWSM)
- Oracle Business Activity Monitoring (BAM)
- Oracle JDeveloper 11*g* (11.1.2.4.0)
- JDeveloper Extension - Oracle SOA Composite Editor (11.1.2.4.0)
- Oracle Database Express Edition 11*g* Release 2
- Oracle Service Bus Release 11*g*R1 (11.1.1.7.0)
- Oracle Service Registry (11.1.1.6.0)
- Oracle BPM Suite 11*g*R1 (11.1.1.7.0)
- Oracle BPA Suite 11*g* Release 1 (11.1.1.7)
- JDK 6

Who this book is for

This book is primarily written for the following:

- SOA Developers: To develop SOA Composite applications
- Administrators: To install, configure, deploy, troubleshoot, and for performance tuning of SOA Suite Platform
- Enterprise/Security/System/Infrastructure architects: To design composite applications, create infrastructure and system architecture, and to design security solutions
- Business Analysts/QA Testers, Project Managers, and Engineers: To design SOA services and business processes, monitor and test composite applications, and oversee &/ manage SOA projects

Conventions

In this book, you will find a number of styles of text that distinguish between different kinds of information. Here are some examples of these styles, and an explanation of their meaning.

Code words in text are shown as follows: "To avoid the install error message, provide the location of JDK/JRE while running the setup.exe file from the command line."

Any command-line input or output is written as follows:

```
setup.exe -jreLoc C:\Oracle\Middleware\jdk160_24
```

New terms and **important words** are shown in bold. Words that you see on the screen, in menus or dialog boxes for example, appear in the text like this: "You'll see the **Middleware Home Directory** screen (if needed, update the install directory), click on **Next.**".

[Warnings or important notes appear in a box like this.]

[Tips and tricks appear like this.]

Reader feedback

Feedback from our readers is always welcome. Let us know what you think about this book—what you liked or may have disliked. Reader feedback is important for us to develop titles that you really get the most out of.

To send us general feedback, simply send an e-mail to feedback@packtpub.com, and mention the book title via the subject of your message.

If there is a topic that you have expertise in and you are interested in either writing or contributing to a book, see our author guide on www.packtpub.com/authors.

Customer support

Now that you are the proud owner of a Packt book, we have a number of things to help you to get the most from your purchase.

Errata

Although we have taken every care to ensure the accuracy of our content, mistakes do happen. If you find a mistake in one of our books—maybe a mistake in the text or the code—we would be grateful if you would report this to us. By doing so, you can save other readers from frustration and help us improve subsequent versions of this book. If you find any errata, please report them by visiting http://www.packtpub.com/submit-errata, selecting your book, clicking on the **errata submission form** link, and entering the details of your errata. Once your errata are verified, your submission will be accepted and the errata will be uploaded on our website, or added to any list of existing errata, under the Errata section of that title. Any existing errata can be viewed by selecting your title from http://www.packtpub.com/support.

Piracy

Piracy of copyright material on the Internet is an ongoing problem across all media. At Packt, we take the protection of our copyright and licenses very seriously. If you come across any illegal copies of our works, in any form, on the Internet, please provide us with the location address or website name immediately so that we can pursue a remedy.

Please contact us at copyright@packtpub.com with a link to the suspected pirated material.

We appreciate your help in protecting our authors, and our ability to bring you valuable content.

Questions

You can contact us at questions@packtpub.com if you are having a problem with any aspect of the book, and we will do our best to address it.

1
Creating Basic BPEL Processes

Over a period of time, people are in the process of finding ways to reuse existing applications to build new applications that are cheaper and faster and achieve interoperability between applications. Loosely-coupled integration of existing applications is required to achieve application agility for timely responses to the changing business requirements. BPEL is one of the leading integration technologies to implement agility for composite applications.

Evolution of web applications

Web applications can be created in multiple ways that depend on the business requirements. There are four generations of web applications which are currently used by the businesses. The first generation web applications were simply informational and static in nature. The second generation web applications enabled interaction with end users and dynamically presented and performed simple transactions online. The third and fourth generation web applications are allowing businesses to perform complex business transactions online that have increased the need for simplifying system integration and reusability of existing enterprise applications with agility.

Evolution of integration technologies

Organizations iteratively work on improving and modifying business processes to stay competitive in the market. This requires application implementations to be more flexible that by design adapt to the changes in business processes. In other words, most enterprise businesses need agility in creating and maintaining applications to run mission-critical businesses functions, and that requires a platform to quickly create and update business process and/or workflow services. Usually these business process services are composite services that depend on the multiple services within and between enterprises. The application's platform, that enables mission-critical business processes online, is easy to maintain if they are developed using technology components such as SOA and BPEL.

This book uses the JDeveloper IDE for designing and validating BPEL services and Oracle BPEL Process Manager (part of SOA Suite) platform, which has a runtime engine, for BPEL services.

An introduction to BPEL

BPEL stands for **Business Process Execution Language**. The standard body for BPEL is **Organization for the Advancement of Structured Information Standards (OASIS)** that produces worldwide standards incorporating industry consensus. The syntax of BPEL is XML-based and the current specification is WSBPEL Version 2.0.

BPEL is a programming language that has a mix of structured (blocks) and unstructured (control-links and events). BPEL is used for designing business processes that integrate web services into end-to-end process flow, and for the orchestration of business services. BPEL is mainly used for orchestrating services. The following figure shows the sample structure of a BPEL process:

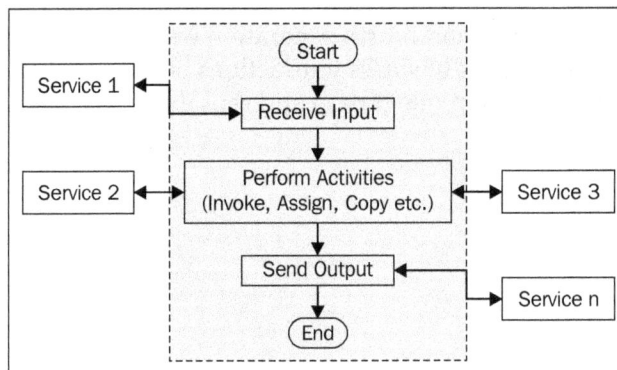

A brief description of BPEL is given as follows:

- BPEL is one of the leading specifications to standardize orchestration logic and process automation between web services.

- The key benefit of BPEL is about leveraging more from existing application assets. BPEL enables legacy applications to be deployed as web services and orchestrated across platforms.

- Identifying and documenting both the existing and new required high-level business process is a time-consuming but essential job.

- BPEL enables developers to develop processes quickly by defining the order in which services will be invoked and provide an easy interface to connect processes from external systems.

- Business Process Execution Language for web services provides a means to formally specify business processes and interaction protocols. BPEL is acting as a glue to bind web services into a cohesive business solution and facilitating their orchestrated interaction within and between enterprises.

- Web service is an integration model created for allowing integration of systems built using heterogeneous tools and technologies. BPEL is one of the core components for defining composite web services to perform complex business functions.

BPEL syntax is based on XML. Therefore, it may not be a good idea to design and develop BPEL code by using a text/XML editor. A visual BPEL editor under JDeveloper IDE helps to develop and validate BPEL code easily without memorizing the BPEL specifications line by line. The following figure shows the interaction between a BPEL process and other services:

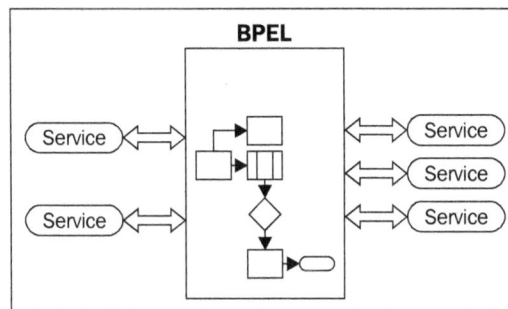

To deploy and execute BPEL processes, one needs Oracle Business Process Manager Engine. Currently Business Process Manager is part of Oracle SOA Suite. This book covers Version 11.1.1.16 of Oracle SOA Suite.

The following figure shows details of the components that interact with a sample BPEL service:

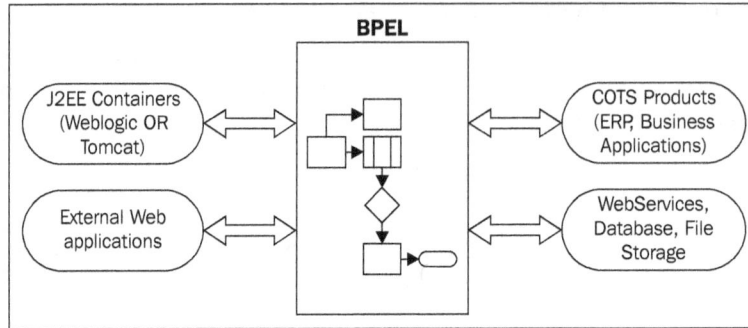

OASIS **Web Services Business Process Execution Language (WSBPEL)** is a vendor-neutral specification.

BPEL process manager is one of the components of the Oracle SOA Suite. The Oracle SOA Suite is a combination of multiple applications created by Oracle developers and deployed in a WebLogic container. For example, SOA Infra.ear, Adaptors, B2B, and so on.

Four separate main components/engines are included in SOA Suite. Each of these components has been created by Oracle developers using JSP, Servlets, EJB, JMS, RDBMS, and other system components.

- BPEL Processes
- Mediator
- Business Rules
- Human Task

BPMN (BPM Suite) is another component that can configure along with SOA Suite. SOA Infra is the core application. Similar to any enterprise web application, SOA Suite uses a database for storing the metadata information. For example, SOA Infra application uses database schemas for storing all the application information.

Oracle SOA Suite, along with JDeveloper IDE, enables the following:

- Design and develop business services
- Manage business services
- Orchestrate services in to SOA composite applications
- Provide a runtime engine for deploying and managing SOA composite applications

The following figure shows different service components of an SOA Suite:

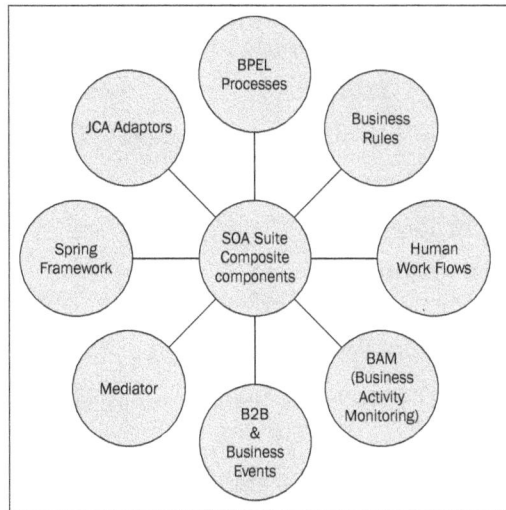

JDeveloper packages various SOA components as SOA composite applications. SOA composite applications may contain some or all of the following components:

- BPEL processes for process orchestration
- Human workflows for modeling human interactions such as approving a salary increment for an HR system
- Mediator for routing and transforming the messages (Oracle Service bus can be used for the same purpose
- Spring framework for integrating Java interfaces to SOA Composite applications
- Business rules for acting as a simple rules engine

Since Oracle SOA Suite runs on top of WebLogic container, you can deploy normal J2EE components as part of SOA composite applications; however, it may not be a good idea to use SOA Suite as a normal J2EE container. Separate the J2EE components and deploy it in another instance of WebLogic instances. Some of the J2EE components are listed as follows:

- Oracle **Application Development Framework (ADF)** is a Java framework initiated from the original **Model View Controller (MVC)** framework
- EJB service for adding enterprise services
- J2EE technologies such as JSP, Servlet, and JSF for web applications
- JMS for messaging

Following are the Oracle SOA Suite management applications and services as part of the SOA Suite installation:

- **Welcome Page**: `http://{hostname}:{port}`
- **Admin Server**: `http://{hostname}:{port}/console`
- **Enterprise Manager (EM)**: `http://{hostname}:{port}/em`
- **Dynamic Monitoring Service (DMS)**: `http://{hostname}:{port}/dms`
- **B2B**: `http://{hostname}:{port}/b2bconsole`
- **Web Services Inspection Language (WSIL)**:
  `http://{hostname}:{port}/inspection.wsil`
- **Web Services Manager (WSM)**: `http://{hostname}:{port}/wsm-pm`
- **Composer**: `http://{hostname}:{port}/soa/composer`
- **DefaultToDo**:
  `http://{hostname}:{port}/workflow/DefaultToDoTaskFlow`
- **Worklist**: `http://{hostname}:{port}/integration/worklistapp`
- **MessagingService endpoint**:
  `http://{hostname}:{port}/ucs/messaging/webservice`
- **MessagingServices preferences**:
  `http://{hostname}:{port}/sdpmessaging/userprefs-ui`
- **SOA-Infra**: `http://{hostname}:{port}/soa-infra/`

> Please note, that for all the service endpoints, you need to replace the hostname and port. For example:
>
> http://{hostname}:{port}/console
>
> Where `{hostname}` is a parameter that you replace with the hostname or IP address of your installation, `{port}` is the port number on which the server is listening for requests (`7001` by default).
>
> Example of the personal installation URL is as follows:
>
>   http://localhost:7001/console/

The concept of composition is to create enterprise solutions by assembling instead of building from scratch. Object-oriented programming allows for reusing the code within the applications. The concept of composite applications allows for reusing the existing applications.

As shown in the following figure, a brand new building is created by assembling pre-built components to cut down the construction time. Similar to creating a new building by assembling components, BPEL allows for creating business processes from existing services:

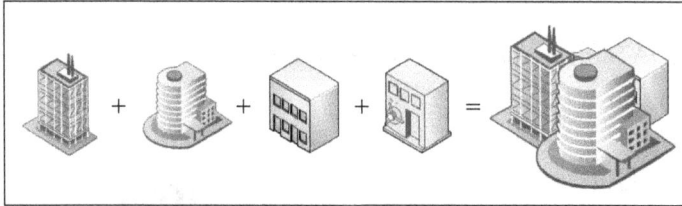

Installing and configuring BPEL Process Manager

This section focuses on setting up the development environment to design and develop business process services using BPEL. The following figure shows the typical environment system components for designing and developing a BPEL service:

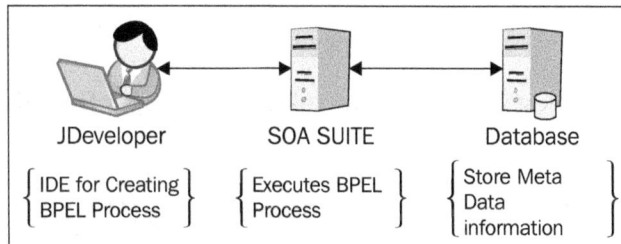

BPEL Process Manager is part of SOA Suite for Version 11.1.1.6. The development environment for creating and updating BPEL Process Manager requires the JDeveloper IDE with SOA Suite extension, a database with SOA Suite Schemas, and an SOA Suite.

The following are the steps to be followed:

1. Install Oracle JDeveloper
   - Install JDeveloper
   - Install SOA Extensions

2. Install SOA Suite Database Schemas

3. Install Oracle SOA Suite

Step 1 – install Oracle JDeveloper

Setting up the development environment involves three major steps. As shown in the following figure, the first step is to install JDeveloper and SOA Extensions:

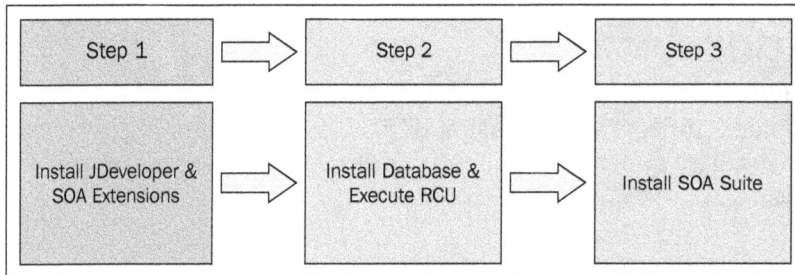

As shown in the following screenshot, download JDeveloper from the Oracle's website:

Release Downloads for Oracle JDeveloper 11g (11.1.1.6.0)
This page consolidates all download links for Oracle JDeveloper. Visit the Installation Guide for Oracle JDeveloper for an overview of the installation process and the Oracle JDeveloper Certification Information for platform specific information.

The downloads below are provided for customers under the OTN JDeveloper License Agreement. Current customers should download their software via our Oracle Software Delivery Cloud, which offers different license terms.

○ Accept License Agreement   ○ Decline License Agreement

Oracle JDeveloper 11g (11.1.1.6.0) (Build 6192)Installations

This is the release of Oracle JDeveloper 11g (11.1.1.6.0) (Build 6192). See the Documentation tab for Release Notes, Installation Guides and other release specific information. You can also view the List of New Features and Samples provided for this release.

Studio Edition: 11.1.1.6.0

Windows Install (Size: 1227 MB) ▼ [Download File]

> Install JDeveloper 11.1.1.6.0 or a newer version. Please note that installing JDeveloper Version 11.1.1.6 installs the following products preconfigured and ready to use with JDeveloper:
> - WebLogic Server Version 10.3.6
> - JDK

1. Install JDeveloper by executing `jdevstudio11116install.exe`. One of the major steps for the installation process is configuring a new, or using an existing, middleware home directory. This will install WebLogic along with JDeveloper, as shown in the following screenshot:

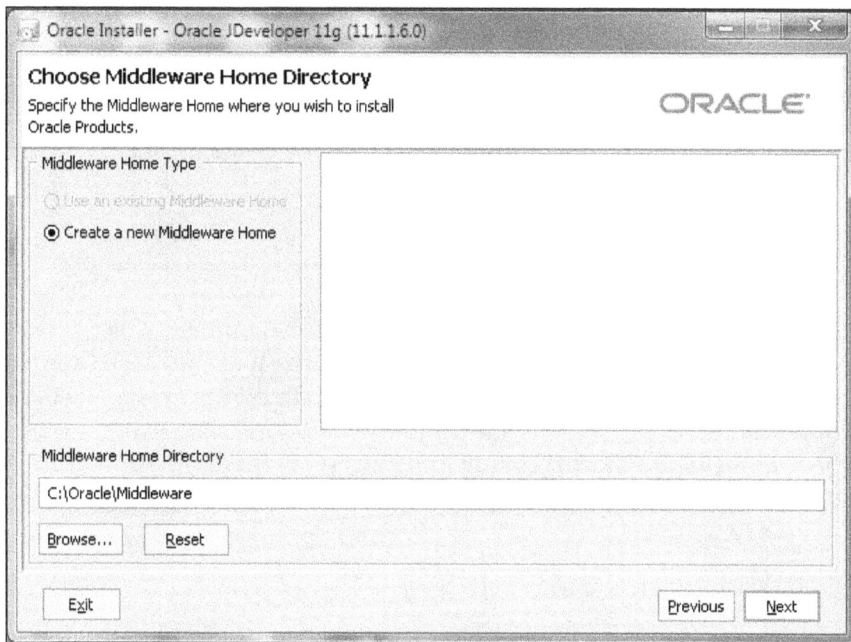

2. You'll see the **Middleware Home Directory** screen (if needed, update the install directory), click on **Next**. Then select **Complete** and again click on **Next**.

3. The next screen will list the Middleware Home and Product Installation directories. Click on **Next**. We recommend keeping the default selection of **All Users**, as shown in the following screenshot and click on **Next**:

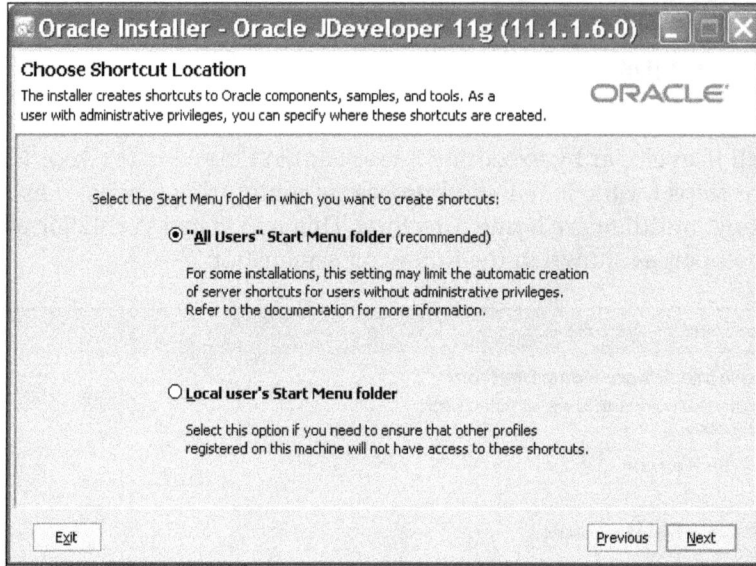

4. On the next screen you will find the installation summary. Click on **Next** on the **Installation Summary** window that will start installing the Oracle JDeveloper. On completion of the installation, you will see the congratulations window, as shown in the following screenshot. Please check the **Run Quickstart** option and click on **Done**:

5. On next window, click on **Launch Oracle JDeveloper 11g** and select the **Default Role** option and leave **Always prompt for role selection on startup** selected, as shown in the following screenshot and click on **OK**. On the next window, make sure to associate the file types of JDeveloper Application, JDeveloper Project, Java Source File, and Java Server Page with JDeveloper:

Installing SOA extensions

The SOA extension for JDeveloper contains SOA Composite Assembly, BPEL PM, Mediator, Human Task, Business Rules, and Adapters. These components are deployed and configured as part of SOA Suite installs. The JDeveloper extensions are only for design.

Perform the following steps to install SOA extensions. An alternative approach is to download the SOA Composite Editor – JDeveloper extensions from **Oracle Fusion Middleware Products Update Center** from Oracle's website.

1. Select **Check for Updates** from the **Help** tab, as shown in the following screenshot and then click on **Next** on the Welcome window:

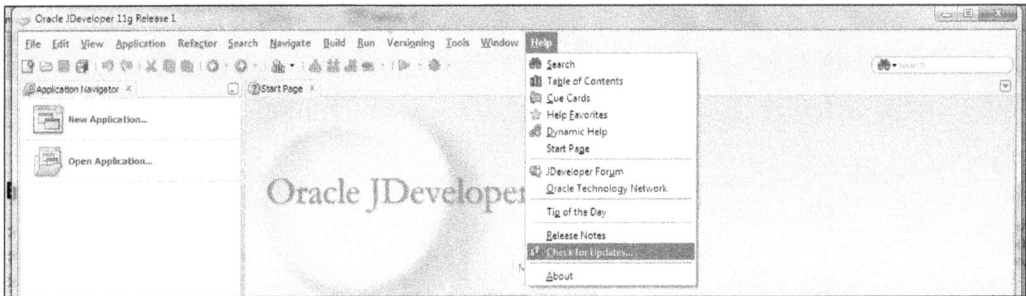

2. Select **Oracle Fusion Middleware Products** and **Official Oracle Extensions and Updates**. Make sure you are connected to the Internet. Another alternative is to download the SOA extensions in the hard disk and manually configure it in JDeveloper:

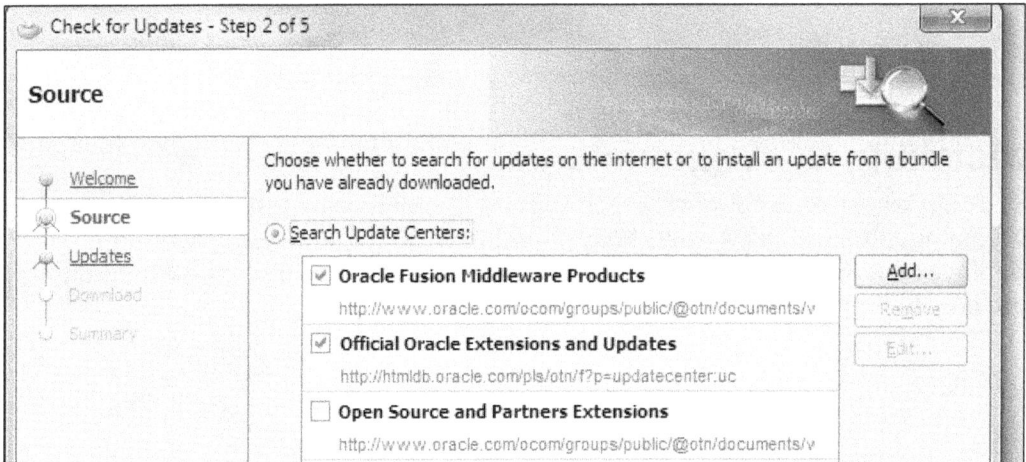

3. Select the SOA composite editor. This will install the SOA extensions required for creating and updating BPEL services. Click on **Next**:

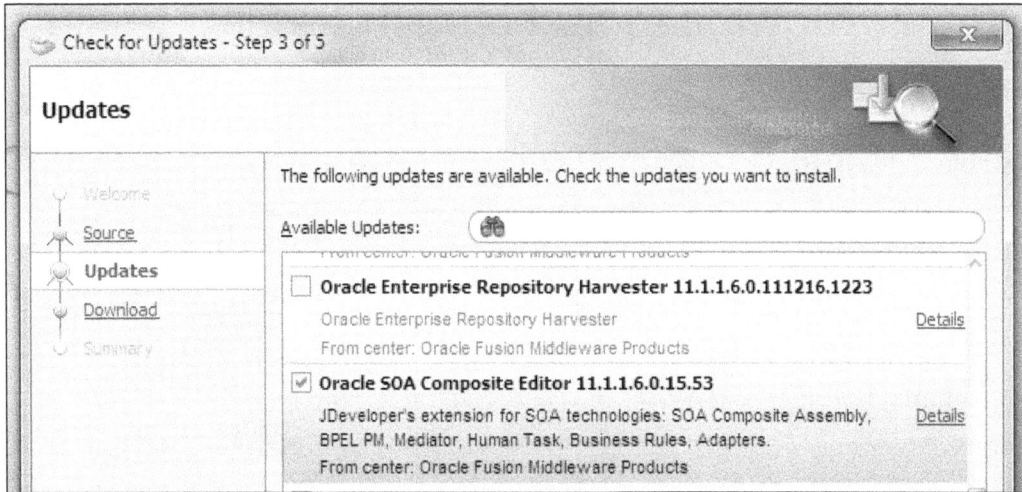

4. On the next window, it will display that it is downloading and installing the SOA extension for the JDeveloper. On a successful install, you will see the **Installation Summary** window, as shown in the following screenshot. Click on **Finish** to complete the SOA extension install and restart the JDeveloper. This completes the installation of JDeveloper with SOA Suite extensions:

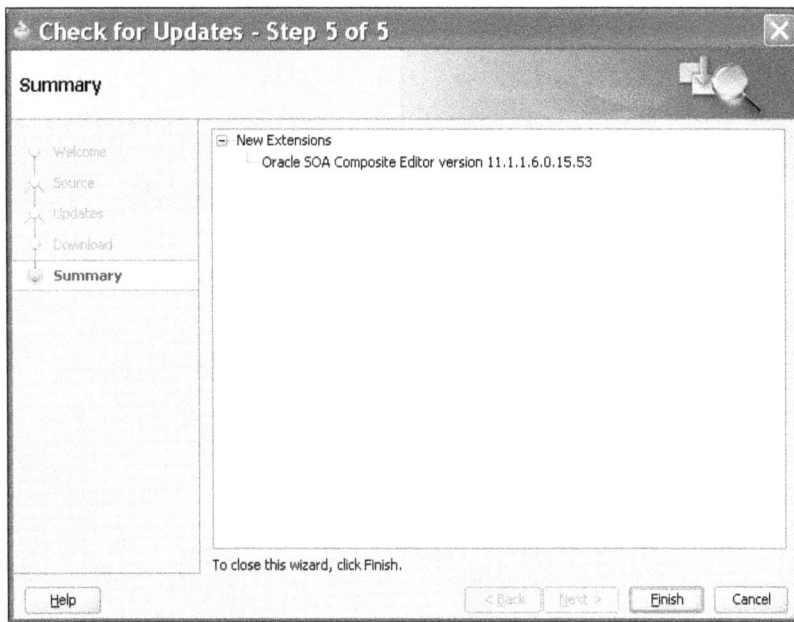

Step 2 – download and install Oracle Database

As shown in the following screenshot, the second step is to install a database and execute an RCU script for creating SOA schemas:

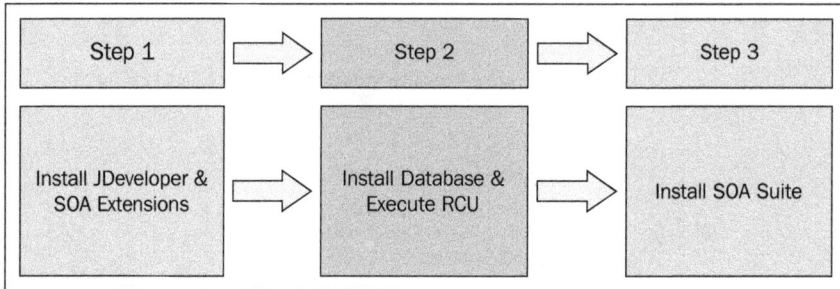

This step assumes that you have got an Oracle database server installed and you have database admin privileges to run **Repository Creation Utility (RCU)**. In the case of personal Oracle Express Database, start the database service if it is not running. One can use the **Start Database** option from the Start menu options.

Open a Windows shell command prompt and run `sqlplus system/{password}@XE as sysdba` to log in to Oracle Express Database.

The default limit of `processes` is not sufficient for creating the SOA Suite schema. Set the `processes` to `600` for all the SIDs, as given in the following lines of command:

```
SQL> alter system reset sessions scope=spfile sid='*';
SQL> alter system set processes=600 scope=spfile;
```

Make the changes effective immediately with the following command:

```
SQL> shutdown immediate
```

Using system Start menu's **Start Database** menu options start the Oracle Database service.

Validate the system settings with the following steps:

1. Connect to the database using a Windows shell command prompt and run `sqlplus system/{password}@XE as sysdba`.

   `SQL> show parameter session`

   `SQL> show parameter processes`

```
C:\WINDOWS\system32\cmd.exe - sqlplus system/weblogic123...    - □ ×

C:\Documents and Settings\User>sqlplus system/weblogic123@XE as sysdba

SQL*Plus: Release 11.2.0.2.0 Production on Sat Jul 28 09:05:29 2012

Copyright (c) 1982, 2010, Oracle.  All rights reserved.


Connected to:
Oracle Database 11g Express Edition Release 11.2.0.2.0 - Production

SQL> show parameter session

NAME                                 TYPE        VALUE
------------------------------------ ----------- ------------------------------
java_max_sessionspace_size           integer     0
java_soft_sessionspace_limit         integer     0
license_max_sessions                 integer     0
license_sessions_warning             integer     0
session_cached_cursors               integer     50
session_max_open_files               integer     10
sessions                             integer     922
shared_server_sessions               integer
SQL> show parameter processes

NAME                                 TYPE        VALUE
------------------------------------ ----------- ------------------------------
aq_tm_processes                      integer     0
db_writer_processes                  integer     1
gcs_server_processes                 integer     0
global_txn_processes                 integer     1
job_queue_processes                  integer     4
log_archive_max_processes            integer     4
processes                            integer     600
SQL>
```

2. Set the `RCU_JDBC_TRIM_BLOCKS` variable as `TRUE` before creating the schemas using RCU if your database is Oracle XE.

   > RCU_JDBC_TRIM_BLOCKS is an environment variable with the operating system. Please note, that RCU_JDBC_TRIM_BLOCKS is *not* a variable in Oracle XE!

3. In Windows, you need to navigate to **Control Panel | Advanced system settings | Advanced**. From under **System Properties**, click on **Environment Variables**. An **Environment Variables** dialog appears. From under the **System variables** section, click on **New**. A **New System Variable** dialog appears. Set the **Variable Name** as RCU_JDBC_TRIM_BLOCKS and **Variable Value** as TRUE, as shown in the following screenshot:

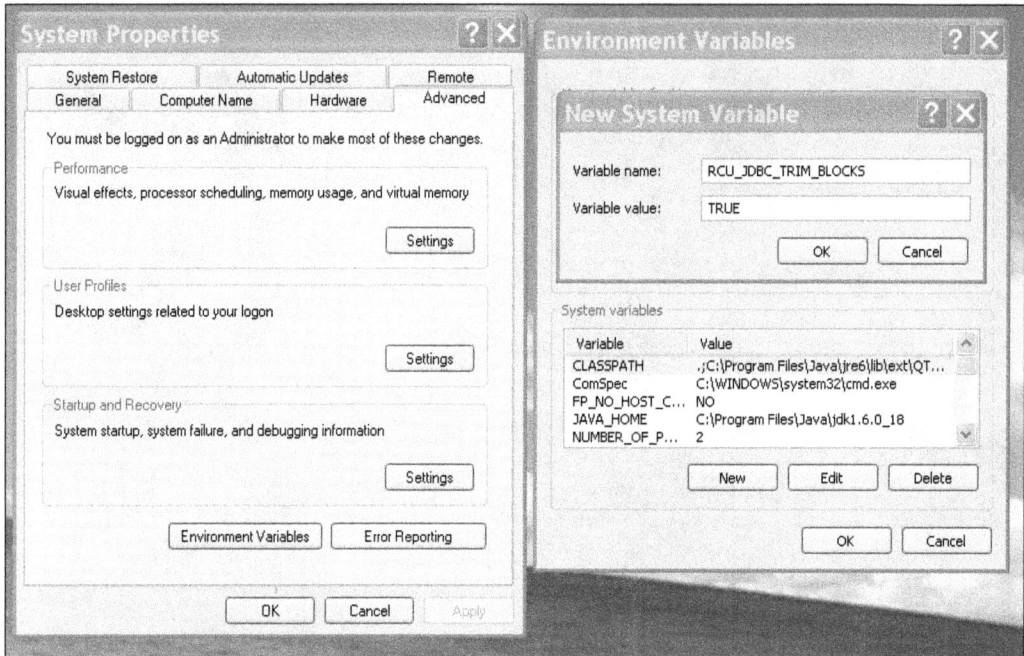

4. For creating RCU schemas, execute `rcu.bat` from the `bin` folder located at `{FullPath}\rcuHome\BIN`. Please note, that `rcu.bat` won't work with the files and folders names having a space in them. It will display the repository creation utility (RCU). Click on **Next** on the **Welcome** window that will take you to the **Create Repository** step, as shown in the following screenshot:

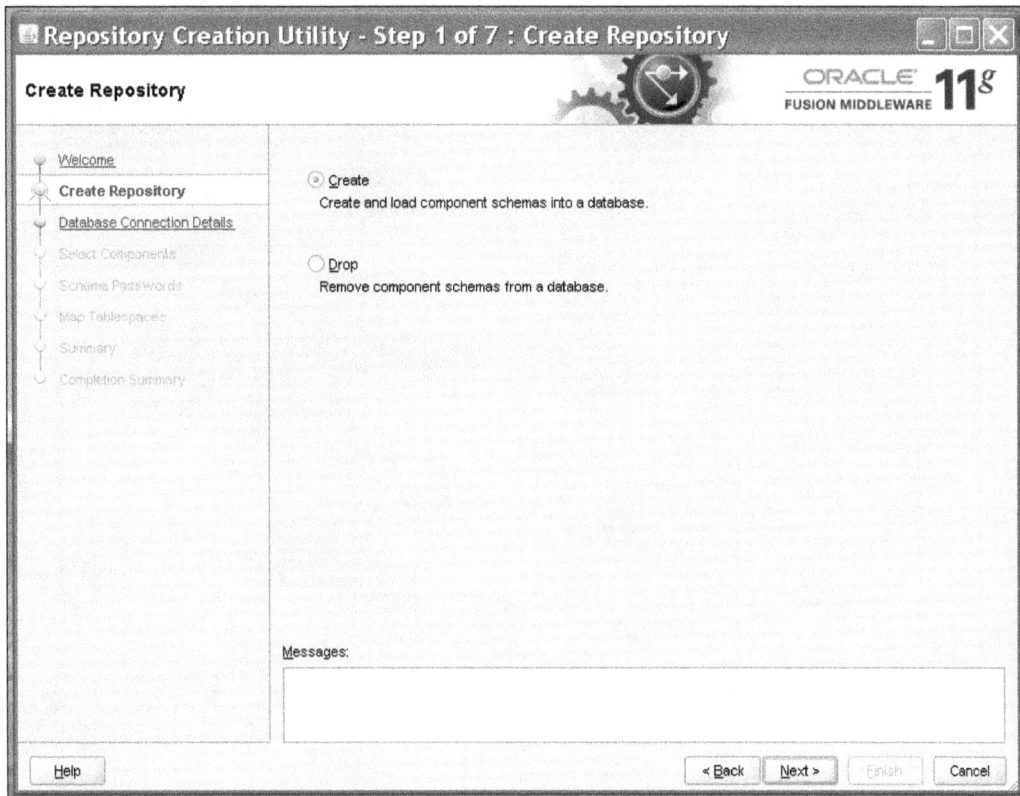

5. Click on **Next** and enter the database information. Look in the `tnsnames.ora` or `listener.ora` files located in the Oracle Database install directory for the database information. As shown in the following screenshot, ensure that you use the exact information from the `tnsnames.ora` file as the database information. For example, enter the value for **Host Name** as the database server hostname. If you are running the Repository Creation Utility on the database server itself, you may use **Host Name** as `localhost`, as shown in the following screenshot:

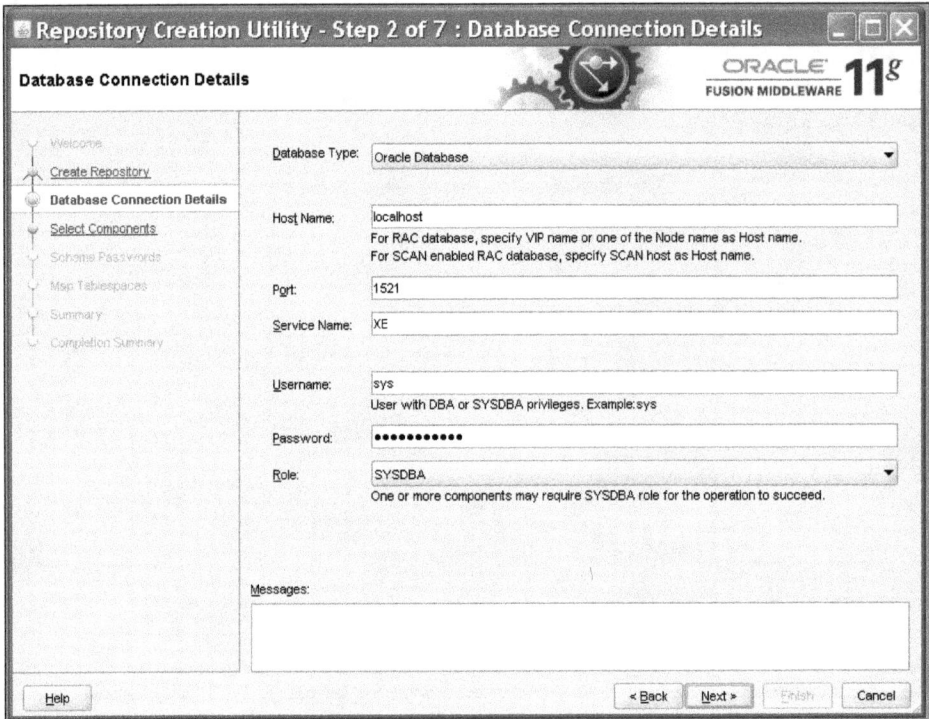

6. You can ignore the database support warnings. It will initiate the installation step of **Checking Prerequisites** with all the green ticks, as shown in the following screenshot. Click on **OK**:

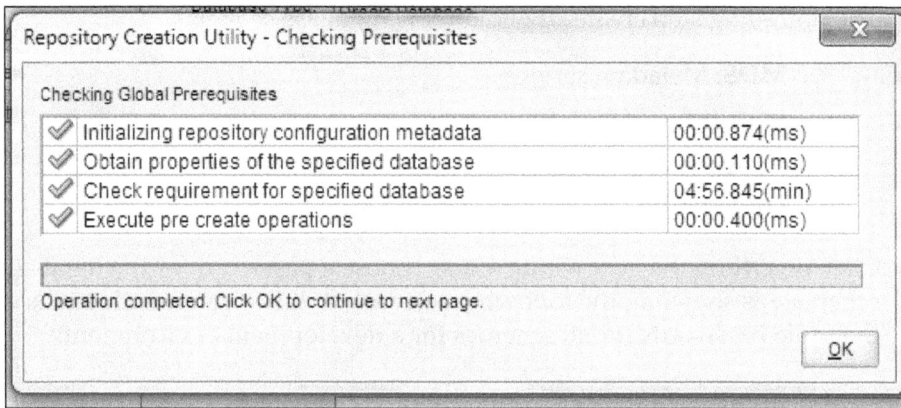

7. The next screen allows you to add a prefix with database schemas. Usually the prefix DEV is used for development environments, PROD for production, and so on. Select the **SOA** and **BPM Infrastructure** components on the next window that will allow you to select **Metadata Services**, as shown in the following screenshot. Dependent schemas are selected automatically. If you choose to select other components, these install instructions may not match your experience. Also, you may have to increase processes in XE (you will get a message telling you what is required):

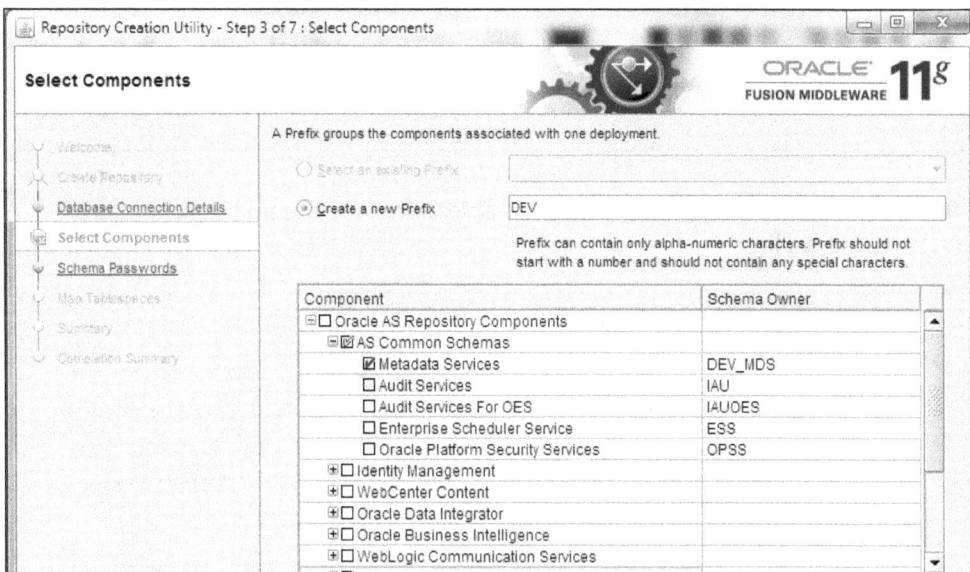

The preceding step creates the following database schemas:

- ° **MDS**: Metadata service
- ° **SOA Infra**: SOA Infrastructure
- ° **ORA BAM**: Business Activity Monitoring Service
- ° **ORA SDPM**: User Messaging Service

8. Click on **OK** on the next window and choose a password for the database schemas, as shown in the following screenshot. It is recommended to keep the same passwords for all schemas for a development environment:

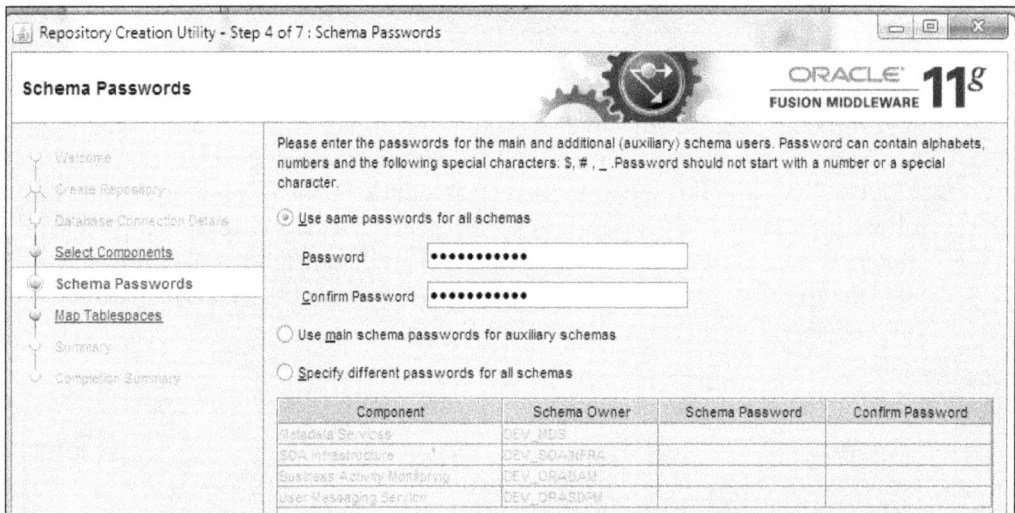

9. On the next window it will create tablespaces for the all the schemas created earlier:

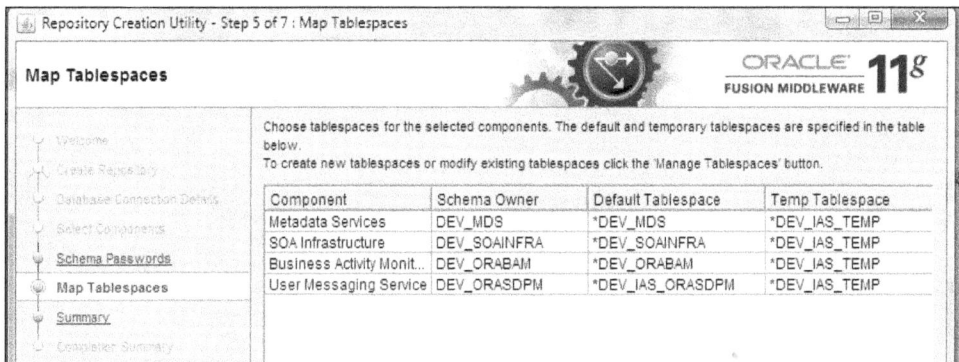

10. Click on **OK** to create tablespaces in the database:

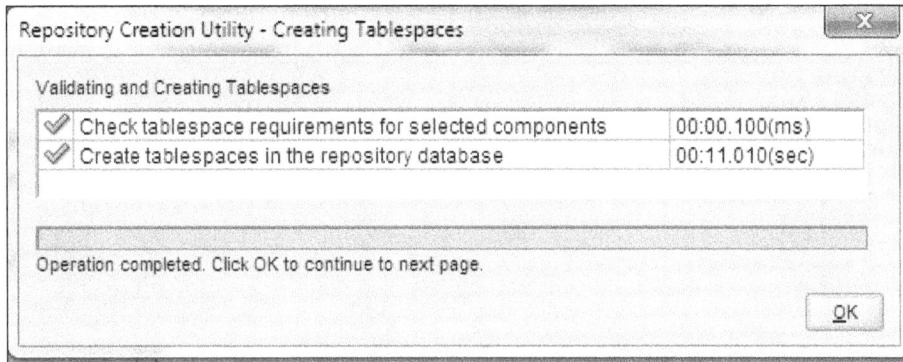

Repository Creation Utility - Creating Tablespaces

Validating and Creating Tablespaces

✓	Check tablespace requirements for selected components	00:00.100(ms)
✓	Create tablespaces in the repository database	00:11.010(sec)

Operation completed. Click OK to continue to next page.

OK

11. Click on **Create**. This will create all schemas in the database, as shown in the following screenshot. On the next window, click on **Close**. That completes the creation of database schemas for the SOA Suite:

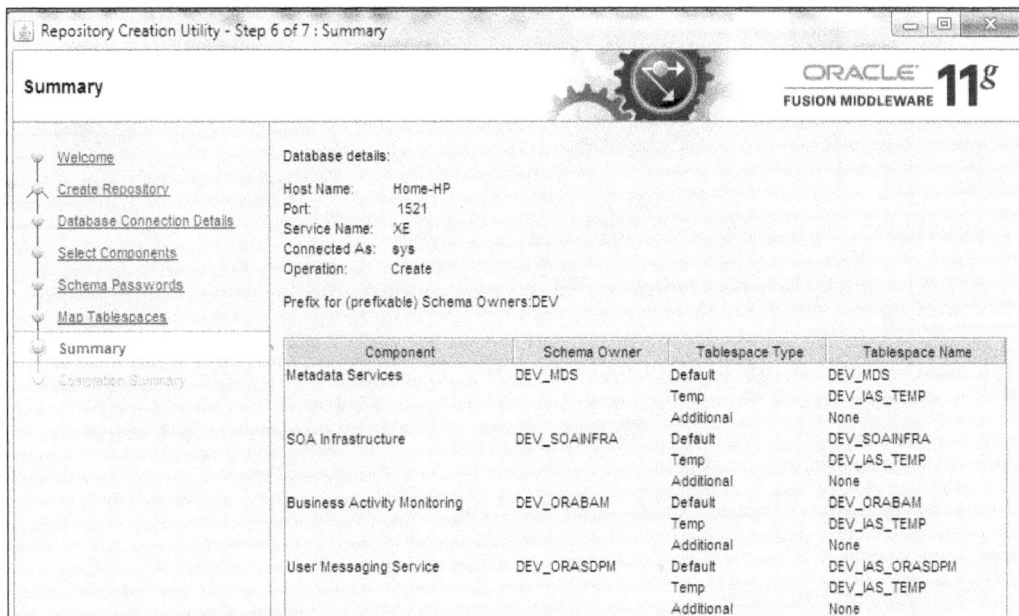

Repository Creation Utility - Step 6 of 7 : Summary

Summary

ORACLE **11**g
FUSION MIDDLEWARE

Welcome
Create Repository
Database Connection Details
Select Components
Schema Passwords
Map Tablespaces
Summary
Completion Summary

Database details:

Host Name:	Home-HP
Port:	1521
Service Name:	XE
Connected As:	sys
Operation:	Create

Prefix for (prefixable) Schema Owners:DEV

Component	Schema Owner	Tablespace Type	Tablespace Name
Metadata Services	DEV_MDS	Default	DEV_MDS
		Temp	DEV_IAS_TEMP
		Additional	None
SOA Infrastructure	DEV_SOAINFRA	Default	DEV_SOAINFRA
		Temp	DEV_IAS_TEMP
		Additional	None
Business Activity Monitoring	DEV_ORABAM	Default	DEV_ORABAM
		Temp	DEV_IAS_TEMP
		Additional	None
User Messaging Service	DEV_ORASDPM	Default	DEV_IAS_ORASDPM
		Temp	DEV_IAS_TEMP
		Additional	None

Step 3 – install Oracle SOA Suite

As shown in the following figure, the final step is to install the SOA Suite.

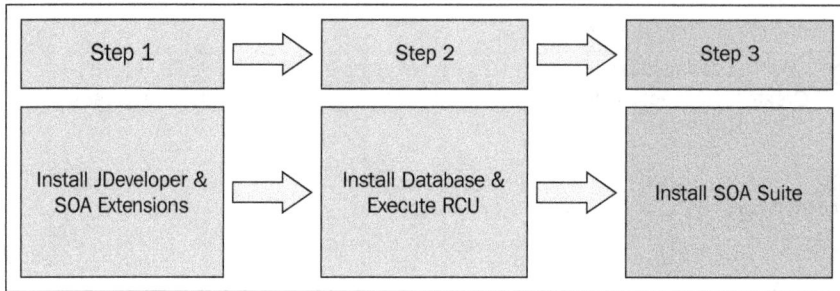

The Oracle SOA Suite Version 11.1.1.6 can be downloaded from Oracle's website.

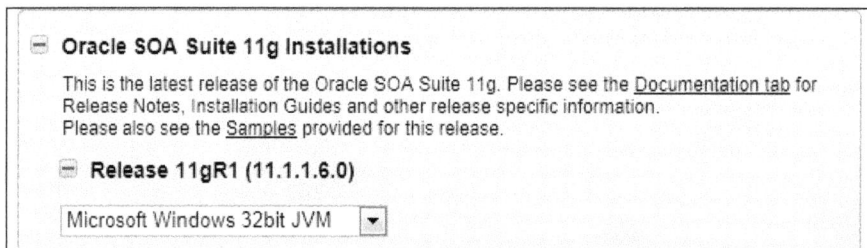

Perform the following steps to complete the installation:

1. Extract all the disks from the ZIP archive into one folder and run `setup.exe` from `disk1`.

2. To avoid the install error message, provide the location of JDK/JRE while running the `setup.exe` file from the command line. You will need to pass `jreLoc` as a parameter to `setup.exe`, as shown in the following command line:

```
setup.exe -jreLoc C:\Oracle\Middleware\jdk160_24
```

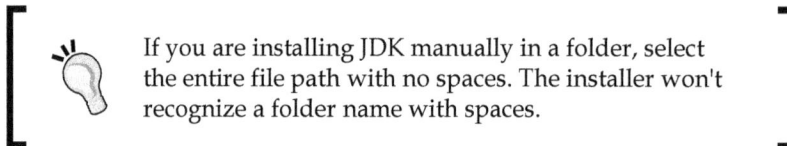

> If you are installing JDK manually in a folder, select the entire file path with no spaces. The installer won't recognize a folder name with spaces.

3. It will launch the install window, as shown in the following screenshot. Click on **Next**. On the next window click on **Skip Software Updates** and then click on **Next**:

4. It will start the SOA Suite installation and that will perform the **Prerequisite Checks**. On successful checks, we will get all the status as green, as shown in the following screenshot. Click on **Next**:

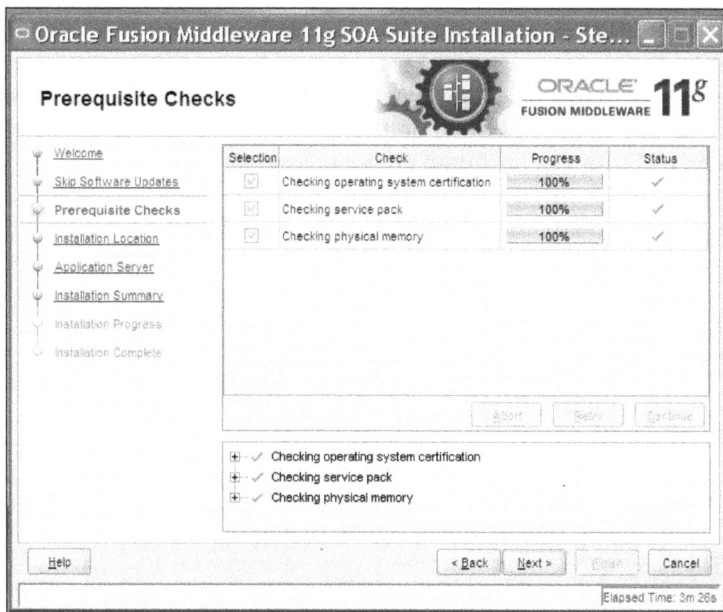

5. Please make sure that you have already installed WebLogic as a standalone install or as part of the JDeveloper install. On the next window, as shown in the following screenshot, enter the location of **Oracle Middleware Home** and click on **Next**:

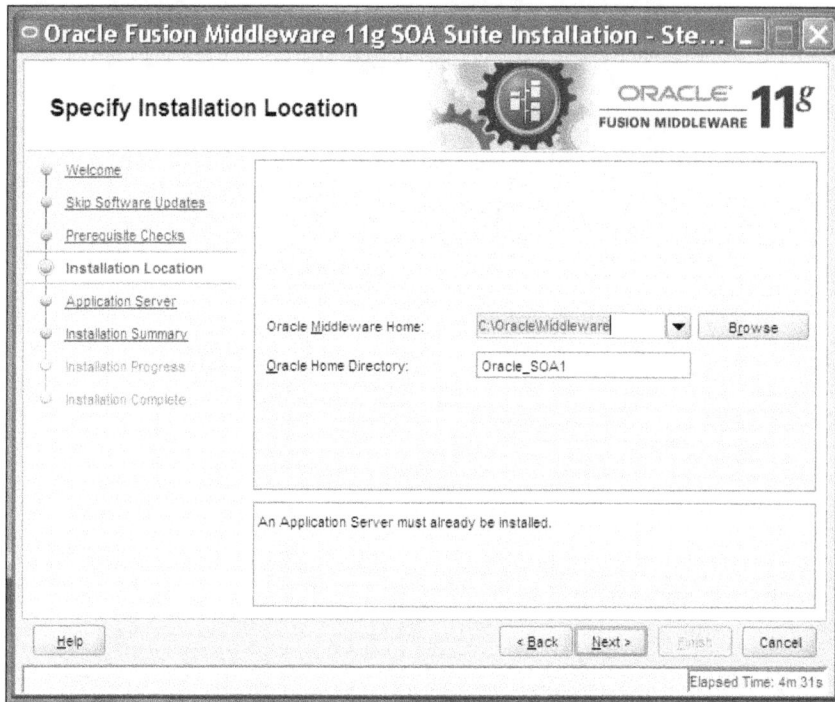

6. On the next window, if you get the warning message that an existing Oracle SOA Suite 11*g* home has been detected, click on **Yes** to upgrade the existing Oracle SOA Suite 11*g* and then click on **Next**:

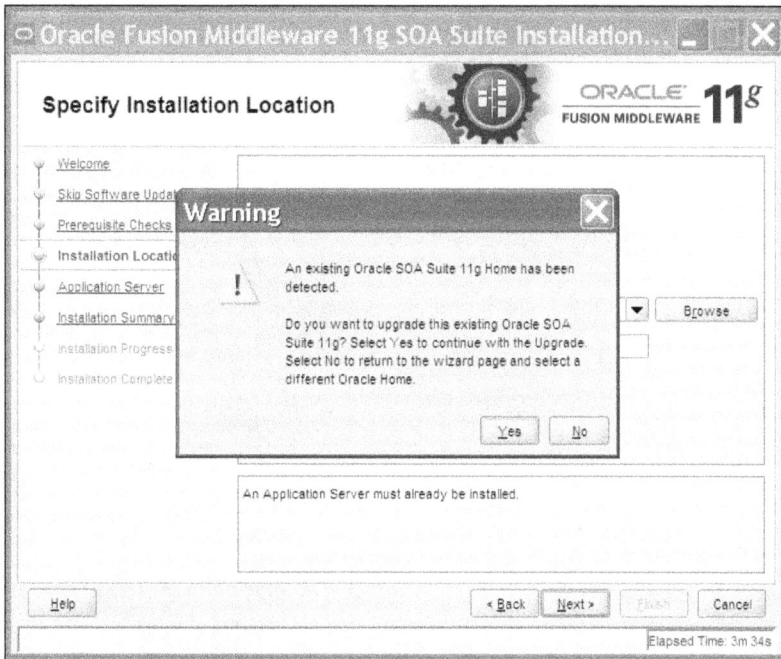

7. On the next window, we will get the installation summary, as shown in the following screenshot. Click on **Install** to start the SOA Suite installation:

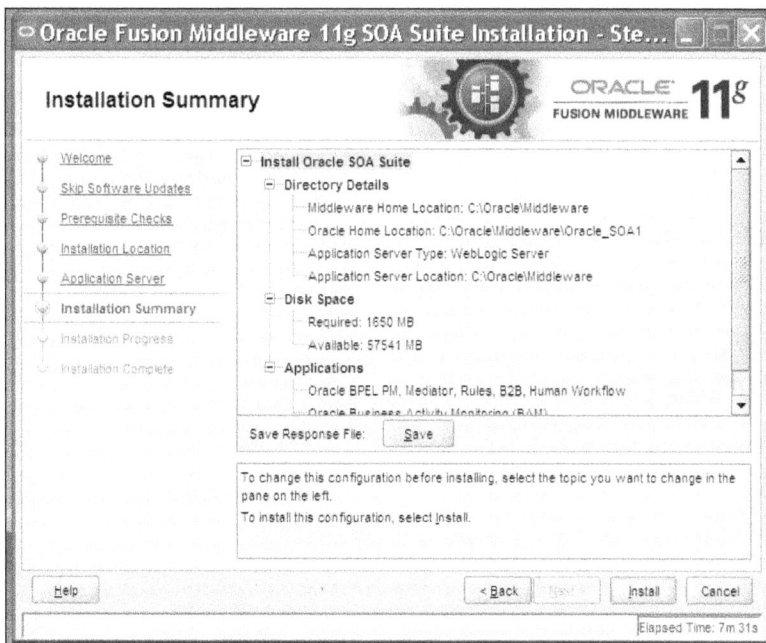

8. On the next window, you will get the installation progress window that may take a few minutes to finish the install. On completion of the install, click on **Next** and that will take you to the **Installation Complete** window, as shown in the following screenshot. Click on **Finish** to complete the Oracle SOA Suite installation:

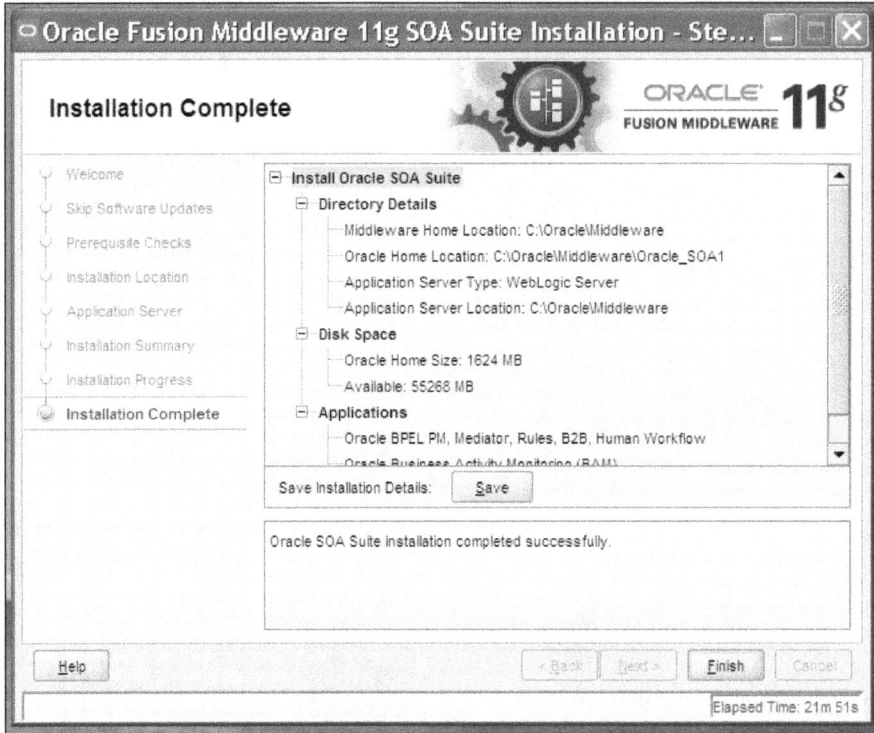

Creating an SOA Suite domain

A typical development environment consists of the following:

- One admin server
- One managed server

However, you can perform the development with a single admin server as well.

A production environment will usually be a clustered environment consisting of multiple managed server and single admin instances.

To create an SOA Suite domain, perform the following steps:

1. Ensure that you choose **Oracle SOA Suite for developers** instead of **Oracle SOA Suite** in the **Domain Configuration** wizard.

2. Execute `config.bat` from command prompt, as shown in the following screenshot:

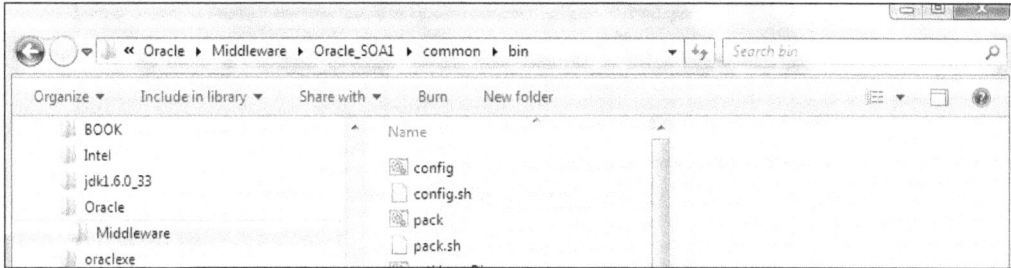

Alternatively, you can select **Configure Application Server** from the Windows Start menu, as shown in the following screenshot:

3. As shown in the following screenshot, select the **Create a new WebLogic domain** radio button and click on **Next**.

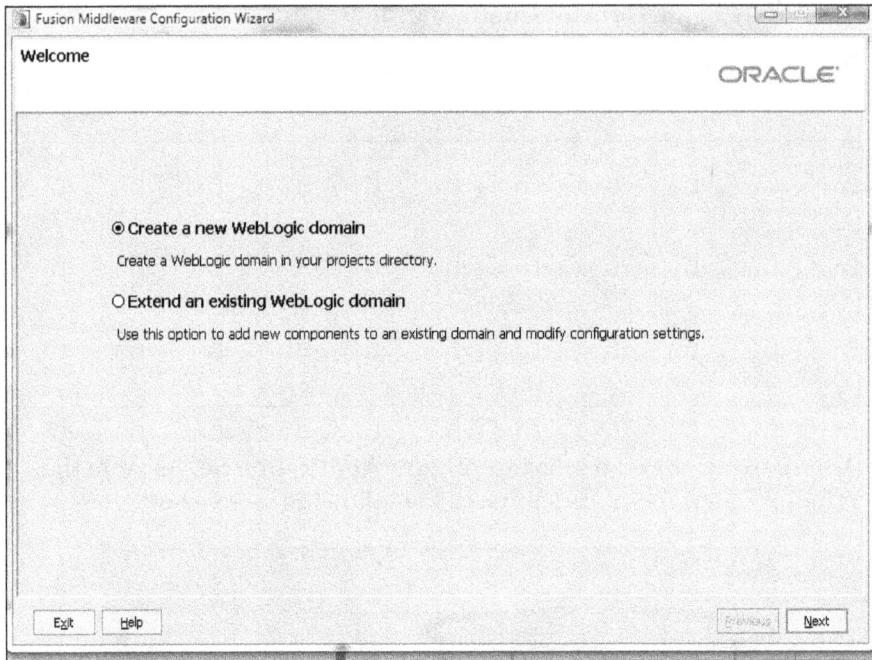

4. As shown in the following screenshot, select the Oracle products and then click on **Next**. On the next window, enter the desired domain name, domain location, and application locations, or leave the default values for them and click on **Next**:

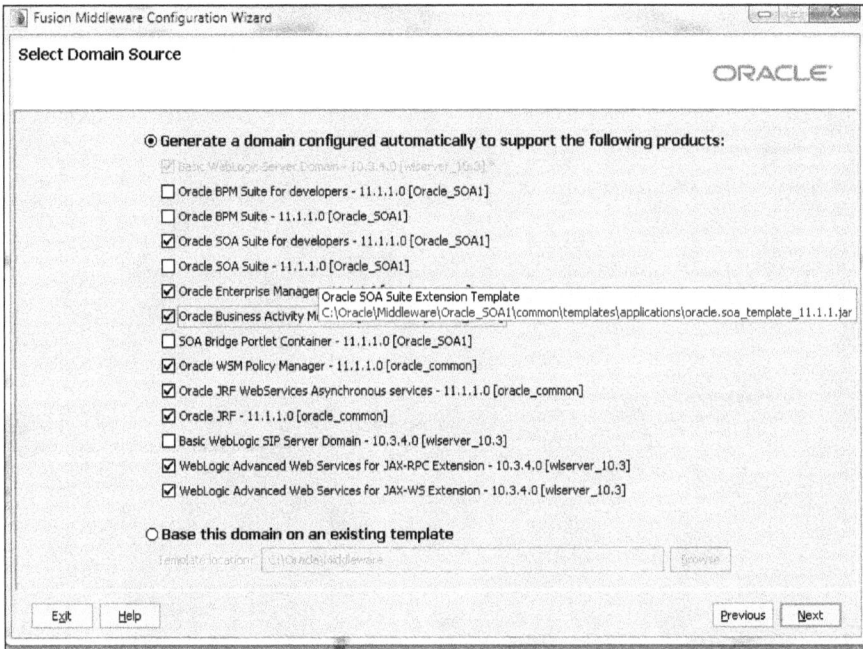

5. Enter the user password and click on **Next**, as shown in the following screenshot. Store the password at a safe place, you will need it later:

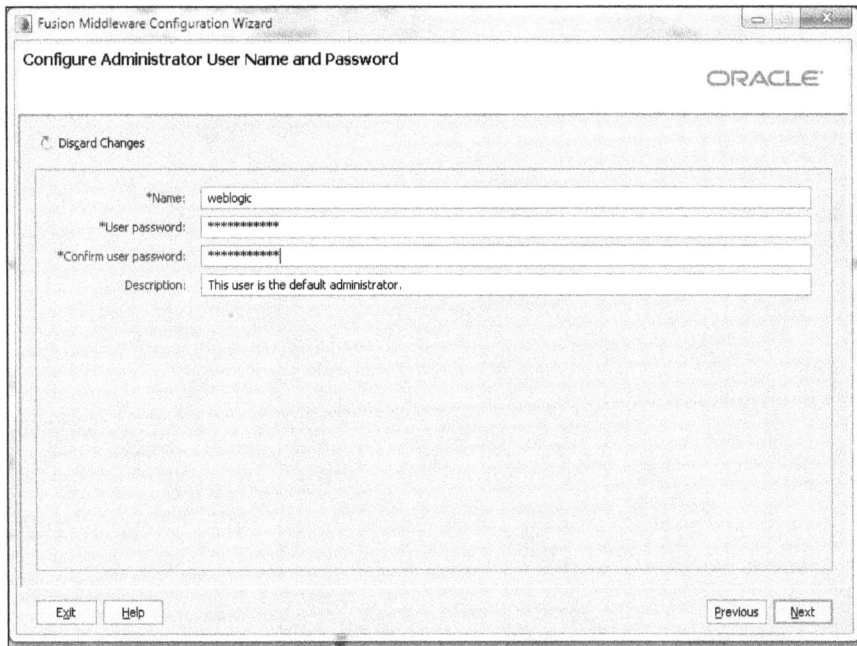

6. On the next window, select **Development Mode** and select the **Sun SDK 1.6** from under **Available JDKs** (in the following screenshot, the only available JDK is **Sun SDK 1.6**). Click on **Next**:

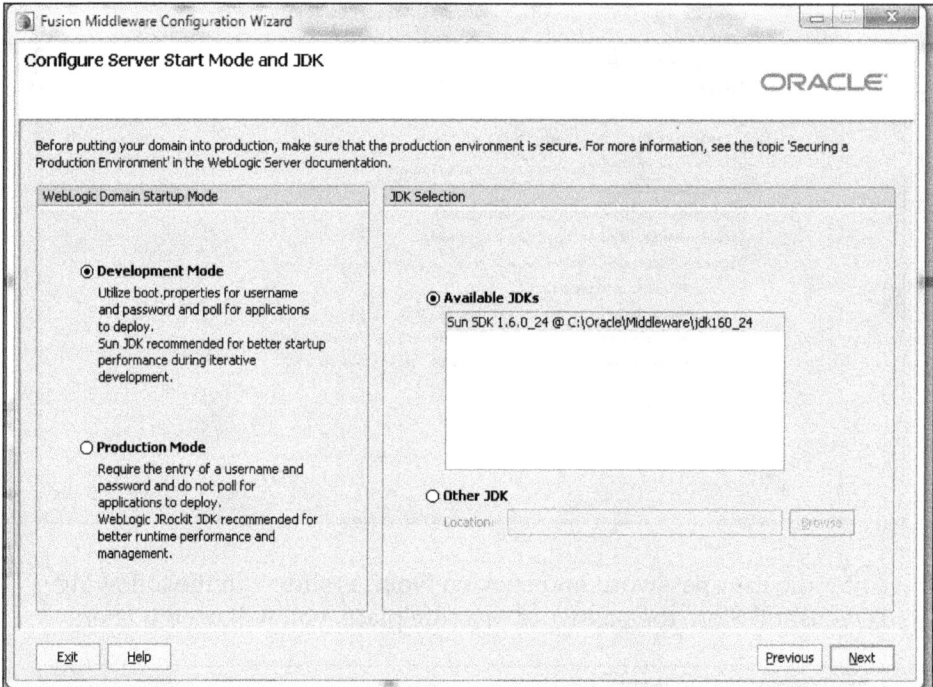

7. As shown in the following screenshot, enter the database information. Do not modify the schema user session. Please select and enter the data in the order as shown in the following screenshot:

8. If you receive a connection error do the following:

   ○ Ensure that the database is up and running.

   ○ Make changes to **DBMS/Service**, **Host Name**, and **Port** number. Check for the `tnsnames.ora` file for correct entries. Always use the same information used for RCU.

Sometimes, you may get the following error:

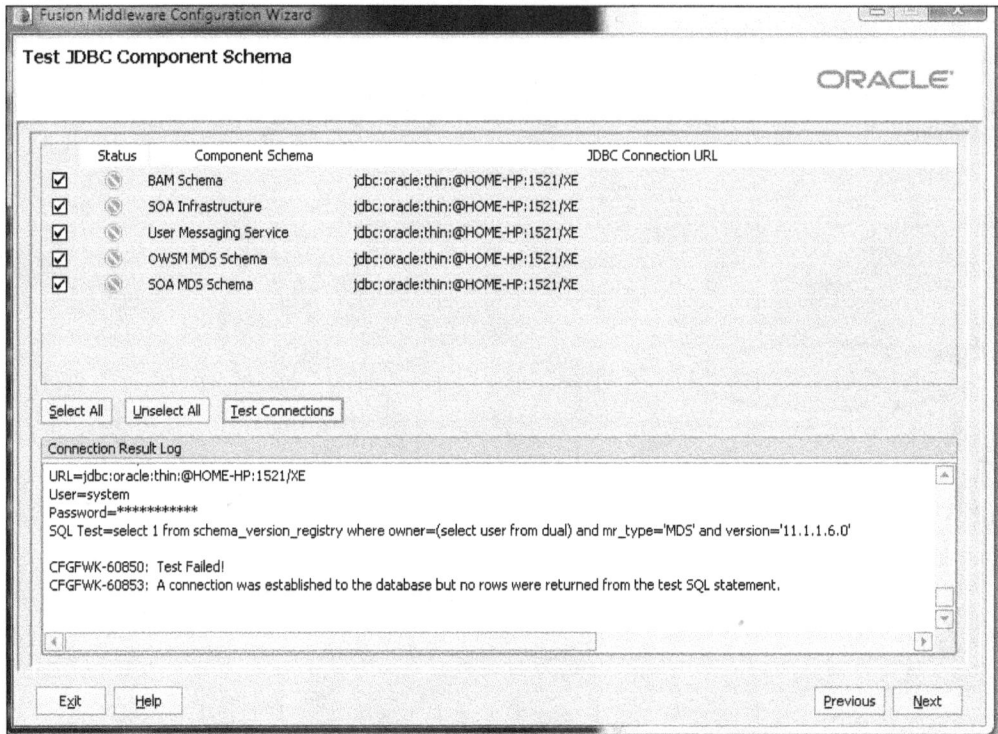

To resolve the preceding error, please ensure that you created schemas with the correct RCU version and are able to connect to the database with the username and password provided in the preceding screen.

> Please note that we should not modify the username to the schemas. The username is selected by the utility. Change only the password. For a development environment, always prefix the schema with DEV.
>
> Ensure that all the steps described in the RCU install session executed, including steps for changing the number of default Oracle database processes.

9. Shut down and start the database after the changes. The preceding changes are required only in the case of the database connection error messages. Test the JDBC connections for the SOA Suite database schemas and make sure it is green for all the schemas, as shown in the following screenshot. Click on **Next**:

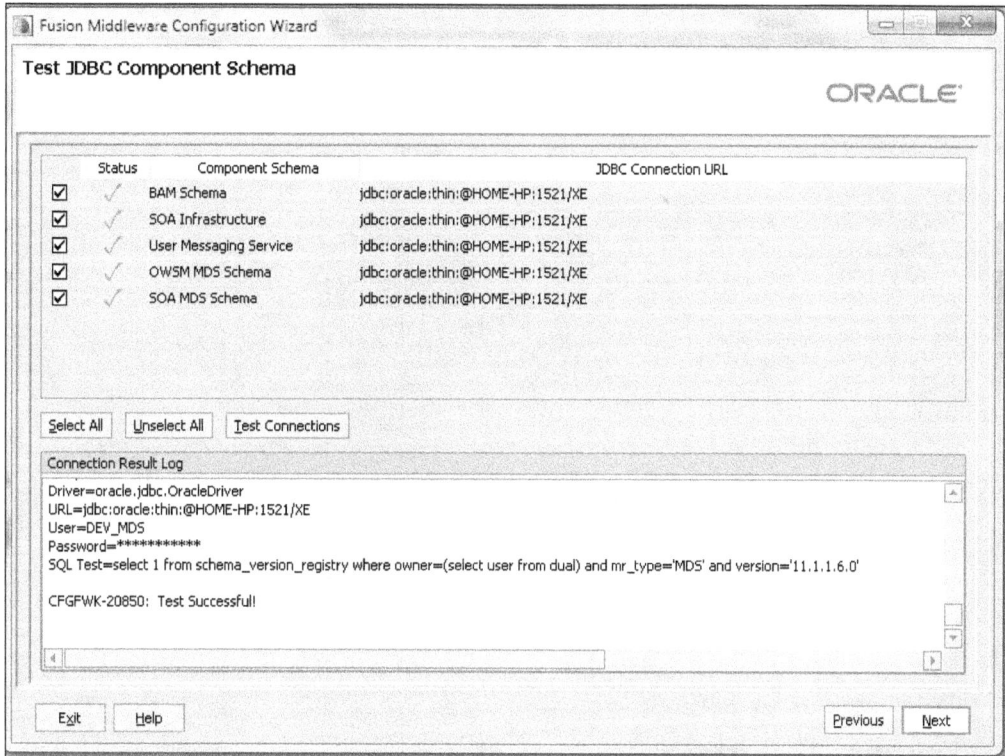

10. On the next window you will see the configuration summary, as shown in the following screenshot. Clicking on **Create** will start writing the WebLogic domain setup files for Oracle SOA Suite. On the next window, you will see the progress of writing the domain setup files. Click on **Done** to finish setting up the WebLogic domain for Oracle SOA Suite:

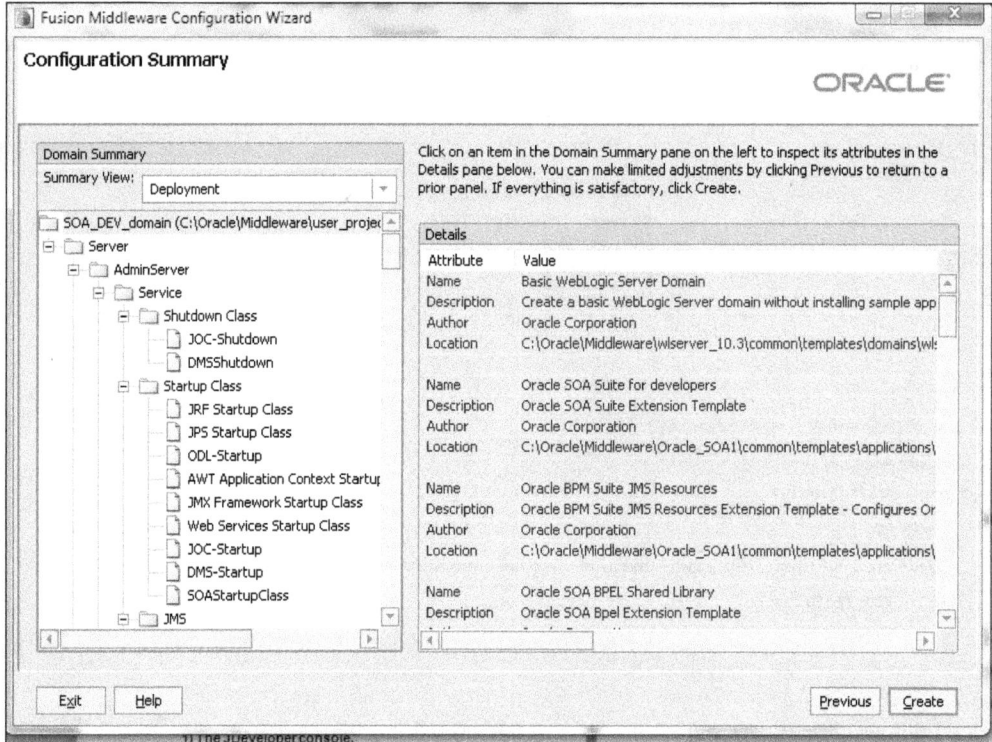

11. Now, to start the admin server, go to the domain's `bin` folder for which you wish to start the administration server using the following command:

```
cd $BEA_HOME/user_projects/domains/<domain_name>/bin
```

   ° For Windows execute `startWebLogic.cmd`
   ° For Linux, execute `startWebLogic.sh`

To start WebLogic, execute the `startWeblogic.cmd` script from the command prompt. Server logfiles are located as `$BEA_HOME/ user_projects/ domains/ <domain_name> /servers/<ServerName> /logs / <ServerName>.log`.

One can confirm that the WebLogic administration server started properly by looking at the message **Service started RUNNING** in the server logfile.

Creating sample BPEL business processes

1. Start JDeveloper from the Start menu with the default role. In JDeveloper, from the **Application** tab, click on **New** and select **SOA Application** and then click on **Next**, as shown in the following screenshot:

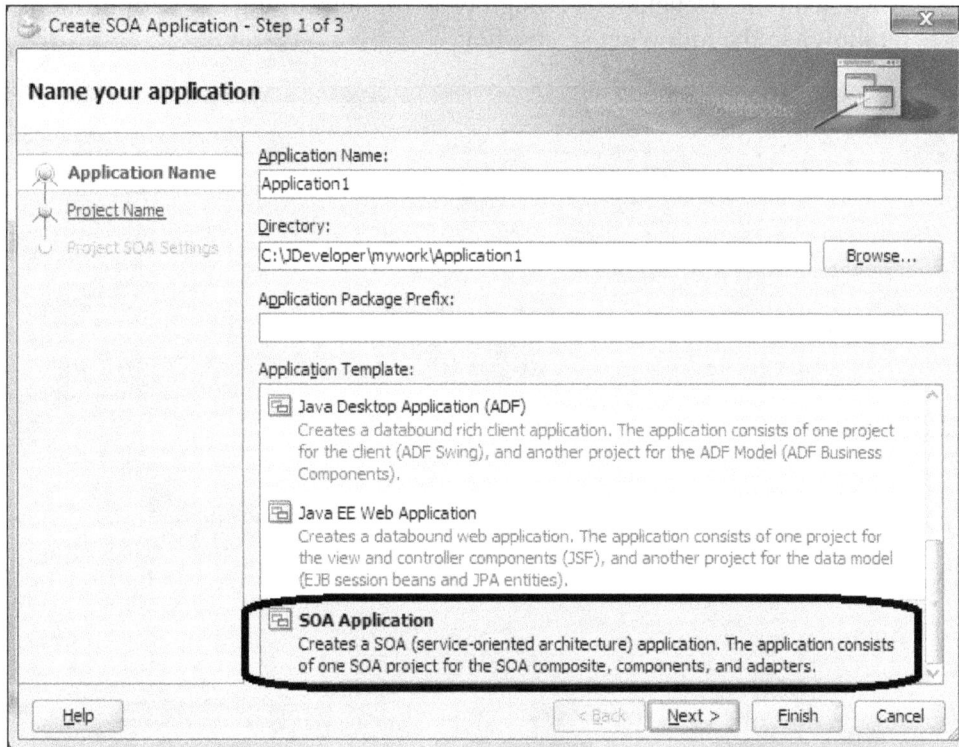

2. Enter the **Project Name** and click on **Finish**, as shown in the following screenshot:

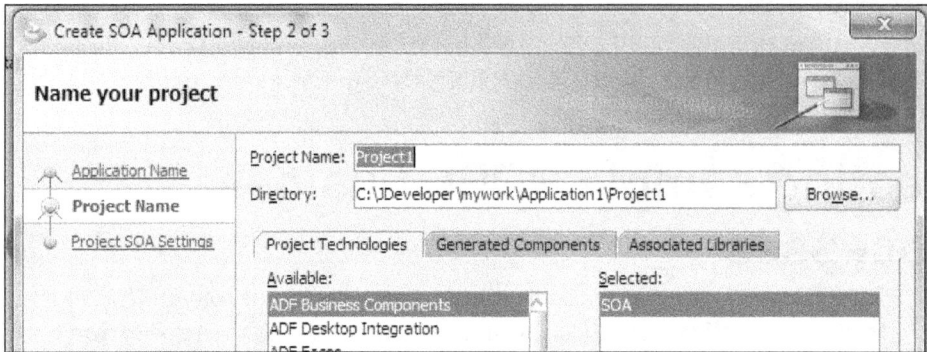

3. It will load the JDeveloper's Design view for developing SOA applications, as shown in the following screenshot:

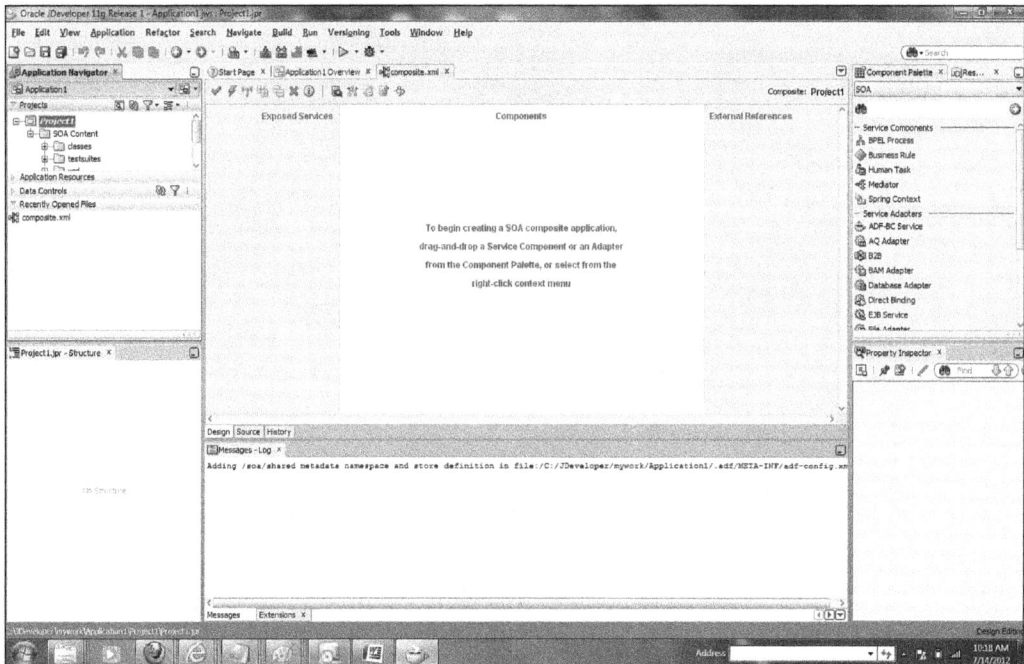

4. Drag-and-drop a **BPEL Process** from **Component Pallet** to the JDeveloper canvas. The Create BPEL Process screen will appear on the JDeveloper console.

5. As shown in the following screenshot, you can name your BPEL process. In this case the name is the default **BPELProcess1**. In the **Template** field, select **Synchronous BPEL Process**. Executing Synchronous BPEL processes returns a result. The Asynchronous BPEL processes may not return any value:

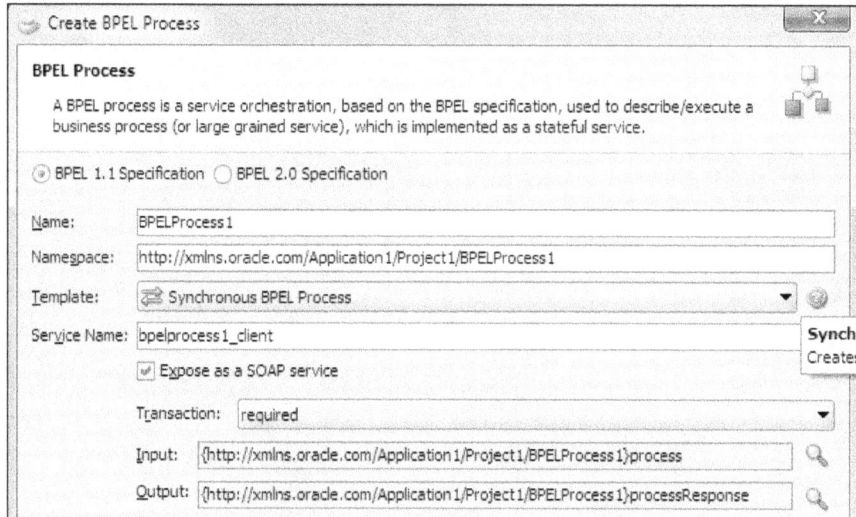

6. As shown in the following screenshot, double-click on **BPELProcess1** to view the BPEL:

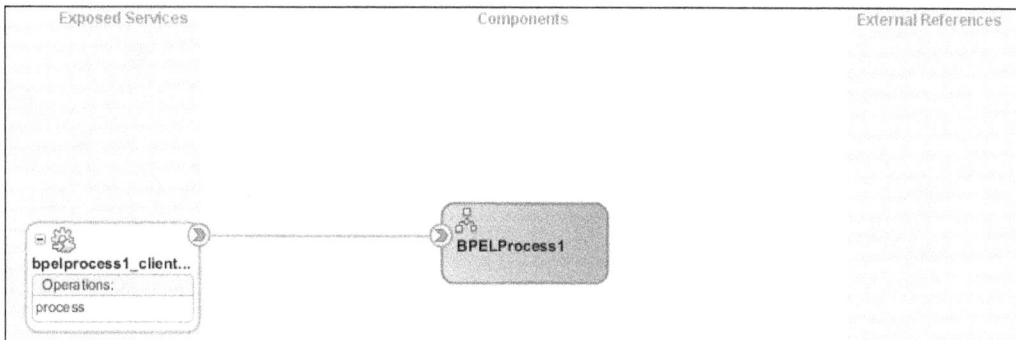

7. After double-clicking on the BPEL process, a window, as shown in the following screenshot, will appear:

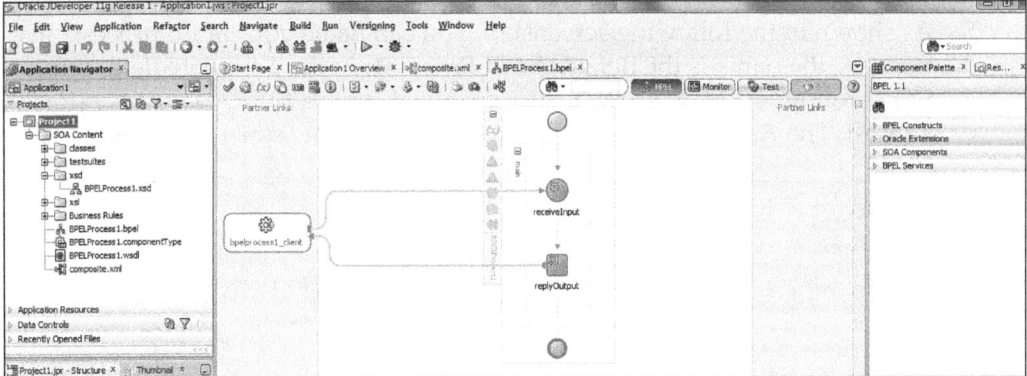

8. The next step is to debug the basic BPEL process. Currently, the business process has only **receiveInput** and **replyOutput** activity. Click on **Run** (or **Make**) to compile the project, as shown in the following screenshot:

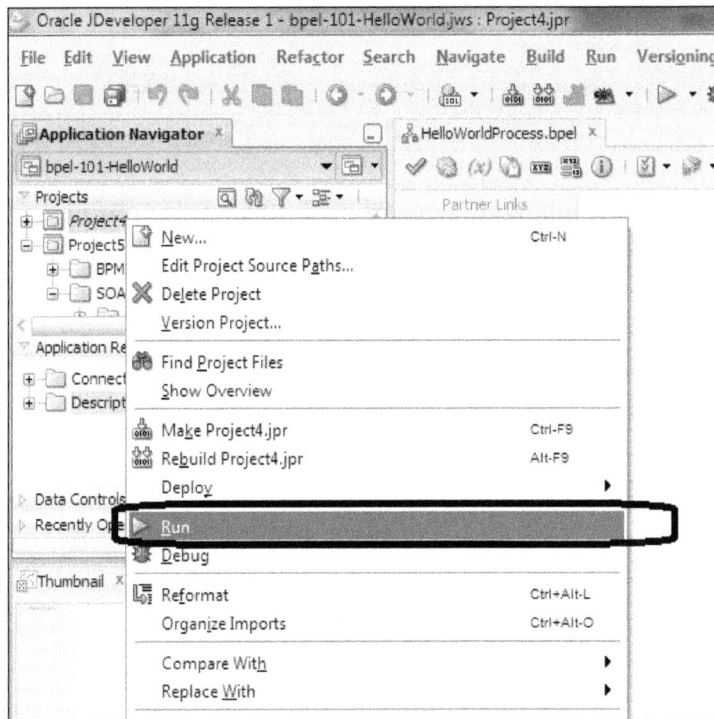

9. After selecting **Debug**, the following dialog is displayed as no **Default Run Target** was specified in **Run/Debug** page of the **Project Properties** dialog.

10. Use the dialog in the following screenshot to specify the **Default Run Target**. Ignore any warning message about the non-existence of the src folder:

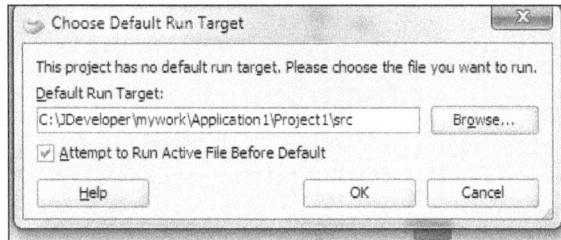

11. From the **Activities** toolbar on the right-hand side of your window, drag an **Assign** activity and drop it between **receiveInput** and **replyOutput**. The following screenshot will appear after the changes:

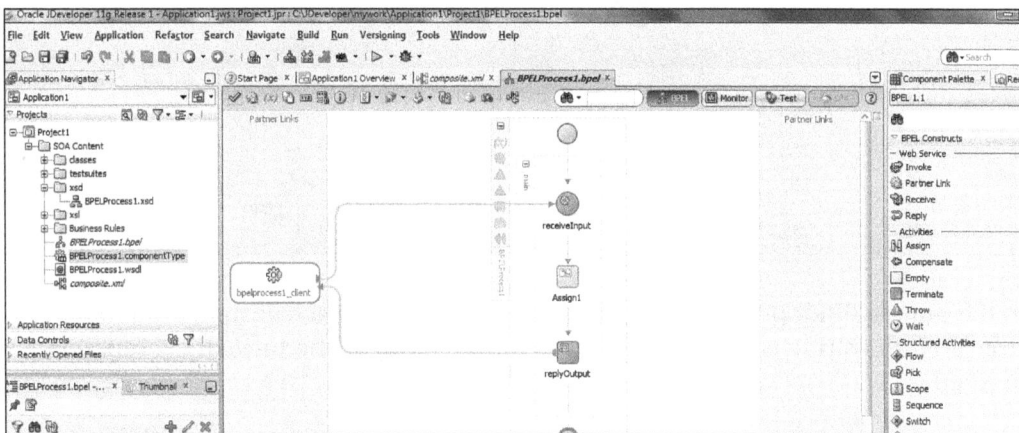

12. You can rename it by double-clicking on **Assign1**.

An **Assign** activity is usually used for manipulating data. For example, **Assign** activity can be used for copying the contents of one variable to another.

Assign activity is mainly used for copying the XML data contained in one BPEL variable to another BPEL variable. The data in a variable is visible and shared among all process activities.

Partner Link represents a link to services. JDeveloper's **Source** tab allows you to make the changes to the sources if required. The following screenshot shows how the **Copy Rules** tab can be used for creating a copy rule and connecting the source and target types:

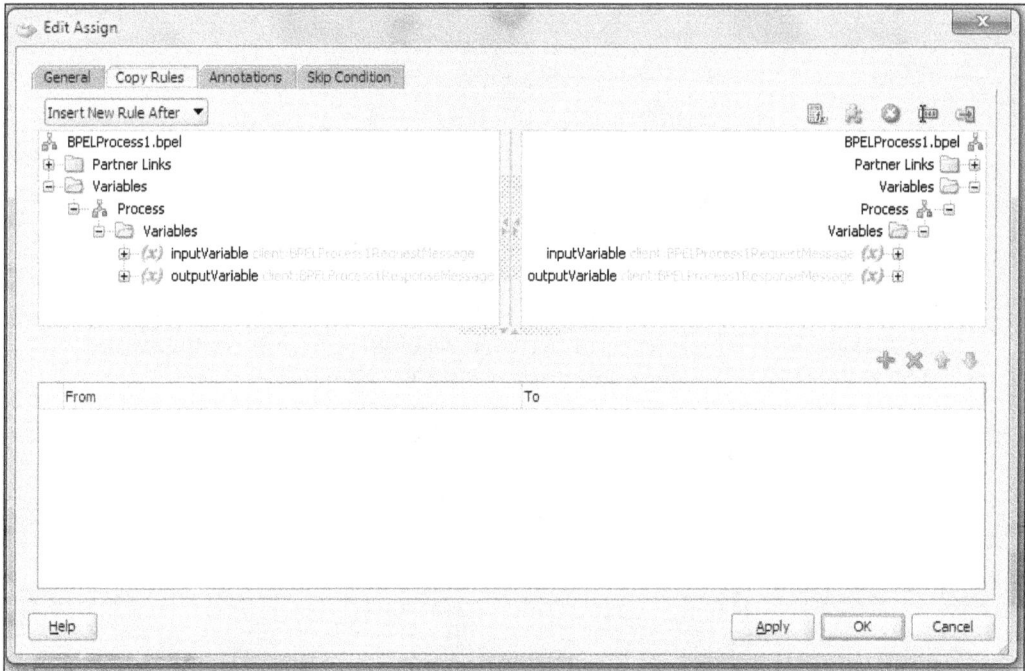

In the sample BPEL process being shown in the preceding screenshot, input data from an input string is being copied to an output string using the concat function of XPath.

XPath is language for navigating through elements and attributes in an XML document and finding information within an XML document. The syntax of XPath's concat function is as follows:

```
fn:concat(string,string,...)
```

It returns the concatenation of the strings. For example, concat("My","first","XPATH function!") gives the output as My first XPATH function.

While copying the value of an input string to an output string, use the concat function of XPath to combine the strings together to manipulate the data. The **Assign** activities in BPEL build the XPath queries.

It is recommended to use the drag-and-drop feature for copying and assembling functions. The source code example of the **Assign** activity is given as follows (you can view the source code from JDeveloper' **Source** tab):

```
<assign>
   <copy>
      <from expression="concat('BPEL working ',
         bpws:getVariableData('input', 'payload', '/p:input))"/>
      <to variable="output" part="payload" query="/p:result/
p:message"/>
   </copy>
</assign>
```

Assign activity in BPEL can do the following:

- Copy data of one XML variable from input to output
- Calculate the value of an expression and store it in a variable

The **Assign** syntax of the copy function is as follows:

```
<copy> <from...> <to...> </copy>
```

Deploying BPEL business processes

1. As shown in the following screenshot, select **Deploy** from the JDeveloper menu and select the project:

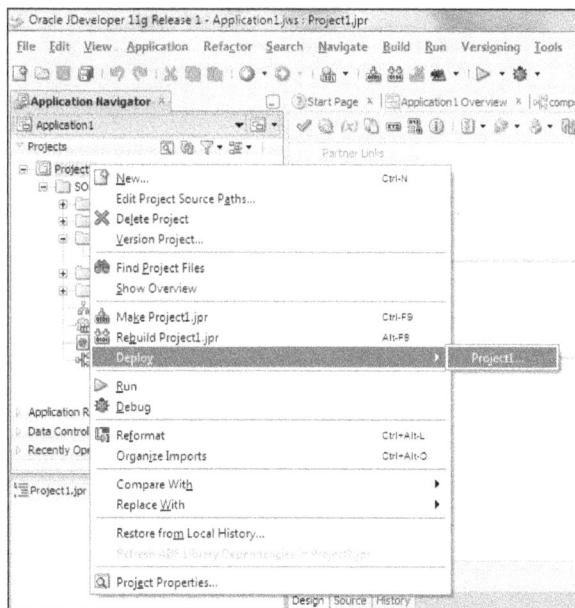

2. Select **Deploy to Application Server**, as shown in the following screenshot:

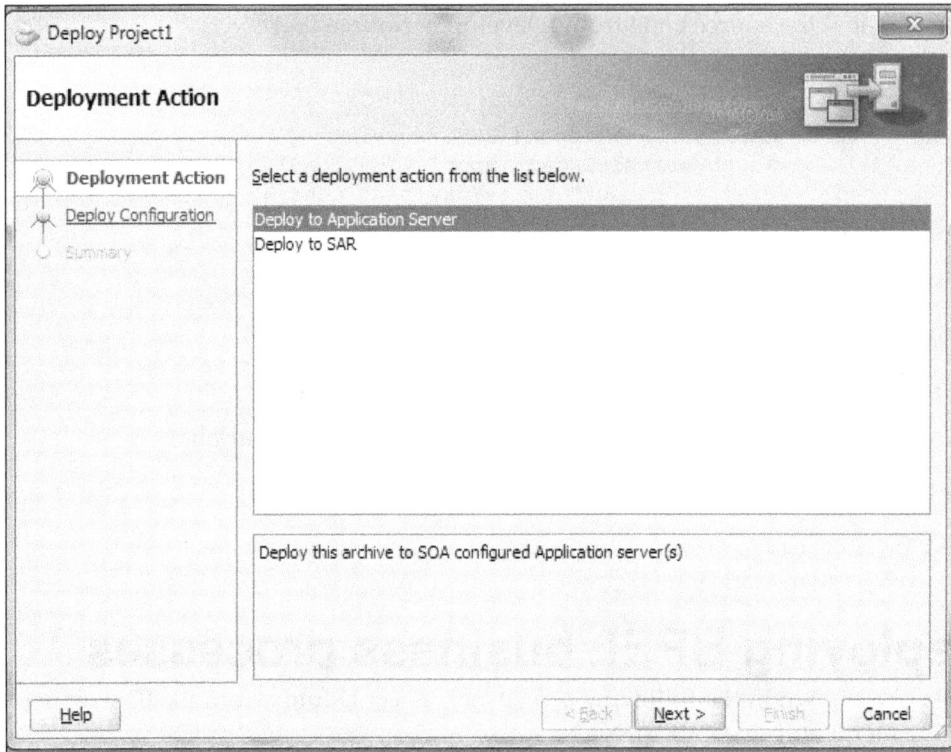

3. Enter a **Connection Name**. For example, enter `Weblogic`:

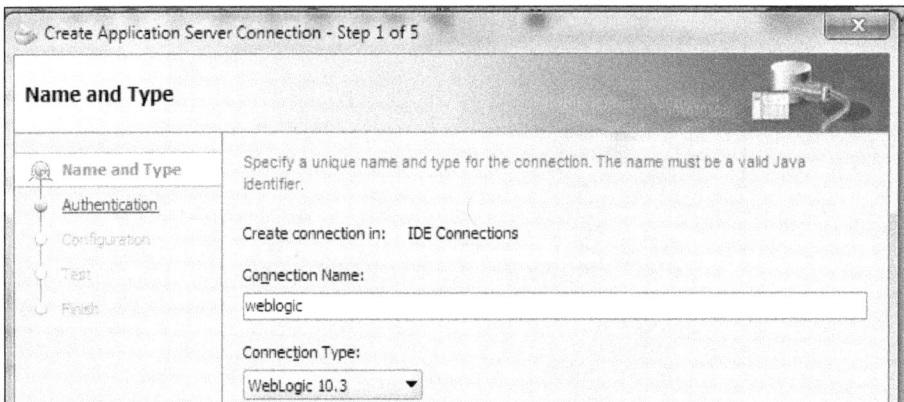

4. Ensure that you start Oracle SOA Suite WebLogic server and database servers. Enter the WebLogic console user ID and password in the next screen.

5. As shown in the following screenshot, enter the server details that you want to deploy the service to. In case of a development integration environment, you may plan to deploy to a remote server. Enter the remote server information:

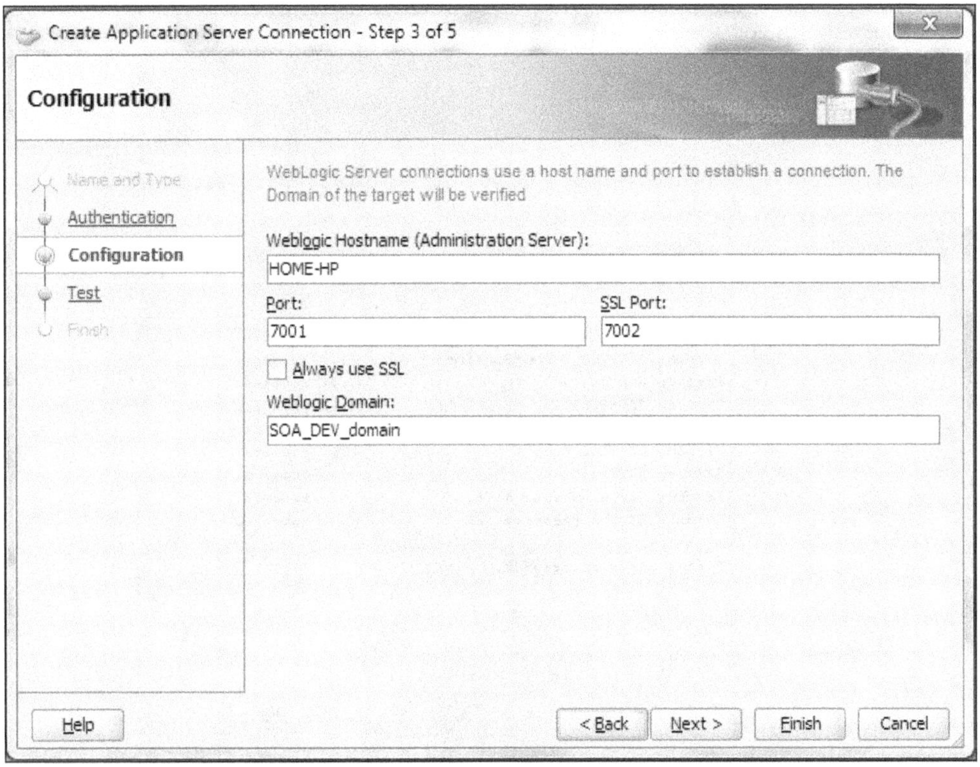

Create Application Server Connection - Step 3 of 5

Configuration

- Name and Type
- Authentication
- Configuration
- Test
- Finish

WebLogic Server connections use a host name and port to establish a connection. The Domain of the target will be verified

Weblogic Hostname (Administration Server):

HOME-HP

Port:

7001

SSL Port:

7002

☐ Always use SSL

Weblogic Domain:

SOA_DEV_domain

Help   < Back   Next >   Finish   Cancel

6. Ensure that the domain name is correct in the preceding screen. Click on **Next**. As shown in the next screenshot, click on the **Test Connection** button for testing the WebLogic connection.

If the application server box is empty, then do the following:

- ○ Ensure that the WebLogic application server and SOA managed server instances is up and running
- ○ Connect to an external WebLogic application server for deploying the services by providing the server information

7. Click on **Next**. In case of errors, ensure that you can connect to the WebLogic console using an external browser. If you are using a proxy for your browser, ensure that you use it while connecting from JDeveloper as well. Update or remove the proxy setting to remove connection errors:

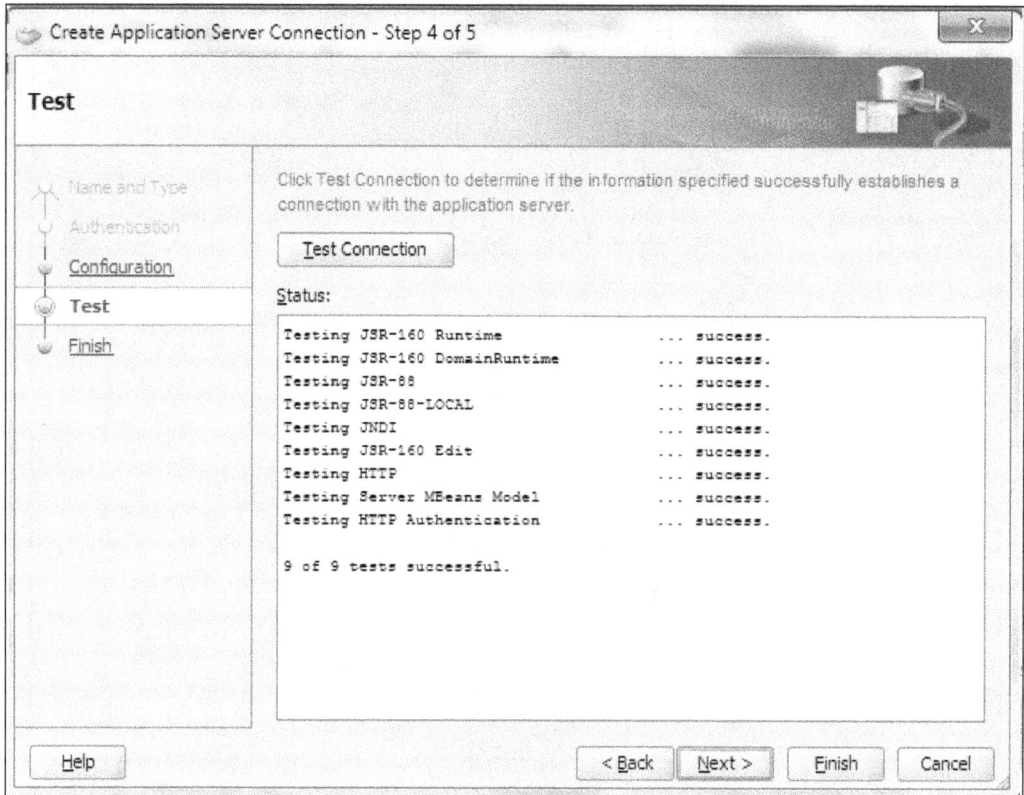

8. As shown in the following screenshot, the next screen will display a message that the creation of the connection is complete. Click on **Finish**:

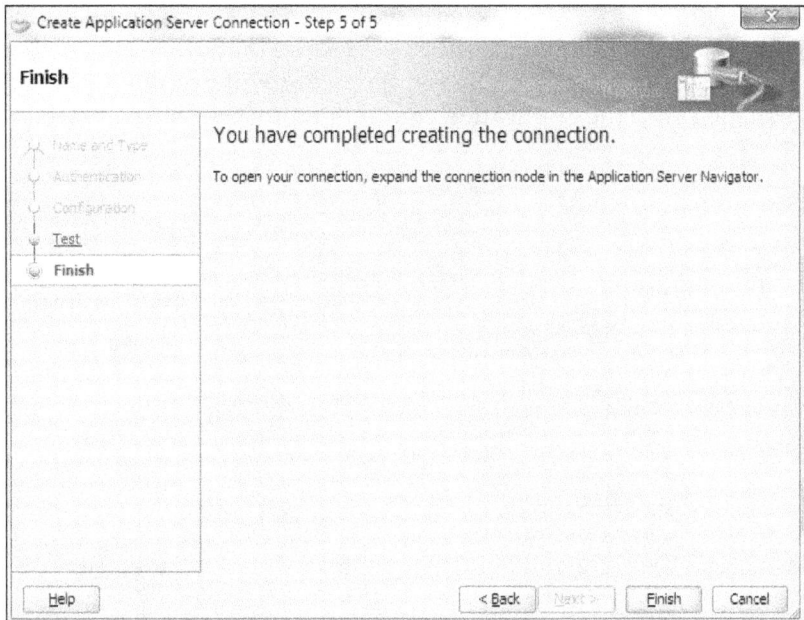

9. Follow the steps and test the connections. Use default port numbers configured while creating the WebLogic domain using the Configuration Wizard. Once connected, JDeveloper will recognize WebLogic in the dialog box, as shown in the following screenshot:

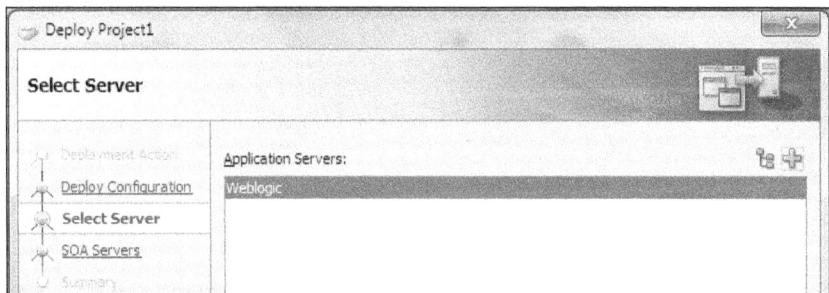

10. The SOA BPEL process manager is required for deploying the BPEL service. If you receive the following dialog box, ensure that the SOA servers are running in the local server, otherwise proceed with selecting the SOA server and finish the application connection process:

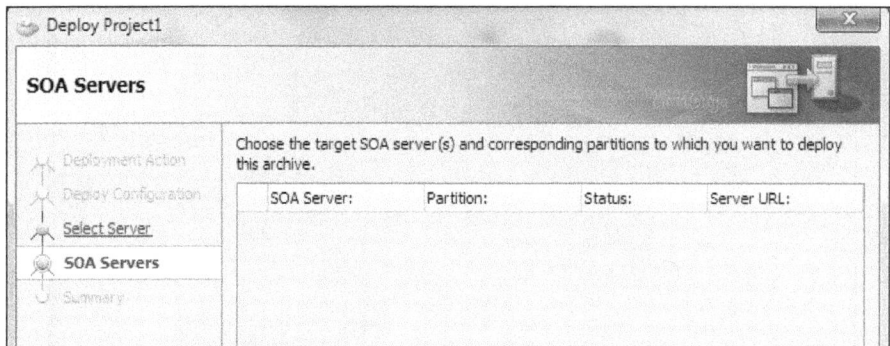

11. JDeveloper shows the following successful validation message:

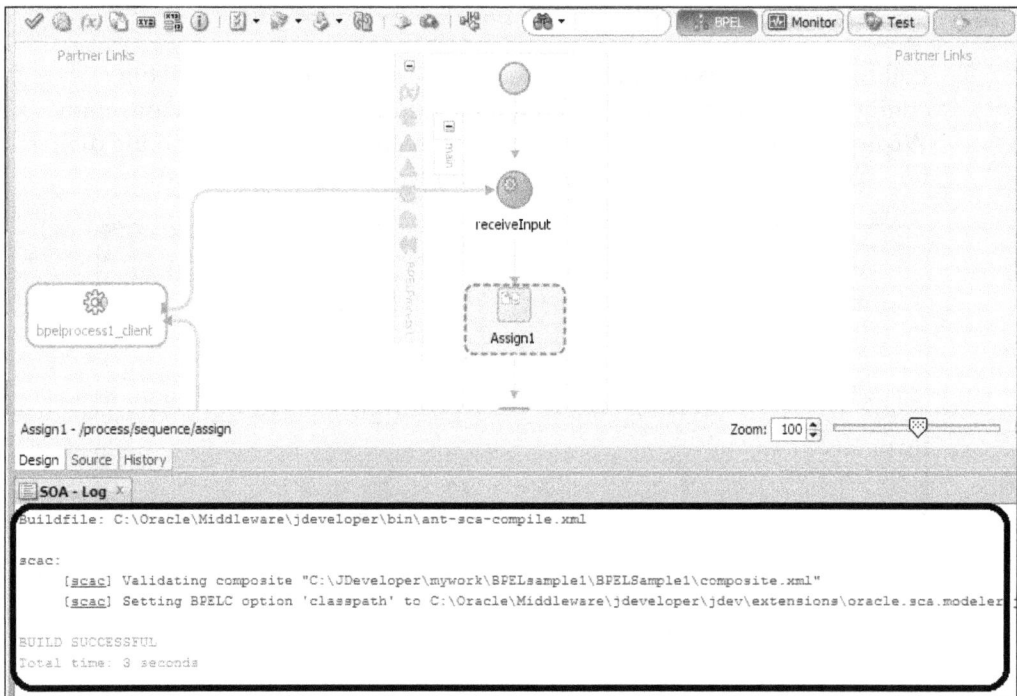

Testing and managing BPEL business process instances

1. To test the BPEL process, log in to Oracle's Enterprise Manager (EM) web interface using the following syntax:

   ```
   http://{hostname}:/em
   ```

2. Log in using an admin user and password:

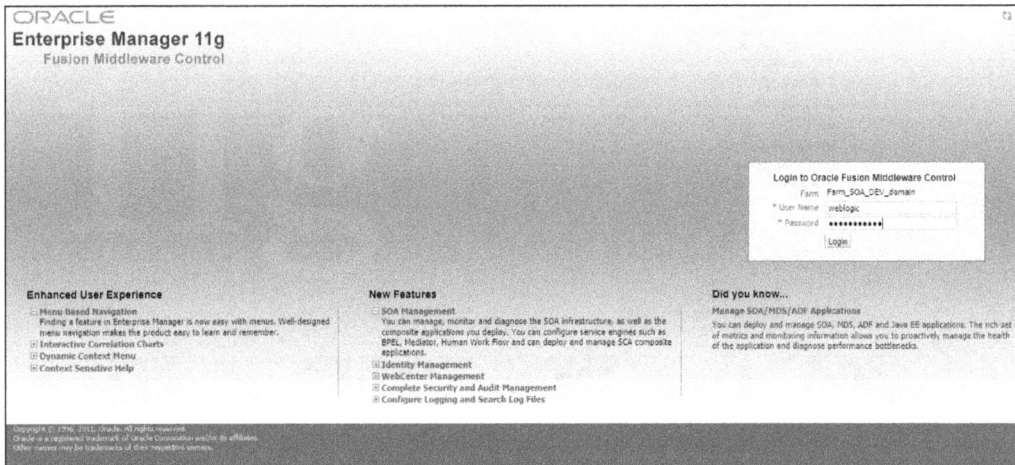

3. As shown in the following screenshot, click on the default domain from SOA node on the left-hand side navigation bar and select **BPELSample1**. Click on the **Test** tab:

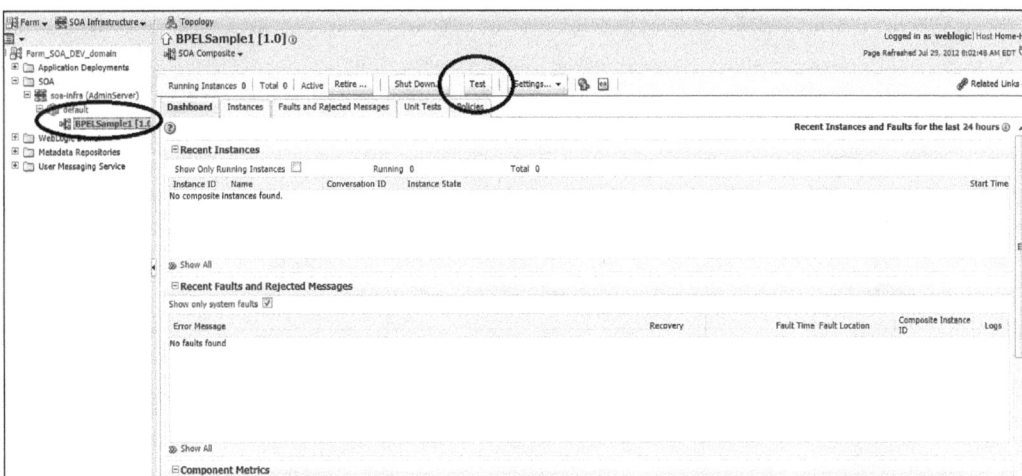

4. Ensure that the WSDL URL is correct and has `http` instead of `https`. Click on the **Test Web Service** button:

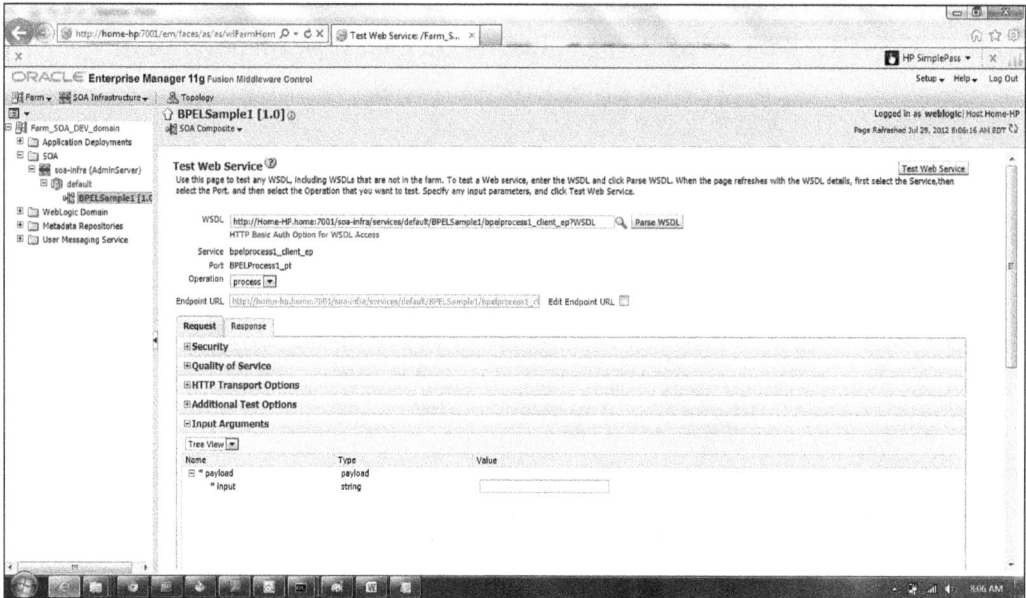

5. The result will be displayed, as shown in the following screenshot:

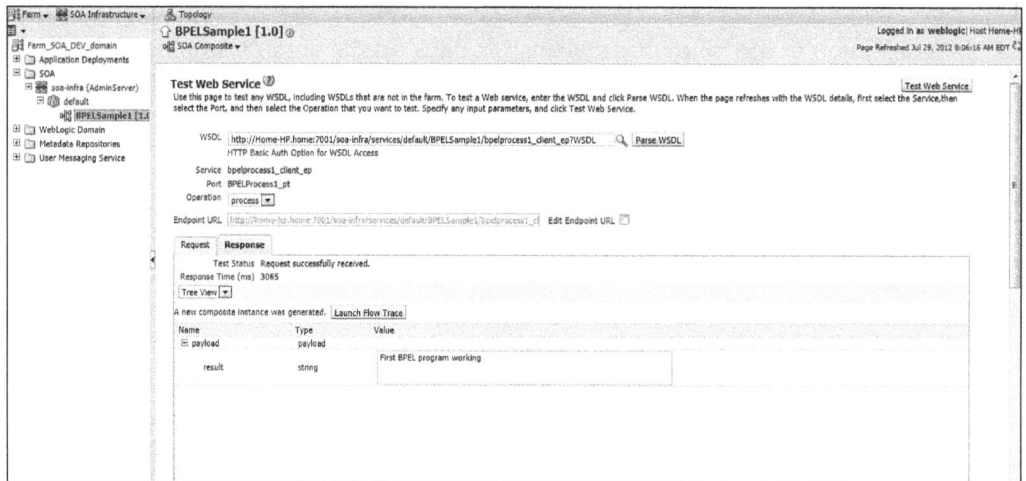

Summary

In this chapter you have developed an understanding of the concept and evolution of BPEL, installing SOA Suite and JDeveloper, creating and deploying basic BPEL services using JDeveloper and SOA Suite, and testing a BPEL service. The next chapter covers major aspects of BPEL language that includes the basic activities, structured activities, human workflow, correlation, and adapters. You will also learn how to create complex BPEL processes using JDeveloper and their use cases.

Configuring BPEL Processes

2

Web applications usually have business logic, workflow, integration with existing enterprise applications such as SAP/JDE/EBS/SDFC, and packages such as Java/ASP.NET. An example of workflow that can be part of a web application is **order processing**. A typical order processing workflow contains references to services, or in other words, consumes services such as create order, process payment, send order to warehouse, check inventory, process, and send order to customers. The order processing service illustrates a typical Business Process Execution Language (BPEL) process scenario.

BPEL is a replacement to simplify your workflow and also, to some extent, a replacement to the custom code that describes and implements the business workflow. Typical web applications require more than one service to fulfill the business requirements. The key challenges are: how to create the services and how to orchestrate the services. We can use BPEL for describing, integrating, and orchestrating a business workflow.

BPEL is an XML-based programming language used for describing high-level business processes. The WS-BPEL standard facilitates the orchestration of business processes and externalizes the processes as services. BPEL also facilitates the interaction either among organizations or between different applications within an organization.

Understanding the BPEL language framework

BPEL is an XML-based language for creating end-to-end process flow. BPEL is based on the WS-BPEL 2.0 specification and built on the **Web Services Description Language (WSDL)** 1.1 specifications.

A BPEL process always starts with a **process element**. A process element must have at least one activity. **Activities** are the core of the BPEL language framework. Usually a process element also has several attributes. The basic structure of the BPEL code is as follows:

```
<process name="ncname">

<!-- Activities  -->
</process>
```

Every BPEL has activities such as `<receive>`, `<reply>`, and `<invoke>`. Activities describe different action steps in a BPEL process that enable the interaction with external and internal services. Note, that Oracle BPEL also allows interaction with JCA adapters and EDN.

The most important concepts of BPEL are activities, partner links, variables, correlation, and handlers. The BPEL processes expose WSDL interface for consumption as web services. WSDL specifies the location of the service, the operations the service provides, and describes how to access them.

BPEL activities

BPEL processes have a series of steps and each step is an activity. BPEL process logic is performed by the activities. For clients, BPEL processes looks like any other web service. In other words, a BPEL process is a web service that coordinates, integrates, and orchestrates the basic web services to serve a business function. OASIS WS-BPEL specifications classify activities in the following categories:

- **Basic activities**: Enables the process behavior such as invoking and performing web services operations, updating variables, and partner links
- **Structured activities**: Enables the control flow logic such as flow control activities

Creating basic activities in BPEL

Launch JDeveloper and perform the following steps to create a basic BPEL process:

1. The first step is to set up the application. In JDeveloper, the term "application" is used for specifying the workspace. An application can have one or more **projects**. An application has a project for defining the models and one or more projects within the same application for accessing and processing the models. The basic deployment unit for an SOA composite is a `.sar` (**SOA Archive**) file that could be part of an `.ear` (**Enterprise Archive**) file. Click on the **Application** tab on the top menu bar of JDeveloper and then click on **New** to set up the application workspace.

2. Once we have created an application workspace, create a new project using the **File** tab on the top menu bar of JDeveloper and then click on **New**, as shown in the following screenshot. Click on **OK**.

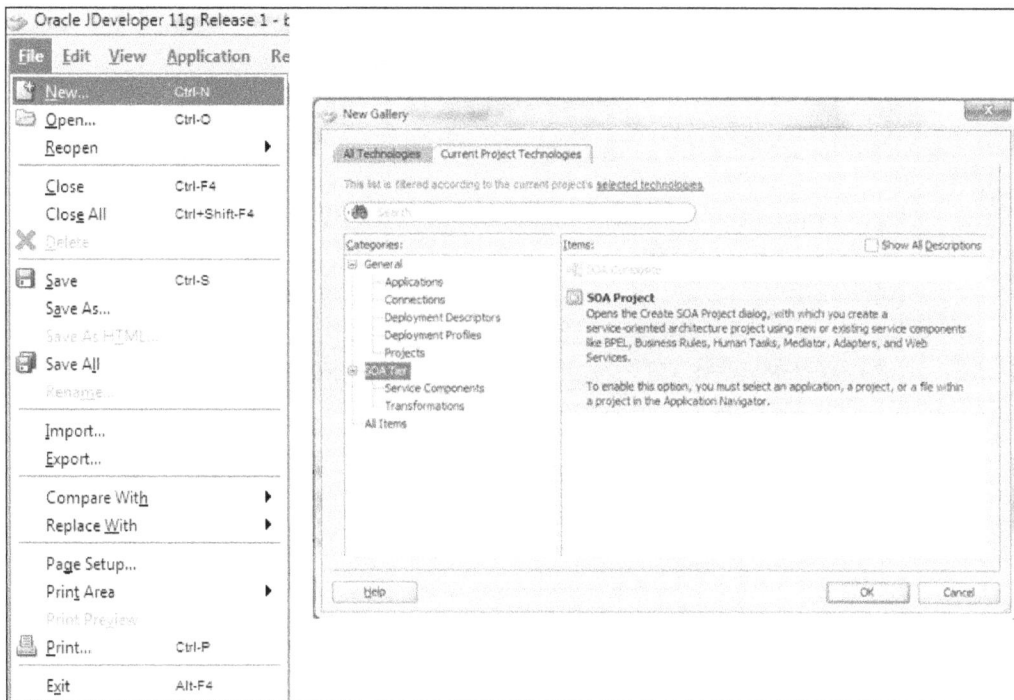

3. Enter the **Project Name**, as shown in the following screenshot, and click on **Next**.

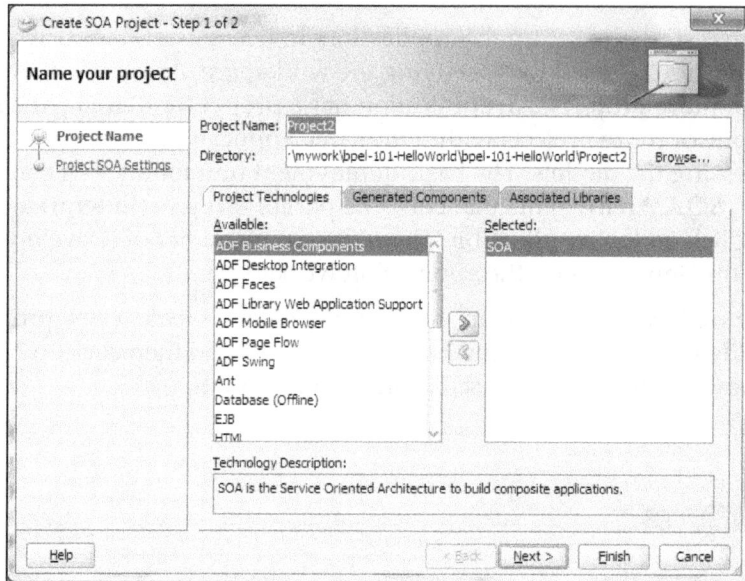

4. Select **Composite Template** as **Composite With BPEL Process**, as shown in the following screenshot:

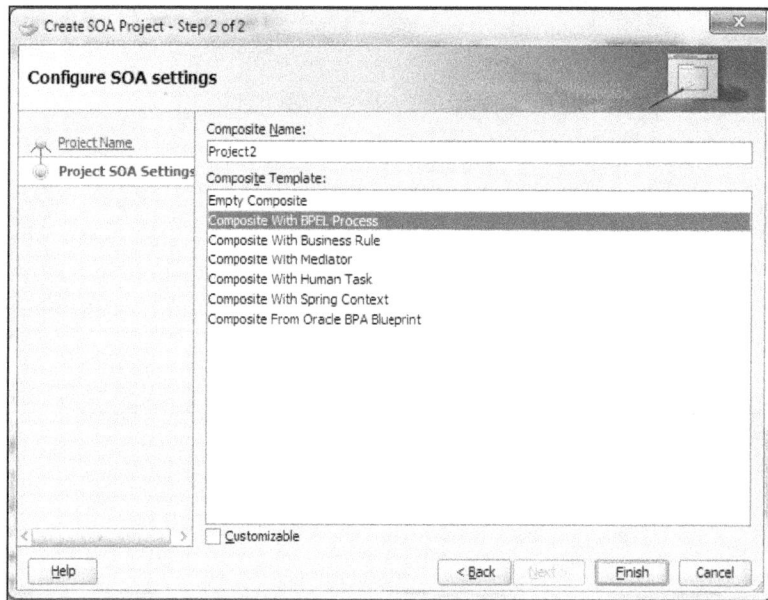

5. Enter the **Name** for the BPEL process. Select **Template** as either **Synchronous BPEL Process** or **Asynchronous BPEL Process** and click on **OK**, as shown in the following screenshot:

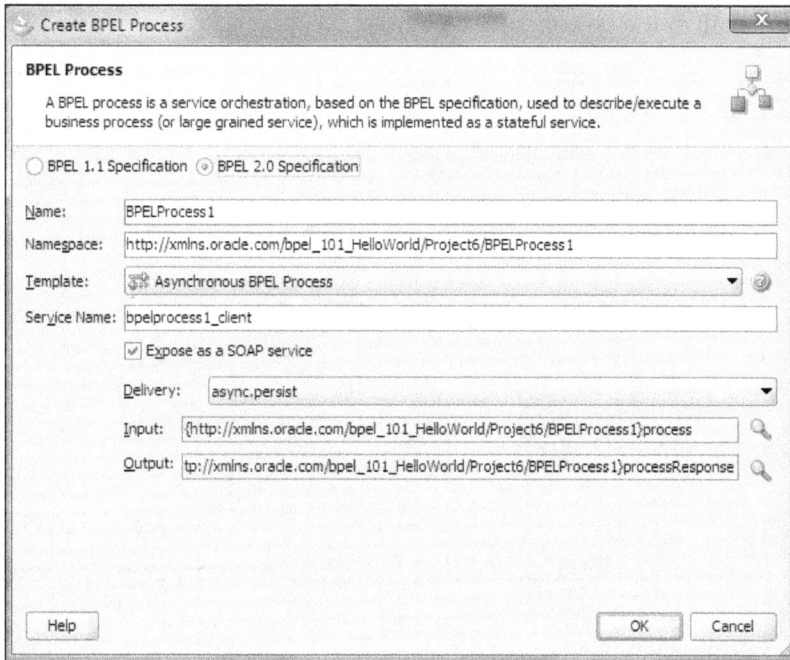

6. It will launch the BPEL process editor, also known as the composite editor, within JDeveloper, as shown in the following screenshot:

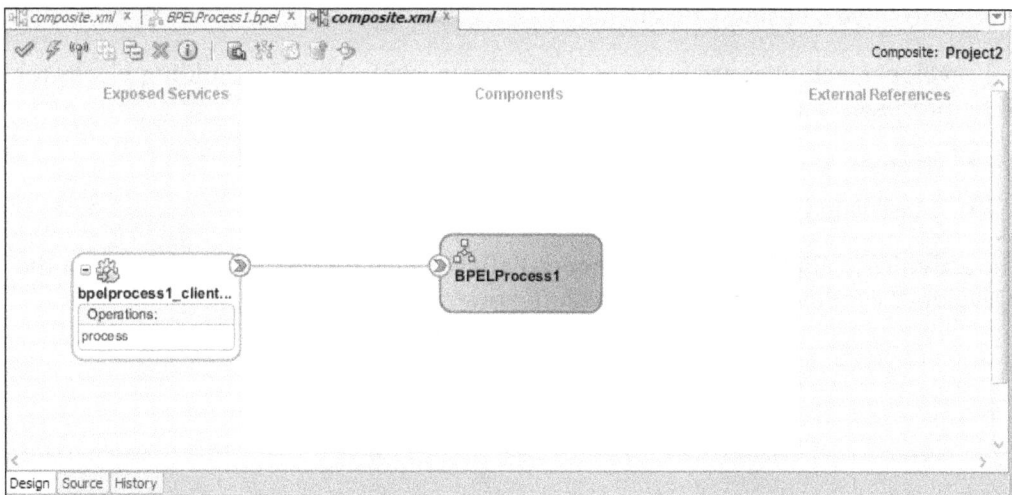

7. Double click on the **BPELProcess1** icon that will launch the **Design** view of
   the editor for defining the BPEL basic activities, as shown in the following
   screenshot. JDeveloper creates the BPEL skeleton with basic activities such as
   <receive> and <reply>. The source code can be viewed by clicking on the
   Source tab at the bottom of JDeveloper.

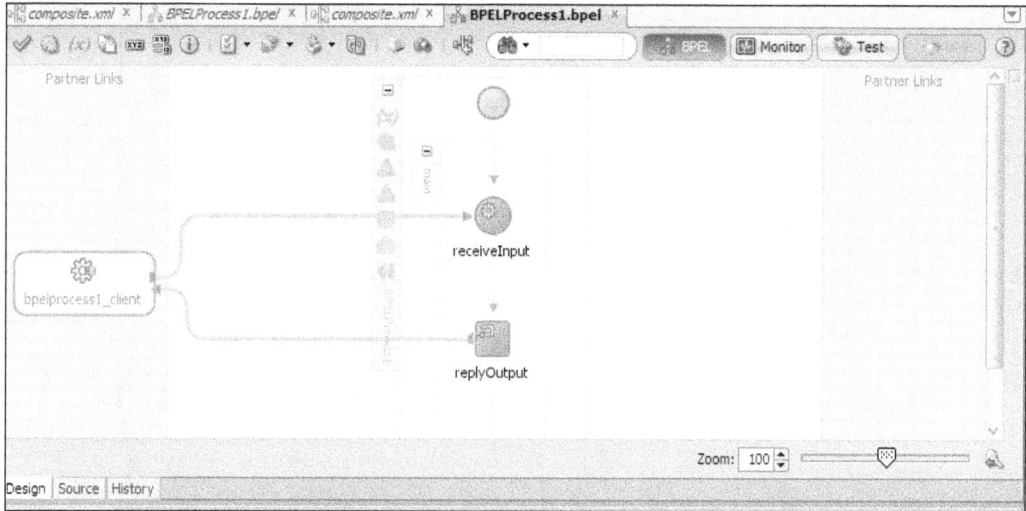

Activities

BPEL is a programming language, and activities provide functions and
operations for creating a BPEL process web service. Understanding the
purpose and usage of the activities are very important for creating a BPEL
process to serve a business function.

In JDeveloper, activities are listed as BPEL constructs and are the building blocks for
BPEL processes. Each of the BPEL constructs has the following:

- Name
- Associated properties — depends on the constructs

The activities available from **Component Pallet** located on the right-hand side of the
JDeveloper window are shown in the following screenshot:

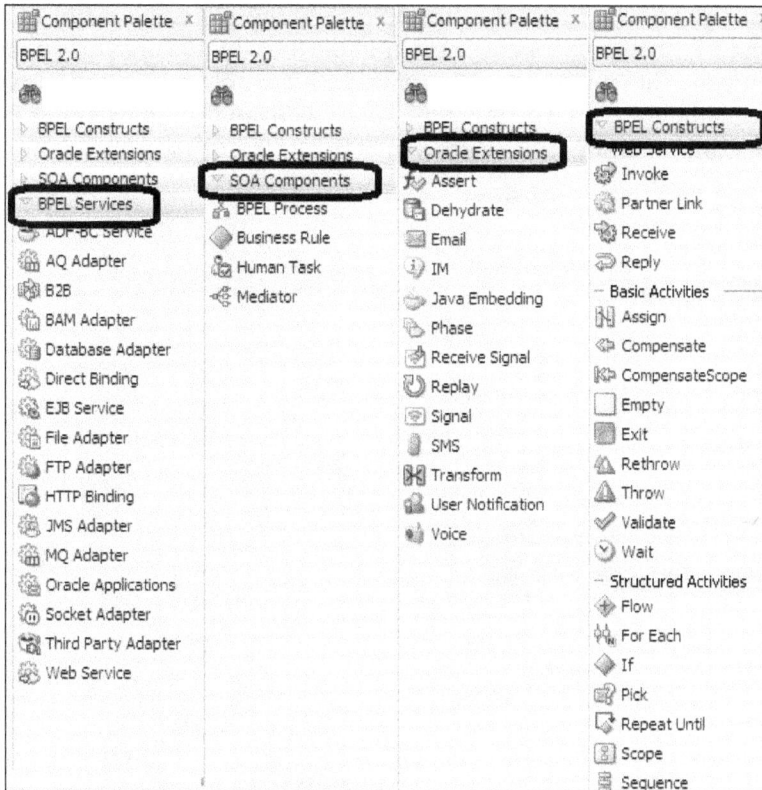

The main BPEL activities are **Receive, Invoke**, and **Reply**. The activities can be added to BPEL by dragging-and-dropping it from the **Component Pallet**, as shown in the following screenshot:

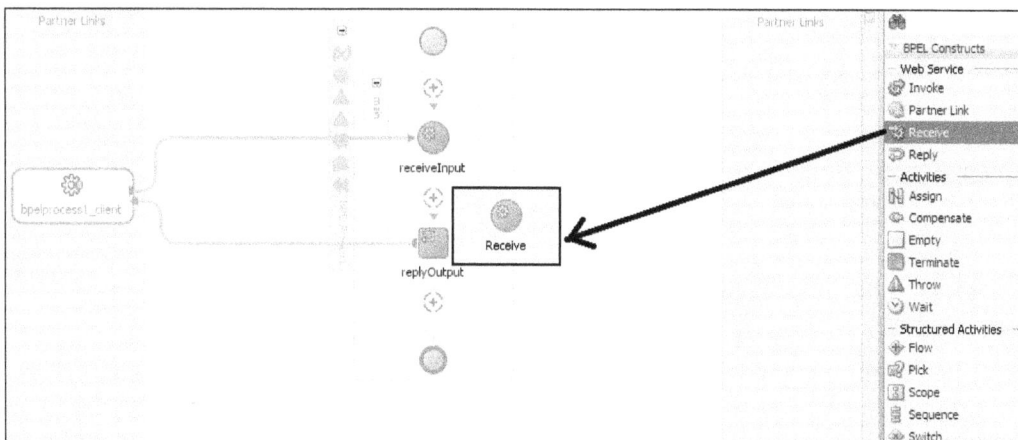

An example of an activity is **Invoke**. The **Invoke** activity is for synchronously, or asynchronously, calling services defined in partner links. For synchronous invocation, specify the input and output variables. Double-click on the **Invoke** activity after dropping it on the JDeveloper canvas from the **Component Pallet** to add configuration parameters, as shown in the following screenshot:

The activities within a BPEL process implementation can be categorized as follows:

- Basic activities
- Structured activities
- Fault and error handling

This following section provides a brief overview and usage of BPEL activities. The activities enable you to perform specific tasks and operations for a BPEL process implementation.

Basic activities

The main steps of a BPEL process are performed by basic activities. The basic activities communicate with web services (receive, invoke, reply), change the content of variables (assign), wait for a certain period (wait), or terminate the process (exit). The following is a brief description of the basic activities:

- **Receive**:
  - ○ Part of the BPEL default template
  - ○ Waits for a client to make a request or processes asynchronous callback responses from external services

- **Reply**
  - ○ Part of the BPEL default template
  - ○ Sends message as Reply after completing the processes

- **Invoke**
  - ○ A BPEL process uses Invoke to make service calls to partner web services
  - ○ Invokes partner web services either synchronously or asynchronously

> In synchronous invocation one needs to specify the input and output variables, while in asynchronous invocation one needs to specify only the input variables.

- **Transform**
  - ○ It is an XSLT Mapper and maps source elements to target elements
  - ○ Transform enables us to convert the document format usually from one XML schema to another XML schema or from an XML schema to another format such as Text, HTML, or PDF
  - ○ Helps working with complex data structures

- **Assign**
  - ○ Provide multiple copy operations such as `append`, `insert after`, and `insert before`
  - ○ Assists in copying and manipulating XML documents and elements

> Assign is mainly used for copying variables and Transform is used for changing the style of the document. Both Assign and Transform activities provide mapping of source elements to target elements; however, Transform is for complex and huge amounts of mapping and Assign is more for straight forward mappings. Assign activity will assign values to variables or initialize the variable for normal transformation. Transform provides validations as well. Transform creates a new document and Assign modifies an existing document.

- **Wait**
    - ○ Sleep for a certain amount of time or wait until a specified time has passed
    - ○ Usually used for waiting for a callback on asynchronous service response or recovering a failed service call after some time

> Two of the available formats of the Wait activity are as follows:
> - CCYY-MM-DDThh:mm:ss (use this format for specifying a wait until the time is reached). For example: <wait until="'2014-05-10T01:02:00'"/> means wait until 01:02:00 A.M., May 10, 2014.
> - PnYnMnDTnHnMnS (use this format for specifying the Time duration for wait). For example: <wait for="'P00Y01M02DT03H04M05S'"/> means wait for a duration of 00 years, 01 months, 02 days, 03 hours, 04 minutes, and 05 seconds.

- **Exit**
    - ○ Assists us to end the process
    - ○ Usually Exit is used to kill/exit a running BPEL process, which is usually done when an exception occurs or data validation fails for an activity within the BPEL process. For example, an invalid order ID will make the BPEL terminate the activity and will not proceed with order fulfillment activities. The Exit activity replaces the Terminate activity from BPEL 1.1

- **RepeatUntil**
    - ○ Provides a mechanism to repeat the execution of a contained activity until a given Boolean condition becomes true.
    - ○ The minimum execution value is one.

- **Compensate**
    - ○ Assists us in implementing recovery business logic when it is either partially or fully executed
    - ○ Compensate activity through compensation handlers allows us to cancel or reverse a previously executed activity
    - ○ A compensation handler defines an undo sequence, for example, cancel order
    - ○ Compensate activity can be invoked either from another compensation handler or only from a fault handler

- **Empty**
    - ° No action activity
    - ° Usually used when you catch an exception and are taking no action

Structured activities

BPEL provides activities for conditional branching based on data (If-Else), parallel execution (Flow), loop activities (While), way to group activities (Scope), executing activities in parallel (Flow), and selective event processing (Pick). Brief descriptions of the structured activities are listed as follows:

- **Scope**
    - ° Assists in grouping activities
    - ° Collection of nested activities with its own set of variables, partner links, exception handlers, message handlers, alarm handlers, and compensation handlers

- **If**
    - ° Assists in branch-out processes within a BPEL process.
    - ° Provides conditional branching such as between two or more branches using if, else if, and else constructs. The concept is the same as other programming languages' switch statement.
    - ° Replaces the switch activity of BPEL 1.1.

- **While**
    - ° While is a looping construct
    - ° Usually used while working with list, retry logic, or callback

- **Flow**
    - ° Facilitates parallel execution or multi-threaded processing.
    - ° Flow enables parallel execution of BPELs activities.
    - ° For example, in a BPEL process, you need to perform two activities: getting the order name and location that can be processed in parallel for a better response time. We can create two BPEL branches and execute both in parallel using Flow.

- **Pick**
  - Pick enables BPELs to implement event-based business logic that forces the process to wait until an event occurs.
  - Pick enables BPELs to wait for message event(s) that are defined on onMessage or time condition alarm event(s) that are defined on onAlarm.
  - Pick is very similar to onMessage in asynchronous JMS processing. The onMessage trigger will process the message once it arrives in either queue or topic.

- **Sequence**
  - Single-threaded processing
  - Enables executing a set of activities sequentially in a BPEL process

- **forEach**
  - Replaces FlowN activity of BPEL 1.1.
  - It is similar to a for loop in a programming language such as Java that enables the execution of multiple activities sequentially or in parallel.

Fault and error handling

Fault and error handling activity in BPEL allows us to implement the recovery from the runtime errors or business constraints. BPEL provides different fault-handling activities such as Catch, CatchAll, and Throw. Brief descriptions of the fault and error handling activities are listed as follows:

- **Catch**
  - Catches an error condition
  - Catch enables BPELs to catch an error or fault by its name. The catch activity gets executed only on failures

- **CatchAll**
  - Catches unnamed error conditions
  - CatchAll enables us to catch errors even by not specifying and/or knowing the name of the error

      °   It could be used if all the errors are handled the same way or in combination of Catch, if some errors needs special handling, and if a subset of them are handled the same way

- **Throw**

      °   Reports an internal fault

      °   Generates custom fault messages inside a business process

Synchronous versus asynchronous processes

To create BPEL, use either the **Synchronous BPEL Process** or **Asynchronous BPEL Process** template from JDeveloper.

> Another useful type of template available is the **One Way BPEL** process. One-way messaging is a type of asynchronous process. Messages are sent from the calling processes; however, no response is expected. It is a one-way call. The **Subscribe to Event** template can be used for subscribing to business events.

The synchronous BPEL default template contains the initial **Receive** activity and final **Reply** activity. We can add more activities between Receive and Reply based on the business process and logic. A typical BPEL requires more activities to process the business logic in addition to Receive and Reply activities.

Usually BPEL contains activities such as Assign for copying and manipulating the XML content.

Usually synchronous BPEL processes wait for Reply until processing is complete while the Asynchronous BPEL Process default template contains the initial Receive and Callback activities. One can add more activities between Receive and Callback based on the business process and logic.

The following figure depicts the typical BPEL structure for synchronous and asynchronous BPELs. The client receives the immediate response for a synchronous BPEL and the delayed response for an asynchronous BPEL.

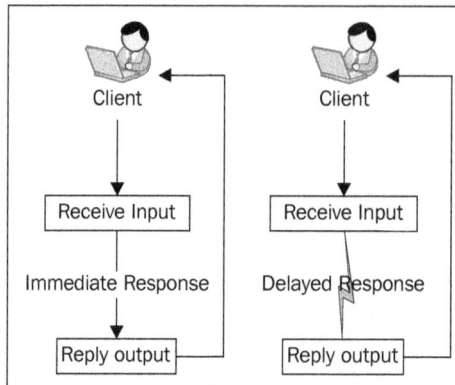

Use synchronous BPEL processes if the BPEL process requires a request-response model. However, creating asynchronous processes is a more flexible and fault-tolerant practice that usually avoids blocking the WebLogic threads.

> Asynchronous services are a call-and-forget service. The response may not return for an asynchronous service. The client can immediately perform other processing work after making an asynchronous service call and doesn't need to anticipate a response immediately.
>
> An update on a database is an example of a synchronous process. BPEL waits until it completes the database update activity and then replies and completes the process.
>
> An example of an asynchronous process can be, getting a credit score from a credit agency system. The asynchronous BPEL provides information about a person to the credit agency and drops the operation. The asynchronous process continues to do processing and it determines when to accept the data from the credit agency.

For asynchronous processes, there is no need to wait for a response before proceeding to the next step. The response can be received as part of a separate process. While creating a BPEL process in JDeveloper, we select either the **Synchronous BPEL Process** or **Asynchronous BPEL Process** template based on the design of business process and logic. The following screenshot shows the **Design** view of JDeveloper for synchronous and asynchronous BPEL processes:

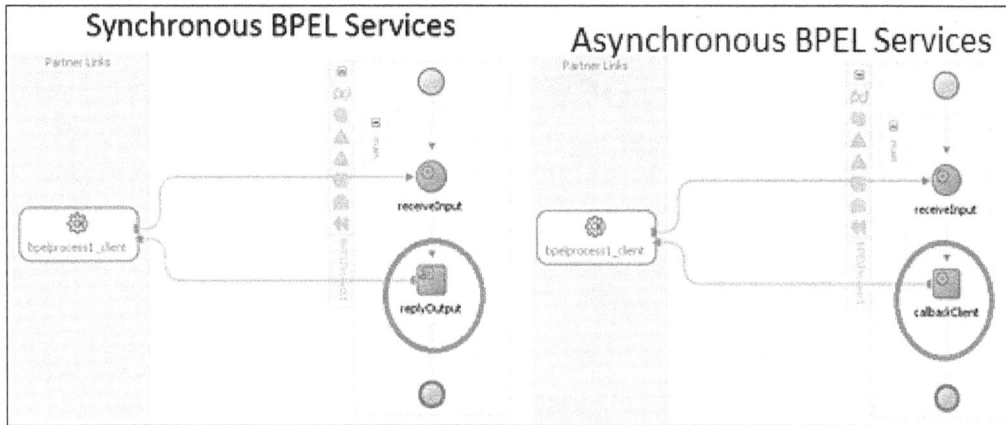

After completing the process, the synchronous BPEL process sends a response back to the client using **replyOutput**. On the other hand, the asynchronous BPEL process calls back the client with the response message using **callBackClient**. Synchronous process provides a reply and the asynchronous process needs to implement a callback using the Invoke activity.

Oracle BPEL Process Manager uses the WS-Addressing technique for message correlation between the sender and receiver. In order to correlate the response messages, Oracle BPEL Process Manager simply adds **Unique Identifier (UID)** in the WS-Addressing headers on the initial request that floats with the **simple object access protocol (SOAP)** packets. You're not required to take any action as Oracle BPEL Process Manager automatically adds the UID and callback address to correlate the response messages.

The following table explains the major differences between synchronous and asynchronous BPEL processes:

Synchronous BPEL	Asynchronous BPEL
Immediate response	Delayed or optional response
Returns the response with a Reply activity	Returns the optional response with Callback implemented with an Invoke activity
Client always waits for a response	Client does not always wait for a response
Client blocks the WebLogic thread until it completes the operation and returns a response	In most cases, client releases the thread after sending the request
Processes are short-lived. Sends a response to invoker immediately	Long-running process. Sends responses to invoker when the process is complete
Default timeout is 60 seconds	No timeout

Selecting the timeout value for synchronous processes

Synchronous processes have a default timeout of 60 seconds. If the synchronous flow takes more than 60 seconds, we must increase the timeout by configuring the Timeout property for the Receive activity.

As shown in the following screenshot, edit the Receive activity and add a **Timeout** value. *Chapter 3, Invoking a BPEL Process*, covers more details of Timeout:

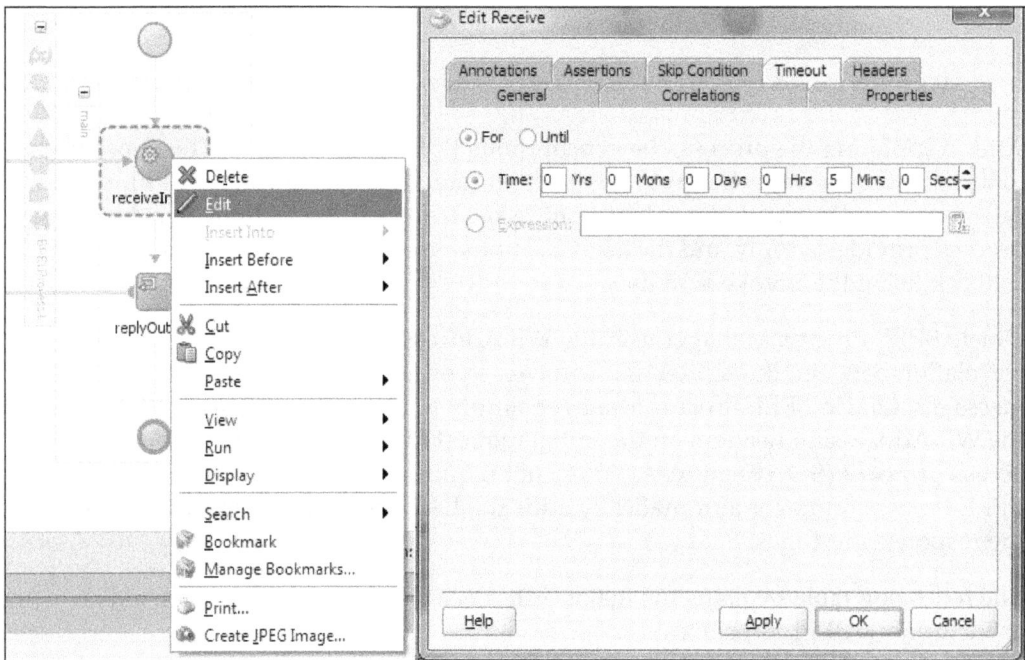

The **timeout** property can be added in the **Partner Link** as well. The following screenshot shows how to add a timeout value for synchronous processes in JDeveloper. Right-click and edit the process that requires the timeout value.

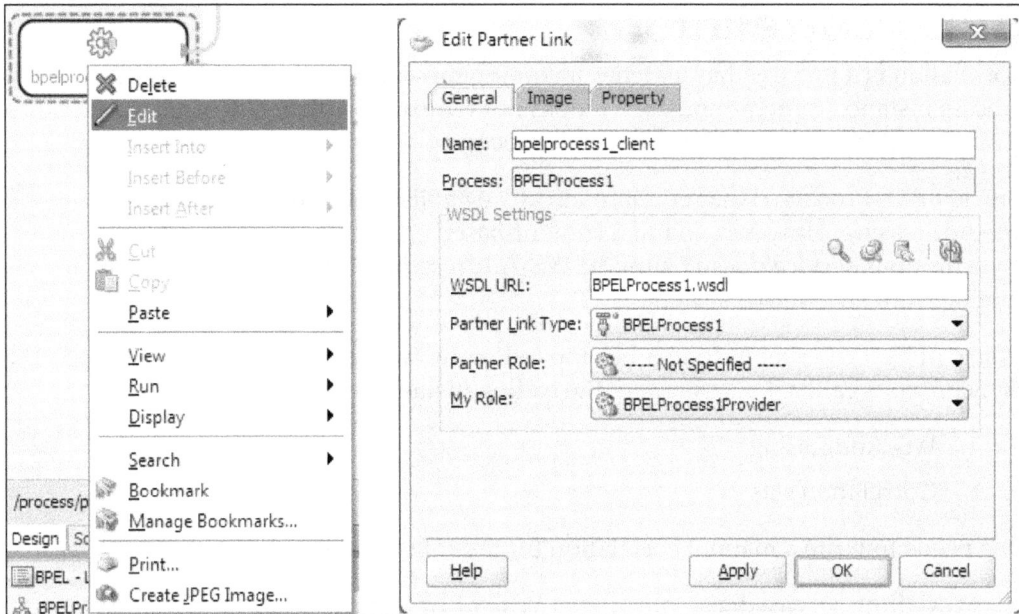

Click on the **Property** tab on the **Edit Partner Link** window. As shown in the following screenshot, click on the green **+** sign to add the **timeout** property. Please note that the timeout value set here is a client timeout:

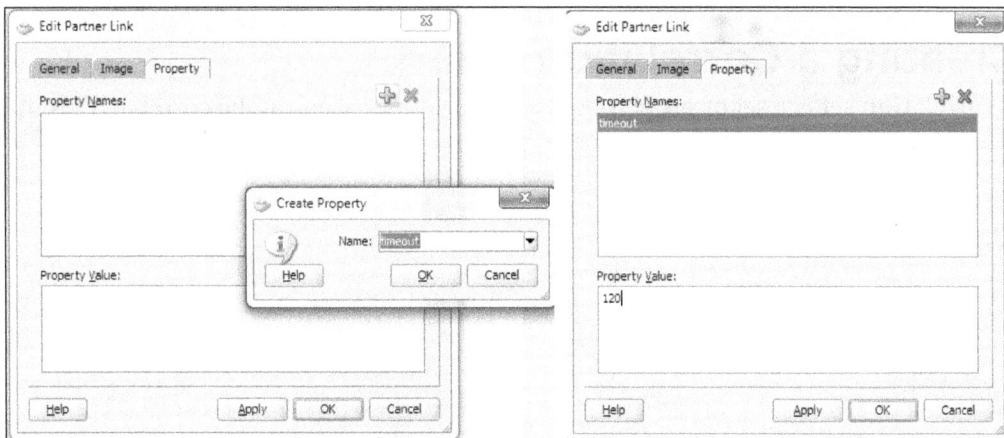

BPEL correlation

Correlation is a process that matches incoming messages to a particular BPEL process instance. Synchronous BPEL does not require correlation. Correlation is only required for asynchronous BPEL processes.

Oracle BPEL Process Manager automatically establishes correlation using WS-Addressing. However, manual content-based correlation is required if the asynchronous service doesn't support WS-Addressing or the BPEL message is coming from an external system.

Oracle BPEL Processor Manager has the following two methods for correlating asynchronous callback messages to the calling instance.

- WS-Addressing
- Correlation sets

One needs to write a manual correlation for the following scenarios:

- Calling service does not support WS-Addressing.
- When the asynchronous call has multiple layers. For example, Service A calls B, B calls C, and C Calls D. Response comes from D to A (instead of D to C to B to A). Another option in this scenario is to manipulate the **replyTo** header without implementing custom correlation.

Creating a Correlation set

A **correlation set** is a set of properties shared by all messages in the correlated group. These properties must be defined in a WSDL file imported into the BPEL process.

The first step is to create a correlation set. In order to create a correlation set, first click on the **Correlation** icon (up and down green arrow icon) on the JDeveloper, as shown in the following screenshot. Second, click on the green plus sign on the **Correlation Sets** window, as shown in the following screenshot that will open the **Create Correlation Set** window. Third, enter the **Name** and click on **OK**. Another option to create a correlation set is to create it from Invoke and Receive activities.

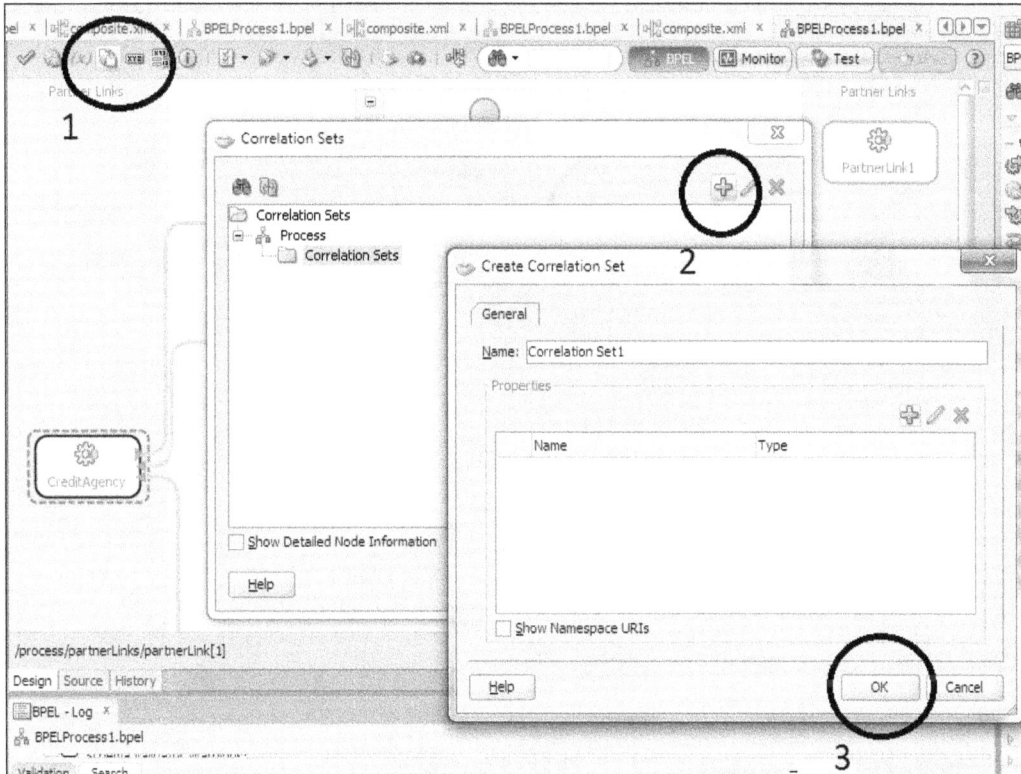

Associating the Correlation set

In JDeveloper, double-click on the Receive activity on BPEL on the **Design** view as shown in step 1 of the preceding screenshot. It will launch the **Edit Receive** window, as shown in the following screenshot. Click on the **Correlations** tab and populate the **Correlation Set** and **Initiate** values, as shown in steps 2 and 3 of the following screenshot. Click on **OK**.

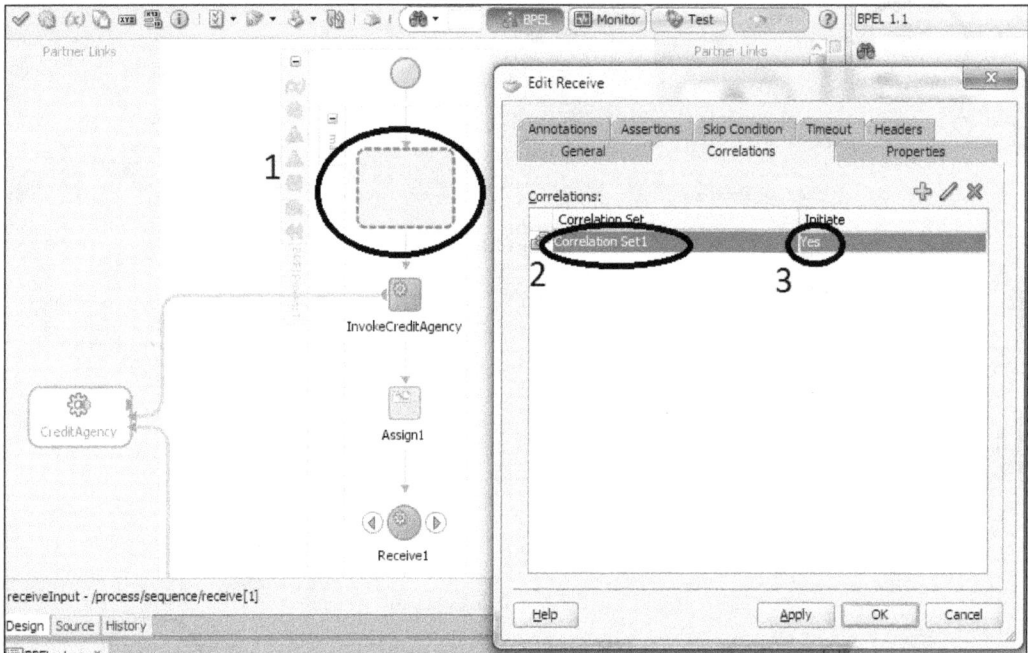

Creating property aliases

Property alias is for telling the BPEL process how to extract the value of the property from the specified message. The property aliases assist us in mapping a property to a field in a specific message part and that can be used in XPath expressions. Multiple property aliases may be required for correlation, such as the one for instantiation and another one for validation.

To create a property alias in JDeveloper, double-click on the **Property Aliases** icon, as shown in the following screenshot. Select the correlation set to associate with a property alias. If the message part is an element or a complex type, you can define an XPath query to identify the location of the property within the element or type. In the **Query** field, add appropriate XPath expressions. An XPath expression is for navigating within an XML document and helps to directly define a part of the XML document.

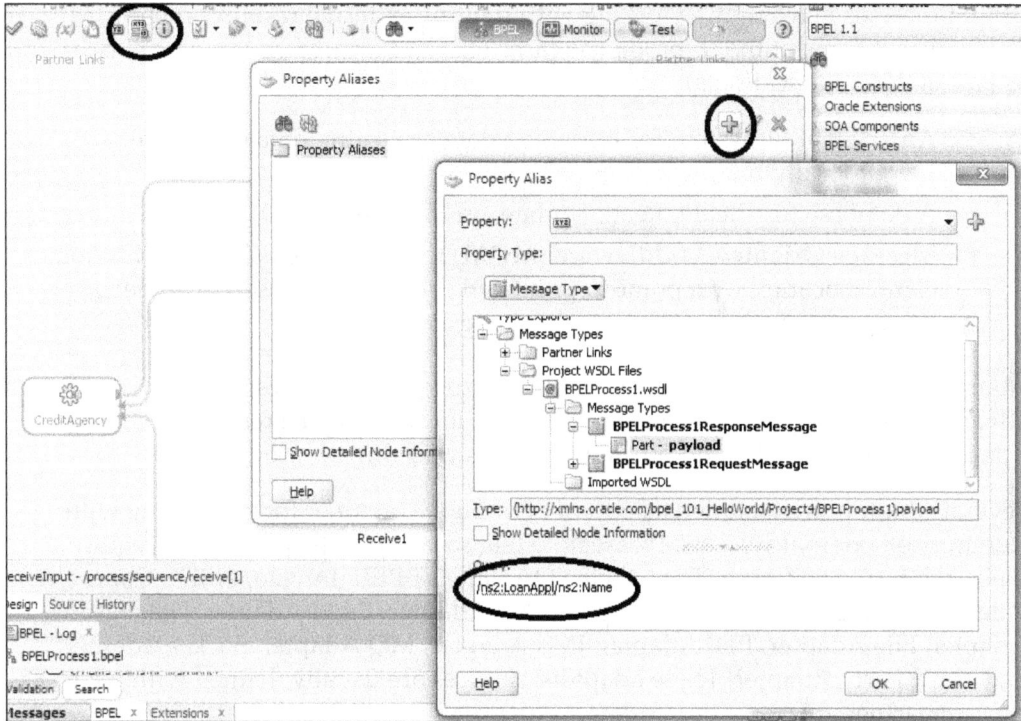

As a final verification, you may review the WSDL file content to ensure that the properties of the correlation set are defined.

Adapters

Adapters facilitate a configurable integration among disparate business systems without worrying about underlying frameworks, tools, and technologies used in implementation of an individual business system. Use of adapters enable reusability of existing applications and systems, therefore, it increases ROI and provides agility for any organization.

The Oracle SOA Suite's adapters are designed and developed using the **J2EE Connector Architecture (JCA)**. Oracle provides adapters to integrate various packaged applications, legacy applications, databases, middleware messaging systems, and web services.

BPEL processes may require working with multiple external resources. The following are some of the common use cases for BPEL processes to connect to as part of your application(s):

- An external filesystem for retrieving data or writing data either over FTP or locally-mounted NFS
- A database for Create, Read, Update, and Delete (CRUD) data
- **Message Oriented Middleware (MOM)** for asynchronous or synchronous communication with point-to-point and/or publish-subscribe model
- An external application such as PeopleSoft

Adapters are used for connecting your BPEL process to other resources. The major advantage is **decoupling**. The resource may be local or may be residing remotely. Usually partner links depend on adapters for connecting to resources.

Several adaptors are included as part of SOA Suite container for connecting with resources or external systems. Please note that some of the adapters may require their own separate license. The Oracle SOA Suite's BPEL JDeveloper IDE **Component Palette** provides out of the box adapters: AQ Adapter, BAM Adapter, Database Adapter, File Adapter, FTP Adapter, JMS Adapter, MQ Adapter, Socket Adapter, and Third Party Adapter. These adapters' services are usually defined within a BPEL process partner link.

Adapters provide an interface for connecting to external resources from BPEL services, as shown in the following figure:

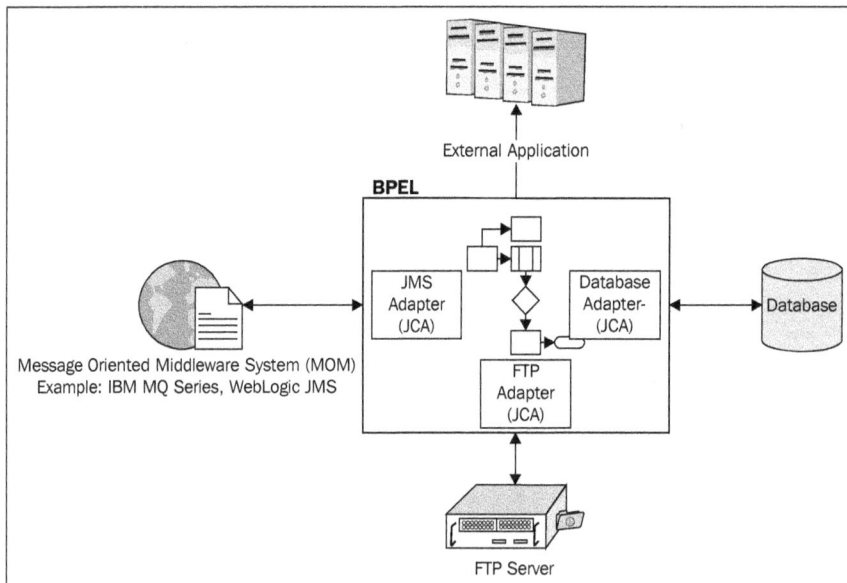

Database Adapter

The Oracle Database Adapter enables a BPEL process to communicate with Oracle databases or any third-party databases such as MS SQL and MySQL through JDBC drivers. One can use a vendor's database for design time and another for runtime because BPEL processes are database-platform neutral.

In order to leverage Database Adapter to create composite web services, one needs to establish database connections. One can establish all the database connections by navigating to **File | New | Connections**, or alternatively one can create database connections on step 3 of the Adapter Configuration Wizard. In order to create a database connection, you need to provide the database details such as **Connection Type, Username, Password, Host Name, JDBC port**, and **Service Name**, as shown in the following screenshot:

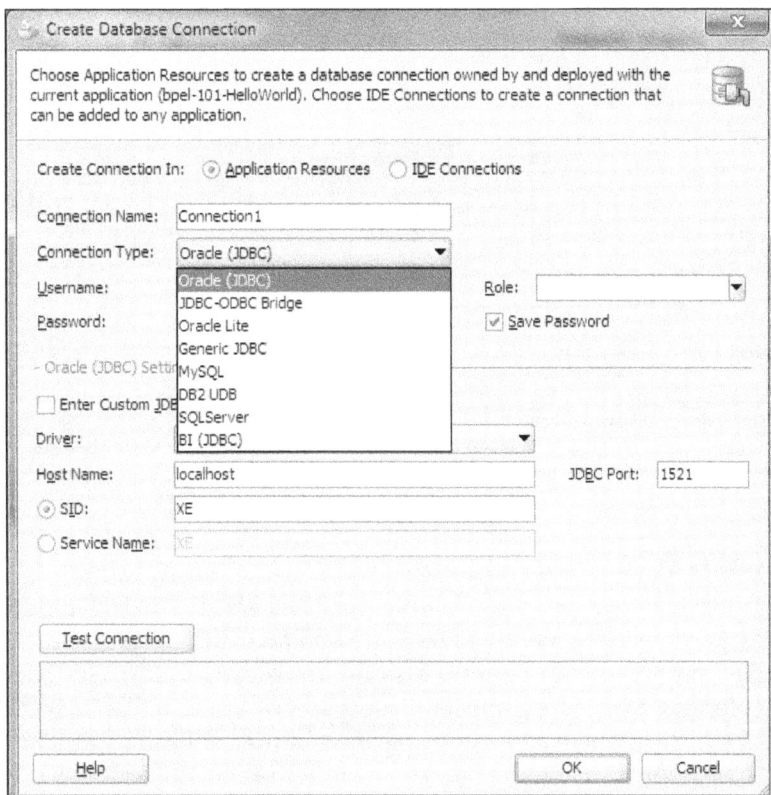

When the Database Adapter is used to poll for database events (usually an INSERT operation into an input table) and to initiate a process; in Oracle BPEL process, it is a partner link tied to a Receive activity. The expression *inbound* (from database into SOA) is commonly used.

When the Database Adapter is used to invoke a onetime DML statement such as an INSERT or SELECT, in an Oracle BPEL process, it is a partner link tied to an Invoke activity. The expression *outbound* (from SOA out to the database) is used.

The following screenshot lists the entire operation types one can leverage as services using Database Adapter to create composite web services within Oracle BPEL Business Process Manager:

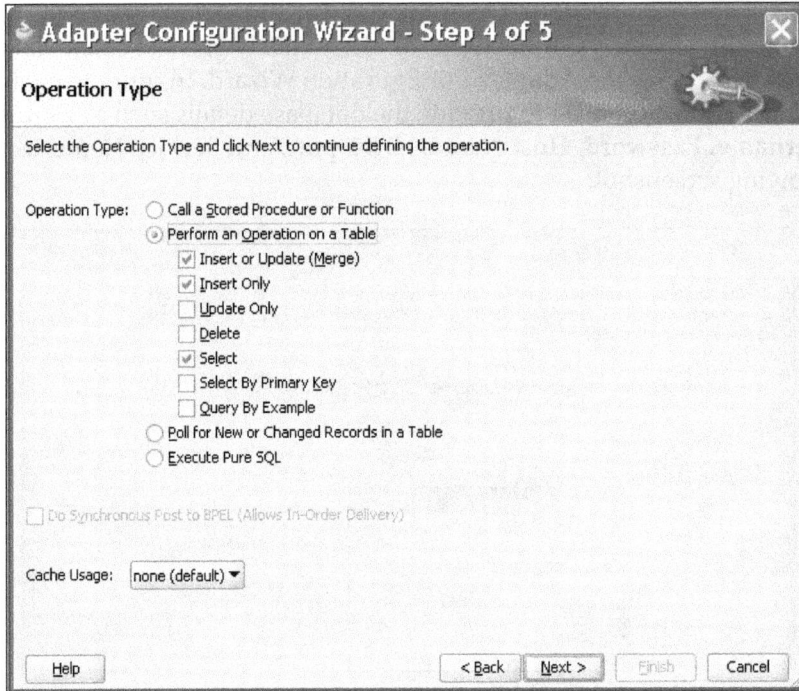

File Adapter

The purpose of the File Adapter is to enable the BPEL service to exchange files between BPEL services deployed in SOA Suite and an external filesystem that is a locally mounted NFS. The File Adaptor also can transform an XML file to text file. The File Adapter has a triggering mechanism that enables or activates transfer of the file once the file arrives in a location specified in the configuration. The polling frequency can be defined using the Adapter Configuration Wizard.

The following screenshot lists the File Adaptor operation types: **Read File**, **Write File**, **Synchronous Read File**, and **List Files** on a local filesystem:

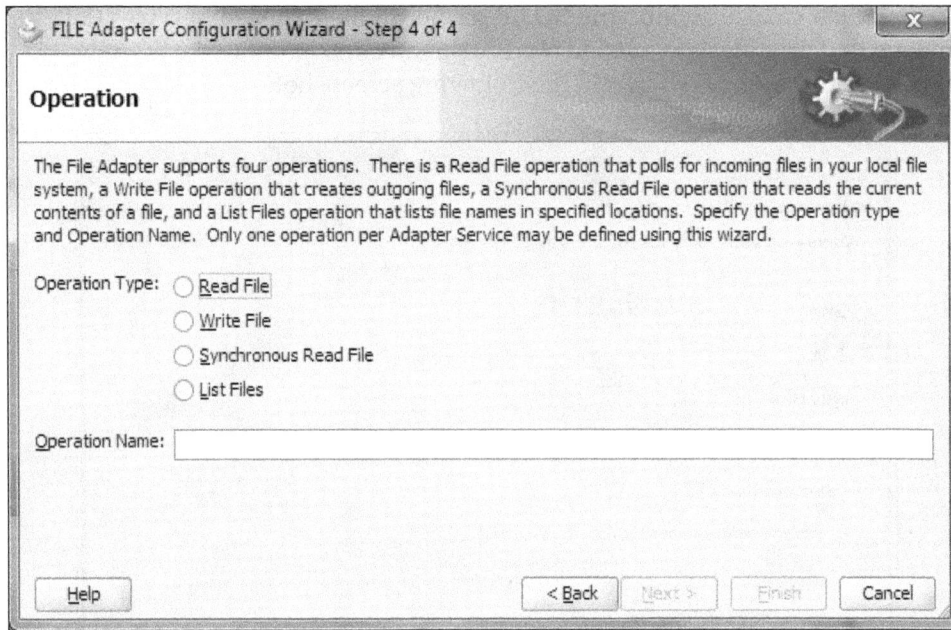

JMS Adapter

The main purpose of JMS Adapter is to exchange messages between a **Message Oriented Middleware (MOM)** such as IBM MQ series, Progress SonicMQ or Apache ActiveMQ, and BPEL services deployed in an SOA Suite platform.

Oracle has certified that the JMS Adapter works with AQ JMS (JMS provides OJMS 8.1.7, 9.0.1.4, and 9.2), WebLogic JMS, and third-party services such as TIBCO JMS, IBM WebSphere MQSeries (IBM MQSeries JMS 6.0), and Apache Active MQ.

The JMS Adapter supports three types of operations: Consume Message, Produce Message, and Request/Reply. The Consume Message operation polls for incoming messages from a JMS destination while the Produce Message operation puts outgoing messages to a JMS destination. The Request/Response operation performs both Consume and Produce operations to JMS destinations either synchronously or asynchronously.

Web Service Adapter

Web Service Adapter assists us in creating a SOAP web service binding component for message delivery. Binding components such as web services make service-oriented architecture (SOA) applications accessible to the outside world. The Web Service Adapter provides two types of service bindings: Reference and Service.

Service binding creates an inbound SOAP service in the **Exposed Services** (left) swim lane that provides the outside world with an entry point to the SOA composite application, as shown in the following screenshot:

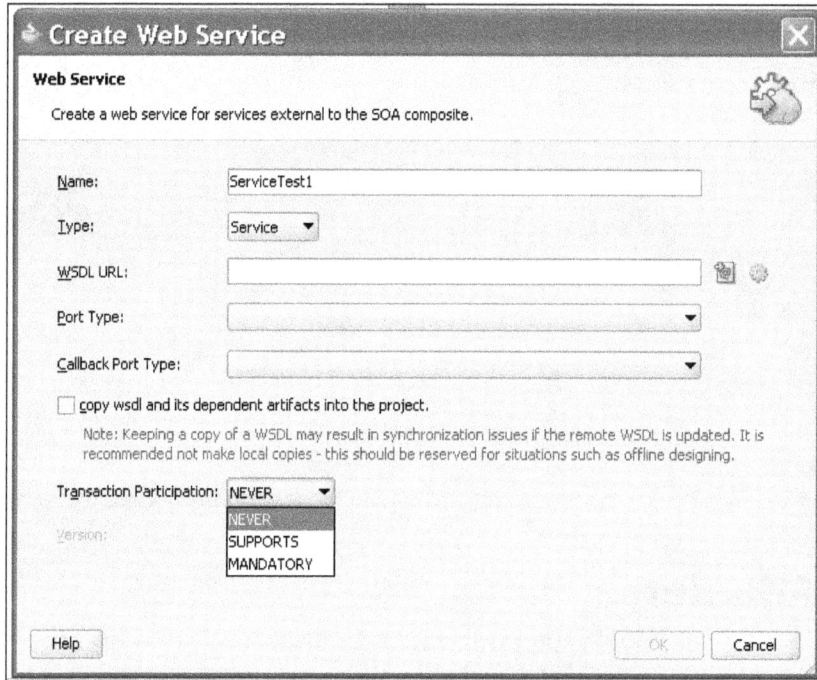

Reference binding creates an outbound SOAP web service in the **External References** (right) swim lane that enables messages to be sent from the SOA composite application to external partners in the outside world, as shown in the following screenshot:

It is recommended that you do not create a local copy of a WSDL and do not update the WSDL location in your file in **Source** view manually. This action is not supported. WSDL location updates made in the **Design** view are supported.

WSDL describes the capabilities of the service that provides an entry point into an SOA composite application or a reference point from an SOA composite application. A service or reference is defined by a port type and, optionally, a callback port type. The WSDL file can define more capabilities (port types) of the target web service, but a service only uses the one defined by the port type.

Transaction Participation configures the level of support for WS-Coordination and WS-AT transactions. WS-AT provides transaction interoperability between WebLogic Server and other external transaction processing systems, such as WebSphere, JBoss, Microsoft .NET, and so on. This enables external transaction managers to coordinate resources hosted on WebLogic Server over WS-AT or vice versa.

Implementing human workflow with Human Task components

There are business use cases that require decision-making by a human as part of the workflow. BPEL provides Human Task to achieve this. The BPEL composite service with Human Task(s) will always be an asynchronous service.

Drag **Human Task** from **Component Palette** to a flow activity of a BPEL process. It will open up a **Human Task** wizard, as shown in the following screenshot:

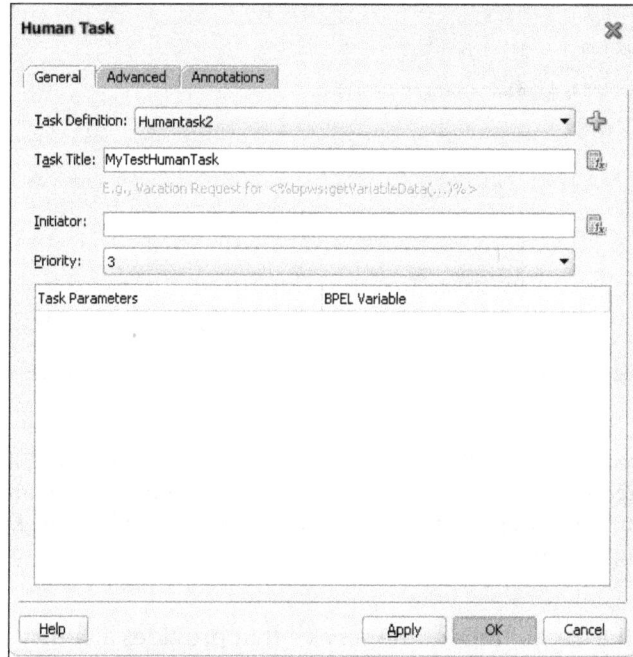

It will pop up a window to let you configure the Human Task's high-level properties, as shown in the following screenshot:

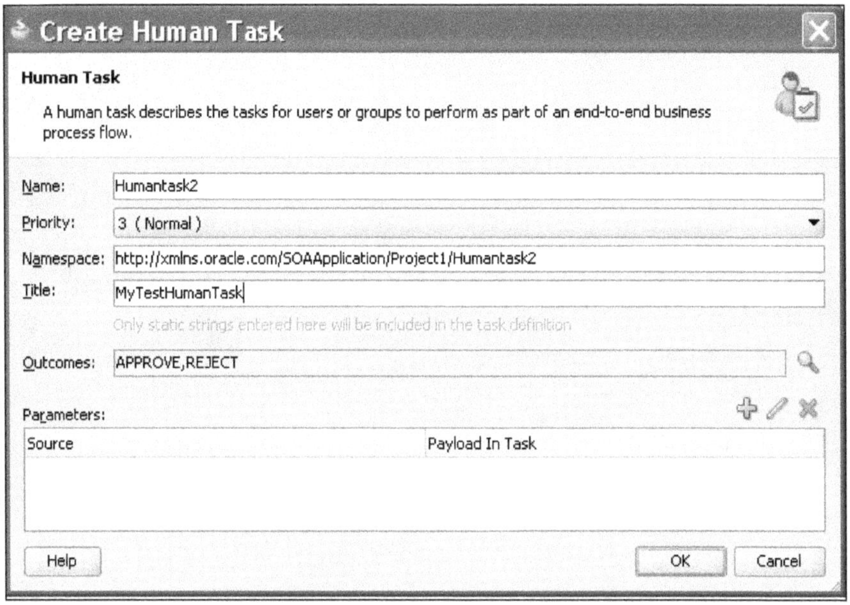

It will open up a component editor to configure the Human Task in detail. One can also open the component editor by right-clicking on the **Human Task** icon on the partner links on the right-hand side of the **Design** panel. On this tab, you can create input data, assignment, notification and events, access, and deadlines to the Human Task.

The following screenshot shows the **Design** view of the Human Task where you could create the next steps for a **REJECT, ACCEPT,** or **Otherwise** outcome for a Human Task:

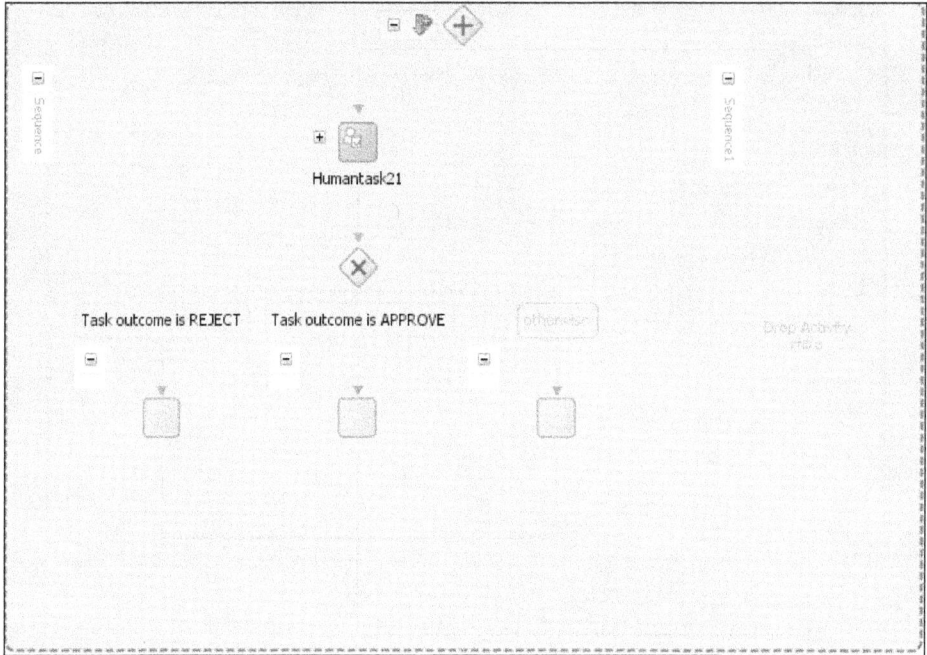

Summary

In this chapter, we learned the details of Business Process Execution Language (BPEL) structure, language framework, adapters, and how to create a BPEL process using Oracle JDeveloper IDE. We also learned the use cases and implementation steps for synchronous BPEL processes, asynchronous BPEL processes, manual correlations, and human tasks. In the next chapter, you will learn how to invoke BPEL processes from Java and vice versa. You will also learn about BPEL processes transaction timeout.

3
Invoking a BPEL Process

BPEL provides an enterprise and cross-enterprise approach for SOA with simple descriptions of how to orchestrate processes and invoke external programs, applications, and/or services. In practice, BPEL is actually extending the existing WSDL standards. WSDL is an XML-based language for describing web services that includes the details of how to consume them.

BPEL does not replace Java, .NET, or any other programming language, rather it complements them. In this chapter, we will talk about interoperability between BPEL and Java. BPEL provides excellent workflow process capabilities; however, one may find competing arguments from associates that it may not be worth it due to investments required in learning and using BPEL, additional infrastructure requirements, and an additional layer for troubleshooting. BPEL won't solve all the enterprise applications' problems, rather it is a tool to simplify reusability of discrete systems and facilitate seamless process agility to design and deploy enterprise class composite applications. The key to success is to realize when and how to use BPEL in implementing composite applications.

Communicating between BPEL to/from Java

To reuse and integrate applications, one can create web services using XML and HTTP. **Web Service Description Language (WSDL)** is an XML-based language for describing web services. The web services can be located and invoked over the Web using WSDL from the service providers.

A WSDL contains an element named `<binding>` which describes how the message is transmitted on the wire and a `<service>` element that contains the location of the web service.

The `<portType>` element in WSDL provides a set of operations for the calling clients. Port type is very similar to the concept of interfaces in Java. Java interface specifies methods that a calling client can consume but only by specifying a method of its own. Similarly, Port type in WSDL specifies the operations available that a calling client can consume but only by specifying an operation of its own.

Usually BPEL process consists of multiple steps that provide an overall process. Each step is called an **activity**. BPEL interacts with external services either by invoking operations on external web services or by receiving invocations from external entities. In simple words, it is either the consumer that invokes operations to others or the provider that receives invocations from others.

Invoking a BPEL process from Java

BPEL is a workflow system that manages coordination and communication for multiple concurrent conversations at the same time. Administrators can view the status of each request in the Enterprise Manager (EM) console.

BPEL provides client interfaces via SOAP, JCA, or native Java. BPEL itself is a service that can be invoked from Java programs. BPEL processes can be invoked using Oracle-provided Java APIs. Usually the BPEL processes are invoked from a Java program using Partner Link.

A BPEL process is available for invocation from standalone Java using one of the following interfaces:

- WSDL Interface
- BPEL Process Manager Java API
- JDeveloper Web Services Proxy
- Business delegate Java interface

Invoking BPEL is similar to calling any other web service from a Java program. BPEL implements a service that is defined in the WSDL. In case you are using Eclipse or NetBeans for writing the Java code, right-click on your project and select **New Web Service Client**. Select the **WSDL** for a BPEL process in the dialog box.

BPEL can be initiated from Java using business delegate Java interface from a locally or remotely used RMI. Partner Link allows BPEL to have conversations with WSDL-defined web services.

In JDeveloper, we can invoke a BPEL process from Java programs using the SOAP interface or native Java interfaces. The following figure shows the structure of invoking a BPEL process:

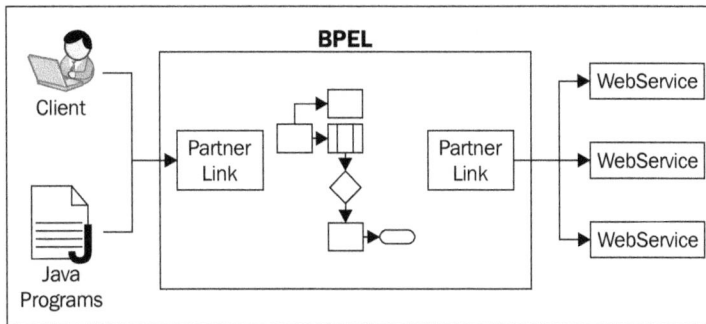

In Java, the invocation of web services is performed using the JAX-RPC library. JAX-RPC Java API enables **Remote Procedure Calls (RPC)** and XML-to-Java and Java-to-XML mapping. Use generic Java API to invoke a BPEL process.

Invoking a service from a BPEL process

BPEL uses Partner Link for invoking synchronous and asynchronous services. BPEL processes may alternatively use the Invoke activity that opens a port in the BPEL service component to send and receive data.

Partner Link

Partner Link provides references to external services. Partner Link is the door for outside services. While editing a BPEL process, one can create a Partner Link to invoke external services. As shown in the following screenshot, drag-and-drop the **Partner Link** to the JDeveloper console and select the **SOA Resource Browser** for selecting the WSDL for interacting with another web service using the standard WSDL interface:

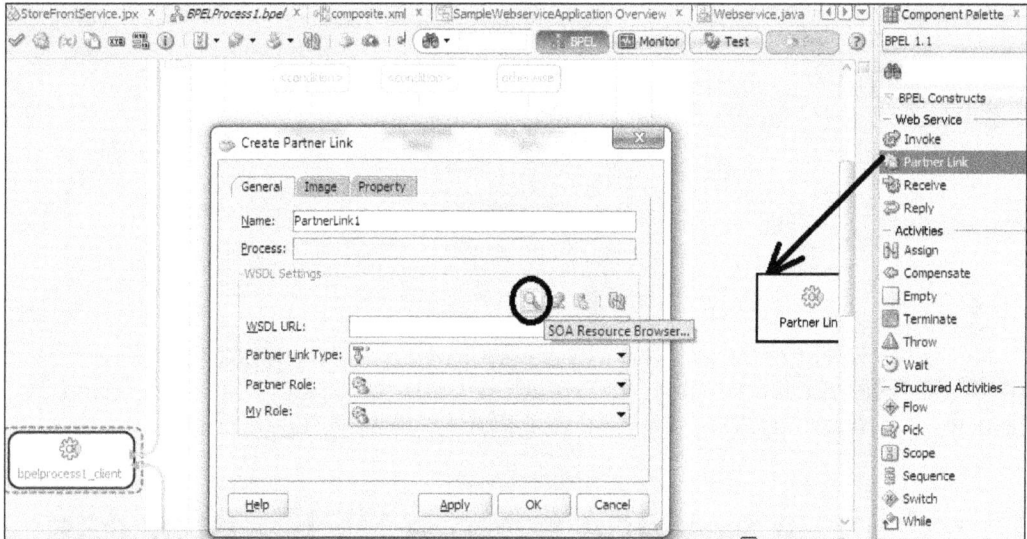

As shown in the following screenshot, select the WSDL file from your filesystem for interacting with another web service. Other options are to locate the WSDL file from **Resource Palette** and **Application** or retrieve WSDL using the WSDL endpoint URL. It is recommended to test and confirm the WSDL URL using an external web browser prior to using in a **Partner Link**:

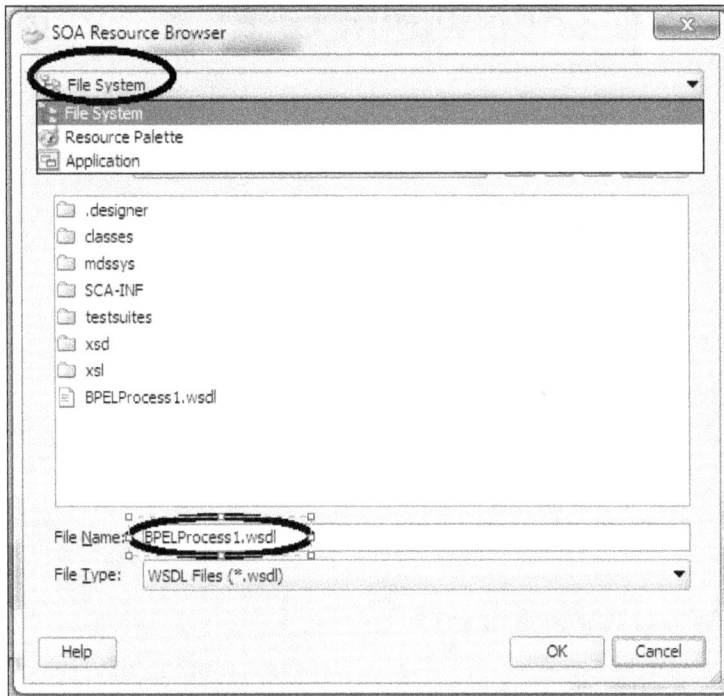

The XML source of **Partner links** is given as follows for reference. The Partner Link Type uses at least one role and describes the details of the external services for exchanging messages:

```
<partnerLinks>
<!-- The 'client' role represents the requester of this service. It is
used for callback. The location and correlation information associated
with the client role are automatically set using WS-Addressing.-->
<partnerLink name="bpelprocess1_client" partnerLinkType="client:BPELPr
ocess1" myRole="BPELProcess1Provider"/>
</partnerLinks>
```

Writing Java code within BPEL activities

To call Java code from BPEL, use the **Java Embedding** activity.

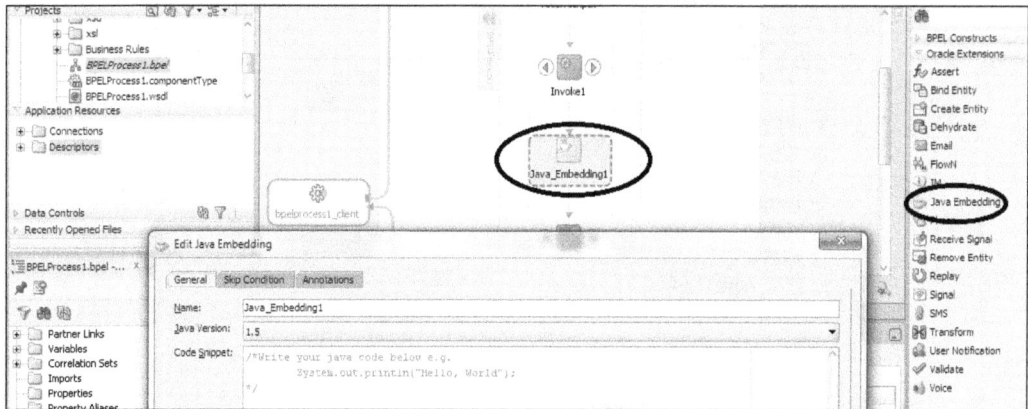

Invoking Java from BPEL

Another option to call Java from BPEL is using SOAP to wrap the Java code as a web service and invoke the web service from BPEL

In order to use a Java method from an already created Java project, you could perform the following steps:

1. Create a `.jar` file of your Java project.

2. To use a Java class from the `.jar` file inside the BPEL process, copy the JAR in the same project's `SCA-INF/lib` folder and include the JAR by going to **Libraries and Classpath**.

3. Use the **Java Embedding** activity for writing Java programs to invoke the method from the `.jar` file.

4. Use `import` statements inside the source code of BPEL to import the Java class. Use the `import` attribute of `bpelx:exec` for importing Java classes and libraries. Examples are listed as follows:

    ```
    <bpelx:exec import="java.util.*"/>
    <bpelx:exec import="myjavaprogram.*"/>
    ```

Configuring BPEL timeouts

Receiving connection timeout-related errors is a common scenario for processing large payload or a large number of message files.

Some of the scenarios that require value changes in the `Timeout` parameter are listed as follows:

- One needs more than 30 seconds for running the composite application with a large payload
- Application logfiles or EM console has timeout errors

There are multiple solutions available to resolve timeout-related errors. The following timeout controls are available in BPEL Process Manager:

- JTA Transaction Timeout aka Global Transaction Timeout
- BPEL EJB's Transaction Timeout
- `syncMaxWaitTime`
- Transaction setting in `composite.xml`

Global Transaction Timeout parameter setting is at the WebLogic container level. Please note that the BPEL Process Manager programs run within the WebLogic platform. The Global Transaction Timeout parameter should be higher than any BPEL program's timeout settings.

It is required to set the timeout values as follows:

```
Global Transaction Timeout ≥ BPEL EJB's Transaction Timeout ≥
syncMaxWaitTime
```

Setting the JTA Transaction Timeout aka Global Transaction Timeout parameters

The Global Transaction Timeout value is set at the WebLogic domain level. This property controls the transaction timeout seconds for active transactions. If the transaction is still in the "active" state after this time, it is automatically rolled back.

Log in to the WebLogic console (`http://{hostname}: {port}/console`). As shown in the following screenshot, click on the **JTA** tab and update the default timeout value (**30** seconds). Restart the WebLogic server after making the changes:

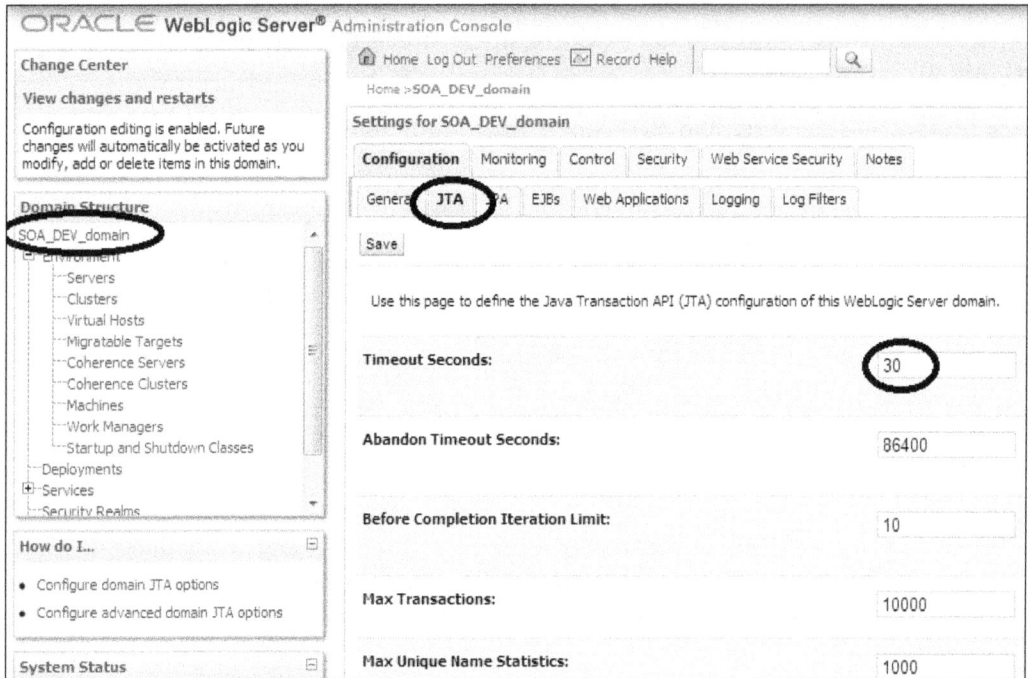

> Please note that changing **Max Transactions** has an impact on the available resources.

Changing the SyncMaxWaitTime parameter

Usually the Oracle BPEL Process Manager generates the following error if the synchronous transactions take more than 45 seconds to complete:

```
nested exception is: javax.transaction.RollbackException: Timed out
```

The solution is to set `syncMaxWaitTime` to `600` or more in the Process Manager console (the default is `45`).

- Log in to Enterprise Manager (EM) (`http://{hostname}:{port}/em`)
- Right-click on SOA and select **BPEL Properties** from under **SOA Administration,** as shown in the following screenshot:

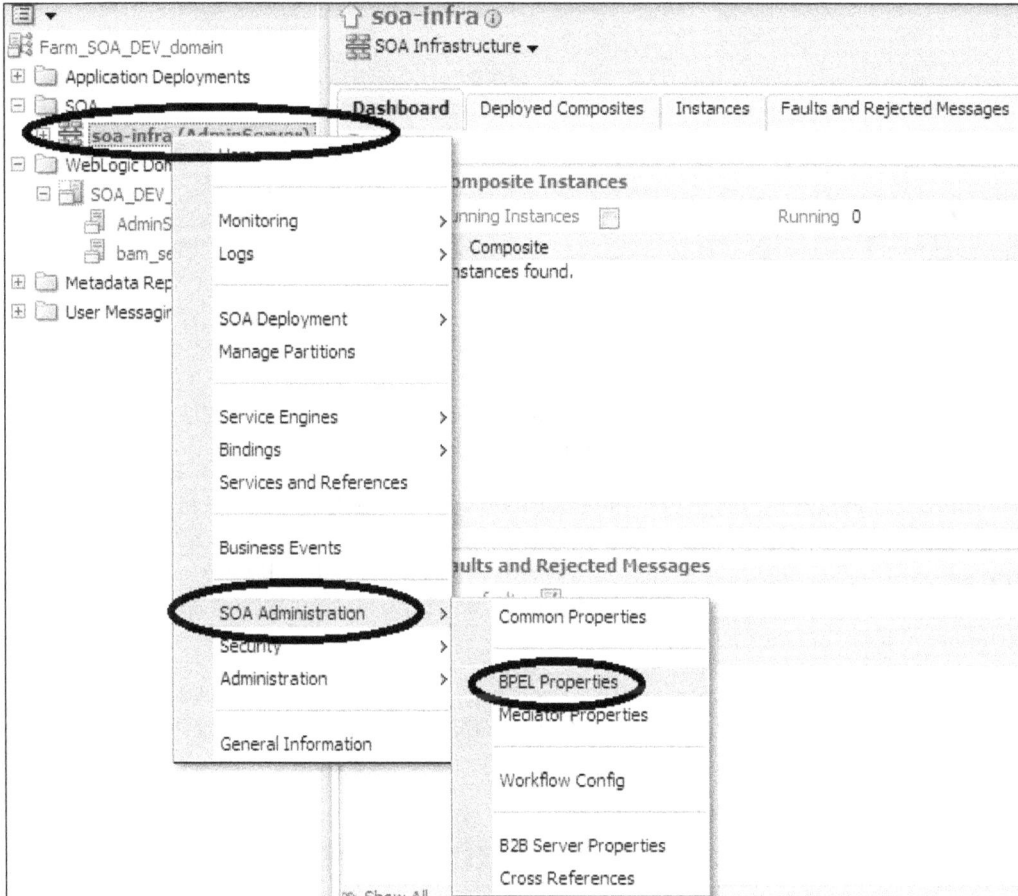

- At the bottom of the **BPEL Service Engine Properties** page, click on **More BPEL Configuration Properties**, as shown in the next screenshot.

- Click on **SyncMaxWaitTime** and in the **Value** field specify the new value in seconds:

Transaction settings

The default transaction setting for SOA Suite is **requiresNew**. Add `bpel.config.transaction` in `composite.xml` for changing the default behavior.

The transaction setting provides a mechanism to handle data when a fault occurs. The implications for setting **Requires** is when the fault occurs and is not handled appropriately, the calling and invoked BPEL operations will roll back together. If the calling BPEL has a `catch` block to commit transactions, you may have a record in the database for calling BPEL.

Change the transaction setting to **Required** for joining with callers transaction instead of creating a new transaction. **requiresNew** will always create a new transaction and commit the data when the operation completes.

BPEL EJB's transaction timeout

1. Log in to Oracle WebLogic Administration console (`http://{hostname}:{port}/console`).

2. Click on **Deployments**, as shown in the following screenshot:

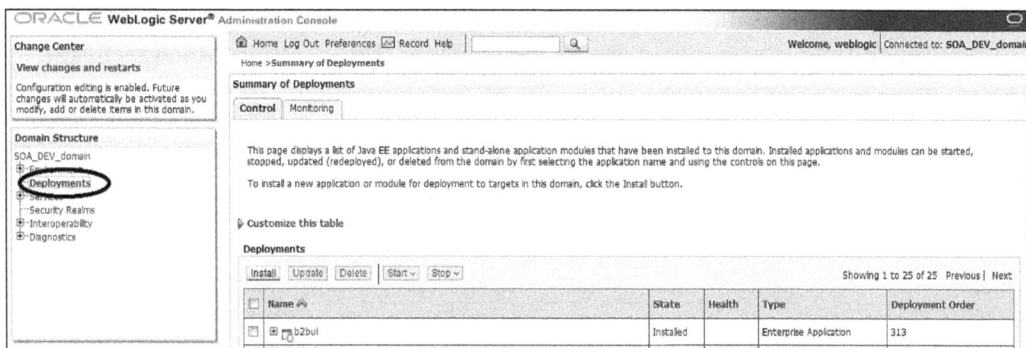

3. As shown in the following screenshot, select EJBs from **soa-infra** from the deployed modules:

4. Update the following EJB's deployment descriptors. Change the **Timeout** setting using the **Configuration** tab. Restart the SOA managed server after making changes to the EJB's transaction timeout.

   ○ **BPELActivityManagerBean**

   ○ **BPELDeliveryBean**

   ○ **BPELDispatcherBean**

   ○ **BPELEngineBean**

   ○ **BPELFinderBean**

   ○ **BPELInstanceManagerBean**

   ○ **BPELProcessManagerBean**

   ○ **BPELSensorValuesBean**

   ○ **BPELServerManagerBean**

5. Repeat the step shown in the following screenshot for all the BPEL EJBs. The following screenshot shows the steps for **BPELActivityManagerBean**:

Timeout for Asynchronous BPELs

For asynchronous BPELs, the timeout period for receiving the response can be defined in terms of seconds, minutes, hours, days, months, or years. The default is indefinite timeout. The timeout response can call other services or return a message to the initial caller.

In BPEL, the asynchronous timeout is implemented with one Invoke and one Pick at the client end and one Receive and one Invoke at the provider end. In the Pick activity, the timeout period can be specified.

Since some of the asynchronous services take a long time to return a response, you can use the Pick activity to perform other duties instead of waiting for a response. The expiration time can be set by using the Wait activity.

As shown in the following screenshot, drag-and-drop the **Pick** activity from the JDeveloper **Component Palette**:

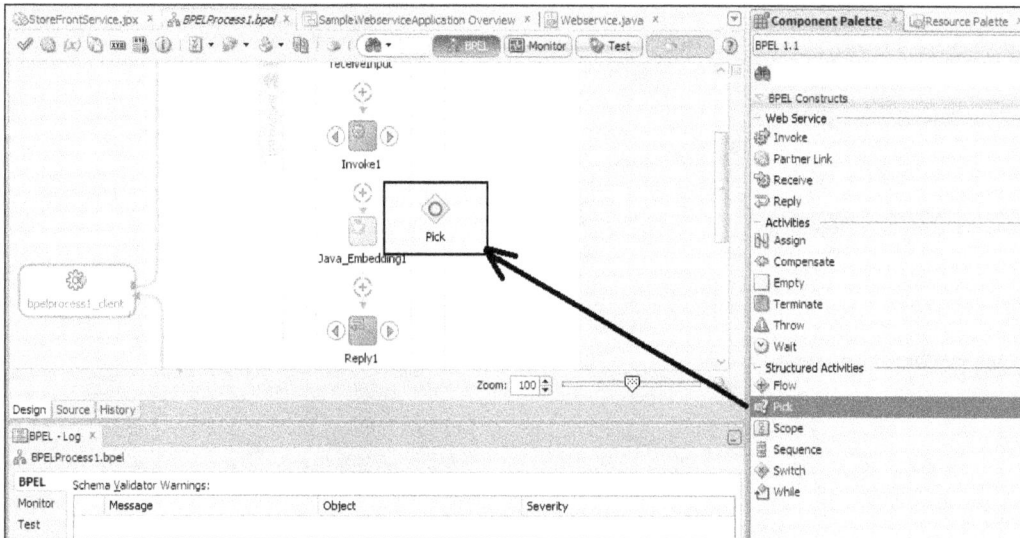

Then double-click on the **OnMessage** branch and add **Partner Link**, **Operation**, and **Variable**:

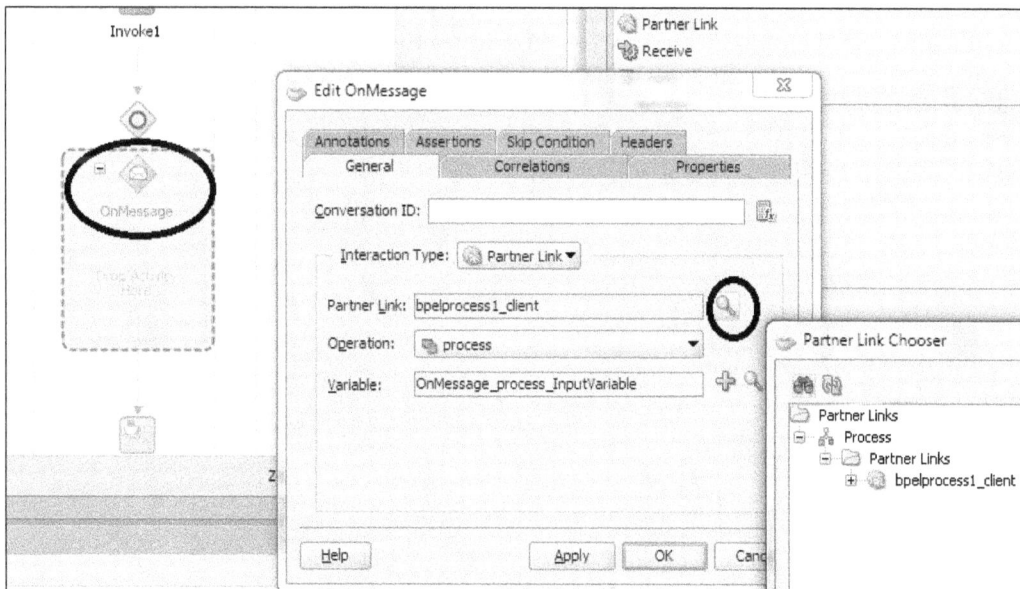

Click on **Add OnAlarm** for adding the **OnAlarm** branch for the Pick activity. The timeout values are specified in **OnAlarm** branch, as shown in the following screenshot:

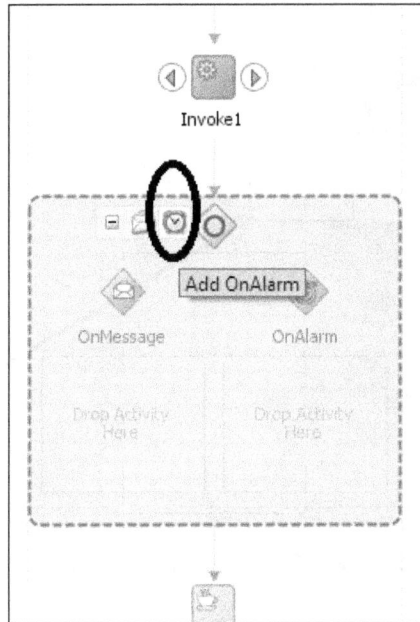

Double-click on the **OnAlarm** branch to configure the timeout. In this example, the BPEL process will wait for 8 hours and 30 minutes.

Use the **For** radio button for selecting the amount of time for wait. Use the **Until** radio button for selecting the deadline for which to wait:

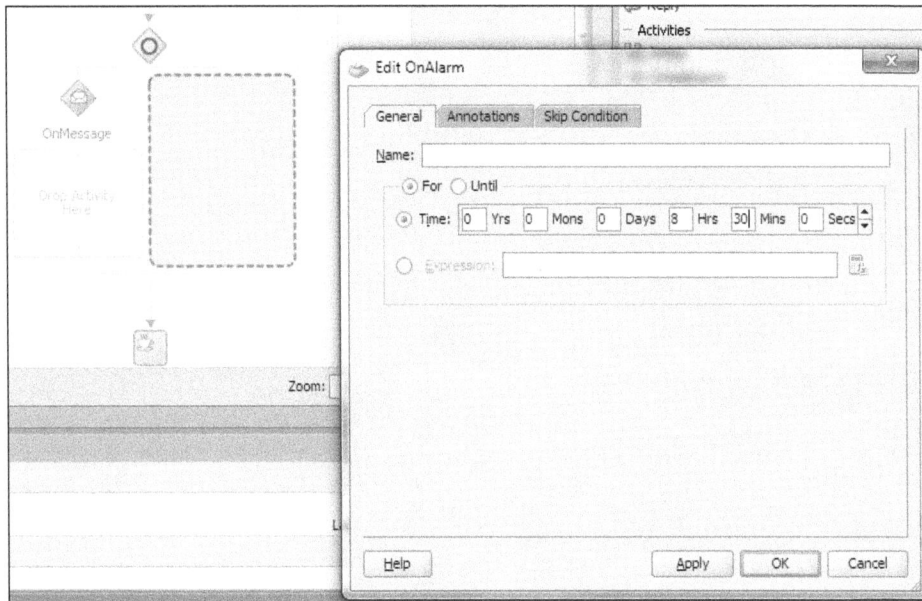

Summary

In this chapter, we discussed how to invoke BPEL processes from Java and how to invoke Java from BPEL processes. The details are also provided for invoking a BPEL from JSP and Servlet. We also learned the importance of setting timeouts and the steps for setting BPEL processes' transaction timeout for synchronous services and configuring timeout using the Pick activity for asynchronous services. In the next chapter, we will learn the basic structure for orchestrating multiple BPEL processes and its key constructs such as flow, scope, and switch.

4
Orchestrating BPEL Services

Interoperability between discrete systems and disparate systems is one of the major challenges for the IT industry and is mission critical for most organizations. Disparate systems provide distinct complementary business functions. Disparate systems are usually designed and deployed using distinct technology stacks. The IT industry has created web services to facilitate the interoperability among discrete and disparate systems.

The underlying foundations of modern web services are XML and HTTP(S). One may find some legacy implementations using simple text messages, or special characters such as comma- or pipe-delimited text messages. In general, web services are XML-based programs that interact over HTTP(S) with interfaces that adhere to the industry standards set forth in the Web Services Description Language (WSDL) from the World Wide Web Consortium (W3C).

The W3C's WSDL standard provides the guidelines to define message types, port types, ports, and operations in a standard way that facilitates different systems to communicate effectively with each other. WSDL specifies the location of the service, the operations the service exposes, and describes how to access them. Web services assist us to convert a legacy application into a web application that can publish its function or message to the rest of the world.

A WSDL XML document consists of six major elements: **definitions**, **types**, **message**, **portType**, **binding**, and **service**, as shown in the following figure:

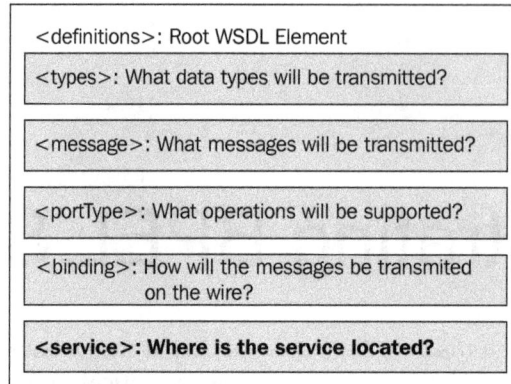

```
<definitions>: Root WSDL Element

  <types>: What data types will be transmitted?

  <message>: What messages will be transmitted?

  <portType>: What operations will be supported?

  <binding>: How will the messages be transmited
             on the wire?

  <service>: Where is the service located?
```

The interaction between the client and web services can be one of the following:

- One way
- Request-Response
- Solicit-Response
- Notification

The One-way and Request-Response are synchronous communications and invocation, that is, Solicit-Response and Notification (or reply) are part of asynchronous communication.

Web services provide interoperability and an ability to conduct simple interactions by using standard protocols. However, systems integration achieved by using web services doesn't provide process agility; it requires a standard way to create a process and an ability to create an integration model. BPEL defines a model and syntax for describing the behavior of a business process and interactions between the process and its partners.

For many years, many software vendors tried to develop and standardize web services and non-standard proprietary-based workflow for creating and managing business processes. Some of the existing workflow tools and runtime engines are complicated and fragmented.

For example, IBM and BEA (BEA is acquired by Oracle) tried to promote **Web Services Flow Language** (**WSFL**) and **XLANG** workflow standards (by Microsoft) that enabled you to create business services.

Currently, most of the software vendors accept Business Process Execution Language (BPEL) as the standard for creating and managing business processes based on the workflow. Some of the software vendors believe Business Process Modeling Notation (BPMN) is the future of business process modeling instead of BPEL.

BPEL provides a standard way that facilitates combining multiple existing functions into a new application and services from a number of distributed and autonomous software components. BPEL addresses the problem of designing, defining, implementing, and deploying composite services.

BPEL helps portability of business processes operating on different software to interact with each other using a set of standard services. The basic underlying standard for BPEL is web services standards such as Web service Description Language (WSDL) and Simple Object Access Protocol (SOAP). SOAP is an XML-based protocol for allowing applications to exchange data over HTTP(S).

The whole concept of SOA is to reuse existing applications of an enterprise. Object-oriented programs allow you to reuse the Java code and Java objects within an application. SOA enables you to reuse application components from within and/or cross enterprise. The location of the application is irrelevant. Using WSDL, the location is independent of the invocation mechanism. Web services can also accept and process messages using the standard XML:

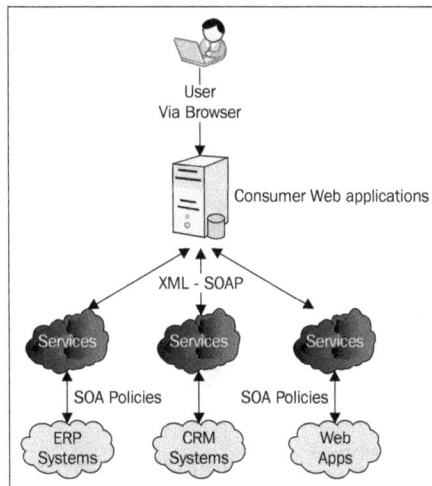

Orchestration

Organizations are moving away from using monolithic, static applications to agile and flexible services-based applications to stay economically competitive in the market. Orchestration allows standards-based interoperable services to be combined and reused quickly, to deliver in changing business requirements. Orchestration of the services is essential for enabling Service Oriented Architecture (SOA).

Process orchestration is a mechanism of combining services and directing and managing their process flows. Business Process Execution Language (BPEL) is one of the leading standards for implementing services orchestration.

As a simple example, to provide an alarm service for clients, we would need the following services:

- **Date service**: This provides a real-time date.
- **Time service**: This provides a real-time time.
- **Alarm service**: This allows users to set an alarm for the pre-defined data and time. It also provides an asynchronous notification to the user when the pre-defined date and time matches with the real-time.

In the following figure, a user is setting an alarm using a consumer application. The alarm service provides the necessary data to the consumer application for notifying a user. The orchestration of multiple services such as Date, Time, Match Date, and Time creates the Alarm Service. The alarm service can be consumed by multiple consumer applications without consuming the Time and Date services directly and by coordinating them:

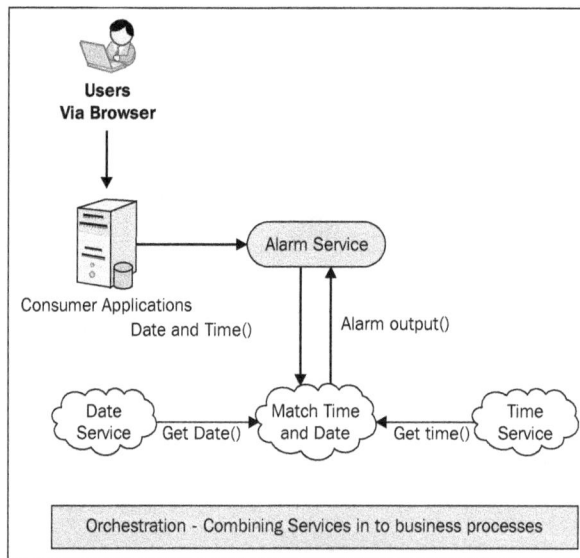

Each of the services has a WSDL interface. Client applications use the WSDL interface to invoke web services.

Coordinating the communication across multiple services is a challenging task. BPEL enables the following based on the input data:

- Invoke one or more services
- Receive responses from one or more services
- Manage the flow of response data
- Provide results to the calling service

While designing the process orchestration, you should ensure to provide dynamic, flexible, and adaptable mechanisms to meet the changing needs of the business. Orchestration allows you to define, change, or redefine business functions as needed. Service orchestration creates dynamic relationships between services that are determined at runtime based on the runtime data rather than at the construction phase.

The approach for orchestration is simple.

- Define the services including purpose, input, and output
- Define the requirement and problem domain
- Identify the available services for use
- Define and identify the flow of information between clients and services

Orchestrations of the services are primarily categorized as either Sequential activities (sequence) or Parallel activities (flow). In some business cases, we may use both in creating a single orchestrated service.

Designing orchestration

Orchestration is the process of combining BPEL services. Defining the style of interaction with the client is the first step of designing a BPEL service. Always consider using the Scope activity to group a set of activities and manage the BPEL variables' scope. Define the XML schemas (XSD) for the message structure after deciding the client interaction style.

As shown in the following figure, the **Partner Link** on the left-hand size contains the service interface (WSDL) to communicate with client applications or other components. The client applications can use the WSDL to invoke the BPEL service.

The **Partner Link** contains the service interface (WSDL) for BPEL services to invoke other external services:

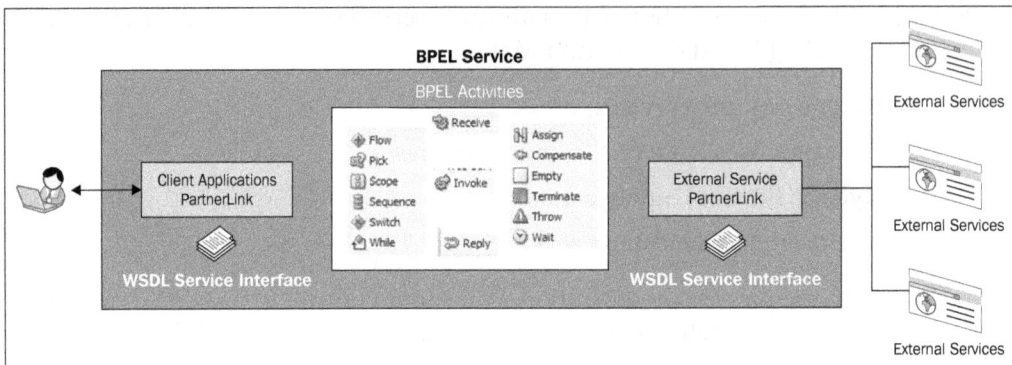

The Oracle JDeveloper's design page has three different swim lanes, as shown in the next screenshot. These swim lanes are as follows:

- The left-hand side swim lane is used to define partner links for communication with clients

- The right-hand side swim lane is used to define partner links for communication with external services

- The center swim lane is used to define the process

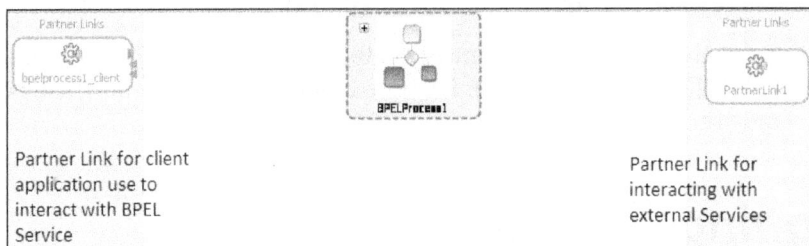

A complete screenshot of JDeveloper's BPEL Designer is given as follows. The designer has **Partner Links** on the left-hand side for clients and **Partner Links** on the right-hand side for external service invocations or configuring adaptors:

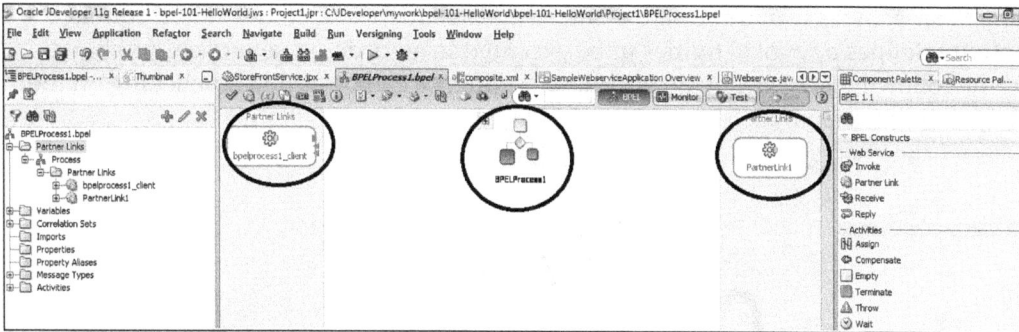

BPEL primarily facilitates orchestrations using Flow, Switch, and Scope constructs.

Flow

The purpose of the **Flow** activity is to manage the processes which are performed concurrently. It can combine the results from two or more activities. As shown in the following screenshot, drag-and-drop the **Flow** activity from JDeveloper's **Component Palette**:

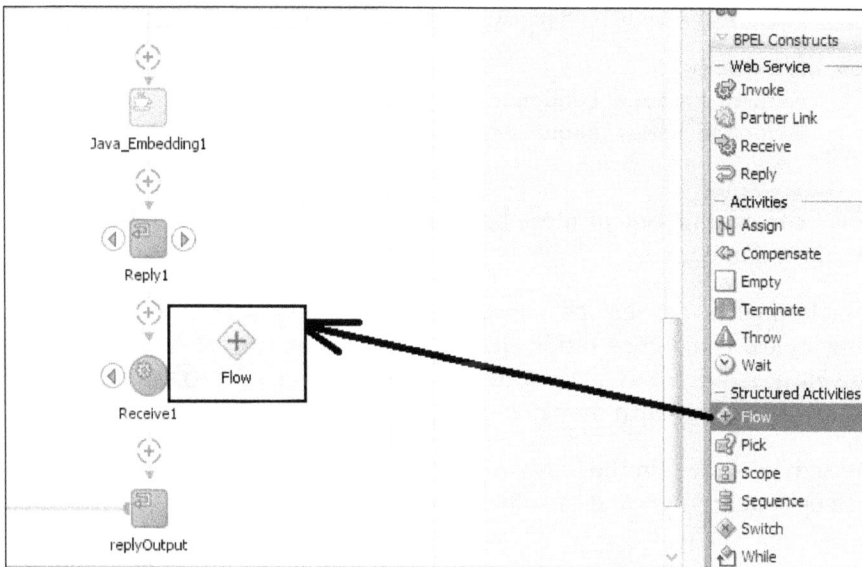

The **Flow** activity usually contains one or more sequence activities. The **Sequence** activity defines a set of activities to be executed in an ordered sequence. As shown in the following screenshot, an additional sequence can be added by clicking on the **Add Sequence** icon:

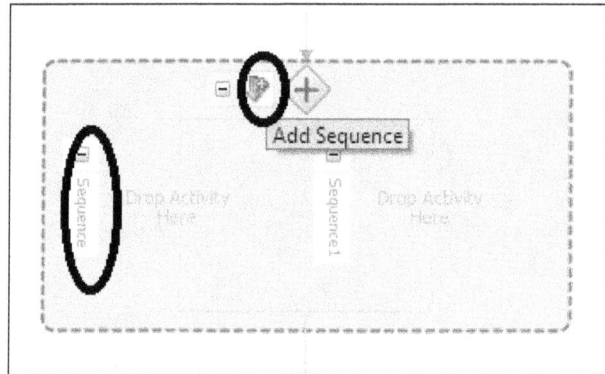

The activities in `<Sequence>` are executed sequentially as expected by the literal meaning of *sequence*.

The source code of BPEL Flow is given as follows for reference:

```
<flow name="Flow1">
    <sequence name="Sequence"/>
    <sequence name="Sequence1"/>
</flow>
```

The `<flow>` can contain one or more branches and activities in each branch are executed at the same time.

The interaction with web services can use both synchronous and asynchronous messaging styles. The orchestration should be able to support both messaging styles. Using the Flow activity, a synchronous and asynchronous BPEL can be invoked concurrently; however, both may not execute at the same time.

The Flow activity shown in the following screenshot has two Invoke activities. One could be synchronous and the other could be asynchronous:

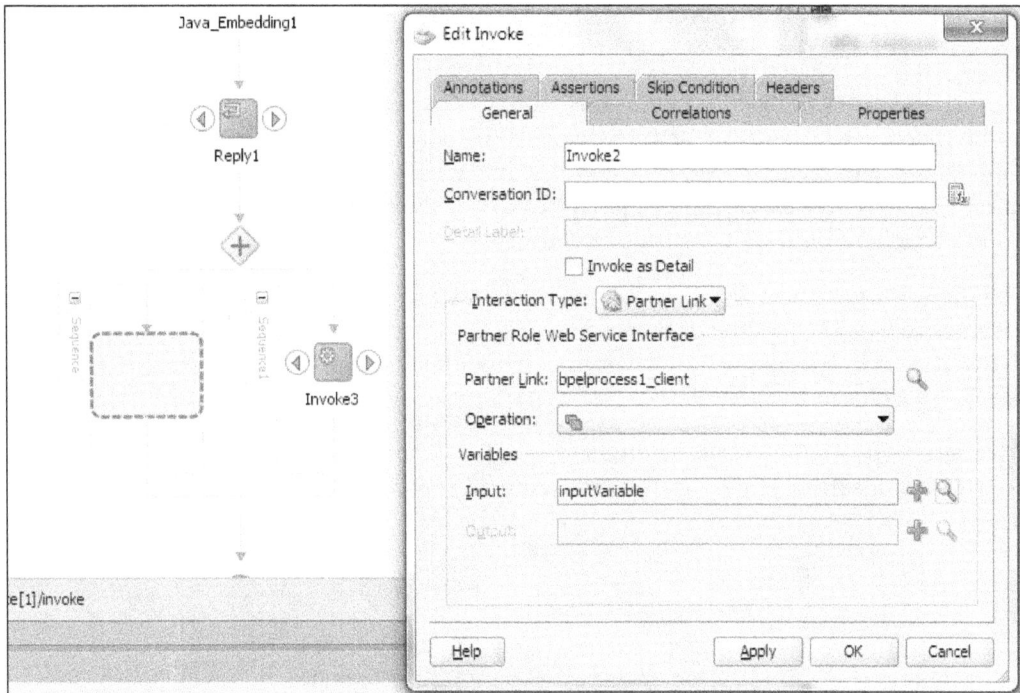

By default, the activities within Flow won't get executed in parallel. The BPEL process manager executes all the activities within Flow sequentially. This will add latency to the application. To avoid this, as shown in the following screenshot, edit the partner link properties and create a property named `nonBlockingInvoke`:

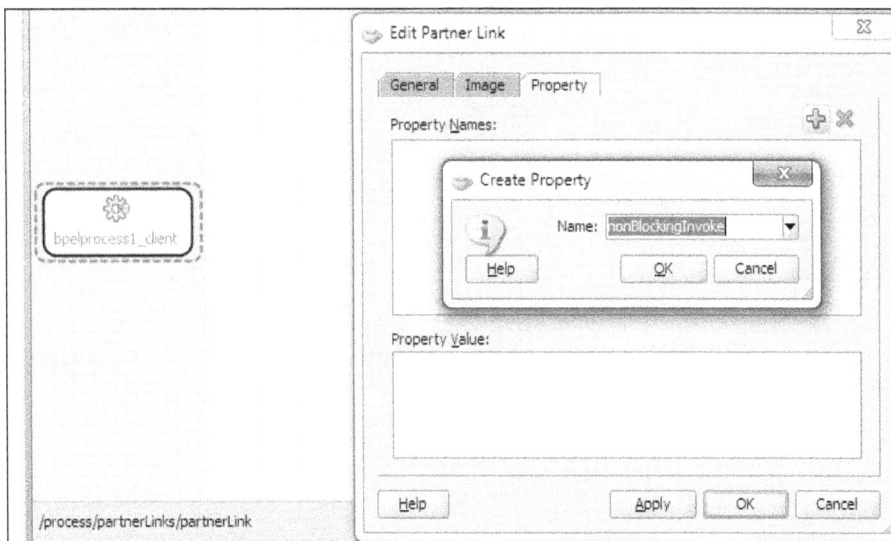

Due to the **nonBlockingInvoke** property, a new thread will be created for the invocation of each partner link.

This thread will call back the main flow thread once the work is complete. As shown in the following screenshot, ensure that this property is set to `true` to create multiple threads for parallel activities. By default, a BPEL process is executed in a single thread. Setting values for this property results in the creation of a dehydration point at each execution of the Invoke activity.

The dehydration point will provide the current state of execution of the BPEL instance to be stored in the database. Storing the process in a database maintains that status of the process and prevents any loss of state if a system shuts down due to unforeseen issues.

Always set the `nonBlockingInvoke` as `True` for partner link that is configured with an Invoke activity as shown in the following screenshot:

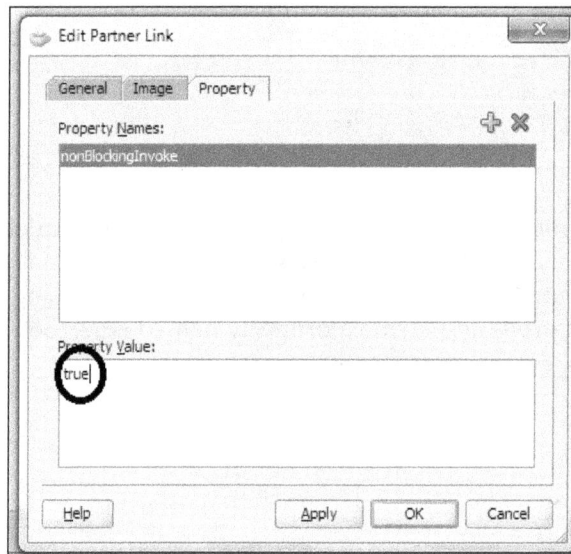

Switch

`Switch` and `While` activities are some of the examples of BPEL activities that create dynamic relationships based on the runtime data. They provide conditional branching with decision points based on the data.

Switch activity is very similar to the Java programming language's `switch` API. It provides conditional branching. The following example depicts the typical structure of a `switch` activity.

```
<Switch>
  <case>
Evaluation  condition -  Do something and exit.
  <case>
Evaluate condition - Do something and exit
<otherwise>
Execute if all the above conditions are false and exit. Usually
exceptions handling are coded here.
```

The Switch activity provides multiple branches; however, only one branch is executed always. If the first `<case>` branch's condition is true, switch won't execute any other `<case>` branches.

The `<otherwise>` branch is optional. This gets executed only if all the `<case>` conditions are false. Usually exceptions are coded here.

As shown in the following screenshot, drag the **Switch** activity from the JDeveloper's **Component Palette**:

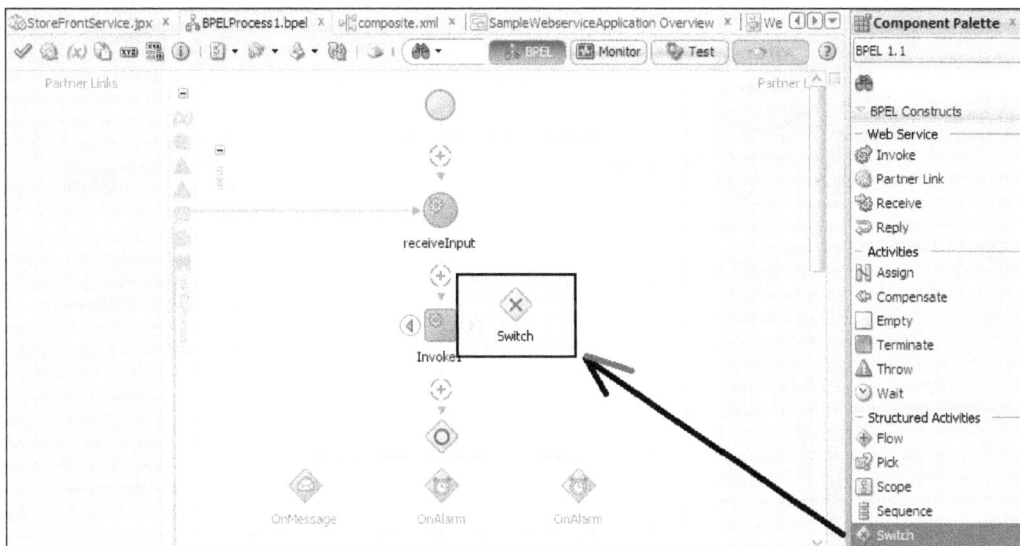

Additional case blocks can be added by clicking on **Add Switch Case**. Click on **Add Switch Otherwise** for adding <otherwise> branches, as shown in the following screenshot:

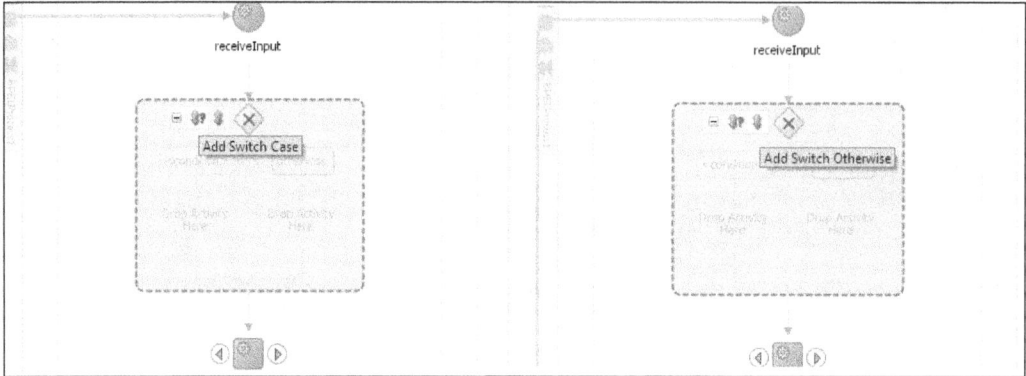

Double-click on **<condition>** and enter values for **Label** and **Description**. Click on the XPath Expressions Builder button for additional expressions, as shown in the following screenshot:

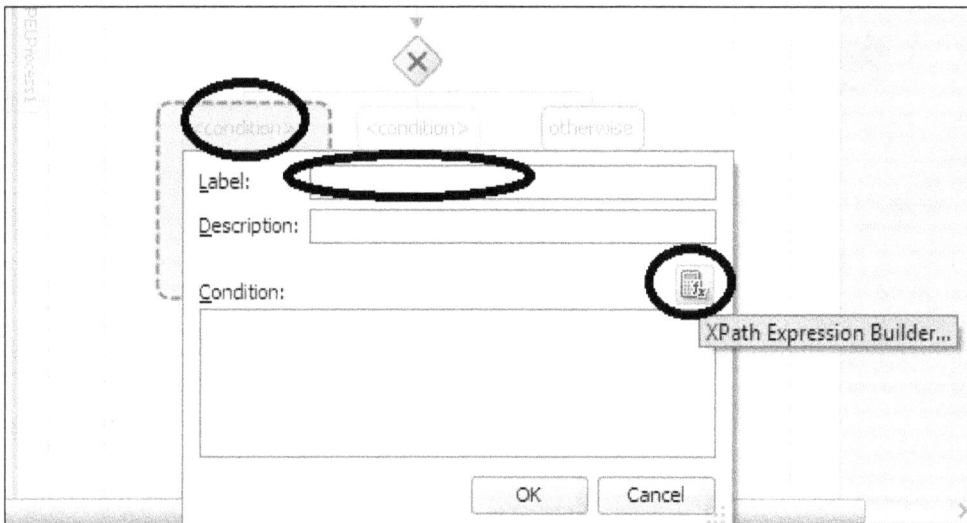

Use JDeveloper's **Xpath Expression Builder** for creating the expressions. In XPath, there are several kinds of nodes such as element, attribute, text, namespace, processing-instruction, comment, and document nodes. It is easy to use the XPath Expression Builder GUI from JDeveloper instead of coding it manually or using a third-party XPath expression builder. Oracle JDeveloper's XPath Expression Builder supports standard XPath language:

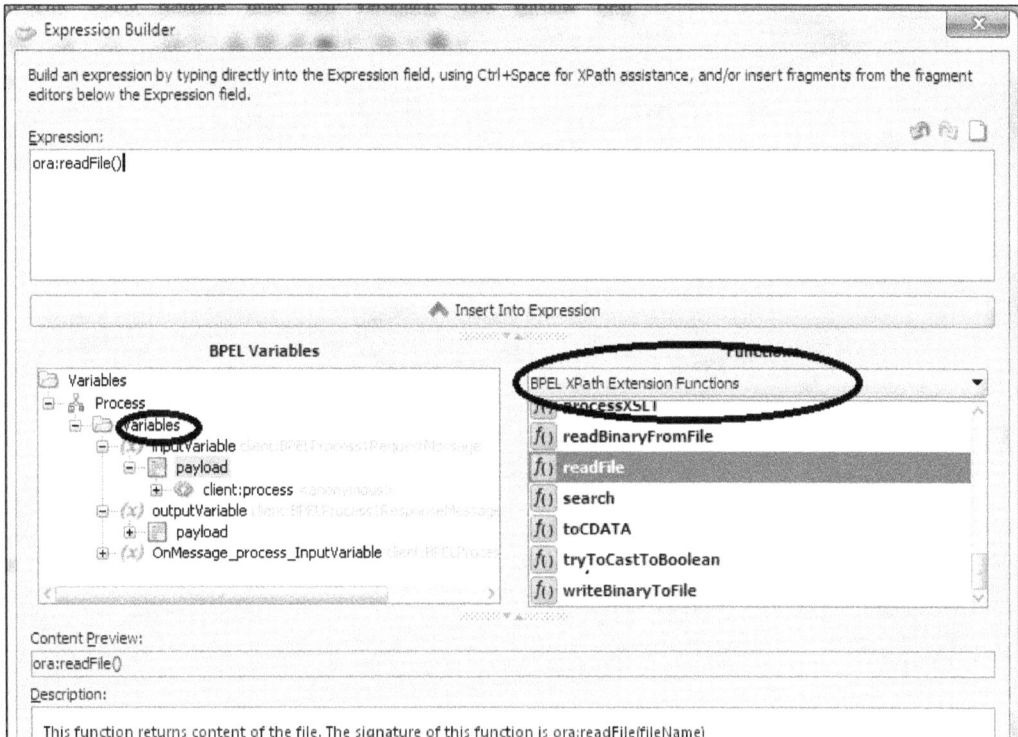

The following example shows how you can communicate with Active Directory using LDAP from your BPEL process and get data from LDAP using JDeveloper's Expression Builder.

XPath expression `ids:getManager(userName, realmName)` will fetch the manager of a given user. If the user does not exist or there is no manager for this user, it returns `null`.

As shown in the following screenshot, select and double-click on the XPath function **getManager()** from **Identity Service Functions** from under the **Identity Service** category:

Select the BPEL variable that requires the manager and click on **Insert Into Expression**. Ensure that you are adding the variable in between the brackets to adhere with the XPath syntax:

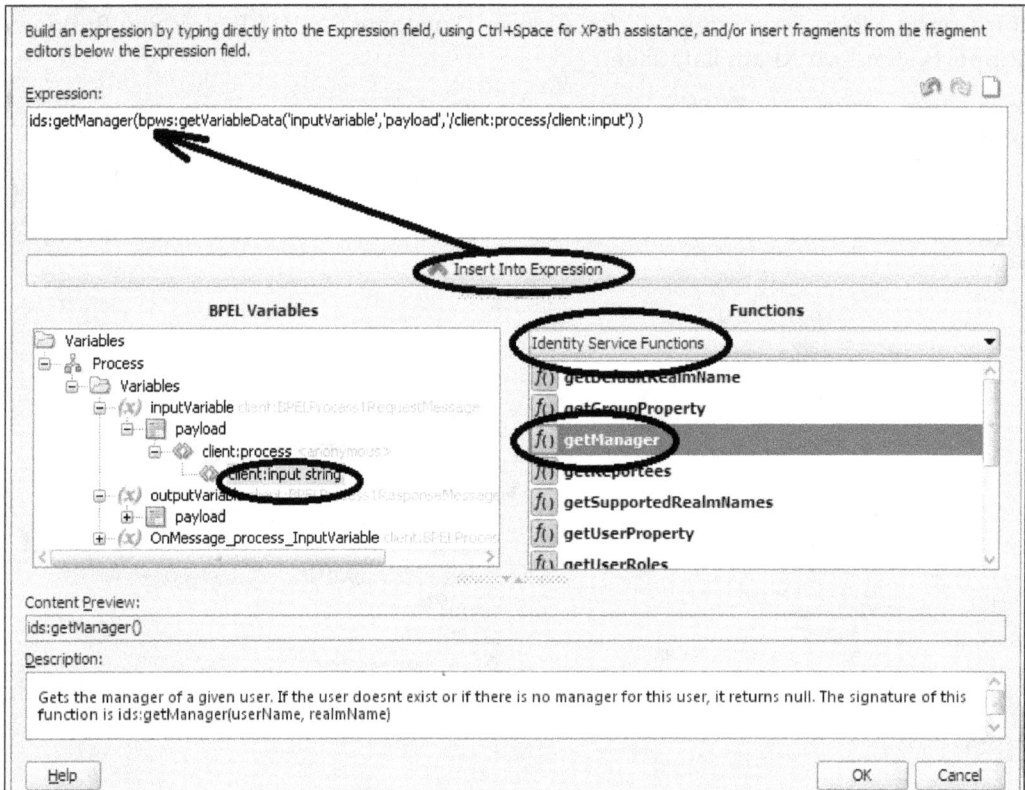

Custom XPath functions

The JDeveloper's XPath Expression Builder provides standard BPEL and Oracle BPEL extension functions.

Even though, the functions of JDeveloper's Expression Builder cover most of the requirements, sometimes, you may have unique business requirements which can be achieved by custom XPath functions. Such custom XPath functions can be called from any XPath expression that is designed in JDeveloper.

For example, you may want to use a custom XPath function to filter or mask sensitive data such as an employee's salary, before sending it to another system or a web service.

If the event carries the employee's ID, you can use a custom XPath function to remove the salary information from the web service response. It is recommended to use the Oracle-provided (`oracle.fabric.common.xml.xpath`) public interface `IXPathFunction` for implementing a custom XPath function in SOA components.

Creating custom XPath functions

To define custom functions, you need to perform the following steps:

1. Create a new Java project in JDeveloper and add the SOA runtime and parser libraries.
2. Write a custom XPath function class.
3. Configure the custom XPath expression function class with JDeveloper and SOA Suite.
4. Deploy user-defined functions to runtime.
5. Start using the custom function from JDeveloper.
6. As shown in the following screenshot, add **SOA Runtime** and **Oracle XML Parser v2** to the libraries of your Java project by choosing **Project Properties**. Right-click on the Java project to view **Project Properties**:

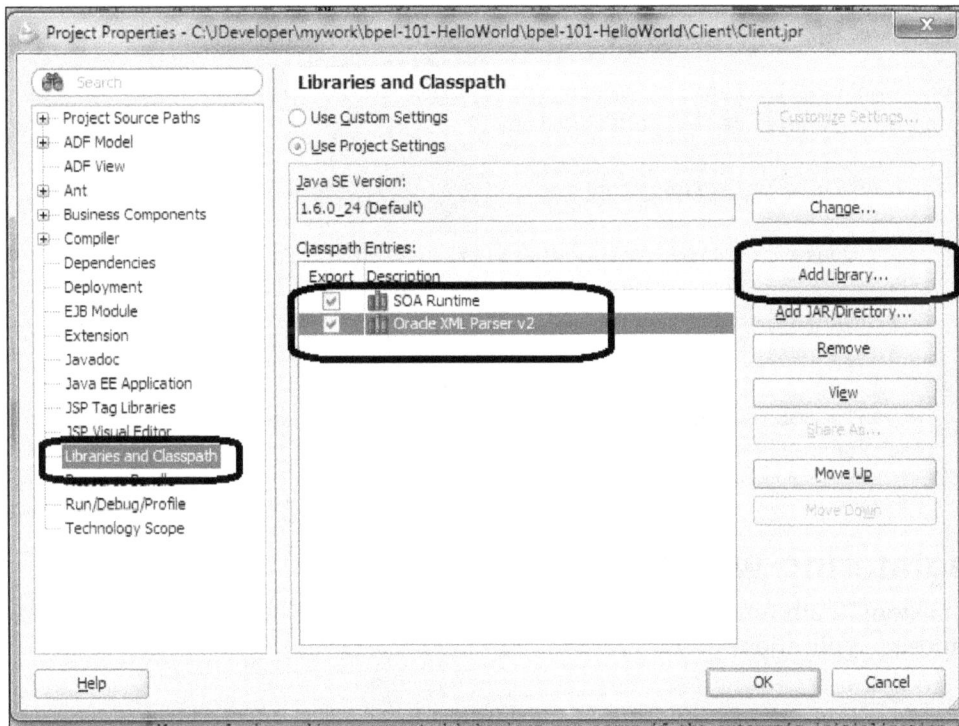

Custom XPath function class

Any method in a custom class can be used as an XPath function with the following limitations:

- The method must be a static class method.

- All parameters for the method must be of a simple type.

- The return type can be void or any other simple type. The class must implement the IXPathFunction interface.

Create a new Java class in a JDeveloper project. Also select the main() method which we would use to test the class.

In the Java class, implement the call method of the IXPathFunction interface. Also add the code in the main() method for testing. The following is the example code:

```
public static Object employeesalaryfilter(
                        IXPathContext iXPathContext,
                        List list
                        ) throws XPathFunctionException {
   return String.valueOf(System.currentTimeMillis());
}
```

Write a class that implements the IXPathFunction interface as follows:

```
package oracle.fabric.common.xml.xpath;
 public interface IXPathFunction
 {
    /** Call this function.
    *
    *   @param context The context at the point in the
    *          expression when the function is called.
    *   @param args List of arguments provided during
    *          the call of the function.
    */
    public Object call(IXPathContext context, List args) throws
 XPathFunctionException;
 }
```

Registering with SOA Suite

The custom XPath function JAR must be added explicitly as it is not part of the SOA composite application.

Define the functions that should be shared by all of the components in `ext-soa-xpath-functions-config.xml`. Define the functions that are specific to BPEL and should not be used by other components in `ext-bpel-xpath-functions-config.xml`. These configuration files must be located in the `META-INF` directory of the JAR file that contains the compiled classes.

```
<soa-xpath-functions
  <function name="get">
    <className> employeesalaryfilter </className>
    <return type="string"/>
    <desc>returns the salary filter</desc>
      </function>
</soa-xpath-functions>
```

Registering with JDeveloper

Add the JAR file to the JDeveloper classpath. As shown in the following screenshot, add the JAR file:

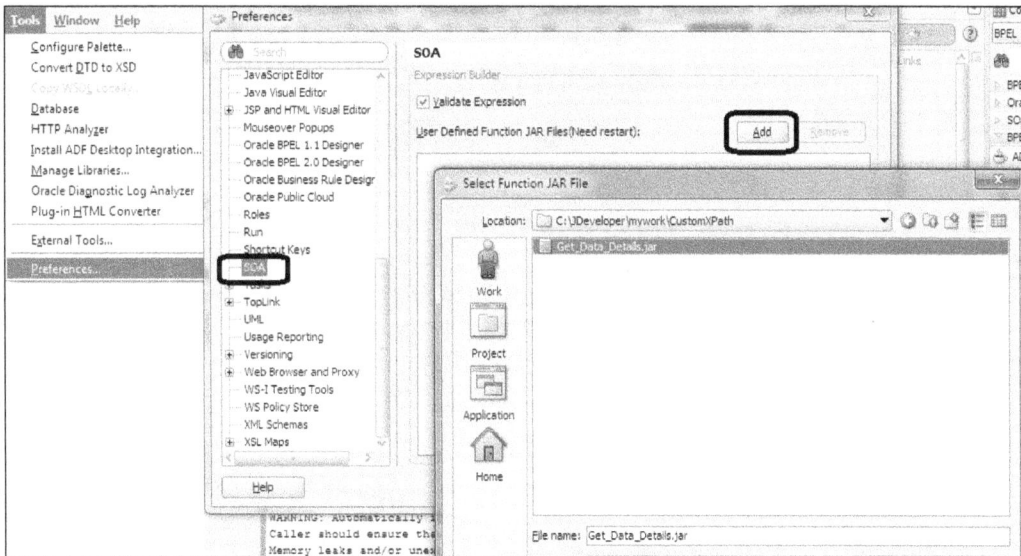

Scope

A Scope activity is to group activities and to define scope-specific variables and handlers. A Scope activity can be nested within another Scope activity. This will reduce the complexity of BPEL service diagrams and will determine the life cycle of BPEL variables.

A Scope activity is also used to handle exceptions. Exceptions occurred at any point in a Scope activity can be handled by the scope's exception handler. If it is not handled, it will propagate to the parent Scope activity, and so on.

As shown in the following screenshot, drag-and-drop the **Scope** activity from JDeveloper's **Component Palette**:

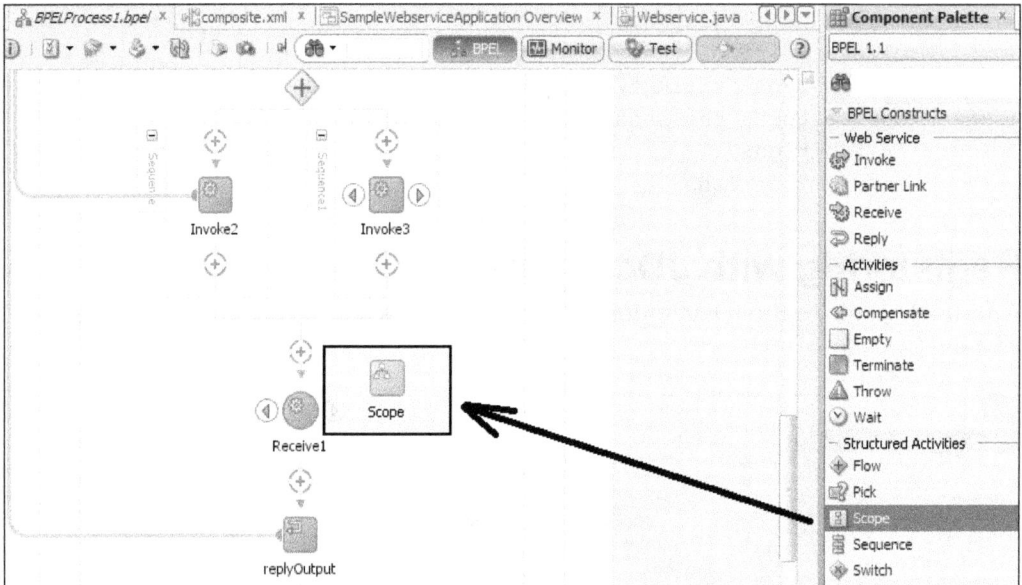

After setting up the **Scope** activity, other activities can be added by dragging the activities from JDeveloper's **Component Palette** and dropping on the **Scope** activity, as shown in the following screenshot. The **Scope** activity encapsulates the recoverable unit of work and allows for separating business processes in to logically separate organized units:

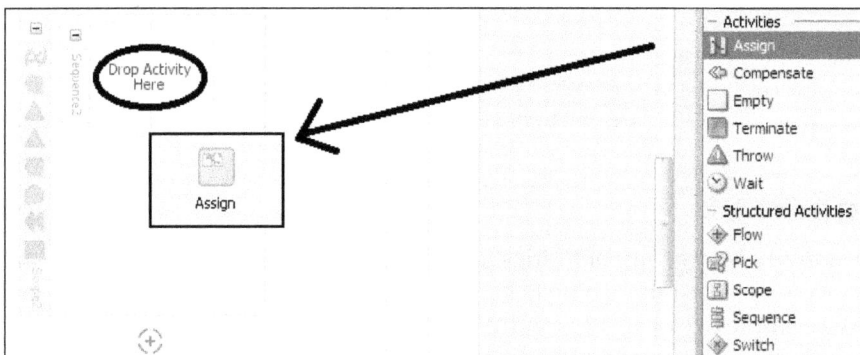

The scope variables can be edited by right-clicking on them and selecting the **Edit** button, as shown in the following screenshot:

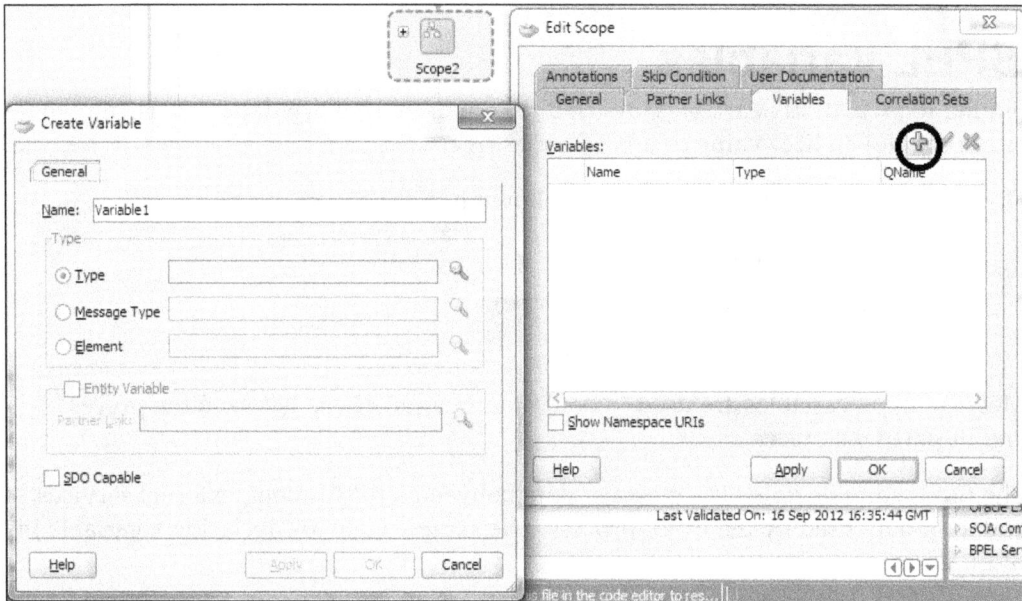

The common scope components such as **Add OnMessage**, **Add OnAlarm**, **Add Catch**, and **Add CatchAll** can be added by right-clicking on the **Scope** activity, as shown in the following screenshot:

The Scope activity provides processing contexts for BPEL variables, exception handlers, organization units' compensation, and event handlers.

BPEL variables

Similar to Java, BPEL Variables are used to contain temporary data. A variable can either contain an XSD value or a WSDL message.

Oracle BPEL Process Manager has the following types of variables:

- XML schema type (Type)
- WSDL message type (Message Type)
- XML schema element (Element)

Message Type variables are used to hold data in interactions between the process and its partner services.

The BPEL variable holds the message data between a BPEL client, external services, and local data used by the BPEL process. The sample code for declaring a variable in BPEL is given as follows:

```
<variables>
  <variable    name="hello_world"
               messageType="Type" />
</variables>
```

Each variable can be declared as a `messageType` or an element. As shown in the following screenshot, select an activity and click on (x) to edit the output and input variables.

Double-click on the input, output, or OnMessage variable to enter the details of the variable:

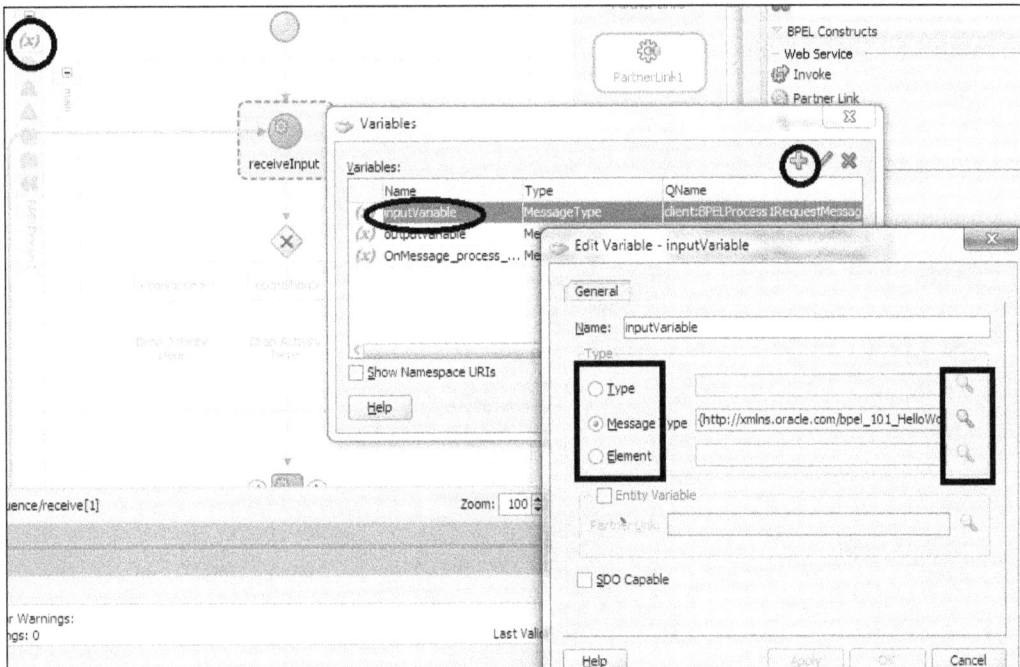

One kind of variable type can be XML schema.

XML schema type (Type): This is the default variable type. These variables can be simple or complex XML schema datatypes. The XML schema types are defined in XML schema files (.xsd) or in WSDL files that are imported into the process. The **Type** attribute is used for defining this variable type.

As shown in the following screenshot, select **Type** and edit it for selecting appropriate XML schema types. The XML schema datatypes can be string, Boolean, float, and so on:

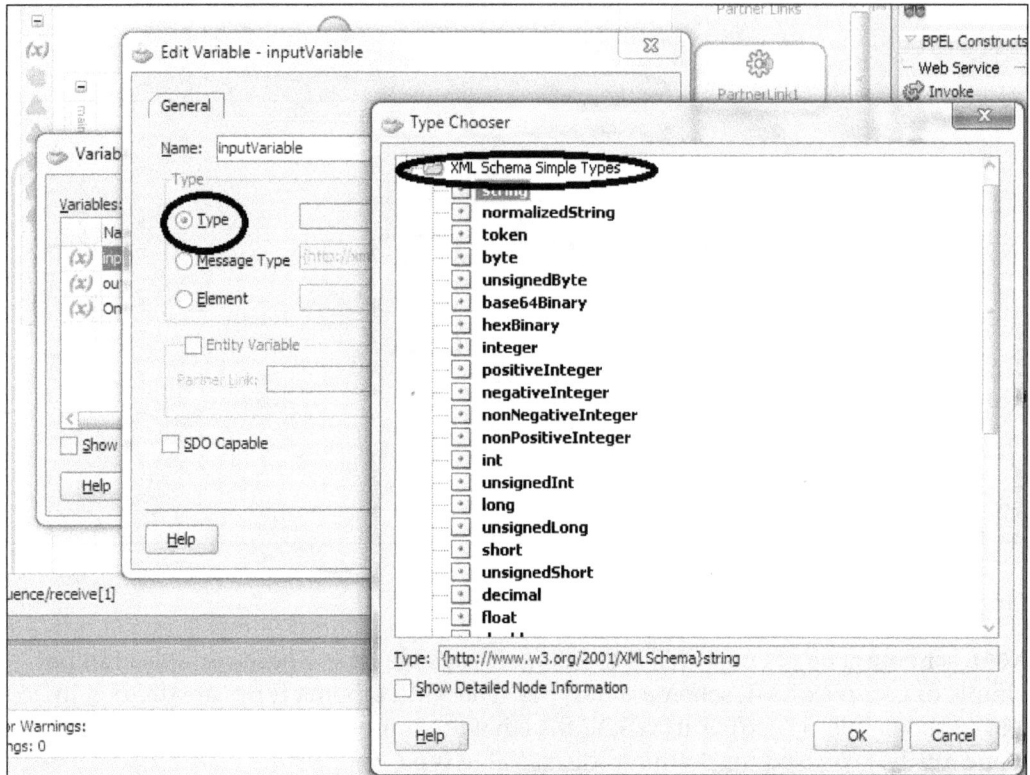

WSDL message type (Message Type): A WSDL message type is used to hold data for interaction between partner links and services. It can be a response or request message.

It is associated with input or output variables for Invoke, Receive, and Reply activities. These variables correspond to the web service message types that are defined in the WSDL files.

As shown in the following screenshot, select type as **Message Type** for entering information about the WSDL message type:

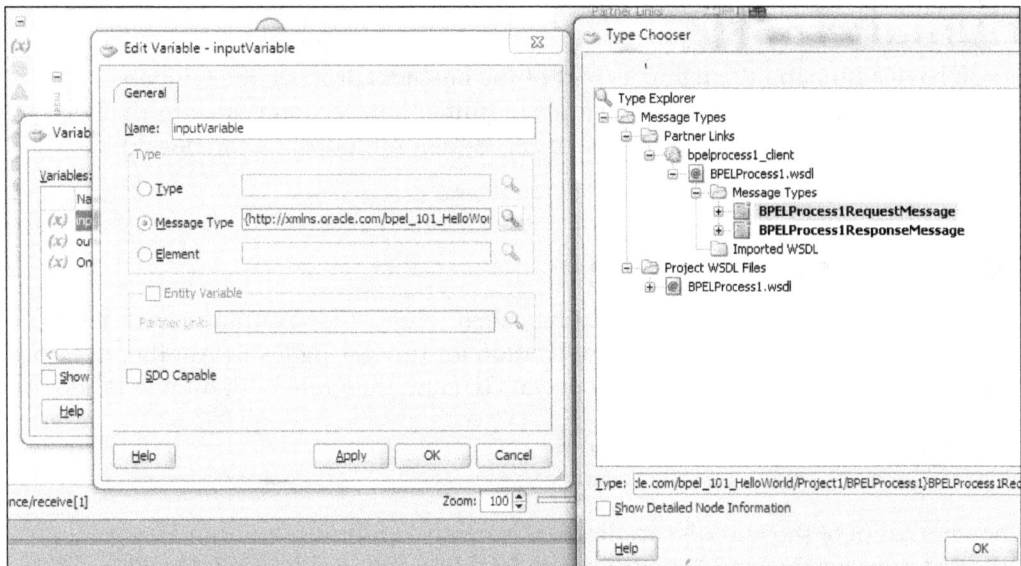

XML schema element (Element): These variables correspond to the project schema file or a project WSDL file of the current BPEL process or of partner links. The XML schema elements themselves are defined in XML schema files (.xsd) or in WSDL files that are imported into the process.

The following screenshot shows the steps for selecting the schema for **Partner Links** as an XML schema element for this variable:

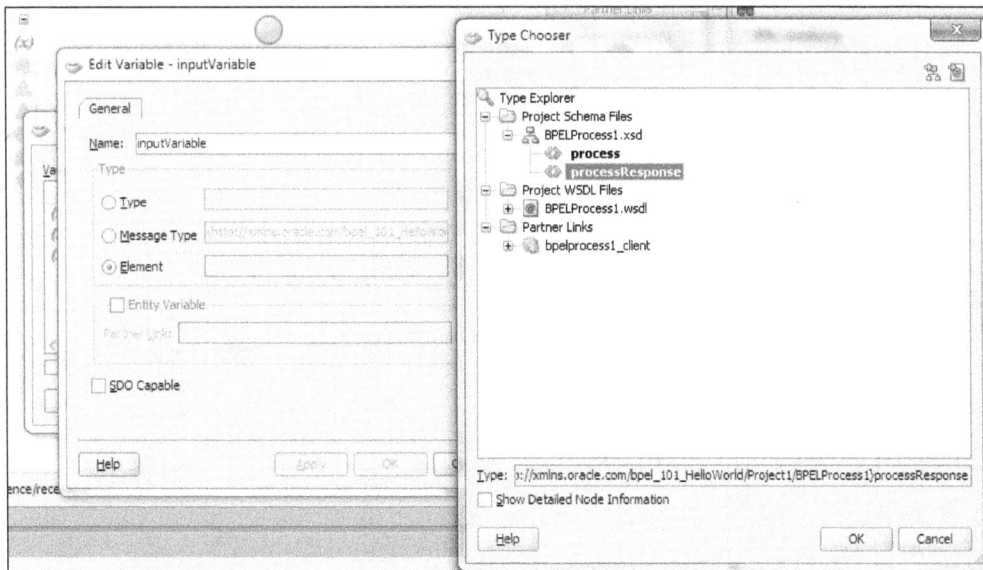

Human Task

If you have a human interaction as part of the business process, the Human Task component is required. An example of human interaction is an approval or rejection by a manager for a purchase order. E-mail notifications can be added as part of the process.

Worklist application

SOA Suite provides a built-in application called worklist for examining and acting on the tasks. **Worklist** is a web-based application for processing tasks. Another option is to use/create a separate application/portal GUI and integrate with human tasks.

The URL for the work list application is
`http://{adminserver-host}:{adminserver-port}/integration/worklistapp`.

The screenshot of the worklist application is given as follows. You can assign different roles for the worklist application GUI based on the user profile. The standard user roles are administrator, process owner, supervisor, and task assignee. You can integrate this with LDAP and get the roles from LDAP. You can filter and search tasks using the worklist's GUI:

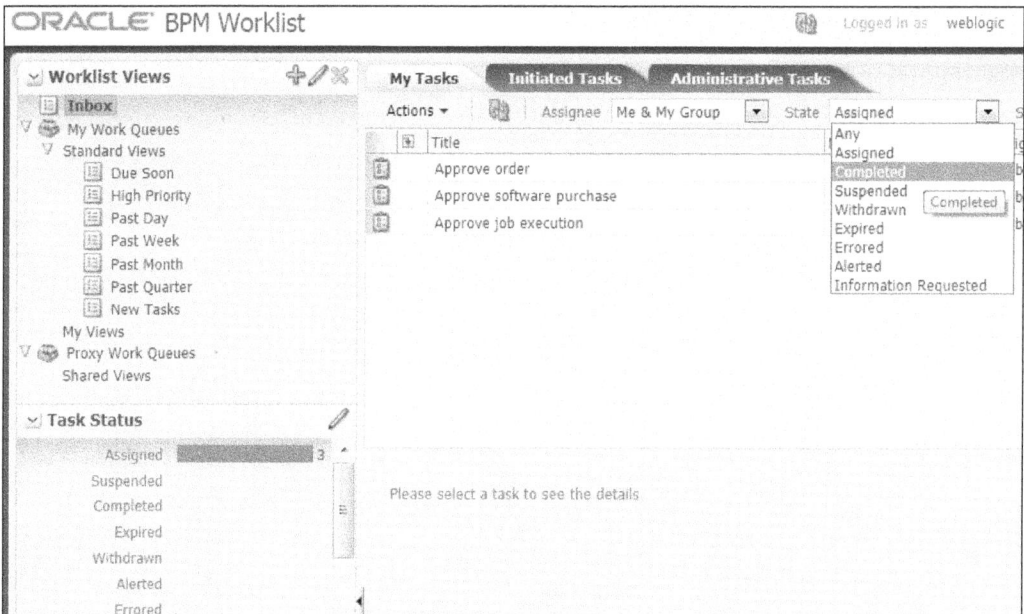

As shown in the following screenshot, click on **Preferences** for configuring e-mail addresses for notification and rules:

Creating Human Tasks

Human Task can be added to the composite application in the following two ways:

- Creating a standalone Human Task
- Creating a Human Task and associating it with a BPEL process

Standalone Human Task – expose as a service

Standalone human tasks are useful for exposing a human service as a service for using with other consumer services and there are no orchestrated activities as part of a human service.

As shown in the following screenshot, drag-and-drop a **Human Task** service component from the **Component Palette** into the SOA composite editor. The outcomes of the tasks, parameters, assignments, and workflow patterns can be configured in the .task metadata file generated as part of creating the Human Task in JDeveloper:

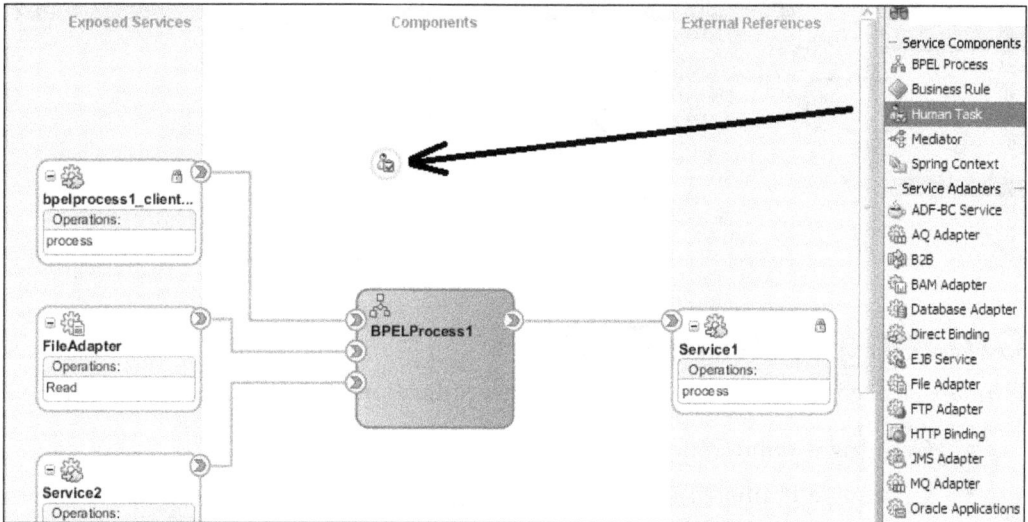

Human Task – part of a BPEL process

Human Task can be part of BPEL's orchestrated business process services. For example, expense approval is required by the manager before completing the expense approval business process.

As shown in the following screenshot, drag-and-drop **Human Task** from the **Component Palette** into a BPEL process:

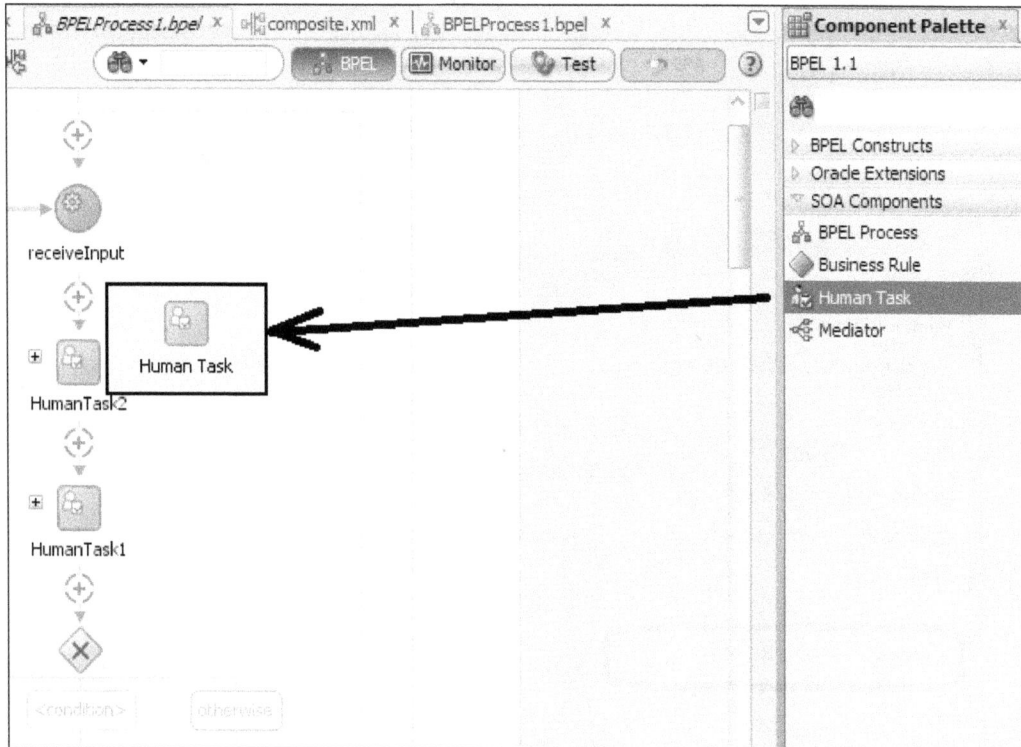

Right-click on **Human Task** and select **Outcomes** and **Source**. Configure task headers by clicking on the **Search** button corresponding to **Outcomes**, as shown in the following screenshot:

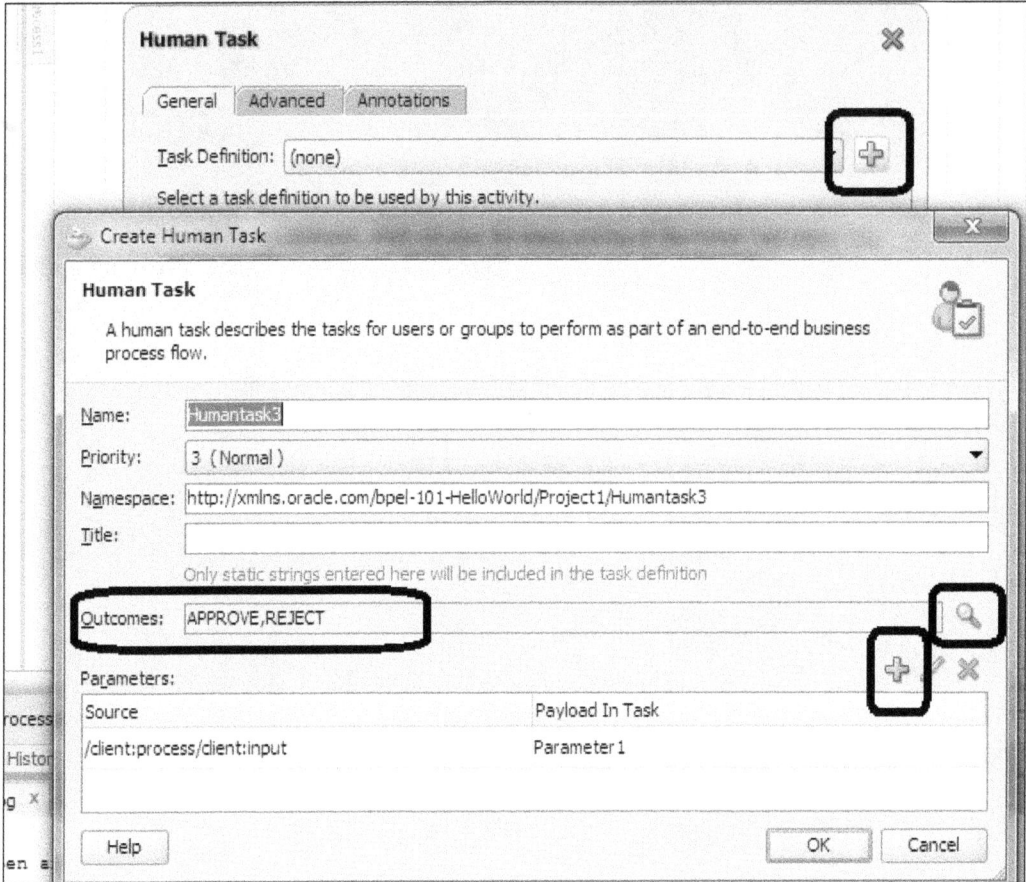

As shown in the following screenshot, usually a Human Task is followed by the `case` statement which has different conditions such as **Approve**, **Reject**, and **Otherwise**:

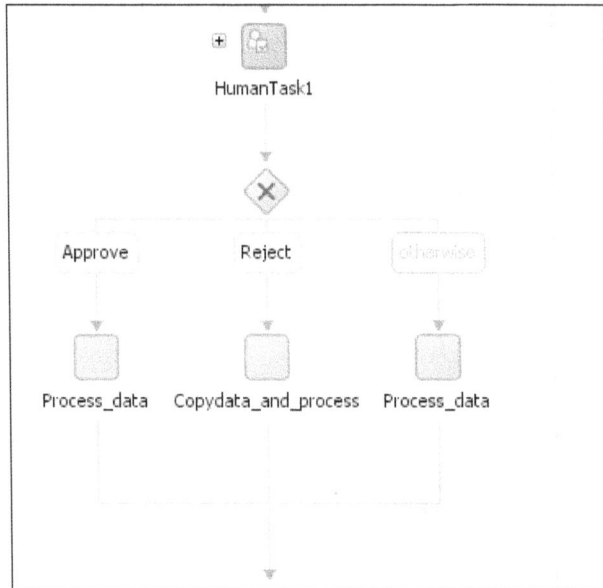

Business Rules engine

SOA Suite has a lightweight Business Rules engine. If you have simple rules, you may use the Business Rules engine that comes with the SOA Suite. If you want to manage complex rules, it is recommended to use an external **Business Rule Management Systems (BRMS)** such as Oracle Business Rules and IBM iLog. External third-party rule engines can connect with the SOA Suite. Configure custom JCA Adaptors or use WSDL for connecting the SOA Suite with an external Business Rules engine.

One of the basic requirements of business is the ability to change the rules without a code change or deployment. SOA Suite Rule engine can be used for editing Business Rule dynamically; however, one of the disadvantages of using SOA Suite Rule engine is that, it does not have a web interface for business analysts to edit the rules.

Adding business rules as part of a BPEL process

As shown in the following screenshot, drag-and-drop the **Business Rule** activity from the **Component Palette** to add business rule as part the BPEL. If you want to create **Business Rule** as a standalone service, drag **Business Rule** and connect it as part of the composite application:

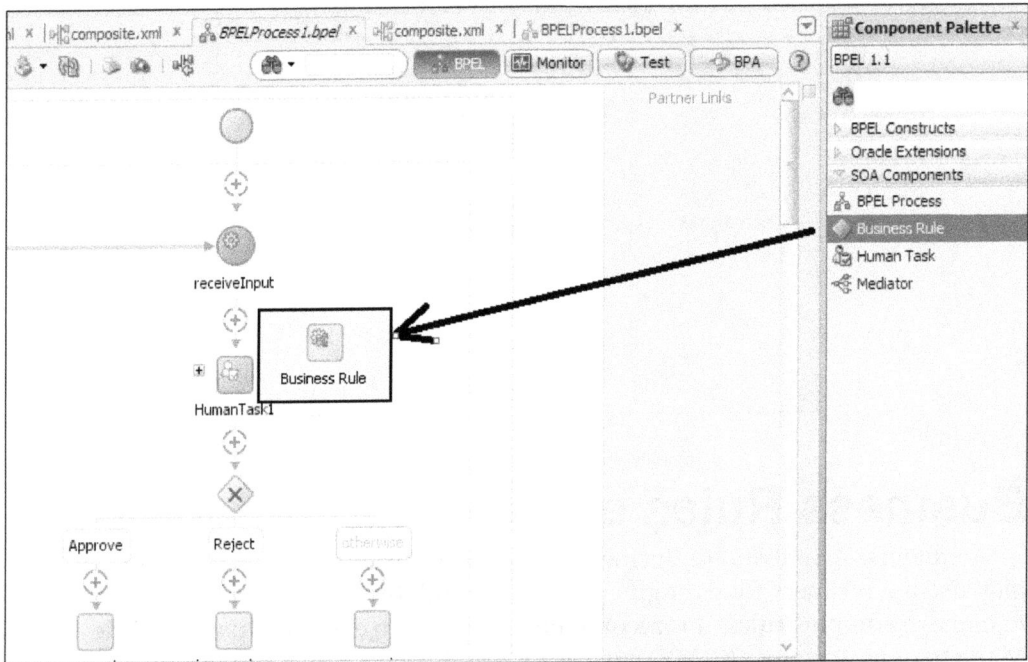

Right-click on the **Business Rule** activity and select **Edit**. Select a Rule dictionary from the drop-down box if already available. If not, please create a new dictionary by clicking on the plus icon. Please ensure that you add appropriate input and output variables from an XSD for the Rule dictionary:

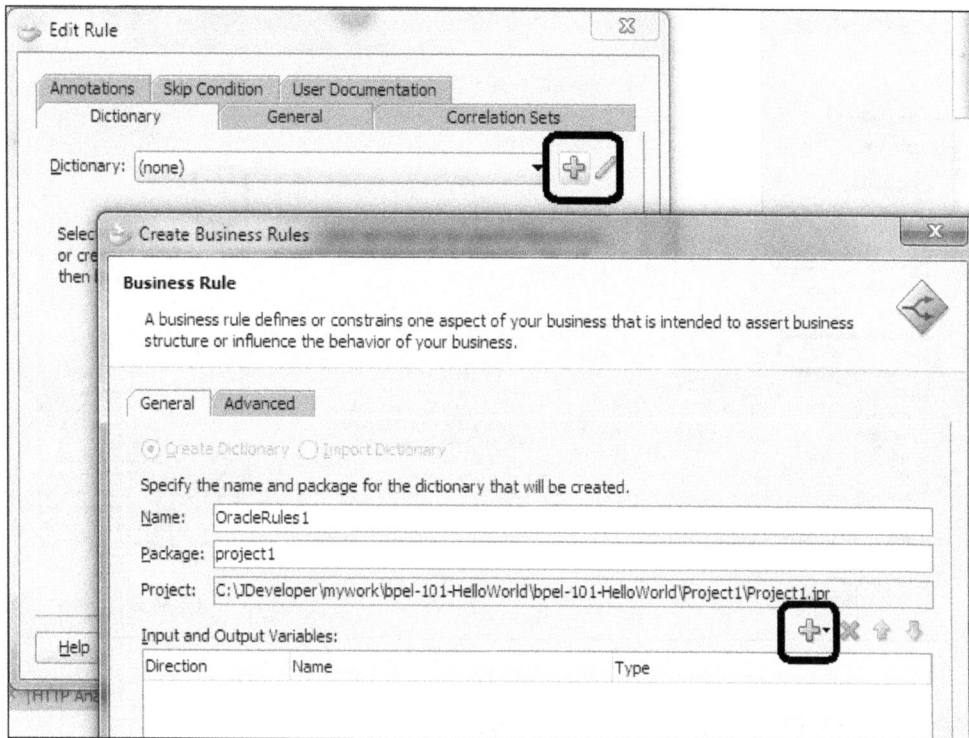

As shown in the following screenshot, after creating the Rule dictionary, JDeveloper opens the **Business Rule Designer**. You can also open it by right-clicking on the **Business Rule** activity and selecting the component editor or by clicking on the Rule from **Application Navigator**:

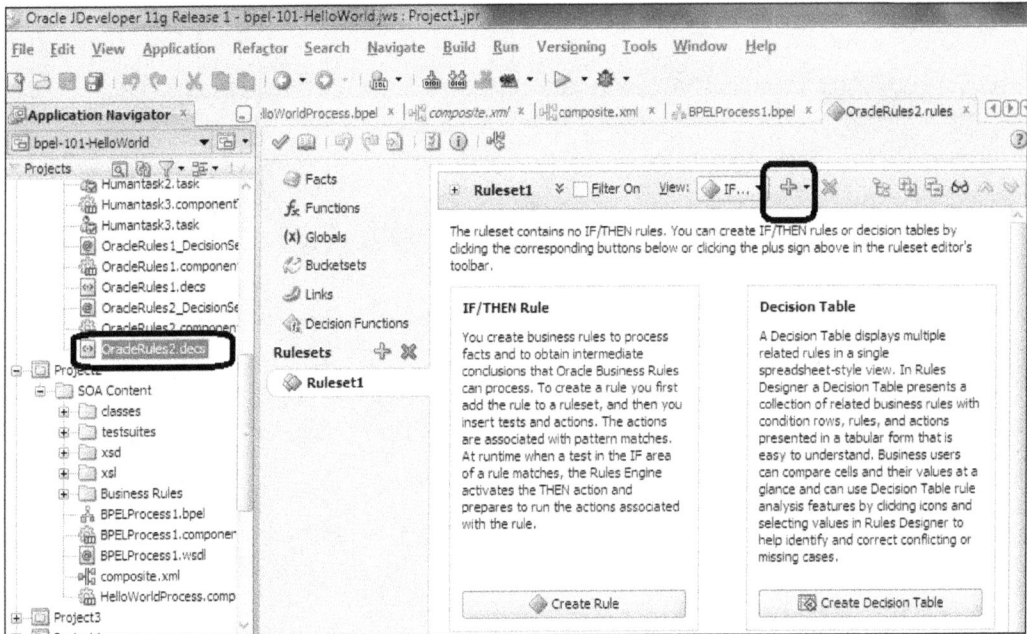

Creating business rules

Most of the rules are IF-THEN constructs which evaluate a condition and perform certain actions. Creating a rule using **Business Rule Designer** creates a .rules file.

Select the Rule set and click on the plus icon to create a rule. As shown in the following screenshot, replace <insert test> with Rule condition and <insert action> with rule actions:

One of the sample rules is given as follows:

```
If creaditscore <= Creditscoreapproval value
THEN
Creditcardapproval (<property>) approval (<result>), Creditcardlimit(
creditcard.limit) )
```

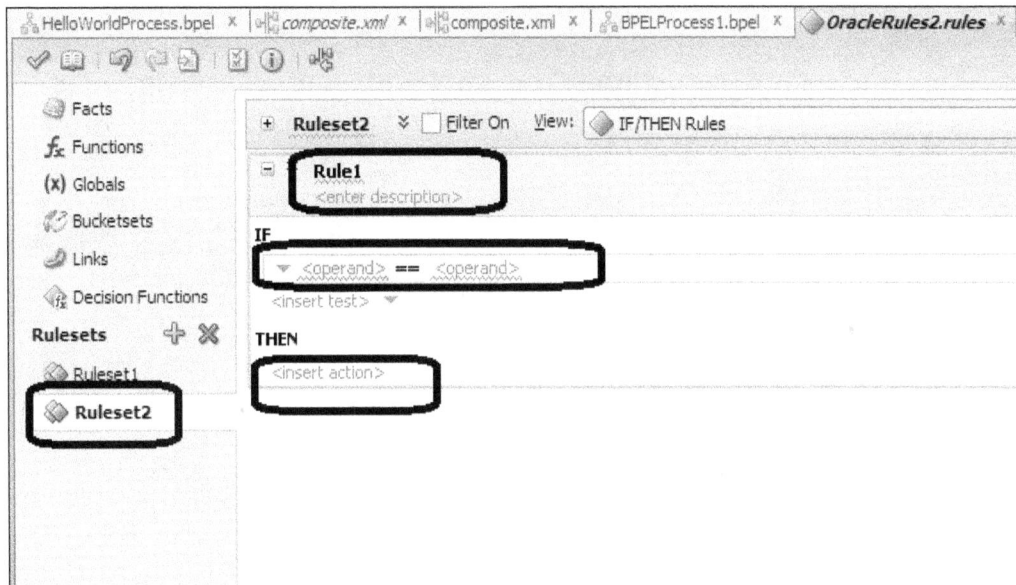

Facts and Bucketsets

It is recommended to create the facts and bucketsets before creating the rules.
Fact types are used for defining the structure of data objects and their methods.
A bucketset limits the values for a fact or property of a fact.

Facts can be created from XML schemas, Java classes, and ADF. All of the Facts types
are imported except for the RL Facts.

As shown in the following screenshot, from JDeveloper's **Business Rule Designer** (right-click on the Rule activity and select component editor) click on **Facts** to create **XML Facts**. The **Java Facts**, **RL-Facts**, and **ADF-BC Facts** can be created by clicking on the appropriate tabs:

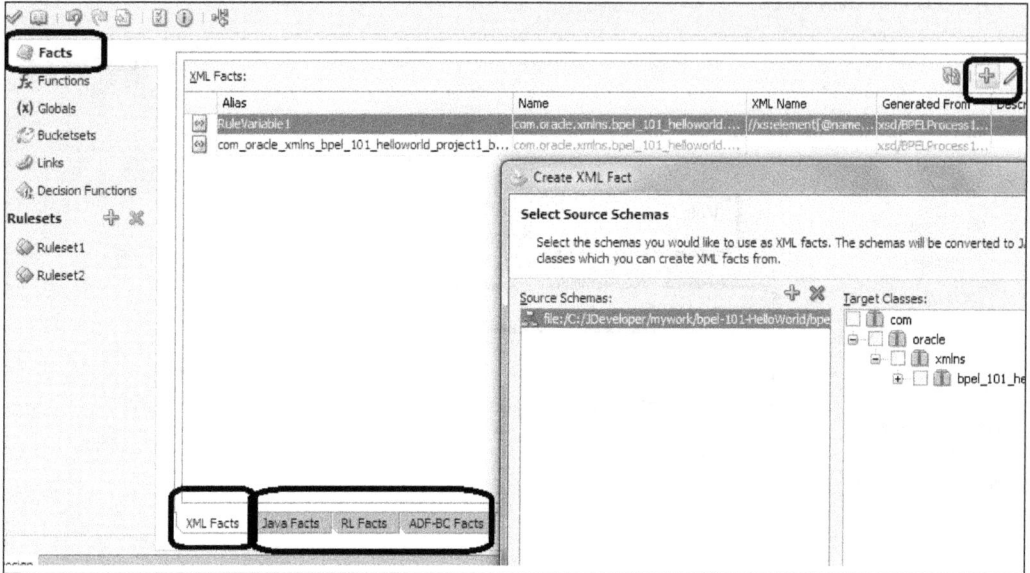

A bucketset can be defined as a value range or a value that is acceptable for a fact. As shown in the following screenshot, from the JDeveloper's **Business Rule Designer**, click on the bucketset for creating the value limits for facts:

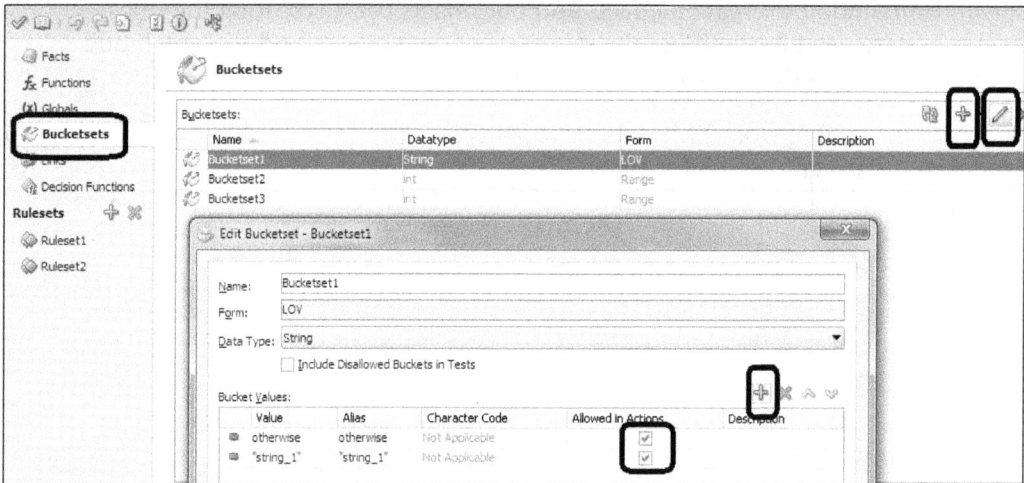

Summary

In this chapter, we have covered fundamentals of BPEL orchestration and steps for how to design a BPEL orchestration, details of using Flow and Scope activities, branching operations by using the Switch activity, how to create and configure custom XPath functions, and XPath expressions, and how to manipulate XML data in BPEL-configured variables. We also learned the use cases of Human Task and Business Rules Engine with BPEL processes. In the next chapter, we will learn how to test and debug an SOA composite application.

5
Test and Troubleshoot
SOA Composites

Testing the strategy, plan, and tactics is mission critical for any IT system implementation for serving business functions. Testing automation has demonstrated its importance and value by reducing the cost and time of testing the lifecycle for agile and iterative implementation of a system. The IT system implementations that are using BPEL Process Manager are usually developed using agile and iterative implementation methodologies to quickly adjust to the business process improvements and changes. In the case of an SOA composite with BPEL Process Manager implementations, to perform an end-to-end functional testing we often emulate external web services as most of the time these services are not available for testing purposes. These external web services are either invoking the SOA composite services or are invoked by the SOA composite service implementation. BPEL Test Suite is used for creating the test cases and emulating services required for testing. In this chapter, we will learn how to test BPEL services and automate such tests using BPEL Test Suite.

Testing SOA composites from the EM

In the Oracle Enterprise Manager console, we can select an individual BPEL service and test it. Click on the **Test** button to test the BPEL process service behind this WSDL, as shown in the following screenshot:

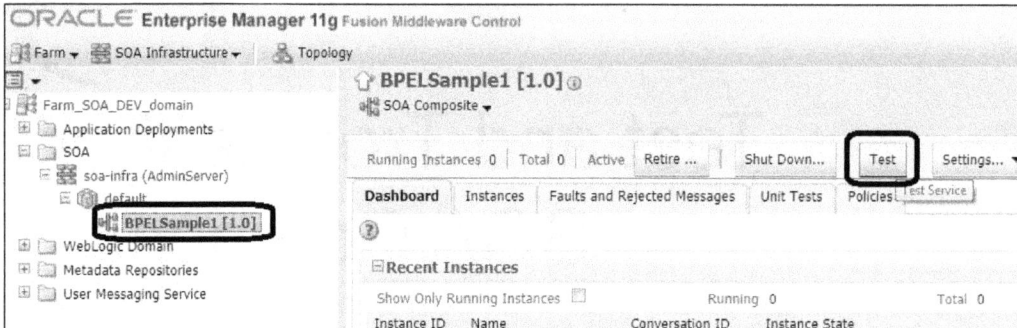

To test a web service, enter the WSDL and then click on **Parse WSDL**, as shown in the following screenshot. Enter the values for **Port**, **Operation**, and **Input Arguments** and then click on the **Test Web Service** button:

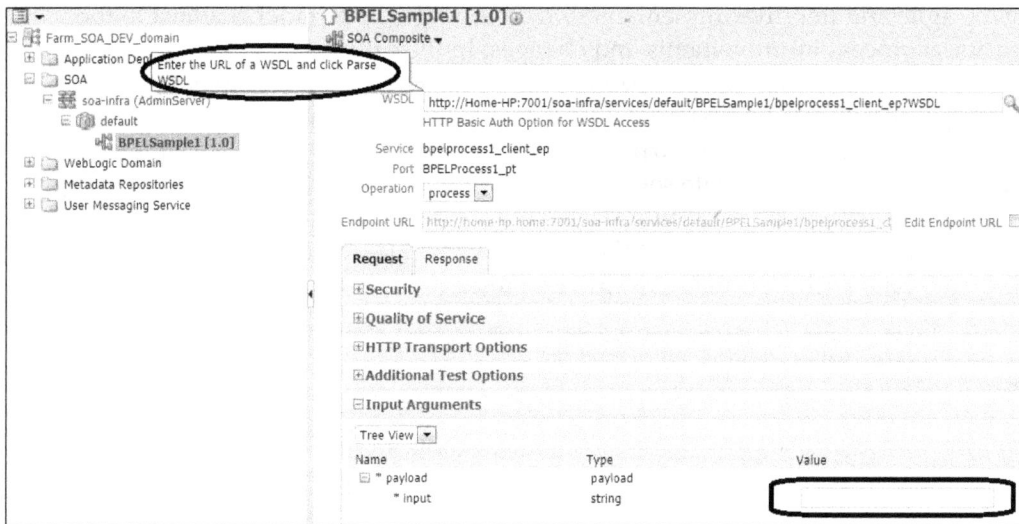

The test results will be as shown in the following screenshot. Selecting the **XML View** option from the drop-down box provides the output data in XML format:

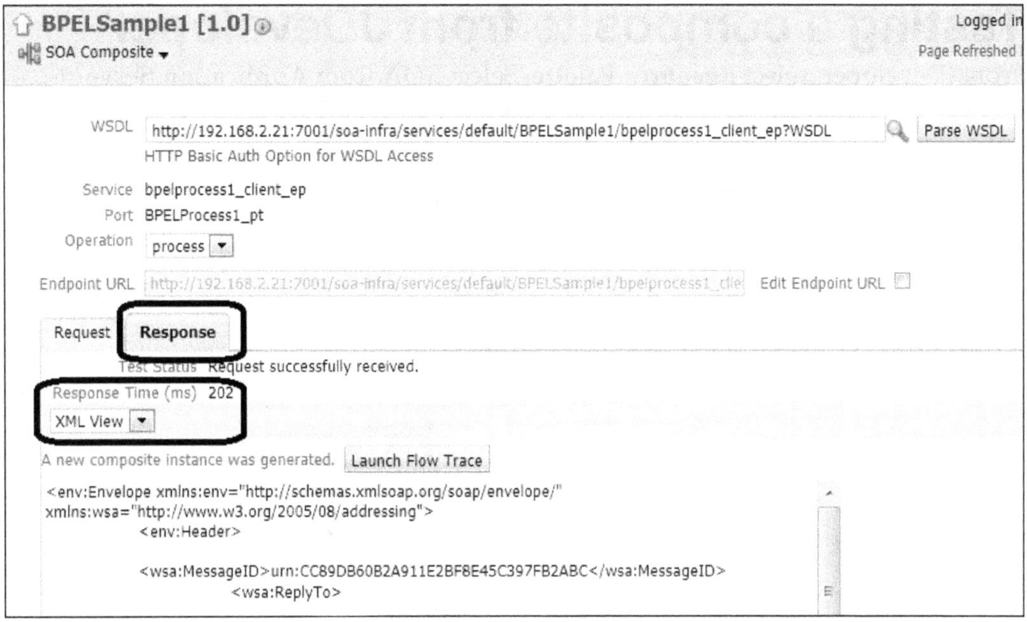

You can also get the audit data, faults, and flow of the response data by clicking on the **Launch Flow Trace** button. (You can get the same information by clicking on the instances). As shown in the following screenshot, select the **Show Instance IDs** check box and click on the BPEL to get the flow details:

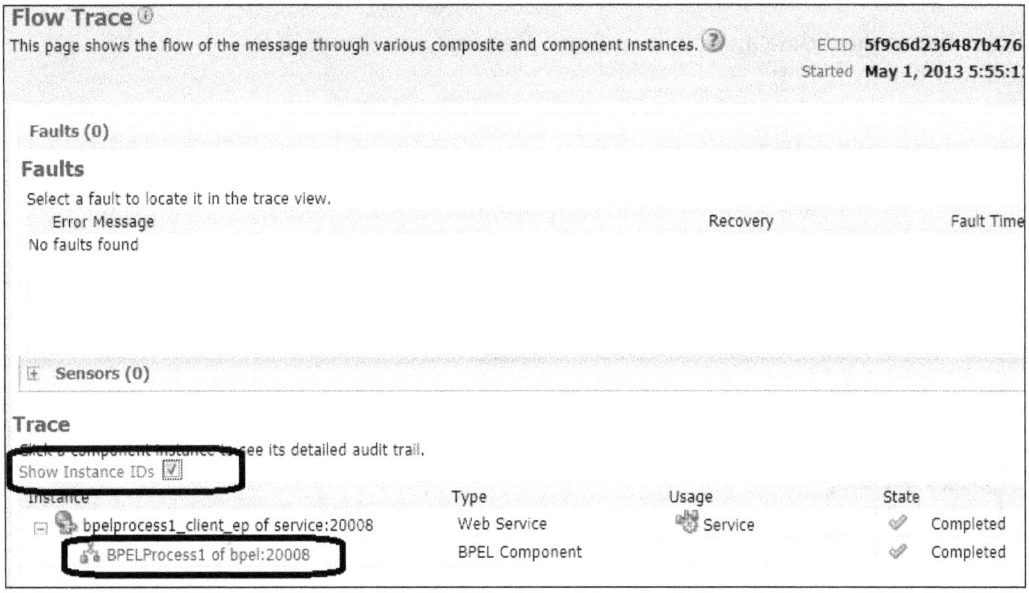

Testing a composite from JDeveloper

From JDeveloper, select **Resource Palette**. Select **SOA** from **Application Server**. Identify the composite application and then right-click on **Test Web Service**, as shown in the following screenshot:

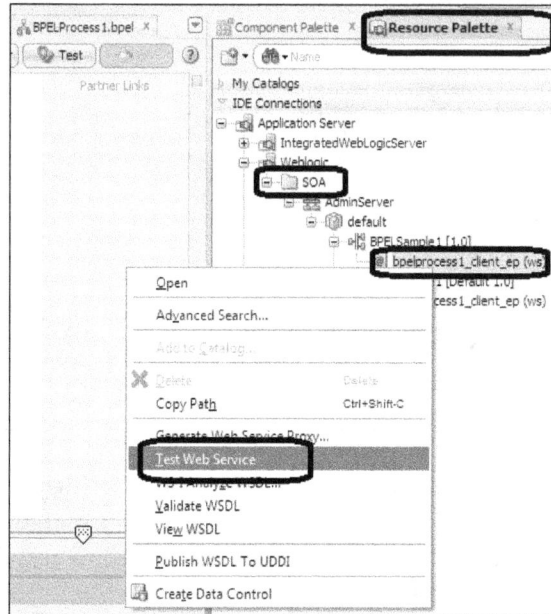

Enter the request data and click on **Send Request**, as shown in the following screenshot:

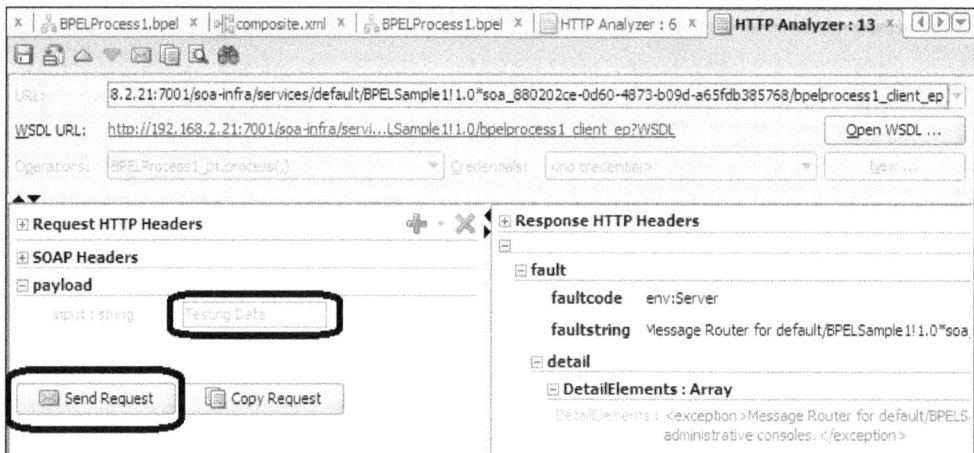

Viewing instances and messages on JDeveloper

The screenshot shows the input and output HTTP header data and instances status on JDeveloper. Click on the **Raw Message** tab to view the SOAP content in the XML format:

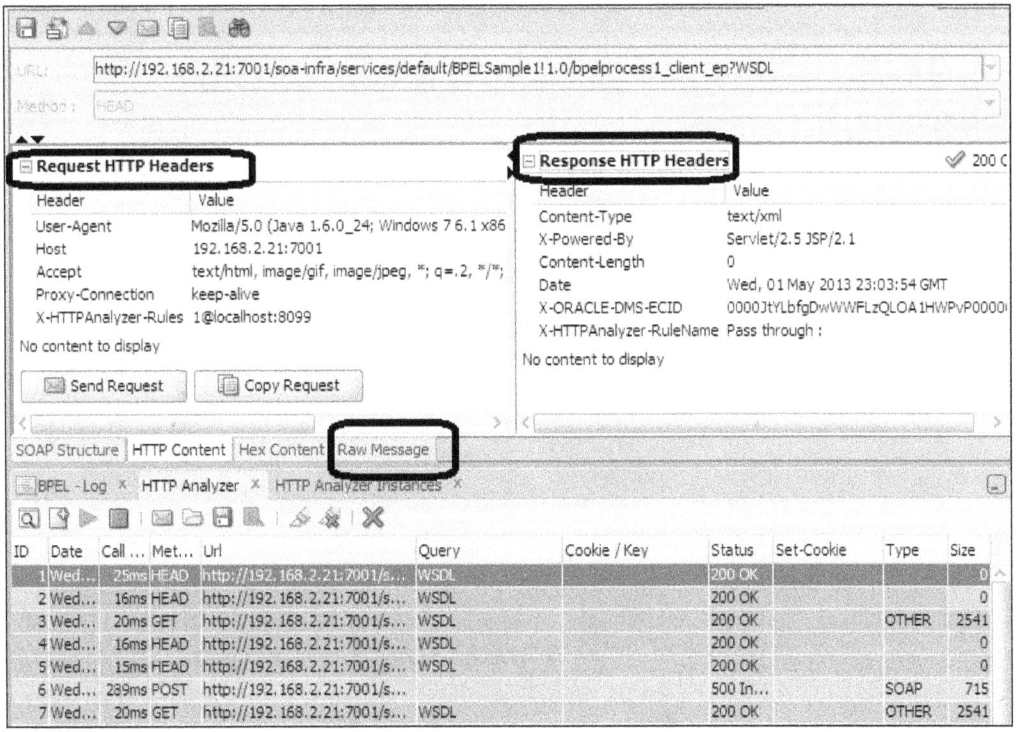

Creating a test suite

For creating a test suite we make use of the following steps:

1. Open the `composite.xml` file of an SOA project implementing BPEL services in the JDeveloper composite editor.

2. Select the `testsuite` folder under the project folder. Right-click on the `testsuite` folder and select **Create Test Suite**, as shown in the following screenshot:

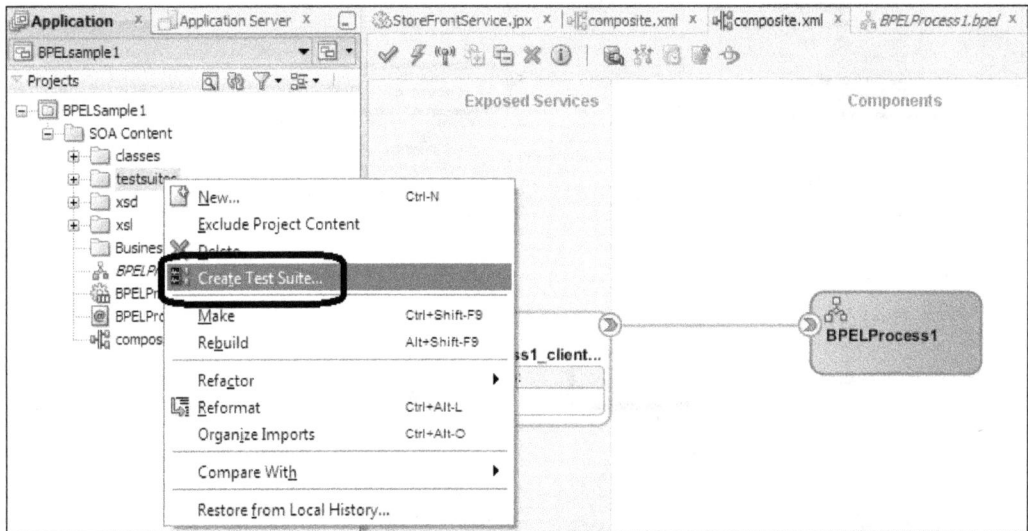

3. Enter the test suite **Name** and then composite test **Name**. It is recommended to keep the self explanatory names for a test suite and test case, as shown in the following screenshot:

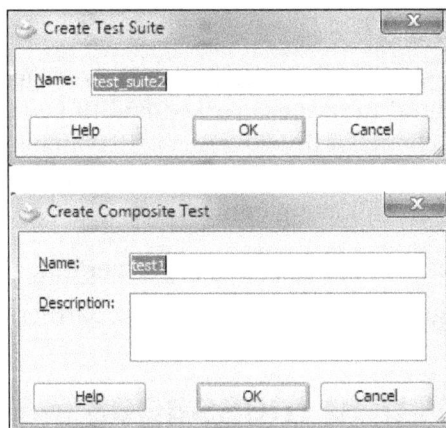

4. An additional test can be created by selecting the **Create Test** option, as shown in the following screenshot:

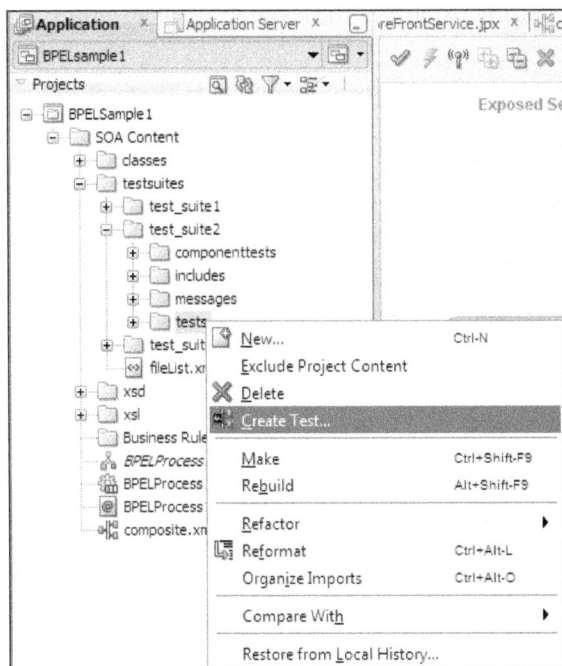

Usually, a test suite contains many test cases but it must have at least one test case. The purpose of the test case is to execute the test, gather test results, and analyze them for validating the business function service works as per the design to meet the business requirements. JDeveloper will generate a test case XML file in the project folder after creating the test case.

Initiating the Test

In a typical BPEL process service, there are inbound messages initiated by the calling client and there are outbound messages invoked by BPEL services via partner link. Since there are no calling clients or invoked services available for testing purposes, you would need to emulate the inbound and outbound messages. BPEL process services for testing needs the following emulations:

- Inbound messages for calling client via partner link
- Outbound messages for invoked services via partner link

Emulating inbound messages

Select the entry point of the BPEL process and right-click on the inbound partner link to initiate the inbound message and then click on **Create Initial Messages** to create an inbound message for the operation, as shown in the following screenshot:

Please note that by creating an initial message, we are simulating the client message.

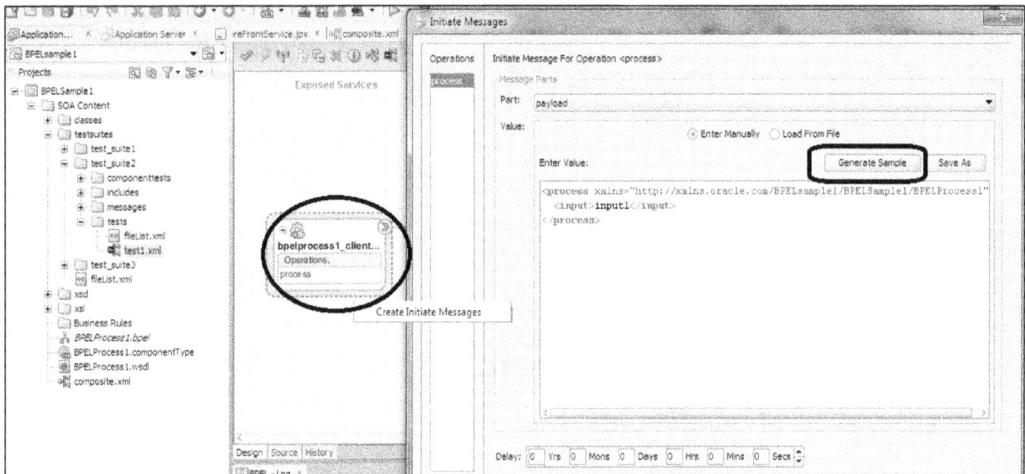

Emulating outbound messages

Select the outbound wire and right-click on **Create Wire Actions**, as shown in the following screenshot:

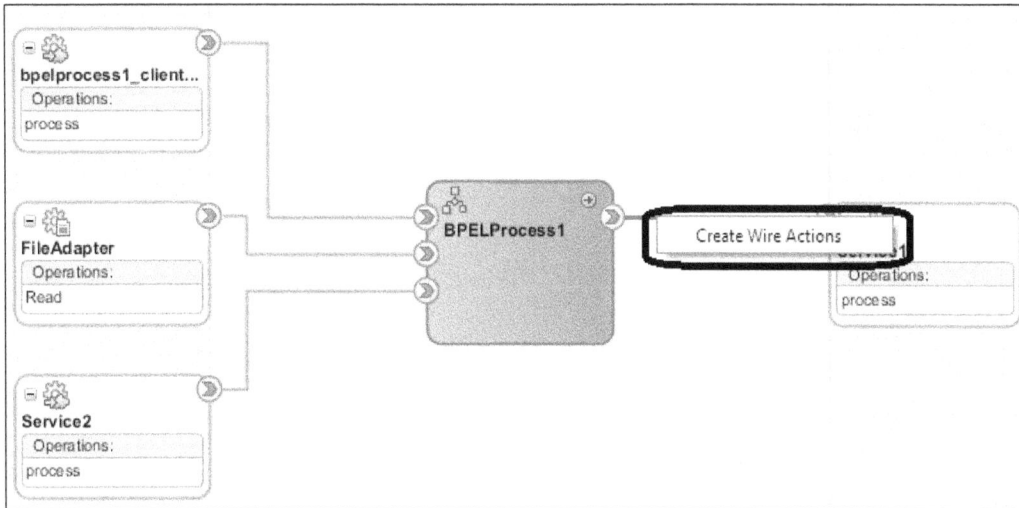

Select **Emulates** and click on **Add Emulate** (**+** sign) to simulate outbound messages, as shown in the following screenshot:

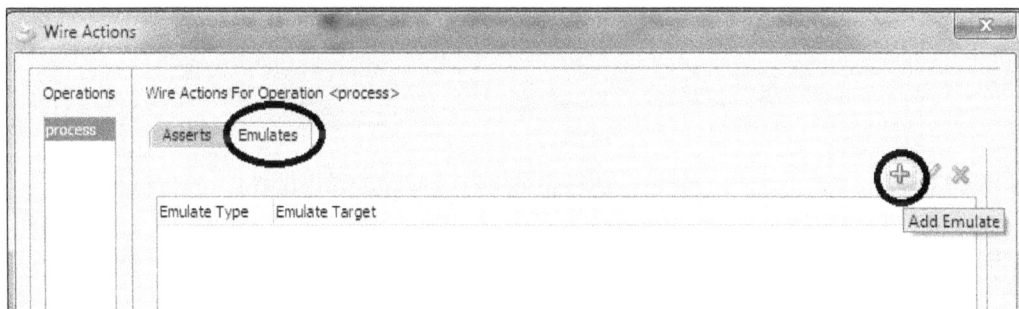

Then, select **Emulate Output** and click on **Generate Sample** to create an outbound message, as shown in the following screenshot:

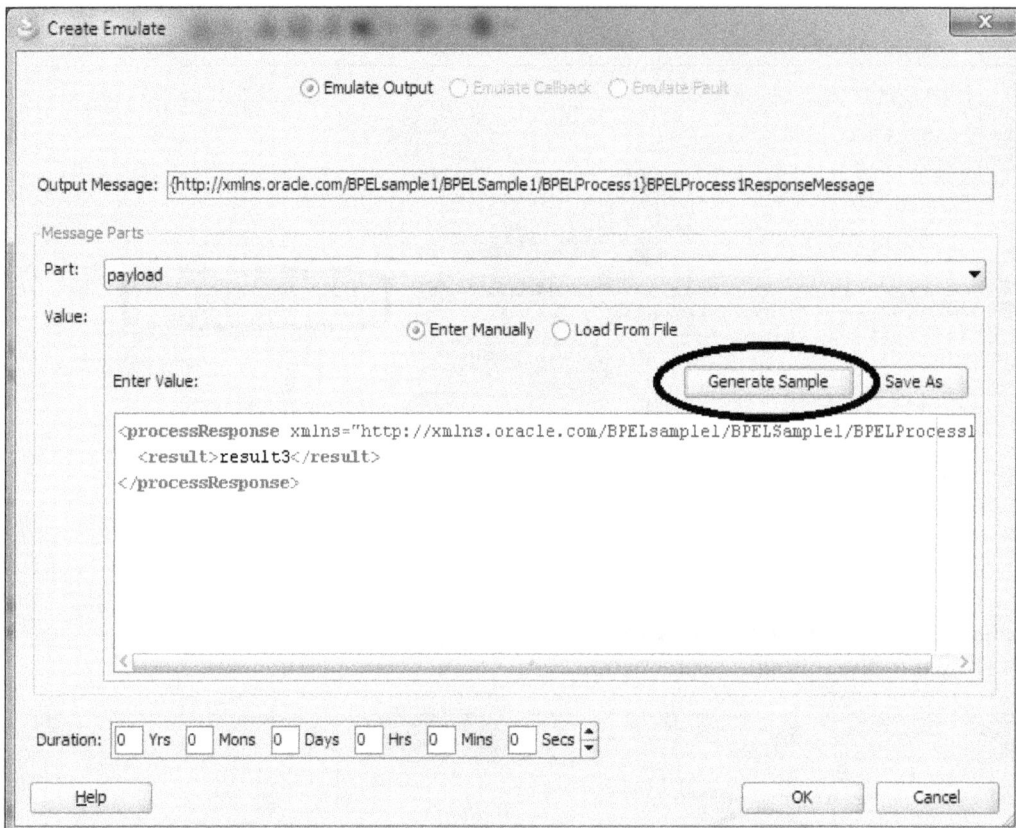

Select **Emulate Callback** to simulate a callback message returned from an asynchronous web service partner, as shown in the following screenshot. Internally JDeveloper creates the **Callback Operation** and **Callback Message** fields by emulating the callback message.

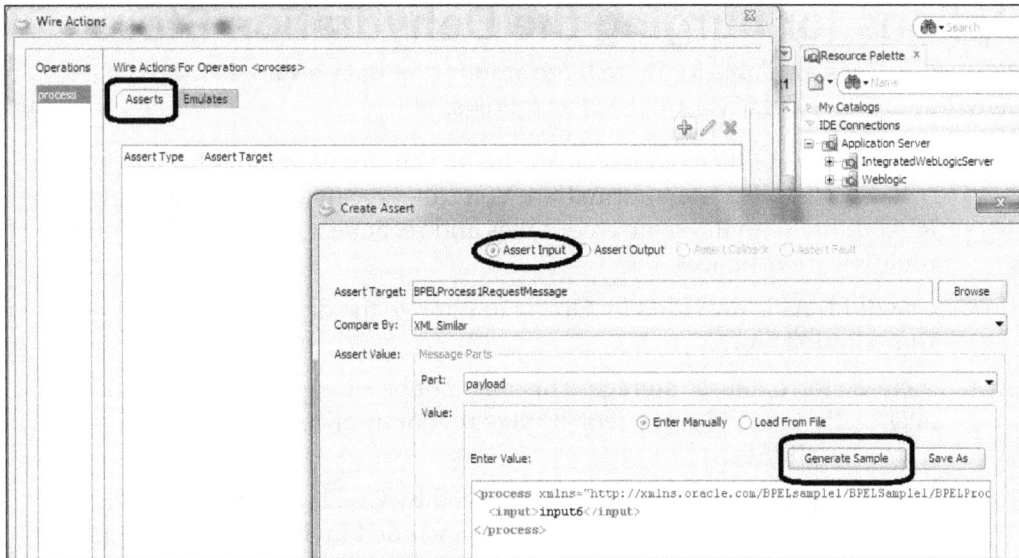

The Dehydration Store

The BPEL Process Manager is a web application created by Oracle. Oracle BPEL Process Manager is deployed on top of J2EE containers such as WebLogic, WebSphere, and JBoss. Oracle BPEL Process Manager uses a database to store metadata, runtime instance information, and the state of each conversation. The database is also used as a Dehydration Store to store the state of the BPEL process services. The process of updating the state of the BPEL process services in the database is called **Dehydration**. The asynchronous and synchronous processes mainly use the **Dehydration Store** to save the state of the process while waiting for asynchronous callbacks. The asynchronous messages also persist in the Dehydration Store.

Over a period of time the Dehydration Store database fills with data unless you purge the data at regular intervals. It is an industry-leading practice to develop data purging frequency based on the data retention policies for audit and troubleshooting needs. It is also a leading practice to trigger the purge of the Dehydration data based on the database disk utilization. Oracle provides the PL/SQL packages to purge data from the Dehydration Store. Due to performance reasons, the database schemas do not have the foreign keys and this complicates the purge of the Dehydration data. There are multiple tables used for the Dehydration Store.

The database schemas are created during the install process using the RCU utility. The database schema DDL for Dehydration Store can be found at `%SOA_ORACLE_HOME%\rcu\integration\soainfra\sql\bpel`.

Options for purging the Dehydration Store

Different options available to purge large amounts of data instances from the Dehydration Store database are listed as follows:

- Drop the SOA schemas created by the RCU utility to remove all the SOA instances and its state information. You can recreate the schemas using the RCU utility with the same credentials and reconnect with the SOA Suite middleware instances.

- Use BPEL APIs provided by Oracle to remove the data from the Dehydration Store.

- Increase the database storage. This may not be a long term option but eventually you will run out of storage if your application has a large number of BPELs.

- Execute the PL/SQL procedures provided by Oracle. Ensure that all the following listed Dehydration tables are included in the data purging process:

  - CUBE_INSTANCE
  - CUBE_SCOPE
  - INVOKE_MESSAGE
  - DLV_MESSAGE
  - WORK_ITEM
  - SCOPE_ACTIVATION
  - DLV_SUBSCRIPTION
  - AUDIT_TRAIL
  - AUDIT_DETAILS
  - WFCOMMENTS
  - WFATTACHMENT
  - WFMESSAGEATTRIBUTE
  - WFASSIGNEE
  - WFTASKMETADATA
  - WFTASK
  - DLV_MESSAGE_BIN
  - INVOKE_MESSAGE_BIN
  - PROCESS_DESCRIPTOR
  - WI_EXCEPTION
  - XML_DOCUMENT

Please note the default purge script provided by Oracle is not sufficient to delete all the data from the dehydration store. Please ensure that you delete the data from all of the preceding tables to clean up the database. The other option is to delete the database schemas and recreate it using RCU without changing the schema name or password.

Troubleshooting

The Oracle BPEL Process Manager has the following two web applications for troubleshooting issues with a BPEL implementation:

- Oracle Enterprise Manager console
- WebLogic admin console

The Oracle Enterprise Manager console application is available at the URL `http://{adminserver-host}:{adminserver-port}/em`. Log in to the Oracle Enterprise Manager console to check the status of **SOA_INRA** application, as shown in the following screenshot.

Ensure that both WebLogic container server and the associated database server is already running; if not first start them by logging in.

The WebLogic Admin console is available at the URL `http://{adminserver-host}:{adminserver-port}/console`. Login to WebLogic admin console. Select **Data Sources** from the left navigation menu and double-click on **SOADataSource**, as shown in the following screenshot:

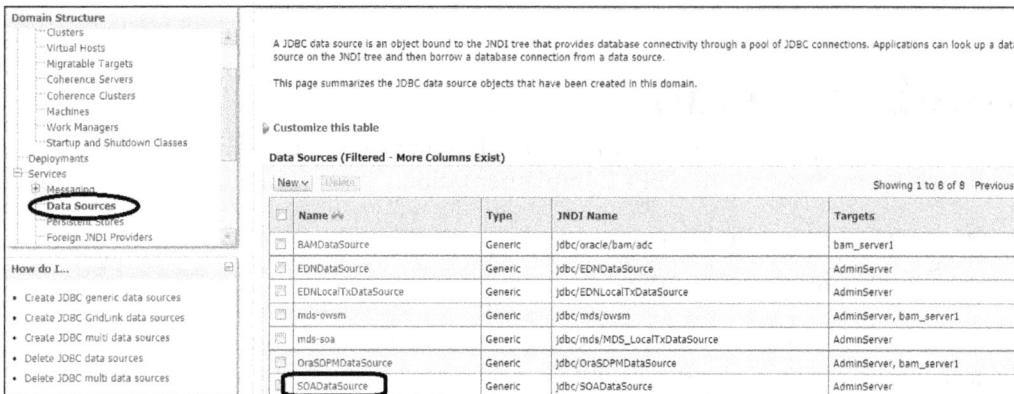

Now, click on **Monitoring** and then **Testing**, as shown in the following screenshot. The console will show the available server instances. Select the server instance and then click on **Test Data Source**, as shown in the following screenshot:

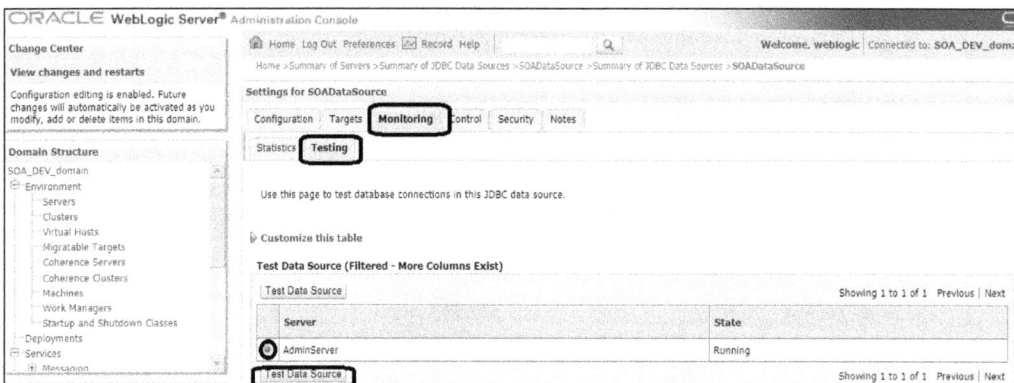

The most common error with the personal development environment is `ORA-12518, TNS:listener could not hand off client connection`.

For Windows servers, use `lsnrctl` status command to identify the TNS listener status, and locations of `listener.ora` and logfiles, as shown in the following screenshot. You may now need to start the database server.

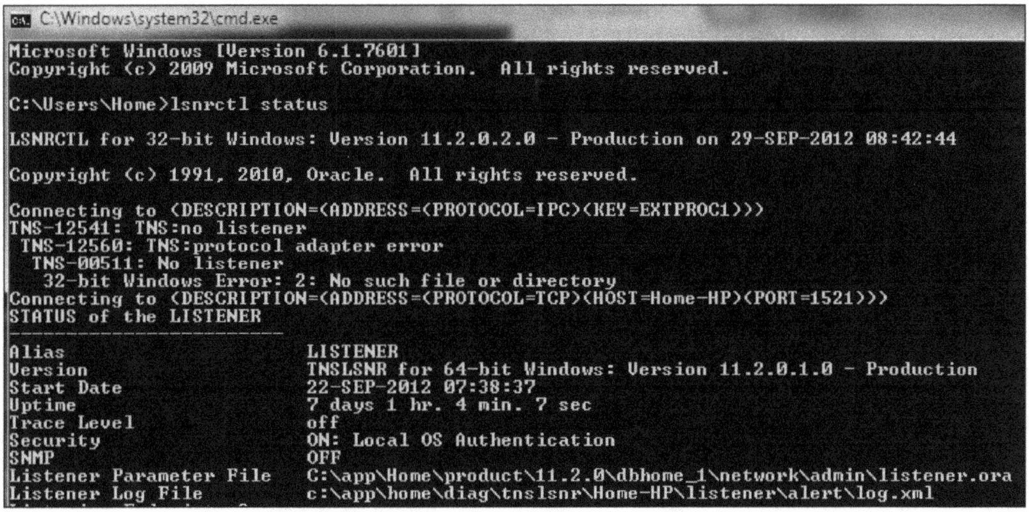

```
C:\Windows\system32\cmd.exe

Microsoft Windows [Version 6.1.7601]
Copyright (c) 2009 Microsoft Corporation.  All rights reserved.

C:\Users\Home>lsnrctl status

LSNRCTL for 32-bit Windows: Version 11.2.0.2.0 - Production on 29-SEP-2012 08:42:44

Copyright (c) 1991, 2010, Oracle.  All rights reserved.

Connecting to (DESCRIPTION=(ADDRESS =(PROTOCOL=IPC)(KEY=EXTPROC1)))
TNS-12541: TNS:no listener
 TNS-12560: TNS:protocol adapter error
  TNS-00511: No listener
   32-bit Windows Error: 2: No such file or directory
Connecting to (DESCRIPTION=(ADDRESS =(PROTOCOL=TCP)(HOST=Home-HP)(PORT=1521)))
STATUS of the LISTENER
------------------------
Alias                     LISTENER
Version                   TNSLSNR for 64-bit Windows: Version 11.2.0.1.0 - Production
Start Date                22-SEP-2012 07:38:37
Uptime                    7 days 1 hr. 4 min. 7 sec
Trace Level               off
Security                  ON: Local OS Authentication
SNMP                      OFF
Listener Parameter File   C:\app\Home\product\11.2.0\dbhome_1\network\admin\listener.ora
Listener Log File         c:\app\home\diag\tnslsnr\Home-HP\listener\alert\log.xml
```

Another common error is `Stuck Messages` that can be caused by many reasons. It is a best practice to configure an alert for stuck messages for asynchronous BPEL processes for Oracle SOA Suite 11*g* Release 1 (11.1.1.6.0) onwards. The global time threshold is used for identifying the stuck messages.

BPEL Process Manager logging

Understanding logfiles available with the Oracle BPEL Process Manager environment is very important for troubleshooting issues. There are multiple logfiles available to trouble shoot issues. Some of the major log files are listed in the following sections.

Domain logs

An example for the location of the domain logfiles is `C:\Oracle\Middleware\`
`user_projects\domains\SOA_DEV_domain\servers\AdminServer\logs`.

The logfiles can be viewed from the Oracle Enterprise Manager console as well.
As shown in the following screenshot, right-click on the SOA infrastructure
domain name from the left navigation pane and select **View Log Messages**.

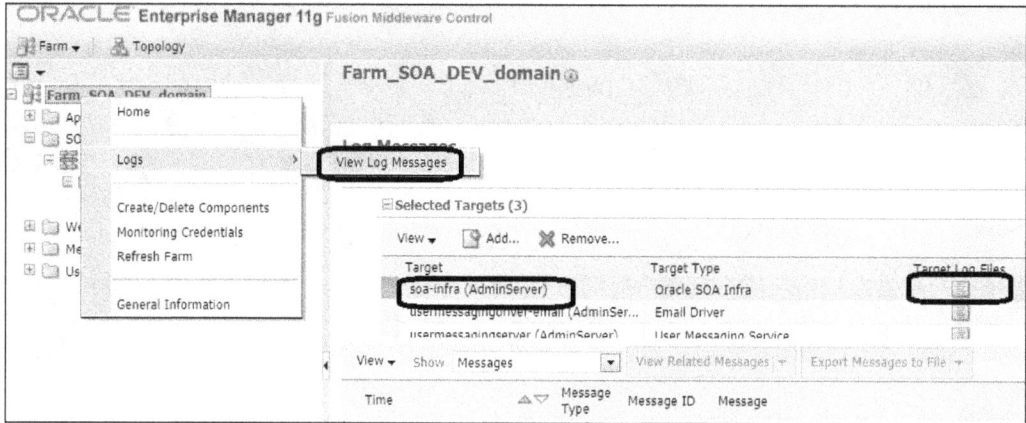

Select **View Log File** to view the content of a log file, as shown in the
following screenshot:

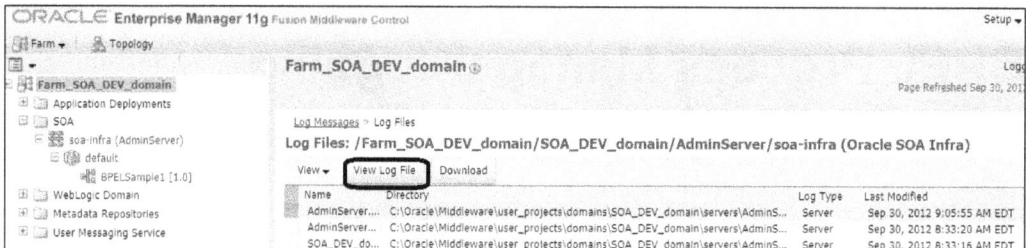

Access.log

The access logfile logs all the interactions with the WebLogic container.

Log in to the WebLogic admin console. Click on the **Servers** option from
the left navigation menu and then click on the server name for example
Adminserver(admin), as shown in the following screenshot:

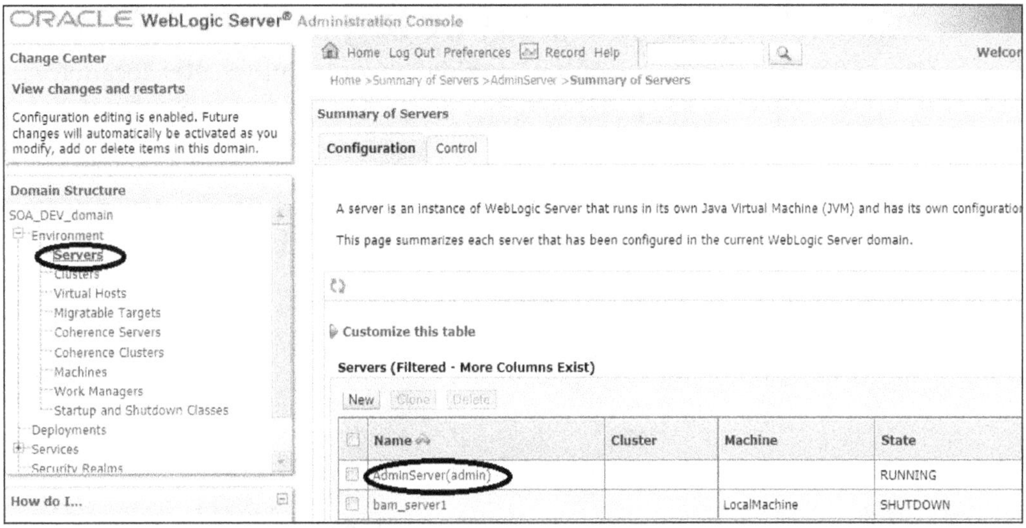

One can set the location of `access.log` properties file by using the HTTP sub tab of the **Logging** tab, as shown in the following screenshot:

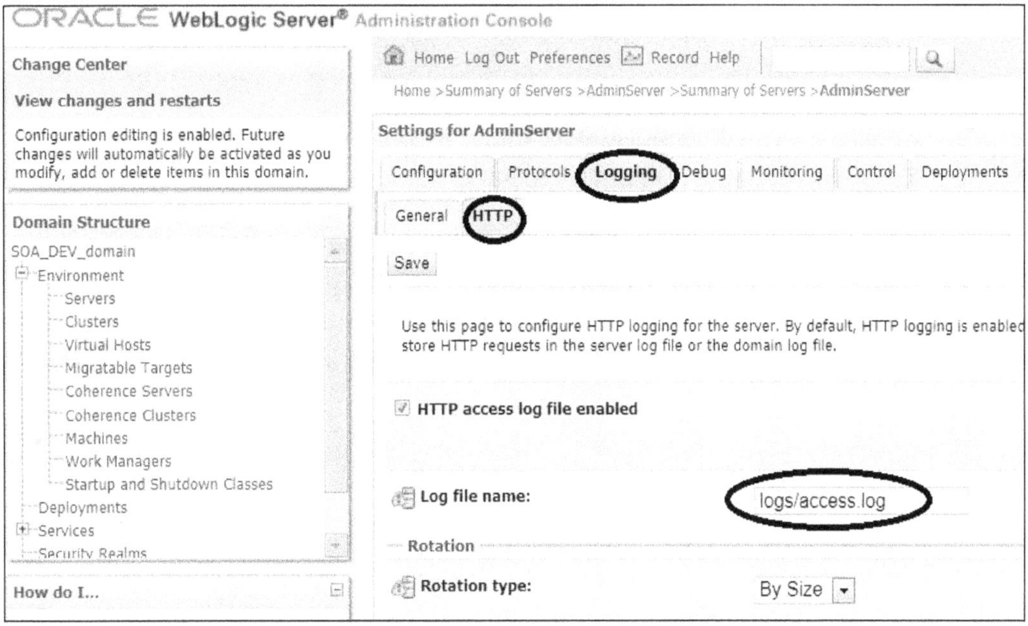

The admin/managed server log

One can select the **General** sub tab of the **Logging** tab for identifying the location of admin and/or managed server logs and changing its properties, as shown in the following screenshot:

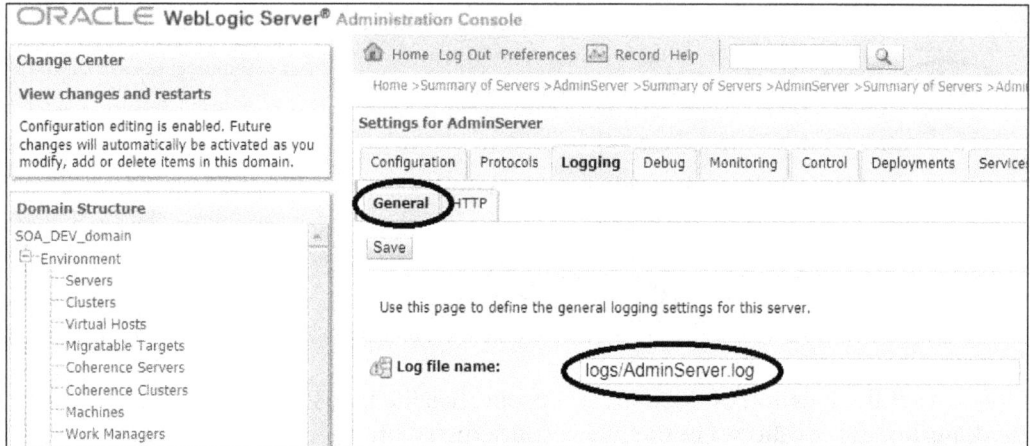

The summary of the important logfiles is as follows:

- AdminServer and Managedserver logfiles
- AdminServer-diagnostic* and Managedserver-diagnostic logfiles
- SOA and WebLogic Domain logfiles
- SOA Composite application logfiles
- Access logs
- JDBC logs

You can view and download logfiles from the Enterprise Manager console. Select logs from SOA infrastructure to view the available logfiles.

The logging level

One needs to set a correct logging level to get the information to either run the operations or troubleshoot issues during development and burn in periods of a BPEL composite service implementation. It is recommended that for the development and burn in periods we set the logging level at the highest possible that is usually development to get all the troubleshooting and runtime behavior information to optimize the BPEL composite services. Now, select **Log Configuration** from the menu of the Oracle Enterprise Manager console, as shown in the following screenshot:

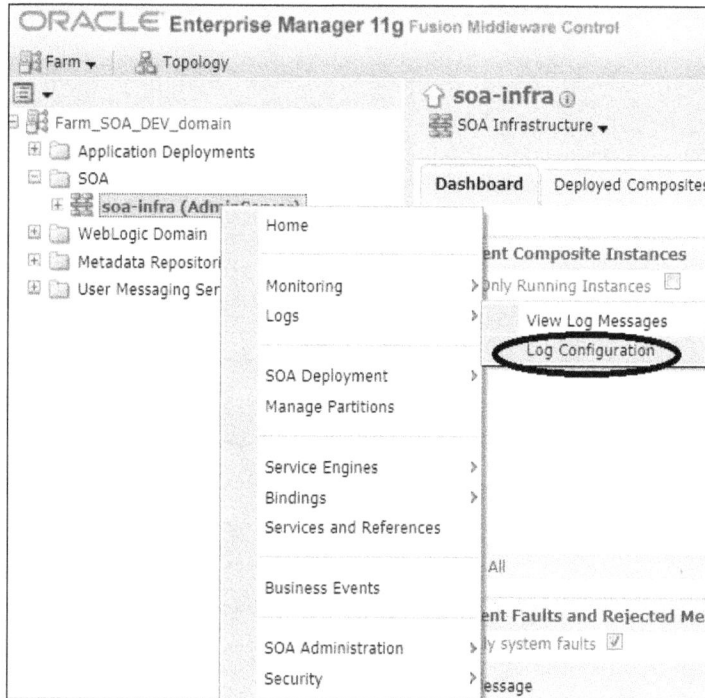

Set the logging levels to the **TRACE:32 FINEST** level to get more information about errors and issues.

If you have not applied the JRF logging templates, the system console will prompt with a message as follows to apply the JRF logging templates to the WebLogic domain:

Key Enterprise Manager features such as monitoring, security and logging are not available because the Java Required Files (JRF) template has not been applied to the server. You can apply the JRF template now to enable these features. The server must be restarted for this operation to complete. Note that the JRF template includes application deployments, startup and shutdown classes, as well as changes to the system classpath.

Click on the **Apply JRF** button, as shown in the following screenshot:

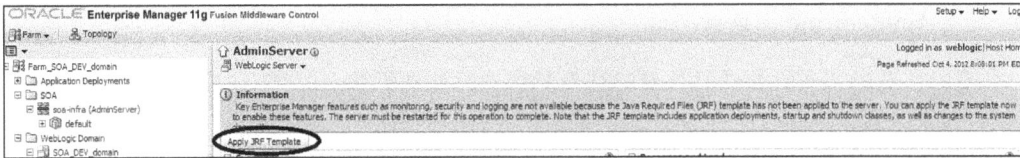

At anytime if you receive a message about domain extension requirement in the Oracle Enterprise Manager console or the SOA Suite admin server logs, please follow the following steps to extend the existing WebLogic domains running the Oracle SOA Suite with the BPEL Process Manager:

1. Invoke `config.cmd` from the SOA domain bin directory.

2. Select **Extend** as an existing WebLogic domain, as shown in the following screenshot:

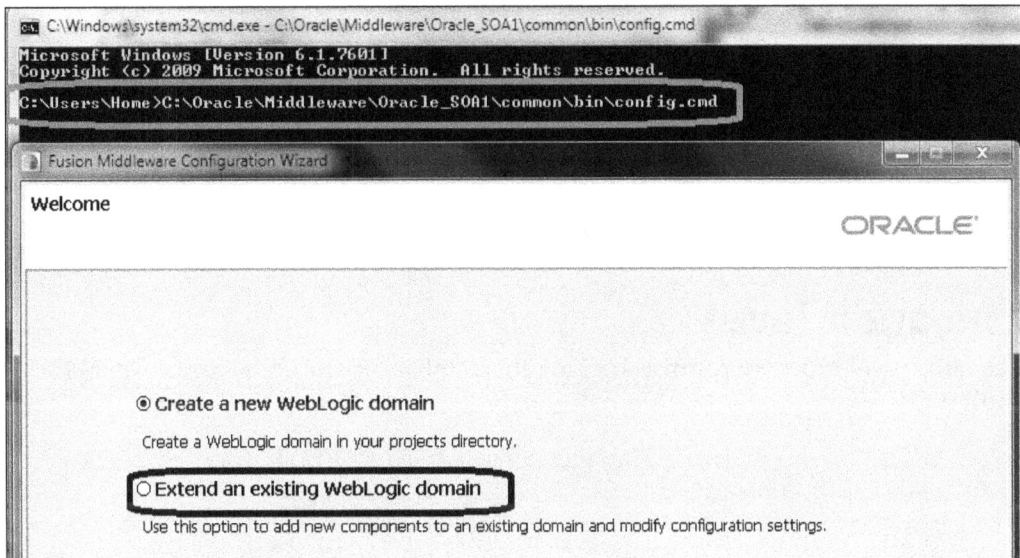

3. An example screenshot is given as follows for selecting appropriate domain extensions for reference. We need to select **Oracle JRF WebServices Asynchronous services**:

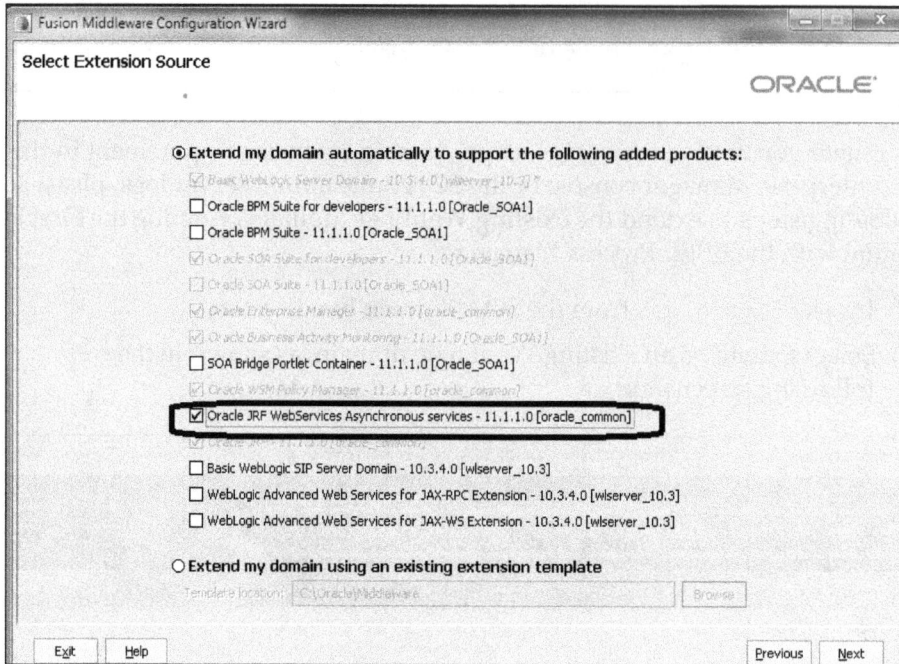

The audit level

The audit level property controls logging the database entries of various events for audit trails.

Log in to the Oracle Enterprise Manager console to edit **BPEL Properties**, as shown in the following screenshot:

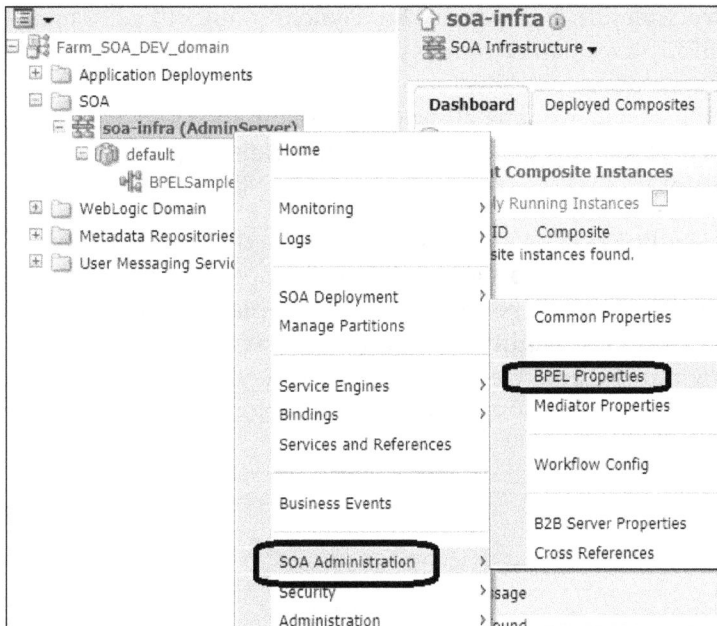

Now, as shown in the following screenshot, select the preferred **Audit Level** for the BPEL Process Manager based on your requirements. You can set the **Audit Level** property as **Off**, if your application does not require storing the audit information in the database; however, it is a best practice to keep the **Audit Level** property to either **Production** or **Development**. Setting it to **Minimal** will keep a log of all the events in the database but will not store any detailed contents such as the values of the variables.

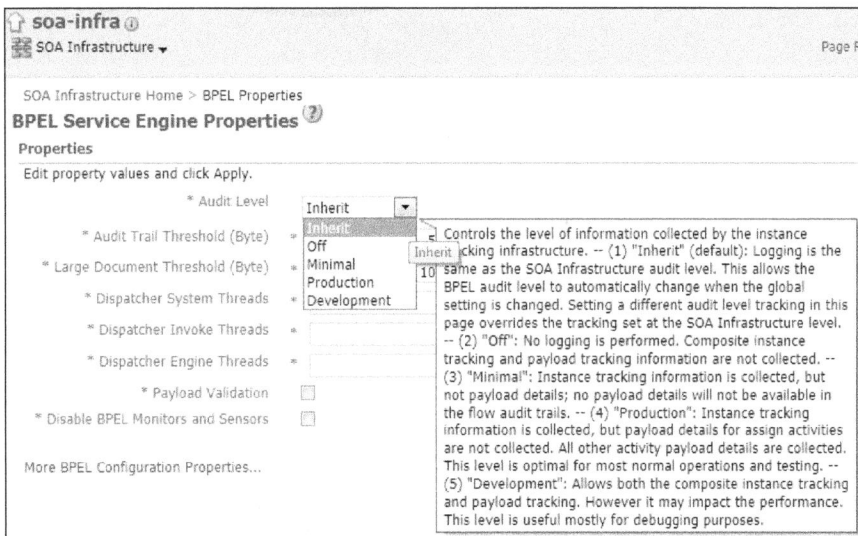

The auto recovery feature is important for asynchronous BPELs. Usually, a synchronous BPEL shows an error message in case of issues during invocations; however, for asynchronous BPELs the caller does not wait for an immediate response. Usually, asynchronous messages persist in the Dehydration Store and are scheduled for execution. In case of any issue, the transaction is rolled back to the last dehydration point.

By default the **Audit Level** property is set to **Production** at **SOA Infra**. It is recommended that you change the **Audit Level** property to **Development** during the development and burn in periods for a SOA implementation, as shown in the following screenshot. The **Audit Level** property, **Development**, captures all the troubleshooting information. Please note that we need to clean up the Dehydration Store periodically to prevent loss of application performance due to running out of database space.

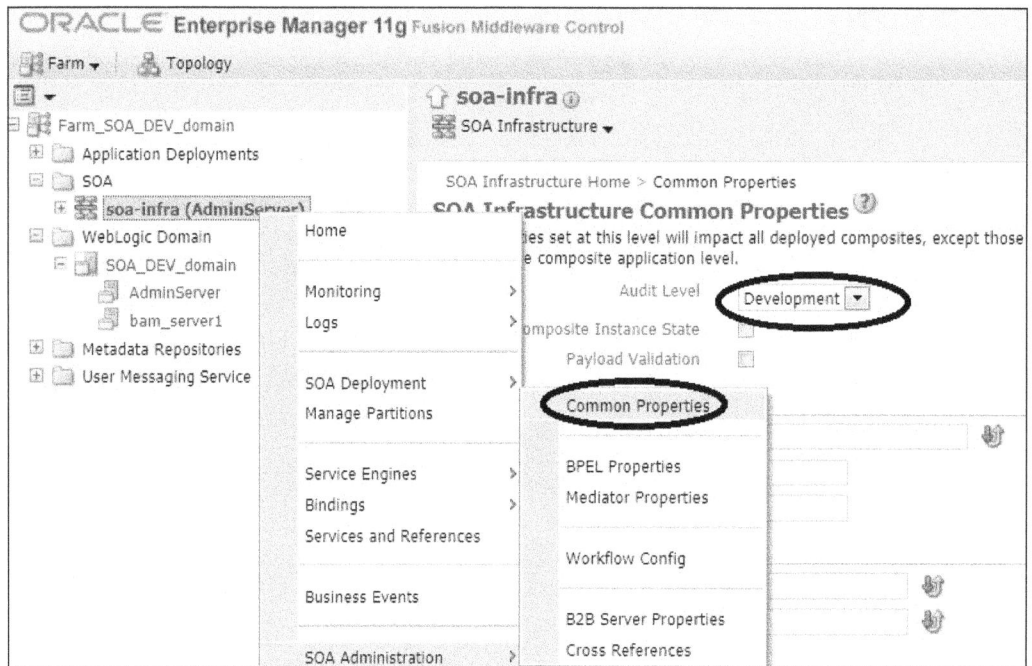

A sample **BPEL Message Recovery** is given in the following screenshot for reference. The EM console shows the BPEL stuck messages from version 11.1.1.6 onwards. The following messages will be shown after clicking on **SOA-INFRA** from the left navigation menu of the EM console. By clicking on the **Show Details...** link, you can get the details of the stuck messages, as shown in the following screenshot:

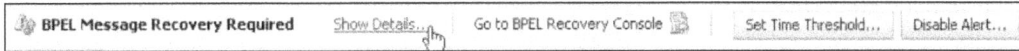

To recover the stuck messages, please use the following steps:

1. Select BPEL from the **Service Engine** option by right-clicking on **soa-infra**, as shown in the following screenshot:

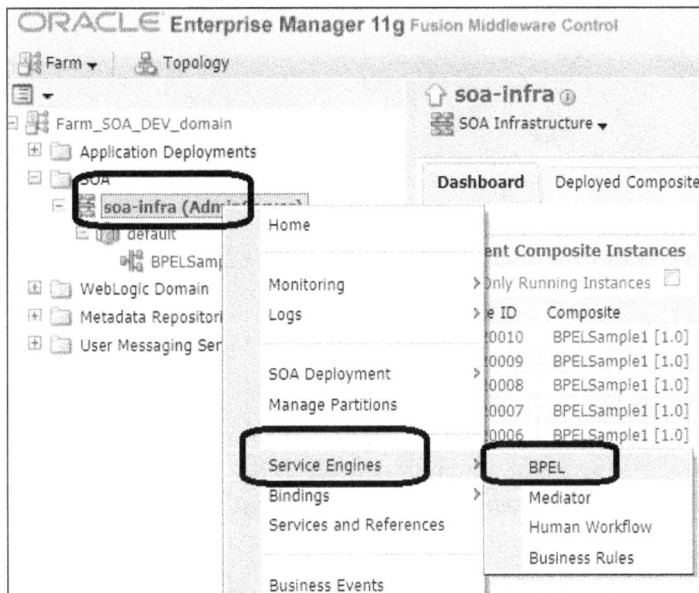

2. Click on the **Recovery** tab and select the instances that require recovery, as indicated in the next screenshot:

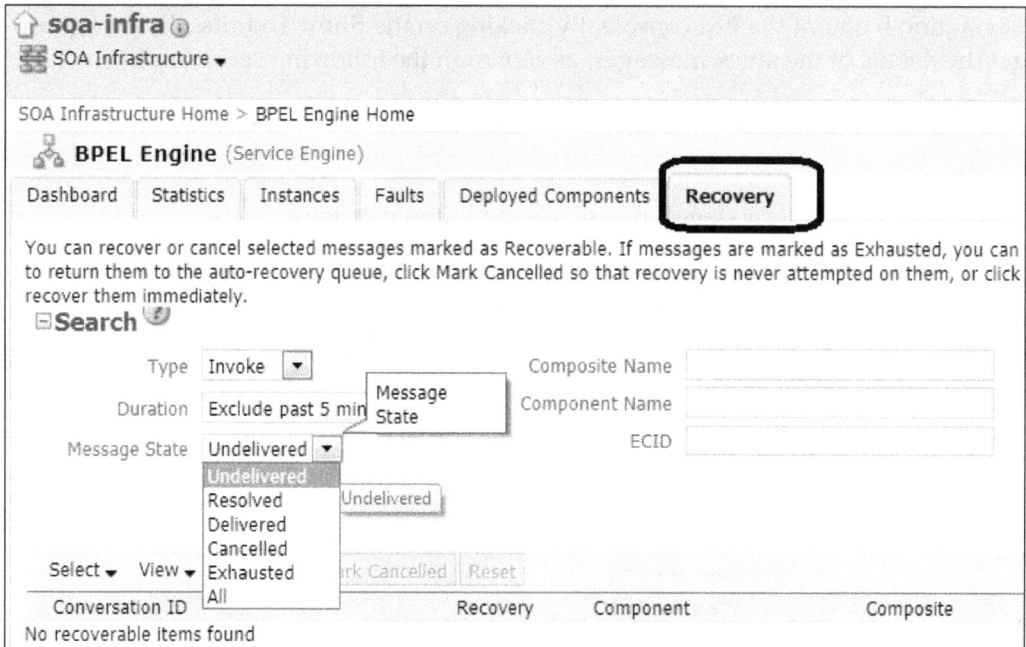

Monitoring

One can use the Oracle Enterprise Manager console for monitoring the BPEL services. Log in to the Oracle Enterprise Manager console and select instances to view the executed and pending instances with status, as shown in the following screenshot:

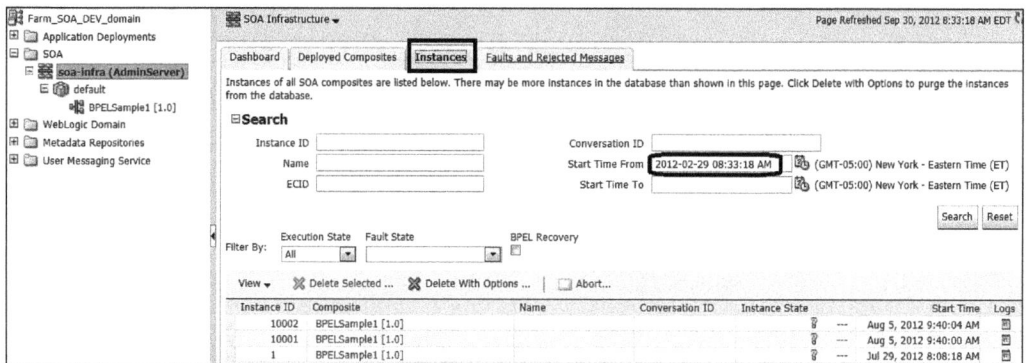

Click on the ID of the instance to get the audit trail information. The audit trail information of a sample BPEL process is shown in the following screenshot:

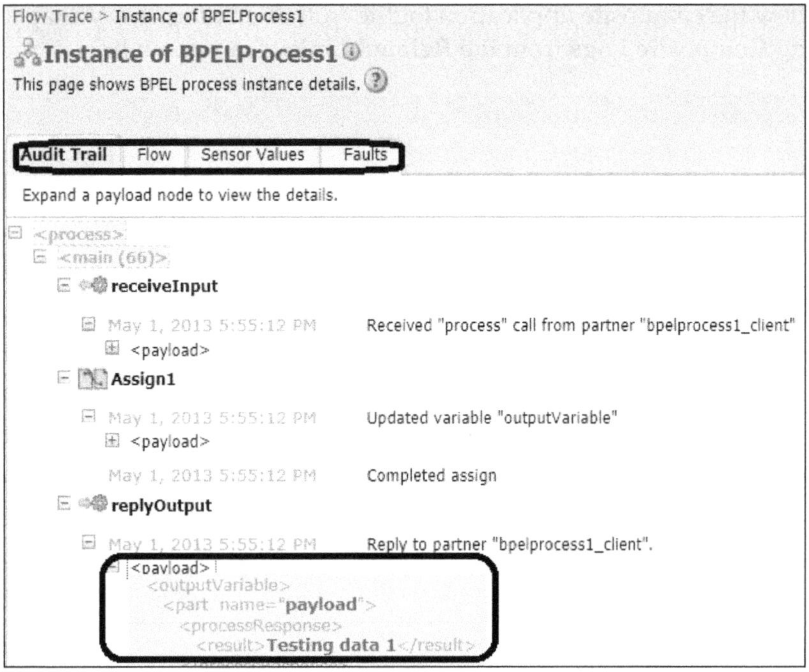

Audit trail explains the details and sequence of events that takes place within the BPEL component. Click on the **<payload>** tag to view the actual message data. The **Fault** page provides details of faults and error messages.

You can also shut down the long running instances by selecting the **Instance ID** and clicking on the **Shut Down** button, as shown in the following screenshot:

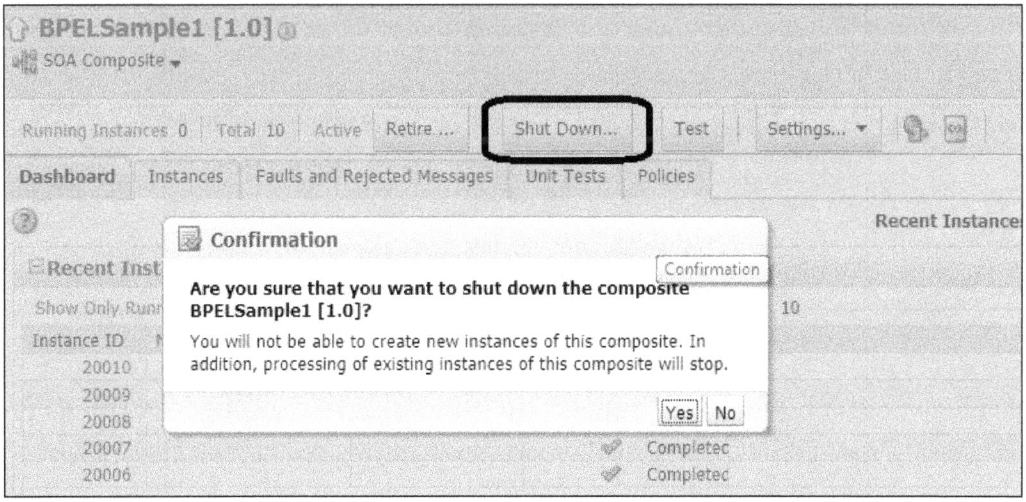

You can view the composite application logfile from the Enterprise Manager console by selecting **Composite Logs** from the **Related Links** drop-down box:

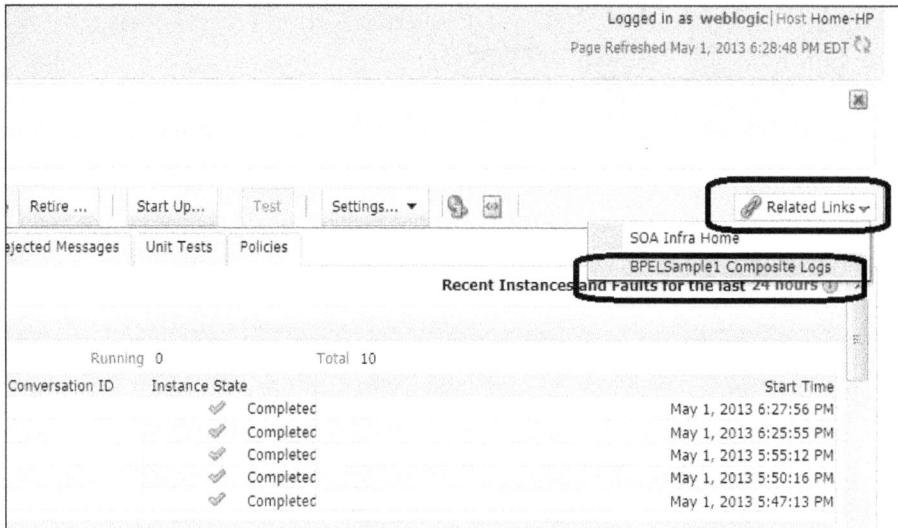

We can monitor the performance and request the processing data by selecting the **Monitoring** option from the Oracle Enterprise Manager console. Select the **Monitoring** option by right-clicking on the domain navigation menu on the left, as shown in the following screenshot:

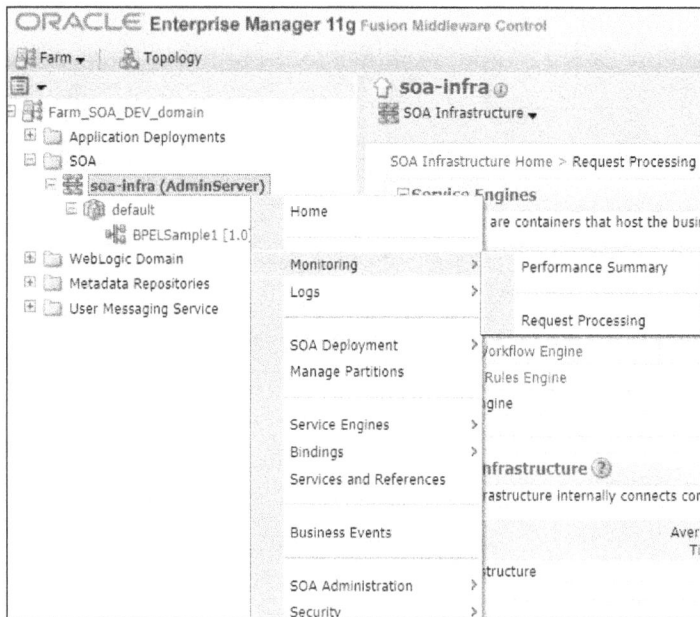

The MBean browser

All the values set using the Oracle Enterprise Manager console and WebLogic admin console can be also changed using systems' MBeans. One can write Java programs and **WebLogic Scripting Tool (WLST)** programs to access MBeans and change the values of MBeans. Select **System MBean Browser** from the Oracle Enterprise Manager console for browsing and changing the values of MBeans', as shown in the following screenshot:

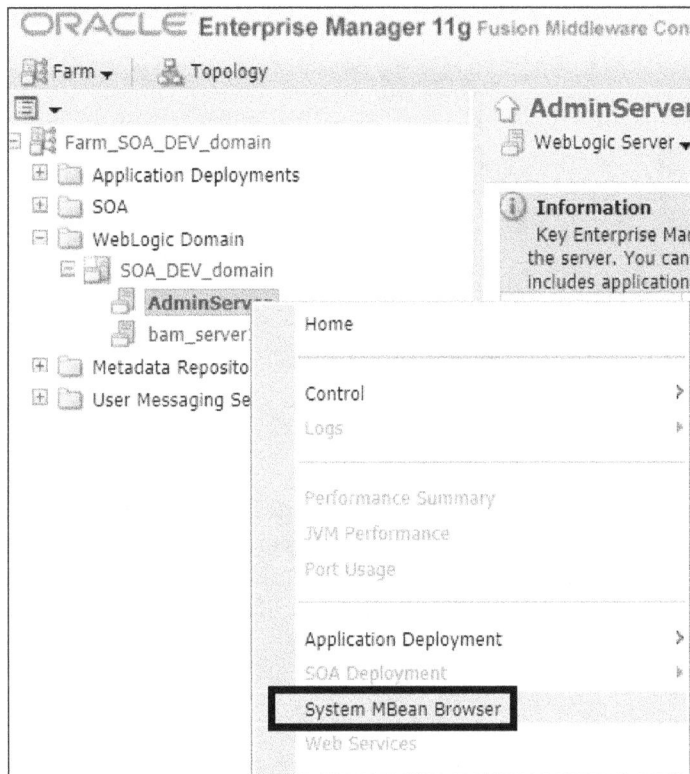

Select the MBean from the left navigation menu and change the values as needed. The following screenshot shows us editing the value of the `AcceptBacklog` parameter. The `AcceptBacklog` parameter configures the size of the wait queue for TCP-client connections while the application is busy processing other requests. One may choose to perform the same using the WebLogic admin console.

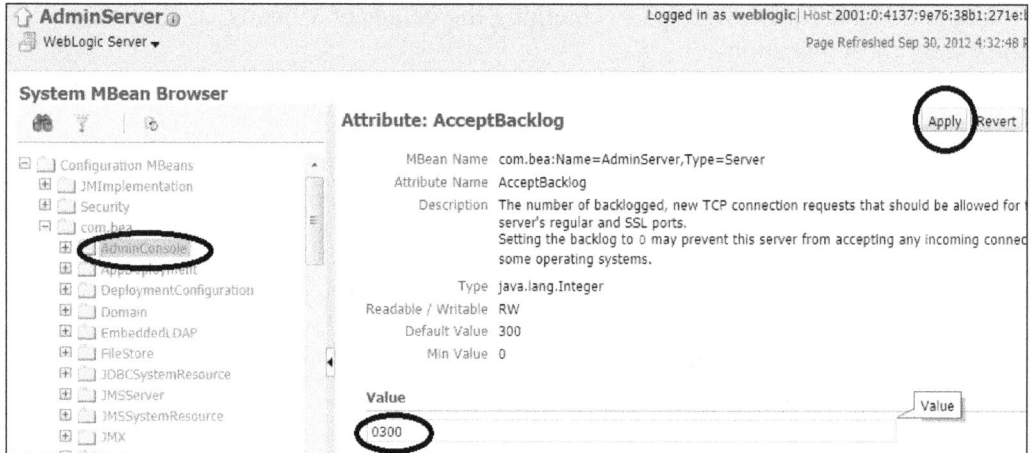

Summary

In this chapter, we learned how to create test suites for BPEL services, create test cases, and emulate inbound and outbound messages for end-to-end functional testing. We also also covered the Dehydration Store purge strategies and SOA composite monitoring. In the next chapter, we will learn to architect and design services using BPEL.

6
Architect and Design Services Using BPEL

In an enterprise, it is rare for us to get an opportunity to design and build enterprise systems from scratch. As enterprise architects, we must deal with the existing application services portfolio to identify commonly used services, and utilize them to implement an enterprise SOA. The architectural design has shifted from creating standalone enterprise systems from scratch to integrating existing systems due to the huge benefits in cost and time to deliver such systems. The standalone system cannot meet the business requirements in an enterprise setup anymore to benefit from economies of scale and scope.

There are several use cases for Business-to-Business (B2B) integration and application to application integration. Usually, many enterprises have application platforms developed using different technologies such as .NET, Visual Basic, Java, PHP, Mainframe, and Commercial Off-The-Shelf (COTS) products. To achieve integration goals, always adopt the service orientation and orchestration approach instead of creating monolithic standalone applications. BPEL allows you to orchestrate, that is, manage and coordinate different web services to achieve specific business requirements. In this chapter, we will learn the industry-leading options to architect enterprise services using BPEL.

Services architecture and design guidelines

The following are the key guidelines for services architecture and design:

- Reuse of existing applications.
- Loose coupling of the interaction between applications.

- Use asynchronous instead of synchronous interaction.

- Use common data formats for exchanging information between applications.

- All available services should be discoverable either manually or automatically.

- Avoid copying the data from one database to another. Always use the data either from the original sources or from a common repository.

Services-based application design

The first step to start designing BPEL services is to document the business process using an easy-to-read visual notation. Services interaction occurs through a standard WSDL format. WSDL is also used to represent the interfaces exposed by the service to the systems outside:

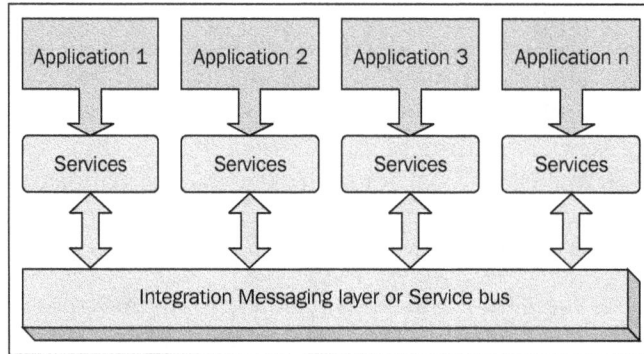

SOA is an IT strategy that organizes discrete functions services from enterprise applications. SOA enables an enterprise to quickly deliver for business requirements by combining and reusing existing discrete functions services.

Usually, a typical SOA environment consists of several applications with multiple interdependencies. The high level flow of a typical service-based application can be given as follows:

- Users log in to a consumer application

- The consumer application authenticates and authorizes the users

- Oracle Enterprise Service Bus (OSB) routes the messages and invokes back office services

- Back office services serve the users' requests

SOA Suite

As an architect, one should know the components available within SOA Suite and how to leverage these components to architect and design the services, and then use these services to create consumer applications faster and cheaper. The list of SOA Suite components with brief descriptions for the capabilities of each component is as follows:

SOA Suite Components	Description
BPEL	✓ Work Flow ✓ Orchestration ✓ Services
Service bus (ESB)	✓ Routing (Mediator) ✓ Messaging, Connectivity and Distribution
Adapters	✓ Connect to External Systems ✓ JAVA Connection Architecture
Web Service Manager	✓ Security and Policy enforcement
Business Activity Monitoring (BAM)	✓ Application Monitoring using Sensors ✓ SLA and KPI Management
Rules Engine	✓ Simple Rules and Editing
J2EE Container (WebLogic)	✓ JSP, Servlet, EJB

Enterprise Service Bus (ESB)

The main purpose of the service bus is to provide routing and transformation between incoming client requests and backend services. The key benefits of the service bus over point-to-point interactions are as follows:

- Enables loose coupling of the interactions between consumers and providers for seamless upgrades and maintenance
- Provides routing and transformation between incoming client requests and backend services
- Eliminates service sprawl by acting as a services backbone
- Provides end-to-end monitoring and centralized management of the SLA (Service-level agreement)
- Provides a centralized search and discovery of services that promote reusability

[💡 You don't require Enterprise Service Bus if you only have a few systems connecting to each other. It may be an overkill to introduce the service bus.]

The following two options are available to use the service bus functionality for your applications:

1.   Use Oracle Enterprise Service Bus (OSB).
2.   Use the Mediator component of SOA Suite.

Point-to-point connections between systems are tightly coupled and do not provide flexibility in the long run. However, as an architect, you should evaluate the pros and cons for introducing OSB as a separate component versus using the Mediator component within SOA Suite. One of the main advantages of using OSB is that you can introduce centralized security, messaging, and management for each interaction between services.

Oracle Service Enterprise Service bus (OSB)	SOA Suite Service bus (Mediator)
✓ Enterprise wide Service bus – Design as federated model	✓ Part of SOA Suite. Mediator provide service bus functionality.
✓ Separate container and console. Require new install, configure and deployment. OSB is not part of SOA Suite install.	✓ Tiny, Light weight Service Bus
✓ Large powerful service bus.	✓ Used for VETRO Pattern (Validate, Enrich, Transform, Routing, Operate)
✓ Great for Enterprise wide integration	✓ Value mapping and cross reference for supporting Canonical Data Model
✓ Message Transformation with XSLT and XQUERY	✓ Message Transformation with XSLT
✓ Not Integrated with SCA	✓ Part of SCA.(Service Component Architecture)
✓ Do not support event publishing and subscriptions.	✓ Support event publishing and subscriptions
✓ Use OSB console for developing business and proxy services	✓ Use JDeveloper for creating services.
✓ OSB provide service virtualization and protocol transformation along with routing.	

Use case of the service bus

The interaction between services can either be point-to-point or via the centralized service bus. The next figure depicts the point-to-point interaction between services.

As shown in the following figure, in order to provide an alarm service to consumer, multiple services needs to be invoked. **Alarm Verification Service** has to invoke the **DATE Service**, **Time Service**, and **Alarm Set Date Service**. The consumer alarm service has to invoke multiple services such as set date and verification service, thereby causing the service sprawl occurring in the system.

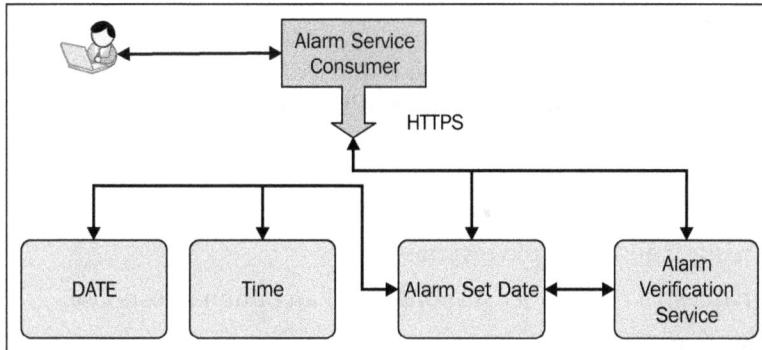

The better approach is to provide a common layer between the calling service and the provider service by using a service bus. The service bus enables loose coupling between the alarm service consumer and the alarm services provider.

The following figure depicts the interaction between services through the service bus:

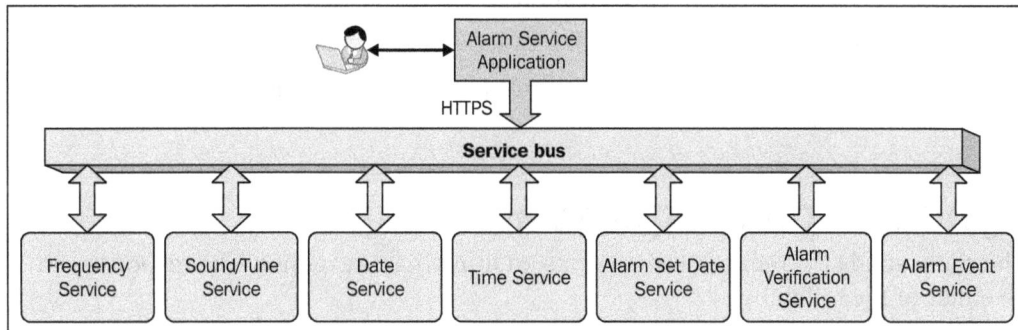

Interaction design patterns

The request will have one or more input parameters, and the response may have one or more output parameters. Deciding the interaction between the client and the service provider is one of the most important decisions during the design of BPEL services. Each service has its own WSDL definition and endpoint. The Partner Link is used for interaction between services.

Primarily, BPEL services are all about the request and response. The following design patterns are used for implementing BPEL services:

- Synchronous request and response
- Asynchronous request and response
- One request and multiple responses
- One request, a mandatory response, and an optional response
- One-way message

Some of the other possible interaction design patterns that are not commonly used are listed here:

- Multiple requests, multiple responses
- Multiple requests, first response (ignore remaining responses)
- One request and one or two responses
- Asynchronous interaction with a timeout using the onMessage activity
- Asynchronous interaction with a notification timer option using the onAlarm activity

Synchronous request and response

The client sends the request and receives an immediate response. The response can be either of the following:

- Response based on the request (The response will contain data)
- Faults/Exceptions (The responses do not have any data)

As shown in the figure, the request can originate from either of the following:

- Client BPEL Services
- Mediator Services
- Oracle Service Bus Proxy / Business Services

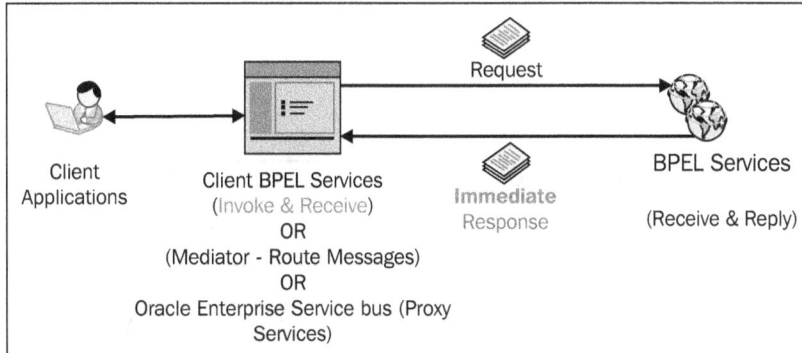

Asynchronous request and response

In asynchronous interactions, the client sends the request, and the service provider may or may not respond immediately.

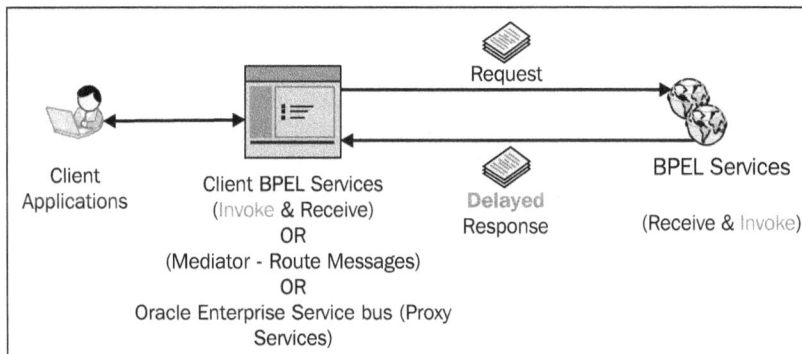

Asynchronous BPEL services use the Invoke activity. The response will usually delay the calling service, and the client may choose to do other activities without waiting for a response. The response could be data or an error message.

One request and multiple responses

The client sends a single request and receives multiple responses. For the client BPEL services, there is one Invoke activity for sending the request, and multiple Receive activities grouped in a sequence. For the BPEL services, there should be one Receive activity and multiple Invoke activities for each reply grouped in a sequence. As shown in the next figure, multiple Receive activities can be grouped together using a sequence:

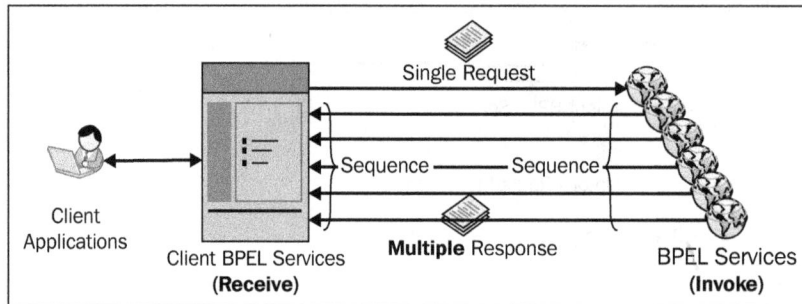

One request, a mandatory response, and an optional response

The client service sends a single request and receives one or more responses. One response must be immediate; the other responses may be delayed.

In this case, a Scope activity is used to group the Invoke activity to send the request and the Receive activity to accept the mandatory response. The OnMessage handler of the Scope activity is set to accept the optional message and the instructions on what to do if the optional message is received. The client will wait for the mandatory reply and continue receiving the same without waiting further for any optional response. The BPEL service also uses the onAlarm handler or the Scope activity to send the optional delayed message if the timer expires.

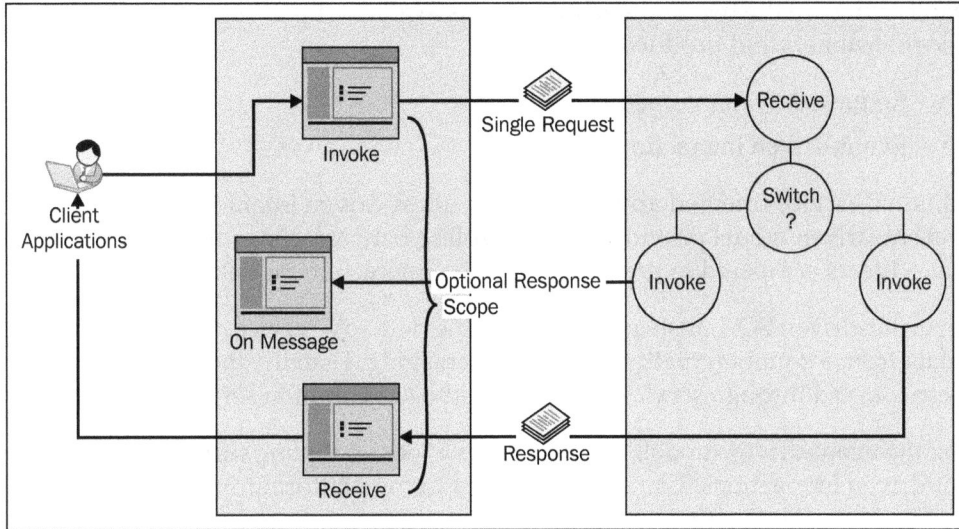

One-way message

The client sends the message, and the service does not reply. This pattern can be used for sending updates to a service with data, and it requires no response in return. As shown in the next figure, the implementation of the one-way message can be done using a Mediator client, BPEL component, or Oracle Enterprise Service Bus.

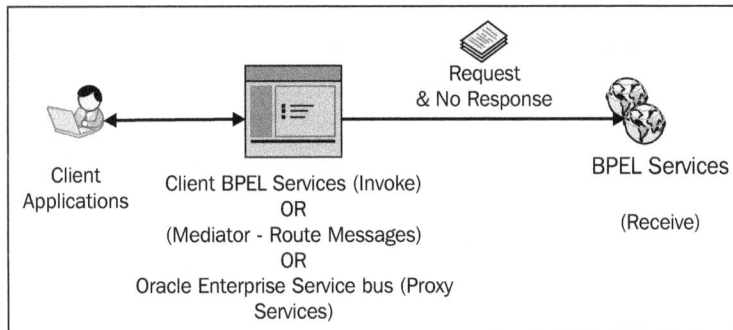

Event-Driven Architecture (EDA)

Service-Oriented Architecture (SOA) and Event-Driven Architecture (EDA) are two complementary architectures for separating service consumers and producers. At present, both architectures are being implemented together.

The following are the two architecture models available for interaction between service consumers and producers:

- Request-driven interaction
- Event-driven interaction

Traditional service-oriented approach uses request-driven interaction. The event-driven model provides loose coupling between consumers and producers compared to the request-driven interaction model.

In an event-driven SOA, instead of pushing the data to a service, the service reads the data from a common platform such as messaging. Usually, the services are loosely coupled through service interfaces and use a common service bus.

Using the event-driven model, you can achieve loose coupling through the event-driven interactions. Use a common messaging platform for reading the data. The invocation is triggered by an event.

For example, a file's arrival to a common SAN/NAS device or a specific data update to a database could trigger an event.

Request-driven interaction

A typical service invocation is that of a service consumer invoking a service producer through a common interface. The invocation can be done either directly through a WSDL file, or through a service bus in the middle. As shown in the next figure, a service consumer invokes a service producer through the service bus:

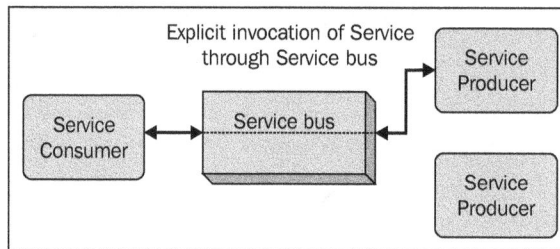

Event-driven interaction

As shown in the next figure, in a typical event-driven model, the service producer produces the data and publishes it on a common messaging platform. The service consumer subscribes to and consumes the data from a common messaging platform.

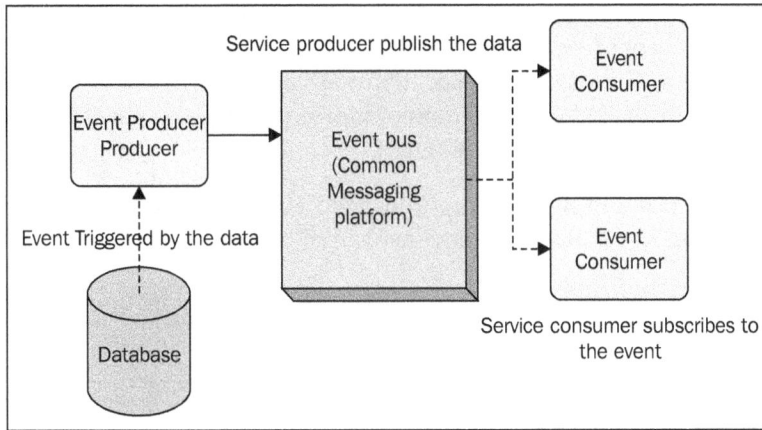

One of the disadvantages of the event-driven model is complexity, due to the additional platform components and configurations over a traditional request-response interaction.

On the other hand, the biggest advantage of the event-driven model is that it provides loose coupling between service consumers and producers.

Human tasks

Human interaction is required for many business use cases that involve some kind of approvals or actions from a person. One of the examples of human tasks is an approval service or termination service. An approver gets notifications about pending tasks from the human workflow, as shown in the next figure. The approver client can take action based on the request. BPEL will process the request based on the input from the approver client. The process may have to wait for the Human Task to complete.

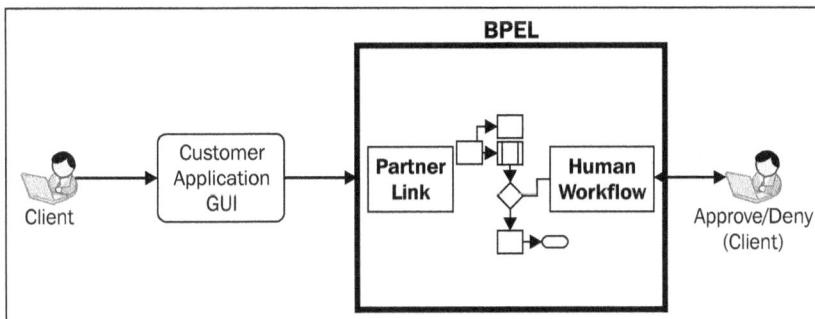

Human tasks have various specifications, such as task properties, people assignments, task owners, task administrators, timeouts, escalations and notifications. Once a BPEL service associated with a Human Task is invoked, a task is created and assigned to a person or a group. Once the person finishes the task, the service is marked as completed.

As shown in the following figure, drag-and-drop **Human Task** from SOA **Component Palette** to the JDeveloper console:

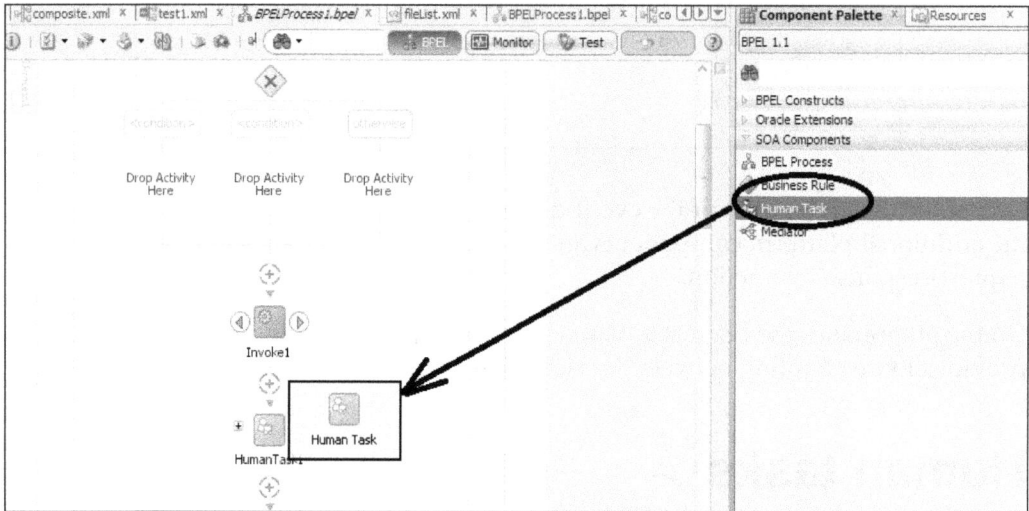

After adding the Human Task from the SOA component palette as a BPEL activity, JDeveloper creates a `.task` file under `SOA Content`.

Double-click on the `.task` file icon to get a Human Task editor, as shown in the next screenshot. The Human Task editor allows you to design the screen and metadata for the Human Task. Usually, Human Tasks are used for approving or denying a particular BPEL flow. Always use a proper title, descriptions, and outcome. The expression builder can be used for building the XPath expression that enables dynamic determination of assignments to the users or groups.

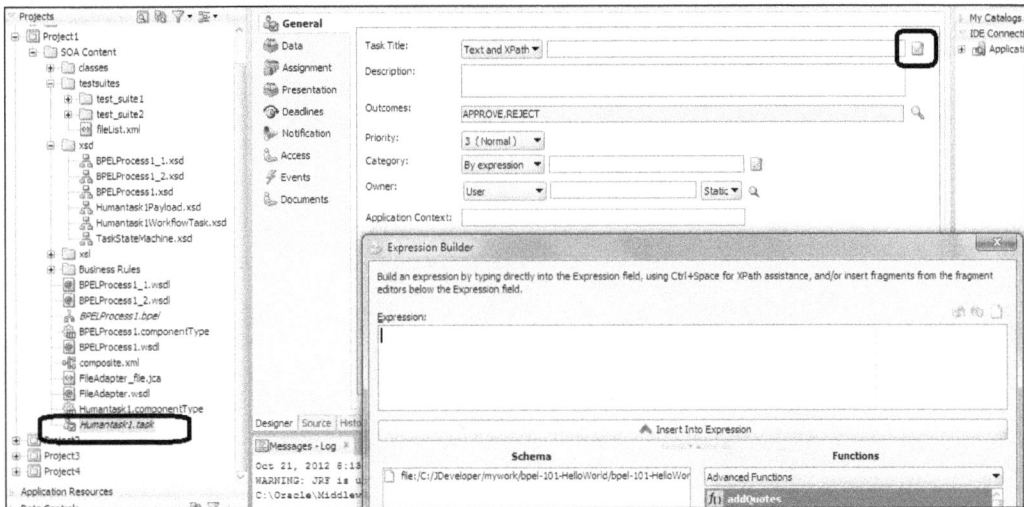

Summary

In this chapter, we learned about the Oracle SOA Suite components and their use cases, interactions, and Human Task design patterns; we also learned about request and event-driven architecture. We also learned to achieve loose coupling using Oracle Enterprise Service Bus. In the next chapter, we will learn the performance tuning of composite applications and SOA Suite platform running BPEL processes.

7
Performance Tuning – Systems Running BPEL Processes

Performance tuning is an important step for any IT system implementation to optimize the systems and software resources needed for serving business functions. In other words, performance tuning enables us to optimize the system cost and performance to stay competitive in the market place. The process of performance tuning is iterative and in this chapter we will look into various systems and software components tuning options to optimize BPEL processes response time, scalability and availability, and underlying systems utilization.

One of the main objectives of performance tuning is to achieve quick response time and more throughput. The application architect should work with business to understand the performance goals and set realistic performance expectations. The architect also needs to work with the infrastructure team to design the system's infrastructure and configuration of SOA components based on the performance expectations. The performance tuning step assists us in identifying the optimal settings for infrastructure and application components.

We should know the current performance level and performance goals before tuning the system. The high-level plan for a performance tuning exercise for an application platform is as follows:

- Document the performance/response time before making any changes also known as the baseline current performance
- Document the configuration parameters for existing systems also known as the baseline current configurations

- Document what is the expected end result and backup the entire system once and also at intermediate points during performance tuning

- Document the performance benefits due to new values of the configuration parameter(s) and update the configuration and performance baselines with suggested values based on the **Service Level Agreements** (**SLAs**)

The **Oracle SOA Suite** is a couple of applications developed by Oracle using J2EE technologies. One of the core applications is **SOA-Infra**, which is similar to any other J2EE web application. The other major components of the SOA Suite are **BPEL Process, Mediator, Business Rules**, and **Human Task**. All the Oracle SOA Suite components are deployed in a WebLogic server platform and also can deploy other platforms such as WebSphere. There are separate tuning parameters available for each of the Oracle SOA Suite applications and sub systems. Depending on your SOA composite application's deployment design one needs to holistically align the configuration parameters of Oracle SOA Suite components in addition to the WebLogic server platform, underlying Java Virtual Machine, Operating Systems, and/or Load Balancers to get the optimal system performance.

Please note that by simply adding more hardware or increasing the hosting system's resources such as CPU and memory you may not improve the performance of an application platform. The application design needs to be capable of utilizing these additional resources for application performance and scalability benefits.

The Java Virtual Machine

The **Java Virtual Machine** (**JVM**) allows you to write programs once and run them anywhere. Usually, JVMs are optimized for an operating system in combination with the underlying hardware platform.

The leading JVM vendors are **Sun HotSpot JVM** and **Oracle JRockit** for Windows, Unix, and Linux platform. Please note that Oracle is the vendor for both JRockit and Sun HotSpot JVMs. The Sun HotSpot JVM is widely used and is the default choice for Oracle SOA Suite implementations. Therefore, we will discuss the Oracle Sun HotSpot JVM performance tuning in detail.

Garbage collection process

Garbage collection (**GC**) is a process of JVM that removes the unused Java objects from the JVM heap to recycle the JVM resources. The configuration of the underlying JVM for the WebLogic servers affects the Oracle BPEL Process Manager performance. The details will be discussed in the following sections.

The Java heap memory space is divided into three sections: young, tenured, and permanent generation, as shown in the following diagram. Minor garbage collection occurs at the young generation space and major garbage collection occurs at the tenured space.

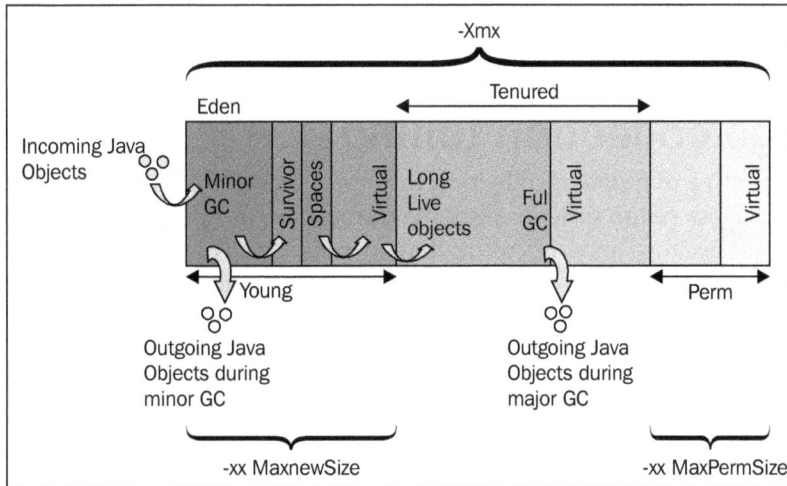

Young generation

Young generation memory space is used whenever we create objects in Java. That is why the young generation memory space is also known as new space. The Java objects enter the young generation space and they either get the garbage collected or move into the tenured generation space. Usually the young generation memory space is smaller than the tenured generation space, therefore it has shorter collection times as compared to the full GC in tenured space. The garbage collection process in the young generation is known as **Minor Garbage Collection (minorGC)**.

Tenured generation

The Java objects in the tenured generation space last longer than the young generation space. Usually, the tenured generation memory space is bigger than the young generation space and it takes more time as compared to minor garbage collection occurring in the young generation. The garbage collection process in the tenured generation is known as **Major Garbage Collection (majorGC)**.

Permanent generation

Permanent generation holds the data needed by VM to describe objects (describing classes and methods). It is recommended that we always allocate enough permanent generation space to load Oracle SOA Suite library classes in a JVM. The default permanent generation size is not sufficient for Oracle SOA Suite. There is no garbage collection process in permanent generation space for a JVM.

Garbage collection tuning

The main objective of garbage collection tuning is to achieve less frequent garbage collection with less pause time. Tuning the garbage collection process for a JVM is very important because an application that spends about 10 percent of its time in garbage collection can lose about 75 percent of its throughput when scaled out to multiple processors.

In this section, we will learn the options to tune JVM to run the SOA Suite optimally. The best way to tune the JVM and eliminate memory-related errors is to adjust JVM memory parameters. The JVM parameters are usually part of the WebLogic server start-up scripts. The default install values are not sufficient and may not provide an optimal runtime performance for an Oracle SOA Suite implementation. You need to ensure that the default JVM parameters are updated. The recommended heap size for Oracle SOA Suite is 4 GB. Some of the major JVM parameters for JDK 6 are as follows:

```
-Xms4096m \ - Minimum Heap
-Xmx4096m \ - Maximum Heap
-Xss512k \ - Set maximum native stack size for any thread
-XX:+UseConcMarkSweepGC
-XX:GCTimeRatio=99 \ - The ratio of GC time to application time
-XX:MaxGCPauseMillis=20 \ - Pause times of 20ms desired.
-XX:PermSize=512m \ - Permanent Size
-XX:MaxPermSize=512m \
-XX:NewSize=1024m \ - Minor GC (Young Generation)
-XX:MaxNewSize=1024m \
-XX:SurvivorRatio=6 \
```

During performance tuning, it is important to ensure that all endpoint applications are responding properly. When you adjust the minimum and maximum heap parameters, please ensure that you adjust the other parameters as well. The PermSize parameter can be constant but the NewSize and MaxNewSize parameters require tuning.

It is recommended for better performance that we keep the same values for following pairs for JVM parameters:

- Minimum heap size (`-Xms`) and maximum heap size (`-Xmx`)
- `-XX:PermSize` and `-XX:MaxPermSize`
- `-XX:NewSize` and `-XX:MaxNewSize`

Choosing the garbage collection algorithm

One of the key JVM parameters is the choice of the garbage collectors. Two of the major garbage collectors are listed as follows for reference:

- Mark and sweep (`-XX:+UseConcMarkSweepGC`)

  Mark and sweep garbage collection algorithm minimizes the garbage collection pause time that enables us to avoid impacting the production transaction during the GC process. This algorithm will run the tenured generation concurrently with the execution of the application.

- Throughput collector parallel collector (`XX:+UseParallelGC`)

  That throughput collector distributes the garbage collection load across CPUs; therefore maximizing throughput.

  It is ideal for using with multiprocessor machines usually with four or more processors.

Select NewSize

Set `-XX:NewSize` to be one-fourth of the size of the maximum heap size. The larger the young generation space means smaller the tenured space. One can't specify the tenured generation size directly; the size of the tenured generation space is determined by the total heap size and `NewSize`.

Tenured generation space size = Total heap size – NewSize

The higher values of `NewSize` will result in a lesser minor garbage collection.

To verify the JVM performance, use Oracle SOA Suite Enterprise Manager Console. Select the WebLogic domain and use the JVM performance to view the performance details.

The other available options are to use the WebLogic Console or JVisualVM.

Select heap size

Set the values of -Xms and -Xmx to around 80 percent of the available physical memory on a server. The remaining 20 percent memory is left for the operating system and other processes. Setting the value of -Xmx to a very high value will result in a slower majorGC that occurs less frequently. Setting too high values for a JVM heap size can cause wasted memory and performance impact during a majorGC. Please note that on a 32-bit OS server(s) a JVM can only use a maximum 2.5 GB.

Garbage collection tool – JVisualVM

JVisualVM is a GUI-based JVM monitoring, troubleshooting, and profiling tool that can be used to diagnose JVM performance, JVM garbage collection processes to tune JVM parameters for an application platform such as Oracle SOA Suite. The JVisualVM tool is part of JDK Version 6 that combines several JVM utilities such as JConsole, jstat, jinfo, jstack, and jmap under one roof.

To start the JVisualVM, go to the bin directory of the JDK install and invoke the jvisualvm application. The Java Visual VM tool provides a view of all the Java parameters set for a WebLogic server environment, as shown in the following screenshot:

Using the JVisualVM tool one can see the live **CPU usage**, **GC activity**, and **Heap activity** for an application such as Oracle SOA Suite, as shown in the following screenshot:

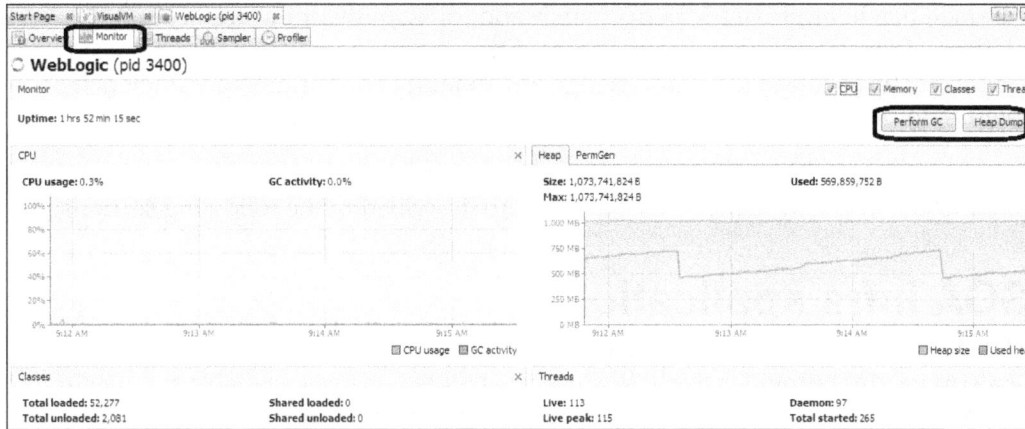

You can also view the JVM performance details for the garbage collection activity by adding the following parameters as part of the WebLogic start-up scripts:

- `-XX:+PrintGC`: Outputs the basic information at every garbage collection

- `-XX:+PrintGCDetails`: Provides the size of live objects before and after garbage collection for the various generations, the total available space for each generation, and the length of time the collection took

- `-XX:+PrintGCTimeStamps`: Provides a timestamp at the start of each collection that helps us correlate garbage collection logs with other logged events

- `Jmap (-histo:live pid)`: Prints memory-related statistics for a running JVM or core file

You are recommended to create a table with JVM parameters and its impact on the performance during the tuning process, as shown in the following table using excel or word. In the tuning process always analyze GC activities for pause time, frequency, and average memory footprint.

Test Time / # of Clients	JVM Parameters	GC Pause Time	Frequency of GC	Response time	Throughput
XX:XX	Eg. Xms - Xmx -Xss- XX:MaxNewSize XX:MaxPermSize XX:NewSize XX:PermSize -XX:SurvivorRatio	Less	Less	High	High

SOA Suite

The SOA Suite's default configuration parameters may not provide optimal performance for your production runtime environment. Tuning the configuration parameters will improve the performance and/or stability of the application platform; however, always document the difference in the performance between before and after changes. Do not change any default configuration parameters if there is no performance or stability benefits for the application platform.

SOA Suite has multiple GUI consoles available to view and update the configuration parameters. The commonly-used consoles are described in the following sections.

SOA infra application

The URL for invoking SOA infra application is `http://{soa-host}:{soa- port}/soa-infra/` that provides the links to various other consoles available for viewing and modifying the configuration parameters, as shown in the following screenshot:

Welcome to the Oracle SOA Platform on WebLogic

Useful links

WebLogic Console
Enterprise Manager FMW Control
SOA Composer
BPM Worklist
B2B Console
SOA Suite for healthcare integration

SOA Version: v11.1.1.6.0 - 11.1.1.6.0_111214.0600.1553 built on Wed Dec 14 13:55:57 PST 2011
WebLogic Server 10.3.5.0 Fri Apr 1 20:20:06 PDT 2011 1398638 (10.3.5.0)

The following composites are currently deployed:

1. default/BPELSample1!1.0*soa_880202ce-0d60-4873-b09d-a65fdb385768
   o Test bpelprocess1_client_ep

The WebLogic console

The URL for WebLogic console is `http://{admin server host}:{admin server port }/console`. The WebLogic console can be used for managing WebLogic server domain, configuring datasources, JMS, configuring security, and monitoring the status and health of the servers.

The enterprise manager

The URL for the enterprise manager console is http://{admin server -host}:{admin server-port}/em. The enterprise manager console can be used for deploying and undeploying SOA composite applications, viewing the filesystem and directory structure of SOA fusion middleware, monitoring the performance of SOA composite applications, and monitoring the status of SOA infra applications. The enterprise manager can be used to perform lifecycle operations such as startup/shutdown of SOA composites. Apart from SOA composites, it is also used to monitor the performance of Oracle's web services and J2EE resources deployed on the WebLogic server.

You can also use the enterprise manager to perform most of the functionalities provided by WebLogic's admin console.

As shown in the following screenshot, you can select the **Performance Summary** option to monitor the performance of the admin, SOA managed server, and BAM instances:

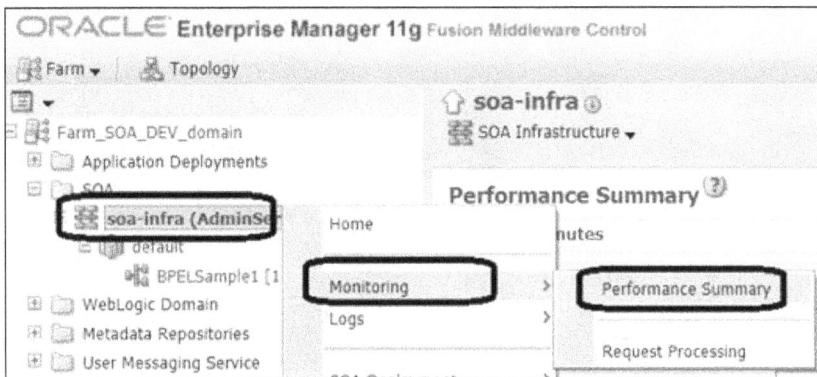

As shown in the following screenshot, you can monitor the performance of an SOA composite application by selecting the **Performance Summary** option under **SOA Composite**:

Dynamic Monitoring Service (DMS)

The DMS metrics tables provide metrics data for fusion middleware. The URL for DMS is `http://{adminserver-host}:{adminserver-port}/dms`. Click on the left navigation menu items to view the details of configuration parameters. A DMS console looks like the following screenshot:

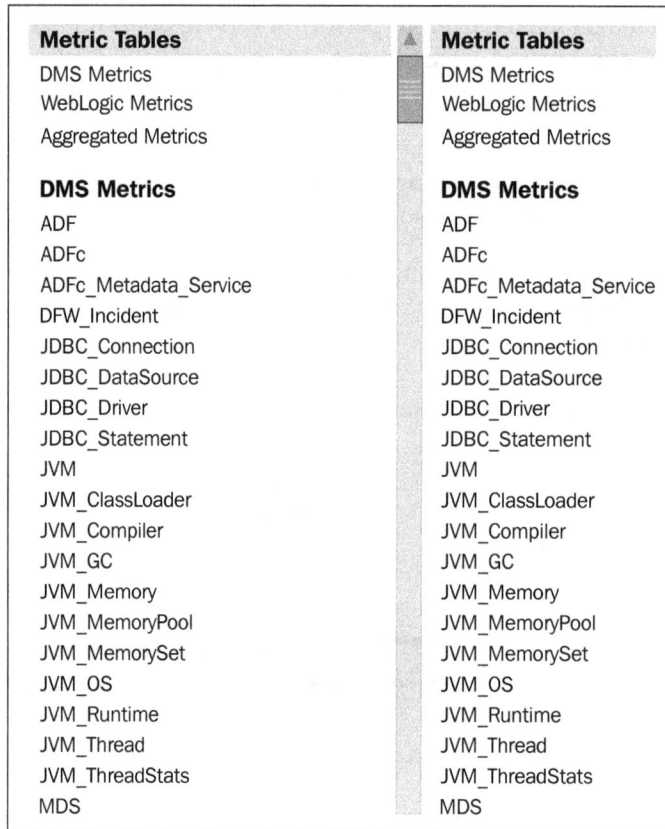

Metric Tables	Metric Tables
DMS Metrics	DMS Metrics
WebLogic Metrics	WebLogic Metrics
Aggregated Metrics	Aggregated Metrics
DMS Metrics	**DMS Metrics**
ADF	ADF
ADFc	ADFc
ADFc_Metadata_Service	ADFc_Metadata_Service
DFW_Incident	DFW_Incident
JDBC_Connection	JDBC_Connection
JDBC_DataSource	JDBC_DataSource
JDBC_Driver	JDBC_Driver
JDBC_Statement	JDBC_Statement
JVM	JVM
JVM_ClassLoader	JVM_ClassLoader
JVM_Compiler	JVM_Compiler
JVM_GC	JVM_GC
JVM_Memory	JVM_Memory
JVM_MemoryPool	JVM_MemoryPool
JVM_MemorySet	JVM_MemorySet
JVM_OS	JVM_OS
JVM_Runtime	JVM_Runtime
JVM_Thread	JVM_Thread
JVM_ThreadStats	JVM_ThreadStats
MDS	MDS

The B2B console

B2B component facilitates the exchange of documents between trading partners. The B2B console URL is `http://{soa-host}:{soa-port}/b2bconsole`. A screenshot of a B2B console is as follows:

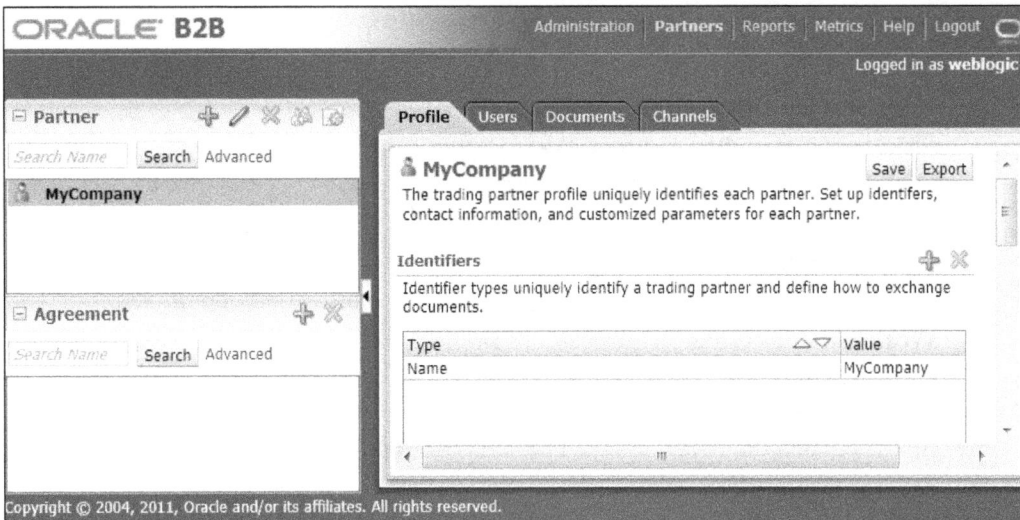

One can make changes to the B2B properties from the enterprise manager console. The B2B properties can be viewed by selecting the **SOA Administration** option and then **B2B Server Properties**, as shown in the following screenshot:

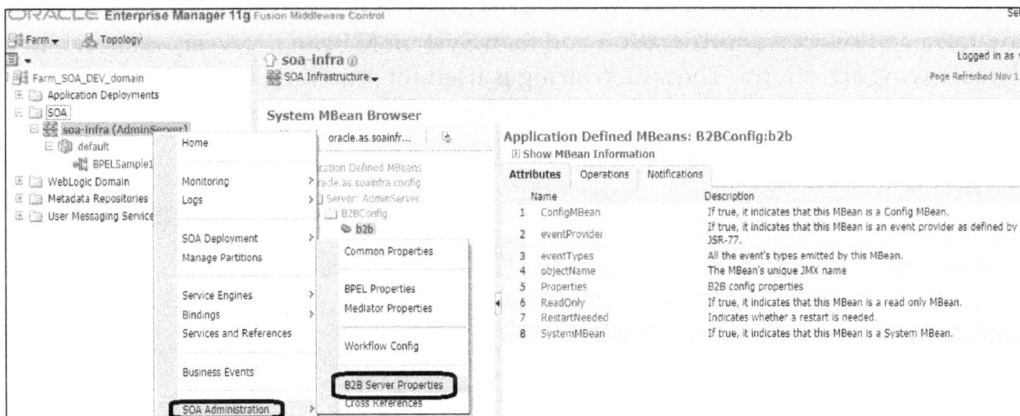

Please make sure to update b2b.inboundThreadCount, b2b.outboundThreadCount, b2b.defaultThreadCount, and MDS cache size to accommodate the messaging load for the production runtime environment. Usually we increase them by 3 to 6 times of the default values to process high volume message loads. The inbound threads responsible for processing the inbound message and outbound threads are responsible for processing the outgoing message from B2B components.

The other available GUIs within Oracle SOA Suite are listed as follows for your reference:

- **Web Services Inspection Language (WSIL)**:
  `http://{soa-host}:{soa-port}/inspection.wsil`
- **Web Services Manager (WSM)**: `http://{soa-host}:{soa-port}/wsm-pm`
- **Composer**: `composer http://{soa-host}:{soa-port}/soa/composer`
- **DefaultToDo**:
  `http://{soa-host}:{soa-port} /workflow/DefaultToDoTaskFlow`
- **Worklist**: `worklistapp http://{soa-host}:{soa-port}/integration/ worklistapp`
- **MessagingService endpoint**:
  `http://{soa-host}:{soa-port}/ucs/messaging/webservice`
- **MessagingServices preferences**:
  `http://{soa-host}:{soa-port}/sdpmessaging/userprefs-ui`

The System MBeans browser

The SOA MBeans can be viewed from the enterprise manager console (`http://{adminserver-host}:{adminserver-port}em`). Right-click on the **soa-infra** and select **Administration** and then **System MBean Browser**, as shown in the following screenshot. The search string is used for searching the Mbeans. You can set the performance tuning parameters on MBeans using MBeans browser:

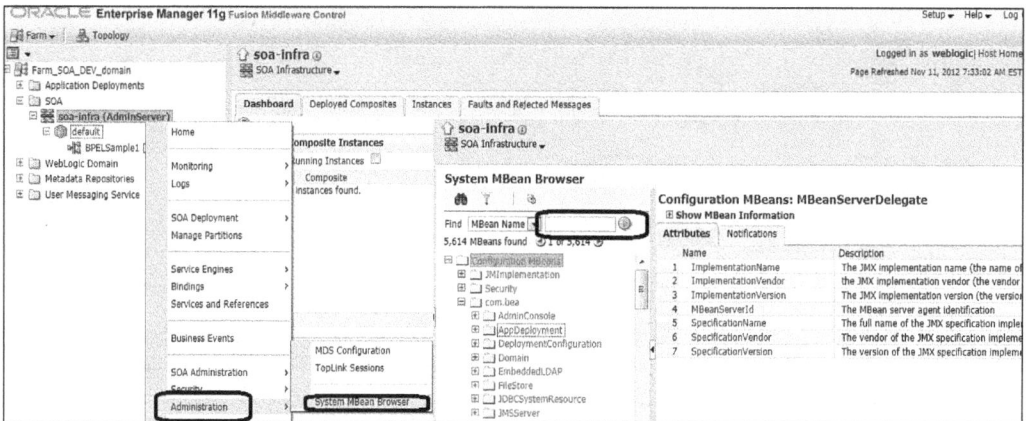

You can view the properties of all the deployed composite applications from MBeans browser including the revision of the application. Click on the composite application name under **Application Defined Mbeans** for making changes, as shown in the following screenshot:

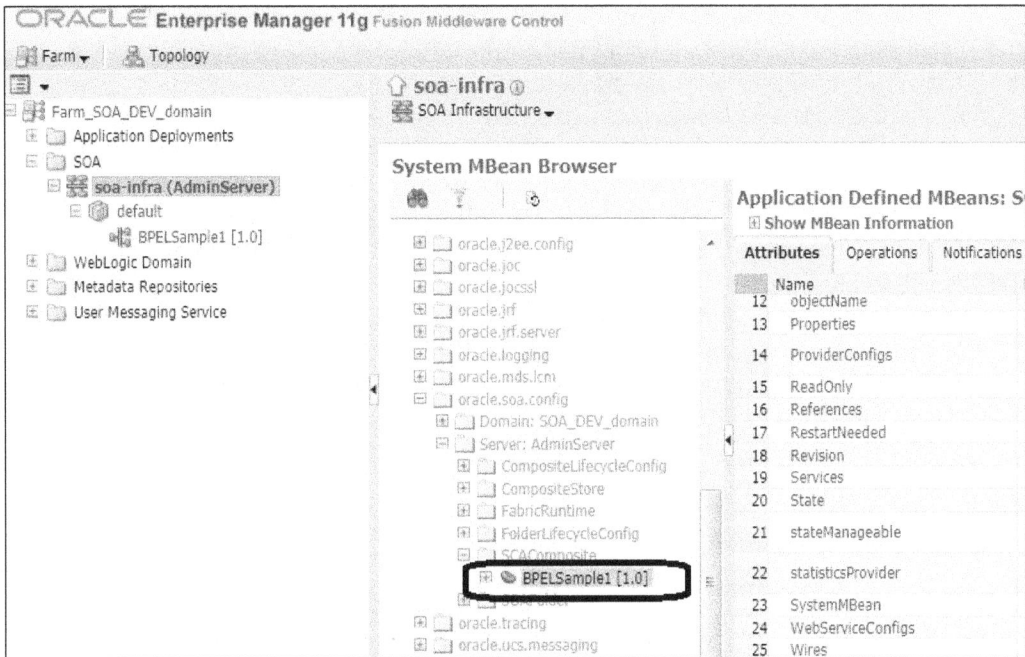

SOA Suite tuning

Some of the major SOA Suite tuning parameters are listed as follows. To achieve high performance, the default parameters require changes.

- **Transaction timeouts**: The default JTA time out of 300 seconds for SOA Suite may not be sufficient for a production runtime. Some of the transactions in the production environment take more than 300 seconds to finish and logfiles show transaction time out exceptions. You will need to increase the transaction time out. Please refer to *Chapter 3, Invoking a BPEL Process,* for detailed steps for setting up **Global Transaction Timeout, BPEL EJB's Transaction Timeout,** and **syncMaxWaitTime**.

- **Database sessions**: Set the process parameter in database > 300. Also set the session parameter > 200. Please refer to *Chapter 1, Creating Basic BPEL Processes,* for details of setting the process parameter for a SOA database.

- **64-bit JVM**: Always ensure that you are using a 64-bit JVM. The 64-bit JVM will allow you to have the recommended heap size of 4 GB. However, for a 32-bit JVM one can get the maximum heap size to 2 GB. On the other hand the 64-bit processor instructions are more efficient than the 32-bit ones.

- **Payload validation and audit level**: Payload validation of incoming messages (while configuring the server URL) decreases the performance. Go to the SOA enterprise manager console to disable the payload validation. The URL for EM is `http://{adminserver-host}:{adminserver-port}//em/`. Right-click on **soa-infra** from the left navigation menu and select **SOA Administration** and then **BPEL Properties** to change the **Payload Validation** and **Audit** settings. As shown in the following screenshot, ensure that the checkbox for **Payload Validation** is unchecked. Usually payload validation is used to intercept the incoming payload data and convert the non schema-complaint data to fault. The payload validation involves additional processing and, therefore, it decreases the overall performance. Setting the **Audit Level** option higher also decreases the performance. One can change the **Audit Level** option by selecting **Off**, **Inherit**, **Minimal**, **Production**, or **Development**, as shown in the following screenshot.

  - **Off**: Highest performance
  - **Production**: Medium performance
  - **Development**: Impacts performance

The **Audit Trail Threshold** parameter sets limits for the audit trial size. The default value is 1 MB. The following screenshot explains how to set the auditing level and disable payload validation:

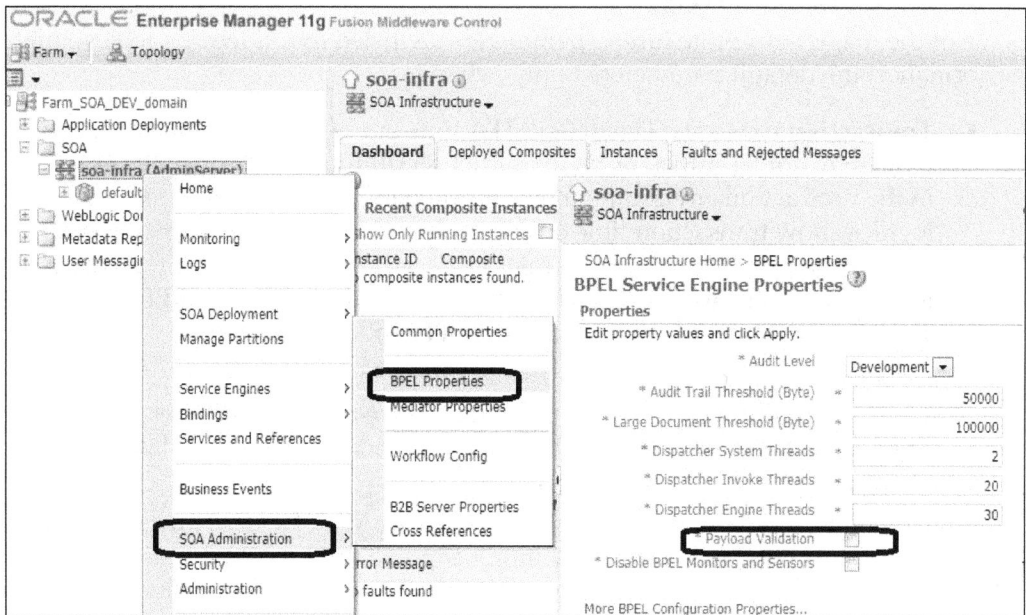

- **The SOA composite application instance state**: Enabling the SOA composite application instance's state decreases the performance of the SOA container and allows you to track the running instance separately. You can use `CompositeInstanceStateEnabled` property to enable/disable the instance state.

- **Mediator worker threads**: Increasing the mediator worker threads results in a performance improvement for asynchronous services. The thread level can be adjusted by changing the **Parallel Worker Threads** configuration parameter available under **SOA Administration | Mediator Properties** in **Enterprise Manager Console**, as shown in the following screenshot. It specifies the number of parallel threads available for message processing. The recommendations for **Mediator Properties** changes are as follows:
  - Increase **Parallel Worker Threads**
  - Increase **Parallel Maximum Rows Retrieved** (x 100)
  - Reduce **Parallel Locker Thread Sleep**

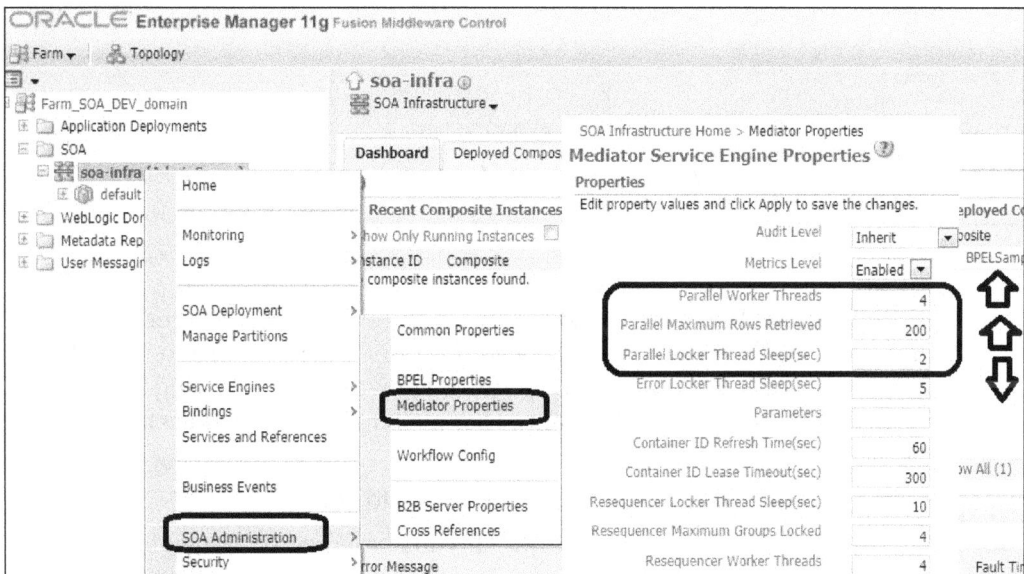

- **Mediator routing rules**: Implementing parallel processing for routing rules of the mediator will improve the performance. The routing rules can be changed using the SOA composite editor. Please note that setting the routing rules impacts the application design.

- **Logging levels**: Set all log levels to **Error** (Severe) in the production environment. You may use the log levels to **Notification** (Info) during development, troubleshooting, and the tuning process. You can modify the log levels of WebLogic components using WebLogic admin console. Use the enterprise manager console to change the log levels of Oracle's loggers. SOA Suite defines a set of Oracle loggers that can be changed only using the enterprise manager console. Please refer to the following screenshot:

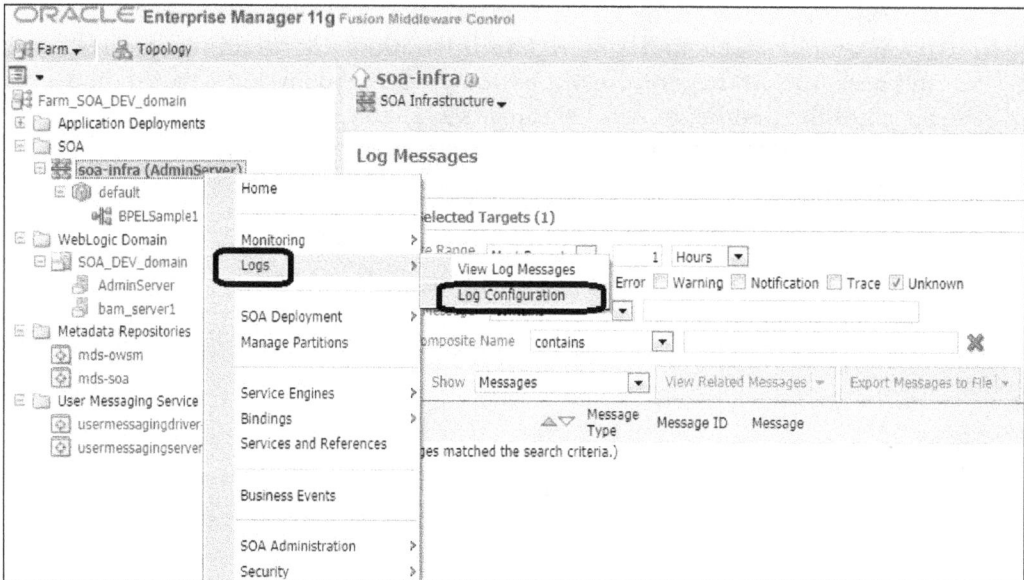

- **BPEL Process Manager Threads**: Login to the enterprise manager console (`http://{adminserver-host}:{adminserver-port}/em/`) and select **BPEL Properties** in the left navigation menu, as shown in the following screenshot. Update the **BPEL Process Manager Dispatcher Threads** settings to support the system load as follows:
  - Increase **Dispatcher System Threads** to at least 10
  - Increase **Dispatcher Invoke Threads** based on the target load
  - The value of **Dispatcher Engine Threads** should be equal to the sum of **Dispatcher System Threads** and **Dispatcher Invoke Threads**

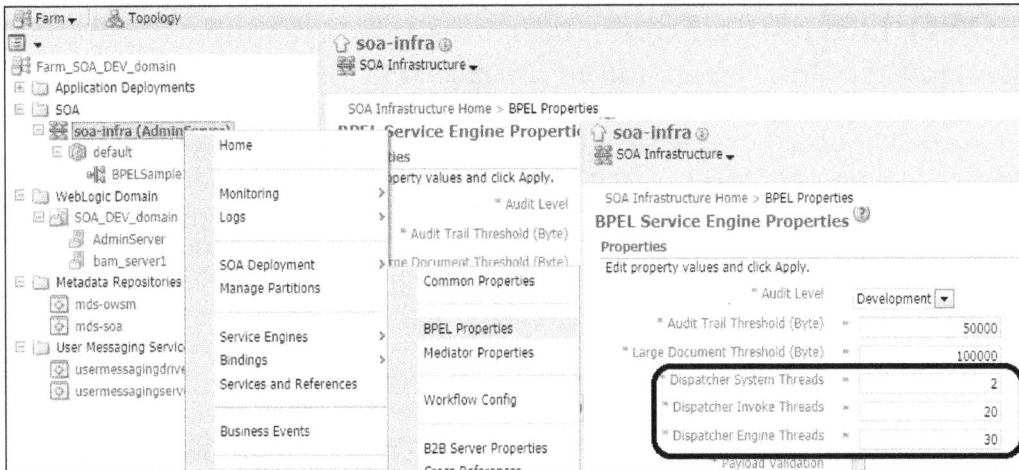

- **JMS modules**: Oracle SOA Suite has many JMS connection factories, queues, and topics for internal use. The changes on these JMS modules are not recommended.

- **Increase the performance of EM Console**: As shown in the following screenshot disable the loading of all metric information to the EM console. Once the production systems are up and running for some time, the EM console load time will be very high and won't be acceptable:

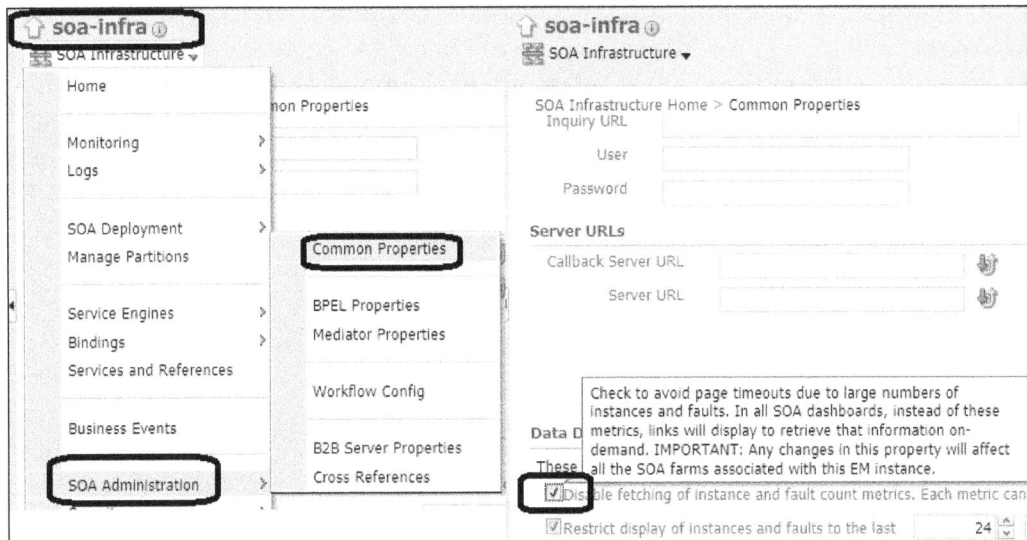

Load balancers

Most of the enterprise implementations of web services will demand high availability. In some cases it will be a global high availability that is usually achieved via the system architecture's designs and deployments leveraging multi sites in active-active or active-passive. The passive site is either standby (manual process to fail over and fail back) or hot standby (automatic process to fail over and fail back) to provide the services if the primary site goes down. The load balancers are also used to achieve the horizontal scalability. Load balancers for web services are implemented at either L7 (application Layer) also known as **Global Server Load Balancer (GSLB)** or **Global Traffic Manager (GTM)**, or at L4 (Transport Layer) also known as **Local Server Load Balancer (LSLB)** or **Local Traffic Manager (LTM)** to achieve high availability and scalability. Layer 7 forwards the user to the appropriate local load balancer, any further requests for the user will directly go the local load balancer within a specified time window configured as part of **TTL (Time to Live)**. The Layer 4 load balancer serves all user requests. In other words, the L7 load balancers provides the user forwarding service while L4 load balancers serves the users as middlemen. In a high-availability environment, both L4 and L7 are used. These load balancers come in both software and/or hardware appliances from various vendors. The major vendors are F5, Brocade, NetScaler, and Cisco.

L4 load balancers are usually implemented to achieve high availability within a data center that provides limited horizontal scalability. One needs to implement L7 load balancers to achieve high horizontal scalability. You will mostly find that L4 and L7 load balancers are implemented as a pair, since most implementations don't need to scale beyond a single load balancer capacity. In implementations where L7 load balancers are not used; the L4 load balancers pair is implemented with one of them as hot standby. It is recommended that if you have got L7 load balancers then make all the L4 load balancers active to optimize the performance and capacity during peak loads.

L7 load balancers/GSLB/GTM configurations are as follows:

- Implement L7 health checks over TCP health checks
- Use low TTL such as 30 secs
- Utilize GEO affinity, if available
- Implement independent endpoints if services are run by different server processes
- Use sites load factors for weighted round robin load balancing algorithm, if available

L4 load balancers/LSLB/LTM configurations are as follows:

- Implement L7 health checks over TCP health checks
- Use least connection load balancing algorithm
- Use SSL offload unless it is a security mandate
- Enable compression and caching
- Enable TCP connection queue

Operating system

Always use a 64-bit operating system instead of a 32-bit one for the Oracle SOA Suite as a 32-bit operating system limits the available JVM memory. Verify the CPU and memory usages under the expected load conditions for the host running the SOA Suite application platform for potential bottlenecks. The CPU usage can be viewed by using the `top` command for Linux. The memory can be verified by using `free -t -m` or `vmstat`. For Windows, use the command `systeminfo`.

File descriptors

The default values of file descriptors in the Linux operating system will not be enough to handle the required number of concurrent connections by SOA Suite. The operating system parameter `ulimit` sets the system-wide resource limit for a user. The default value of 1024 for a user is too low for running an Oracle SOA Suite application. Use the `ulimit` or `sysctl` Linux commands to change the default value to at least `8192` by executing the following command:

```
ulimit -n 8192
```

The following message in the logfile indicates that you need to increase the file descriptors:

```
Too many open files
```

Also, make changes to soft and hard file limits from `limits.conf` located in the `/etc/security` folder for Linux systems

Adaptors

Please make sure that the operating system file descriptor is set very high if you are using file adaptors.

Tuning JCA adaptors are important for optimum performance. Change the following properties in the inbound and outbound JCA files.

- `Threadcount`: By default, the adapter uses the global thread pool. The default value is `-1`. If you have the threading issues on logfiles and have performance issues, then create separate processor threads by changing the value to zero.

- `MaxRaiseSize`: Increase this parameter from default (`10,000`) if you need to process a large amount of files.

- `ConcurrentThreshold`: By default, the translation activities is limited to `20`. Increase this value up to `100` for increasing the translation activities allowed to start in parallel for particular outbound scenarios.

- For database adaptors use indexes, disable delete polling, disable Merge, use connection pooling and synchronous processes.

Database

Tuning of the Oracle database is out of the scope for this book; however, some of the relevant steps for tuning that can be performed as part of SOA Suite tuning are listed in this section. Since SOA Suite is an application running on a J2EE container such as WebLogic, it requires a database for storing meta data. Monitoring and tuning the database associated with SOA Suite provides optimum performance for SOA Suite container and your BPEL composite application.

- Ensure that the initial connection pool and max connection pool are the same. Use a large number for connection pools to avoid running out of database connections.

- Use GridLink database source for Oracle RAC connectivity instead of multi pools. Please refer to *Chapter 10, Architecting High Availability for Business Services*, for details.

- Disable database connections verifications, testing, and profiling.

- Enable statement caching. This improves SOA Suite performance by caching executable statements that are used repeatedly in the database.

Dehydration store

The Oracle SOA Suite saves all the BPEL process statuses in dehydration database tables. The dehydration tables are part of SOA_INFRA schema and created initially during installs as part execution of RCU.

Over a period of time, you need to purge the metadata from the dehydration store to manage the growth of the database. Oracle provides a default purge script for deleting data which is located in {RCU_HOME}/rcu/integration/soainfra/sql/ soa_purge, however, you need to delete additional data to improve the performance and manage the database growth.

The database schema ddl can be found at {Oracle SOA Install directory}\ rcu\integration\soainfra\sql\bpel. You can write SQL statements to delete or update data in dehydration tables. Please refer to *Chapter 5*, *Test and Troubleshoot SOA Composites*, for further details on dehydration.

Init.Ora

Most of the database initialization parameters are stored in the Init.ora file for Oracle database 11*g*. Some of the important configuration parameters related to SOA Suite container performance are as follows:

- Memory_Target: Manage the RAM resource utilization. Instead of setting SGA_MAX_Size, use SGA and PGA as needed.
- Audit_Trial: Database auditing can be enabled or disabled using this parameter.
- Always enable auto extend of Oracle Tablespace to avoid performance and run time issues. Use **Automatic Segment Space Management** (**ASSM**) for permanent table spaces.

Automatic Workload Repository

You can use **Automatic Workload Repository** (**AWR**) for tuning the SOA_INFRA database. AWR is a part of the Oracle database. The Oracle database automatically collects performance information such as snap shots on periodic bases (every hour). The Oracle database takes care of cleaning the snap shot performance data on a regular basis.

As shown in the following screenshot, please login to the Oracle database to run the report:

```
C:\Windows\system32>sqlplus

SQL*Plus: Release 11.2.0.2.0 Production on Sun Apr 28 07:48:45 2013

Copyright (c) 1982, 2010, Oracle.  All rights reserved.

Enter user-name: ^C
C:\Windows\system32>sqlplus system/weblogic123@XE as sysdba

SQL*Plus: Release 11.2.0.2.0 Production on Sun Apr 28 07:49:48 2013

Copyright (c) 1982, 2010, Oracle.  All rights reserved.


Connected to:
Oracle Database 11g Express Edition Release 11.2.0.2.0 - Production

SQL> SELECT DBMS_WORKLOAD_REPOSITORY.Create_Snapshot FROM DUAL;

CREATE_SNAPSHOT
---------------
            609
```

As shown in the following screenshot, execute the following command for creating the AWR report:

```
@?/rdbms/admin/awrrpt.sql
```

```
SQL> @?/rdbms/admin/awrrpt.sql

Current Instance
~~~~~~~~~~~~~~~~

   DB Id    DB Name      Inst Num Instance
----------- ------------ -------- ------------
 2670344913 XE                  1 xe


Specify the Report Type
~~~~~~~~~~~~~~~~~~~~~~~~~
Would you like an HTML report, or a plain text report?
Enter 'html' for an HTML report, or 'text' for plain text
Defaults to 'html'
Enter value for report_type: text

Type Specified:  text


Instances in this Workload Repository schema
~~~~~~~~~~~~~~~~~~~~~~~~~~~~~~~~~~~~~~~~~~~~~~~

   DB Id     Inst Num DB Name      Instance     Host
------------ -------- ------------ ------------ ------------
* 2670344913        1 XE           xe           HOME-HP

Using 2670344913 for database Id
Using          1 for instance number

Specify the number of days of snapshots to choose from
~~~~~~~~~~~~~~~~~~~~~~~~~~~~~~~~~~~~~~~~~~~~~~~~~~~~~~~~~
Entering the number of days (n) will result in the most recent
(n) days of snapshots being listed.  Pressing <return> without
specifying a number lists all completed snapshots.


Enter value for num_days: 3

Listing the last 3 days of Completed Snapshots
```

The sample report will be as follows:

```
Child Latch Statistics                          DB/Inst: XE/xe  Snaps: 606-608
                   No data exists for this section of the report.

%Segments by Logical Reads                      DB/Inst: XE/xe  Snaps: 606-608
-> Total Logical Reads:            1
-> Captured Segments account for   1.7E+07% of Total

             Tablespace                    Subobject  Obj.     Logical
Owner        Name       Object Name        Name       Type     Reads    %Total
SYS          SYSTEM     COL$                          TABLE    35,056   3.5E+06
SYS          SYSAUX     WRH$_SYSMETRIC_HISTO          INDEX    20,928   2.1E+06
** MISSING   TEMP       ** TRANSIENT: 419494 MISSING ** UNDEF  17,712   1.8E+06
SYS          SYSTEM     SEG$                          TABLE    16,832   1.7E+06
SYS          SYSTEM     TS$                           TABLE     7,920   7.9E+05

Segments by Physical Reads                      DB/Inst: XE/xe  Snaps: 606-608
-> Total Physical Reads:           1
-> Captured Segments account for   3.7E+05% of Total

             Tablespace                    Subobject  Obj.     Physical
Owner        Name       Object Name        Name       Type     Reads    %Total
XDB          SYSAUX     XDB$RESOURCE                  TABLE     1,001   1.0E+05
SYS          SYSTEM     VIEW$                         TABLE       709   7.1E+04
SYS          SYSAUX     WRI$_OPTSTAT_HISTGRM          TABLE       623   6.2E+04
SYS          SYSAUX     WRI$_OPTSTAT_HISTHEA          TABLE       371   3.7E+04
SYS          SYSAUX     WRH$_SYSMETRIC_HISTO          INDEX       351   3.5E+04

Segments by Physical Read Requests              DB/Inst: XE/xe  Snaps: 606-608
-> Total Physical Read Requests:   1
-> Captured Segments account for   6.9E+04% of Total
```

Analyzing the entire AWR reports are out of the scope for this book. You can get a lot of information such as CPU and memory usage, standalone and RAC load profile, operating system statistics, wait events, instance and tablespace IO statistics for your database platform without writing scripts.

Summary

In this chapter, we learned to tune the SOA composite applications designed and deployed on the Oracle SOA Suite platform for optimal performance and scalability. We reviewed the industry leading practices for the Oracle SOA Suite platform components such as Oracle SOA Suite component applications, WebLogic server platform, JVM, operating systems, and load balancers. In the next chapter, we will learn about integrating BPEL process manager with Service Bus, Registry, and BPEL deployment.

8
Integrating the BPEL Process Manager with Service Bus, Registry, and SOA Deployment

In a typical SOA composite application deployment using Oracle SOA Suite, the Oracle BPEL Process Manager interacts with multiple enterprise and cross-enterprise systems. In this chapter, we will learn SOA composite application architecture components and integration design patterns for the BPEL Process Manager with Oracle Service Bus and Oracle Registry. In the end, we will review the options available to manage the SOA composite application deployment life cycle.

The SOA composite application architecture

SOA composite application architecture is an organized and managed layered architecture as compared to the legacy application architecture. The primary benefits of the SOA composite application layered architecture are its re-usability, ease of operation, maintenance, and agility.

In a simple application architecture, the user connects to a backend database via a single middleware application server such as WebLogic J2EE container that may provide the lowest possible latency to user requests, as shown in the following diagram:

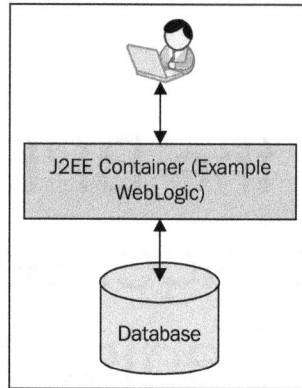

However, simple architectures pose the challenge for an enterprise to achieve business agility and economies of scale and scope. Therefore, as architects, we will be implementing layered application architectures. The key guidelines for designing layered architectures are as follows:

- Keep the published interfaces of a layer backward compatible
- Avoid duplication of services among layers
- The components within a layer should be able to interact with each other
- The horizontal layer should interact only with one consumer and one provider layer
- The vertical layer, also known as the management layer, can have multiple consumer and provider layers

The following diagram depicts an example of an SOA composite application architecture that utilizes multiple layers between a user request(s) and backend database:

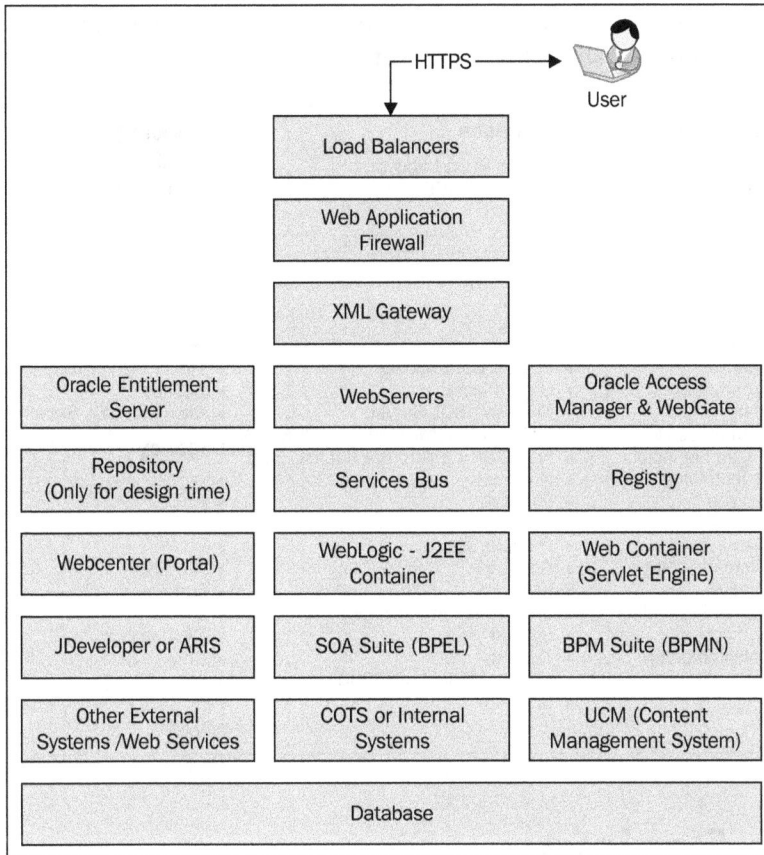

The layered architecture needs standardized and simplified system integration without worrying about the underlying technology stack. The Oracle SOA Suite adaptor's capability is one of the key components to promote the reusability of legacy applications. Some of the available adaptors with Oracle SOA Suite for connecting to external systems are given in the following diagram. Please note that some of these adaptors may require separate licensing from Oracle or third-party vendors.

Applications	Databases	Technology
• Oracle Applications	• Oracle 8*i* and above	• SOAP
• SAP R/3	• IBM DB/2 UDB	• HTTP, HTTP-S
• Peoplesoft	• Informix	• Email-POP3, SMTP, IMAP
• JD Edwards	• Clarion	• FTP, FTP-S
• Siebel	• Clipper	• Flat File
• Clarify	• Cloudscape	• LDAP
• Lotus Notes	• DBASE	• JMS
• Ariba	• Dialog	• Oracle AQ
• AXIOM mx/open	• Essbase	• IBM MQSeries
• Baan	• FOCUS Data Access	• TIBCO Rendezvous
• BroadVision	• Great Plains	• Socket
• Clarify	• Microsoft SQL Server	• Microsoft SQL Server
• Commerce One	• MUMPS (Digital Standard MUMPS)	
• Hogan Financials	• Navision Financials (ODBC 3.x)	**Legacy**
• i2 Technologies	• Nucleus	• CICS
• Lawson	• Paradox	• IMS/DB
• Livelink	• Pointbase	• IMS/TM
• Manugistics	• PROGRESS	• VSAM
• Microsoft CRM	• Red Brick	• ADABAS
• Vantive	• RMS	• Natural
• Walker Interactive	• SAS Transport Format	• Tuxedo
• Remedy	• Sybase	• CA-Datacom
• Salesforce.com	• Teradata	• Screen Scraping
	• Unisys DMS 1100/2200	• CA-IDMS
	• UniVerse	• C-ISAM,D-ISAM,K-SAM,
		• QSAM

Oracle Registry

One of the main goals of implementing **Service-Oriented Architecture (SOA)** is to reuse the existing applications and achieve business agility. To enable reusability and loose coupling, the developers and architects should know the taxonomies of available services within an organization before creating and architecting new applications. Lack of service visibility and traceability leads to redundant services within an organization. The ability to discover and use existing services is one of the key success criteria of implementing service-oriented architecture.

Oracle Registry organizes the existing SOA assets into taxonomy of entities and tModels to assist us in implementing the SOA governance. Ideally, any request of the resources first goes to the enterprise service bus. The enterprise service bus will do a **Universal Description, Discovery, and Integration (UDDI)** look-up (that is similar to a **Domain Name Server (DNS)** lookup) at the registry. The registry will provide the following details for the resources:

- **Who is the service provider?**: The details of the party who publishes the service
- **What is the service?**: The service description
- **Where is the service endpoint?**: The service location, protocol, and port
- **How and Why**: The description for services' specifications and value sets along with taxonomy, WSDL interfaces, and resources

One can configure Oracle SOA Suite for doing a UDDI look-up at registry for the resources. We can establish a UDDI connection for resources from the Oracle JDeveloper during development. It is a leading practice to use the UDDI reference for resources to design and deploy SOA composite application(s).

The initial step is to register the services with Discovery Registry, as shown in the following diagram. The service bus will do the UDDI look-up with Discovery Registry to get the services endpoint before accessing the services directly from the service providers.

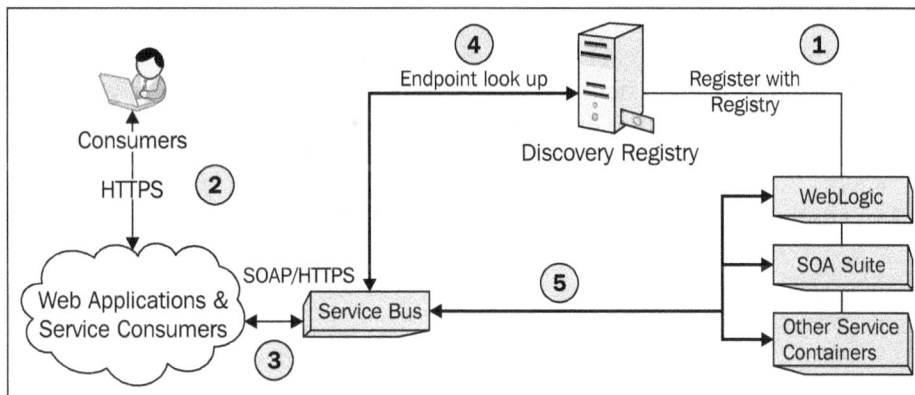

The major reason for first routing the SOA composite application to Discovery Registry is to dynamically identify the endpoint of the services, the SOA composite application then calls the endpoint. This enables decoupling of a SOA composite application from a specific service provider. The services' definitions and their endpoints are stored as resources in the Discovery Registry. In other words, Discovery Registry helps us to commoditize the services and the services can move for operational reason(s) without impacting the requests, that is, SOA composite applications. Usually, registry is used along with the service bus. The service bus can examine the property values to determine the endpoint and other security essentials for a service provider that is the cheaper option from the available choices. The cheaper option is usually evaluated by two factors; first is the performance SLAs and second is the real dollars associated with third-party services.

There are various runtime options for the UDDI look-up with the Oracle Registry while the Oracle Repository is used for design time. Oracle Registry installation has different options to install UDDI look-up registry. The available options are listed as follows:

- **Standalone Registry**: Developers create artifacts and enter details to the Standalone Registry. It is used for a personal development environment.
- **Publishing Registry**: Developers create artifacts and enter details to the Publishing Registry. It is suitable for a development environment.
- **Intermediate Registry**: In the next step, we transfer specifications of services and value sets along with taxonomy, WSDL interfaces, and resources to the Intermediate Registry. It is used for a QA environment.
- **Discovery Registry**: Once the QA finishes the validation, the artifacts are published in the Discovery Registry for the prime time use. It is used for a staging and production environment.

All these install options facilitate the design to deployment life cycle for a UDDI registry. The following diagram shows the design to deployment life cycle model for the Oracle Registry.

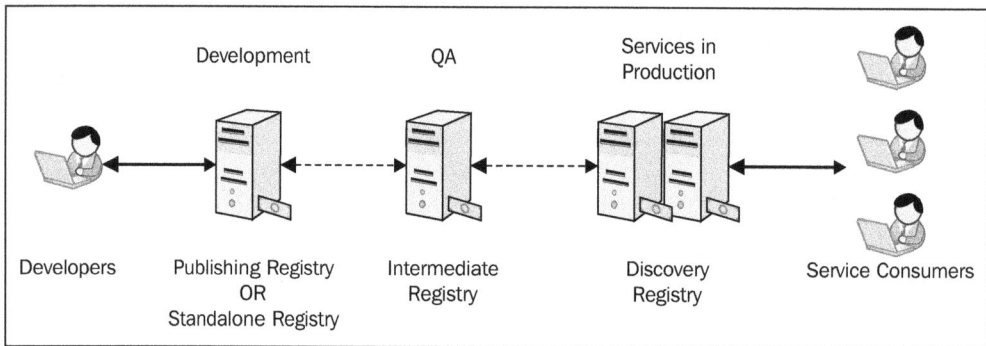

Service Registry install

The following are the major steps for installing Oracle Service Registry:

1. Download the registry install file from the Oracle website.

2. Execute the SQL statements for creating tablespace and database user for the registry (The SQL statements are provided as part of the registry install download).

3. Execute the OSR install file.

4. A sample install console is shown in the following screenshot:

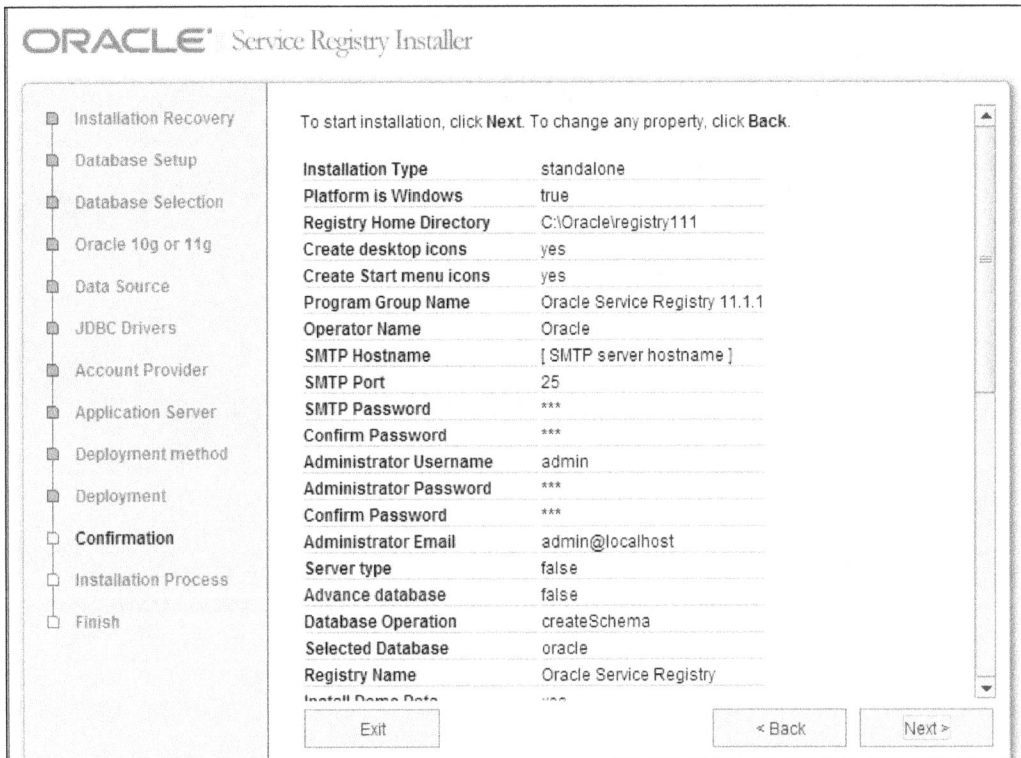

5. After installing the Oracle Service Registry, log in to the registry console using the URL http://{host name}:{port number}/{registry}/uddi/web.

Publish services to registry

You can publish services to the registry using the Oracle Registry console or business service control console. Apart from the registry console, you can publish services from JDeveloper to the registry, using the following steps:

1. Open Oracle JDeveloper.

2. Click on the **File** menu and then select **New...**.

3. Select **UDDI Registry Connection** and then click **OK**, as shown in the following screenshot to establish connection(s) to a UDDI registry:

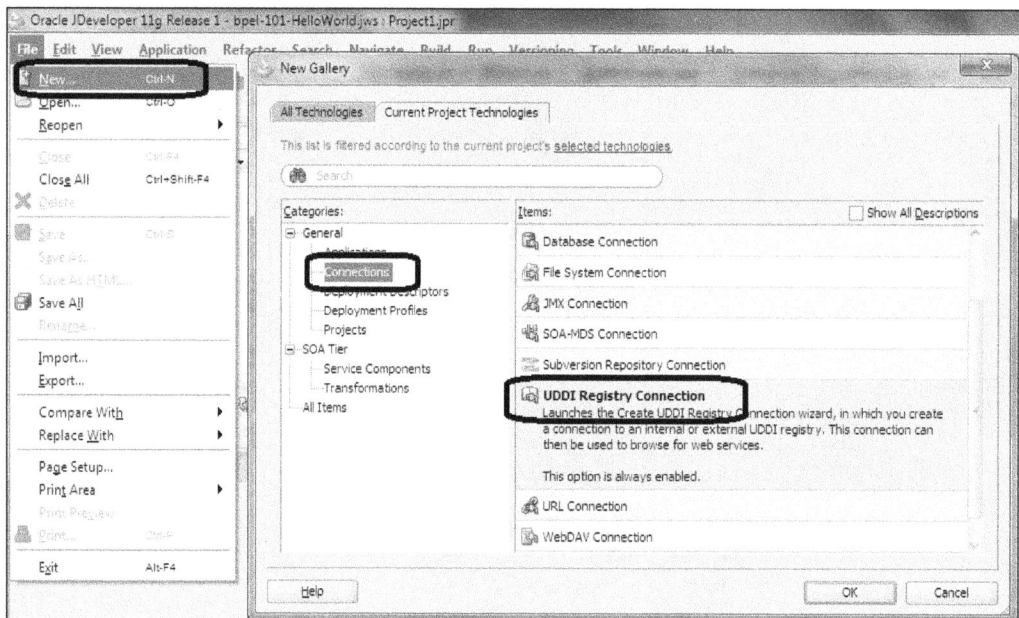

4. Enter the registry URL in the **Connection** window and click on **Finish**, as shown in the following screenshot:

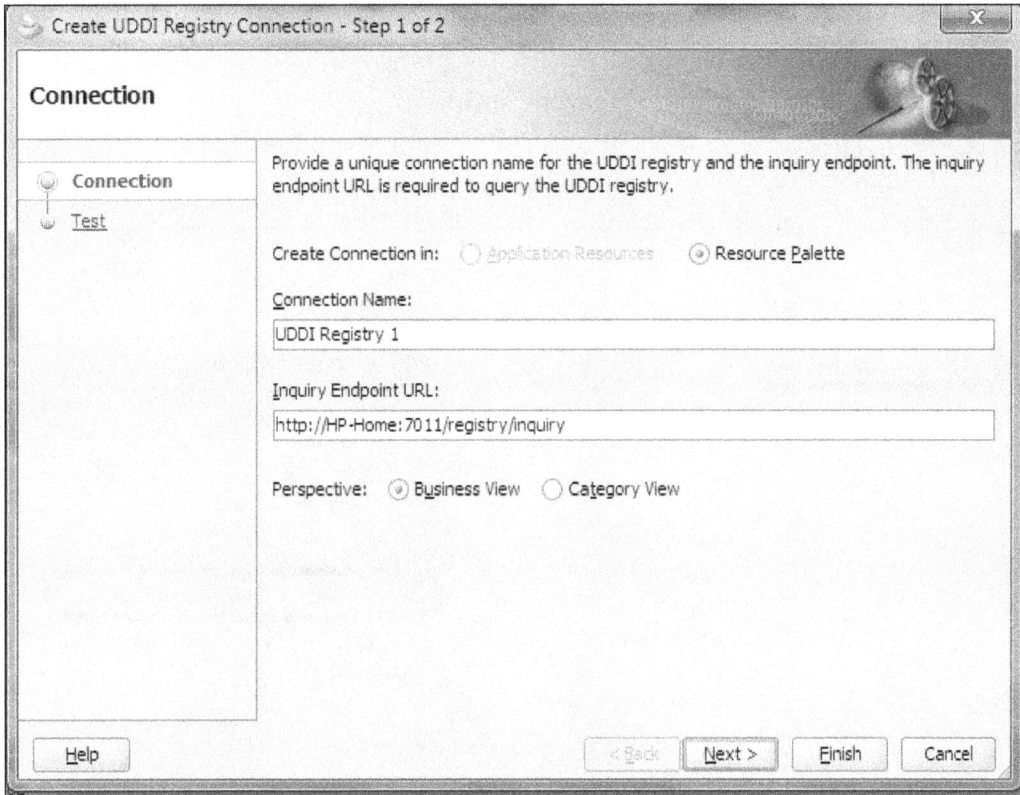

This makes the UDDI registry available on the JDeveloper Resource Palette for designing SOA composite applications.

Consume services from registry

You need to configure the UDDI registry properties with SOA Suite for enabling UDDI look-up and consuming services from the registry. This can be done using the following steps:

1. Log in to the Enterprise Manager Console.

2. Right-click on **soa-infra** and select **SOA Administration | Common Properties**.

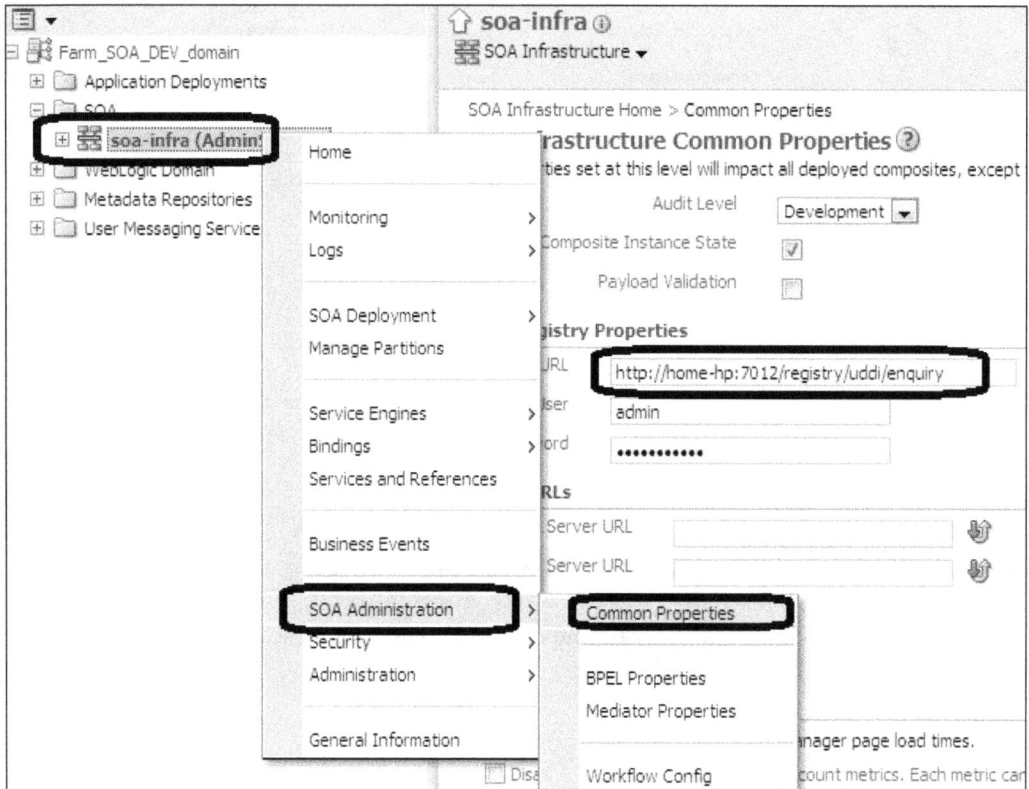

You can add services from the UDDI registry into JDeveloper by right-clicking on the **External Reference** section of JDeveloper and selecting **Web Service**, as shown in the following screenshot:

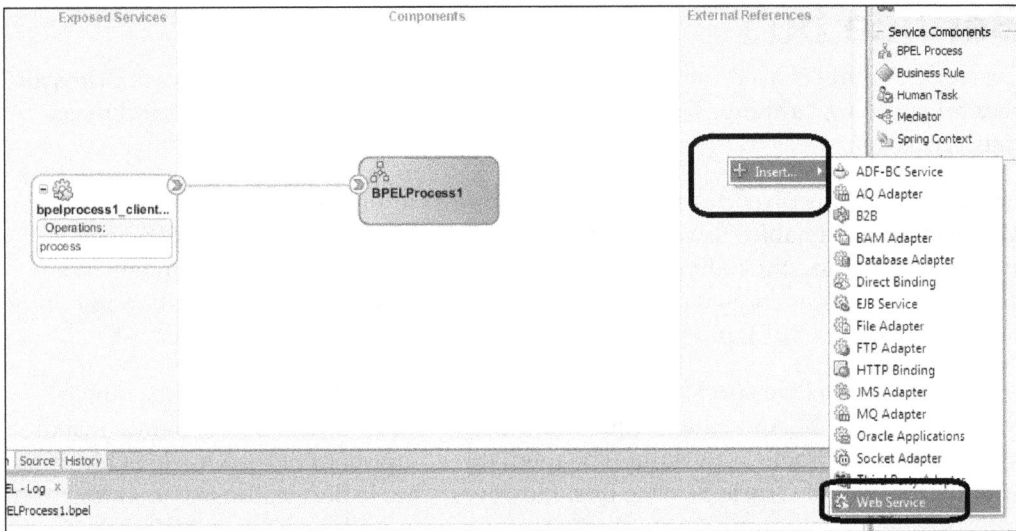

Select the appropriate WSDL file from the local filesystem. You can select **Service** as the **Type** to create an inbound SOA Service and also **Reference** as the **Type** to create an outbound SOAP web service in the external reference. As shown in the following screenshot, you can create a web service to consume services from the registry:

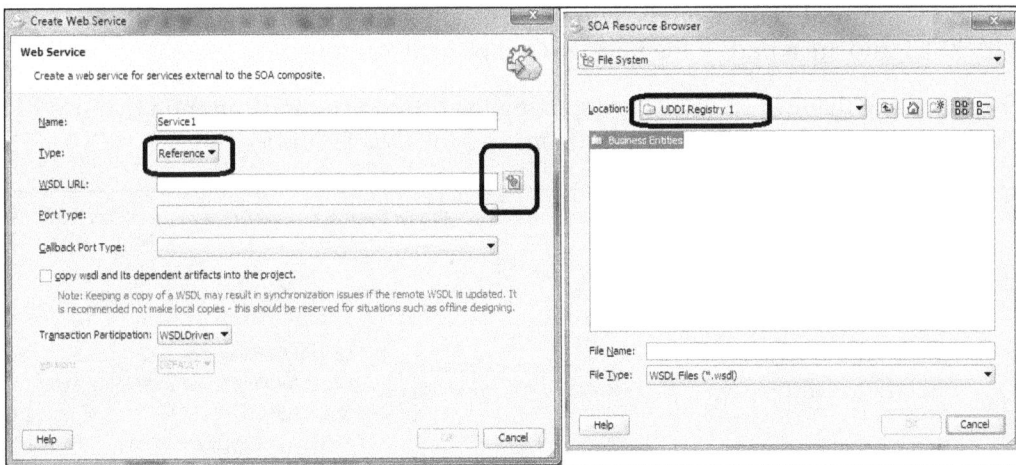

Service bus

Oracle SOA Suite is used for the process orchestration. These processes are primarily stateful and long-running. The service bus is used for routing messages and message transformation.

Oracle Service Bus provides support for communication with Oracle BPEL Process Manager, which enables us to include the BPEL processes in our SOA composite applications. Using the native BPEL transport within Oracle Service Bus, one can expose BPEL processes as web services in the Oracle Service Bus layer allowing other services to invoke BPEL processes.

Oracle Service Bus was previously known as BEA AquaLogic Service Bus, which was a part of the BEA product acquisition. Oracle Service Bus has a separate install as compared to Oracle SOA Suite. The mediator component of the Oracle SOA Suite is similar to that of Oracle Service Bus. However, Oracle Service Bus is great for enterprise-wide integration, message transformation with XSLT and XQUERY, that is, it is large and powerful compared to the mediator component of the Oracle SOA Suite.

The service bus functionality of the Oracle SOA Suite (that is, the mediator component) is a lightweight service bus used for **VETRO (Validate, Enrich, Transform, Routing, and Operate)** pattern, value mapping, and cross-referencing to support **Canonical Data Models**, which are used for minor message transformation with XSLT and are a part of the **Service Component Architecture (SCA)**.

The following diagram shows sets depicting the differences and common features of the Oracle SOA Suite mediator component and the Oracle Service Bus.

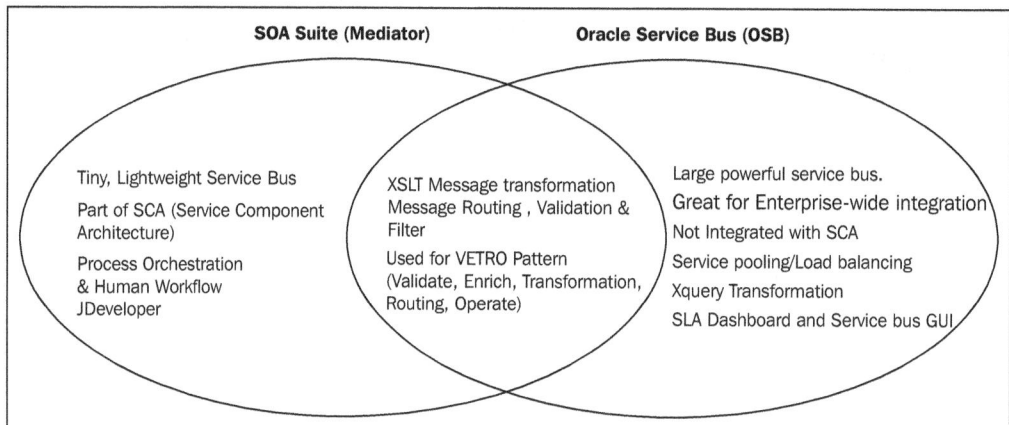

SOA Suite (Mediator) | Oracle Service Bus (OSB)

Tiny, Lightweight Service Bus
Part of SCA (Service Component Architecture)
Process Orchestration & Human Workflow
JDeveloper

XSLT Message transformation
Message Routing , Validation & Filter
Used for VETRO Pattern (Validate, Enrich, Transformation, Routing, Operate)

Large powerful service bus.
Great for Enterprise-wide integration
Not Integrated with SCA
Service pooling/Load balancing
Xquery Transformation
SLA Dashboard and Service bus GUI

Oracle SOA Suite components can be developed using the JDeveloper. The Oracle Service Bus proxy and business services are configured using the service bus console. The service bus console URL usually is `http://{AdminServerName}:{PortNumber}/sbconsole`.

The Oracle Service Bus routes the messages from the service consumers to the service providers (service endpoints) and perform load balancing if required. The service bus has options to remove the non-responsive endpoints out of load balancing. The Oracle Service Bus can perform protocol translation of the incoming messages along with message transformation and dynamic- and content-based routing, as shown in the following diagram:

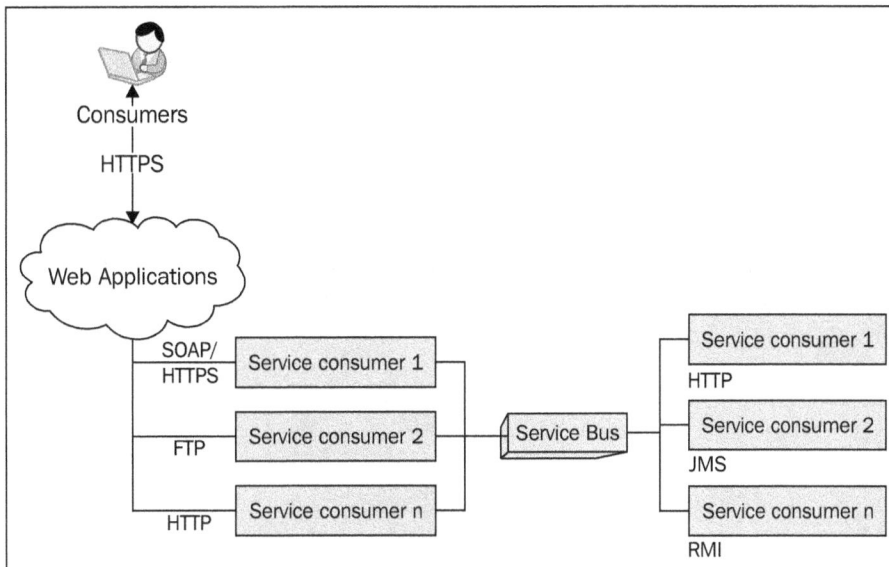

A service bus provides the following functionalities:

- **Avoids service sprawl**: The main purpose of a service bus is to avoid service sprawl in an SOA infrastructure. A service bus provides an option for service consumers to connect once and separate integration logic from business logic. It acts as a centralized connectivity infrastructure with a central management and enterprise-wide use. One service bus can provide connectivity to all services within an organization. For a very big infrastructure with several hundreds of services there are different options available to integrate multiple service infrastructures, such as a federated model where each service bus handles specific business areas.

- **Transformation**: Service bus can transform the service protocol based on the service consumers and providers. For example, transformation between HTTPS, JMS, FTP, SMTP, and so on. Service bus also provides different messaging invocations such as request-response, asynchronous messaging, and one-to-many publishing.

- **Dynamic- and content-based routing**: Service bus provides routing of messages to underlying infrastructure.

- **Service storage and discovery**: Service bus acts as a centralized registry for services (endpoints) and stores service metadata. The services are searchable and organized.

- **Service monitoring and service SLAs**: Service bus can establish thresholds based on different performance parameters such as errors, execution time, and success ratio. Service bus can also configure with an SMTP server and send e-mail notifications.

- **Split and aggregation**: Split the incoming payload messages into multiple service invocations. Service bus provides load balancing across service providers and also aggregates the service responses into a single payload.

Oracle Service Bus uses its native transport to integrate with the Oracle SOA Suite to expose services for BPEL processes also known as BPEL transport, as shown in the following diagram:

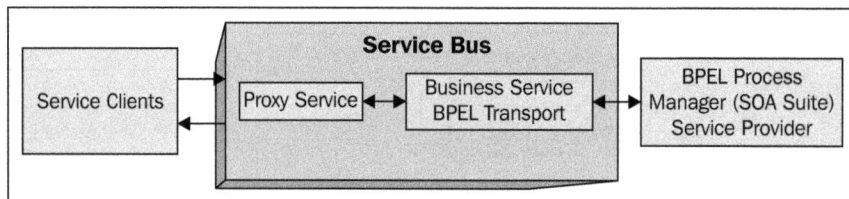

Oracle Service Bus can implement a federated service model as shown in the following diagram. At a higher level, one can implement two separate service buses; the first one configured for external consumers and the second one configured for different business departments within an enterprise. In a very large setup, one can also configure a separate service bus for different application domains within each business department. A centralized enterprise service bus is recommended for central monitoring, reporting, and configurations.

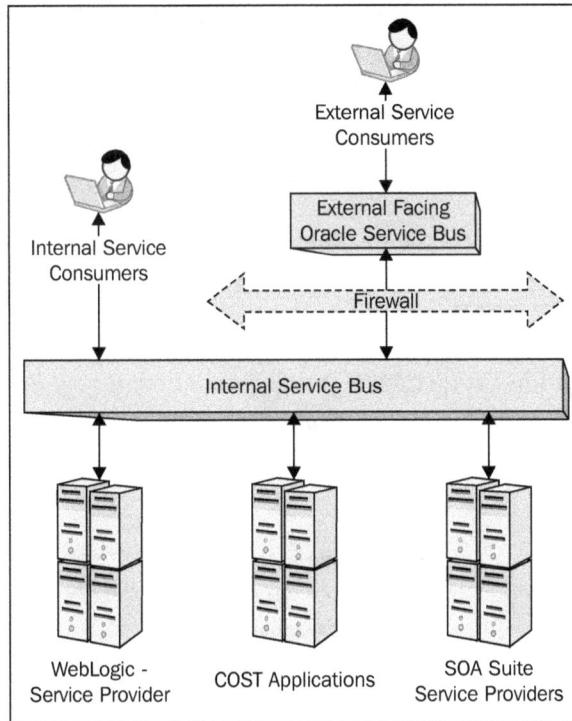

SOA Suite deployment

The **Service Component Architecture (SCA)** is an assembly model for composite services. The specifications for SCA are managed by the standard body OASIS. The SCA specification assumes that any business application consists of a series of services. All the services can be assembled as composite services using the SCA model.

A typical web application written using JSPs and/or servlets is deployed as a .war (web archive) file and an enterprise application written using EJBs and others is deployed as an .ear (enterprise archive) file. Similarly, a SOA composite application written using BPEL is deployed as a .sar (service archive) file. All service components such as business rules, mediator, BPEL processes, adaptors, and others are packaged in a single .sar file called Service Archive.

The deployment descriptor for a .war file is web.xml; similarly, the composite application assembly model uses composite.xml. The composite.xml file conforms to the SCA specifications. The composite application is deployed as a single application unit .sar file.

We can design composite applications without completing all the external service implementations. The alternate approach is to design and implement the external service implementations first before creating the composite application components. The advantage of the alternate approach is that we have all WSDL and XSD documents that are readily available for packaging. The best approach is to use a hybrid model where you can create some external service as a reference to start.

The following diagram depicts the packaging model for an SOA deployment:

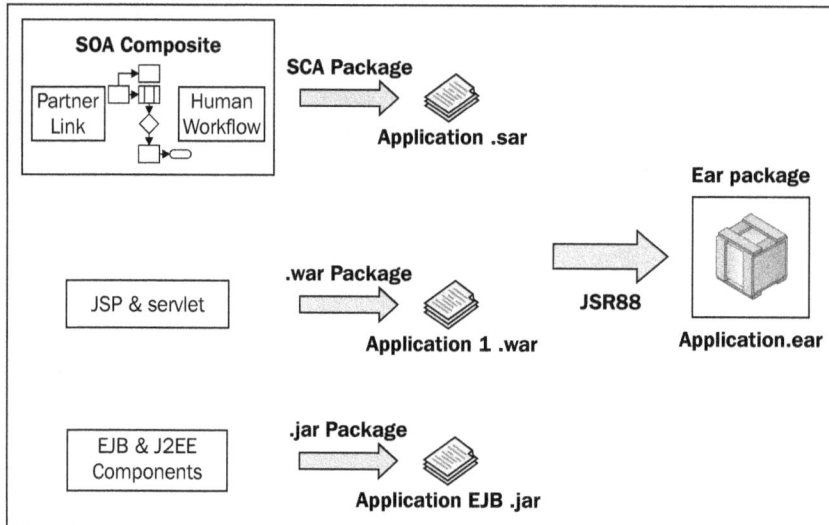

The `composite.xml` file has the elements representing binding, properties, external references, component, services entry points, adaptor configurations, and so on. JDeveloper creates the design and source view of `composite.xml` as you create the BPEL and other components, as shown in the following screenshot:

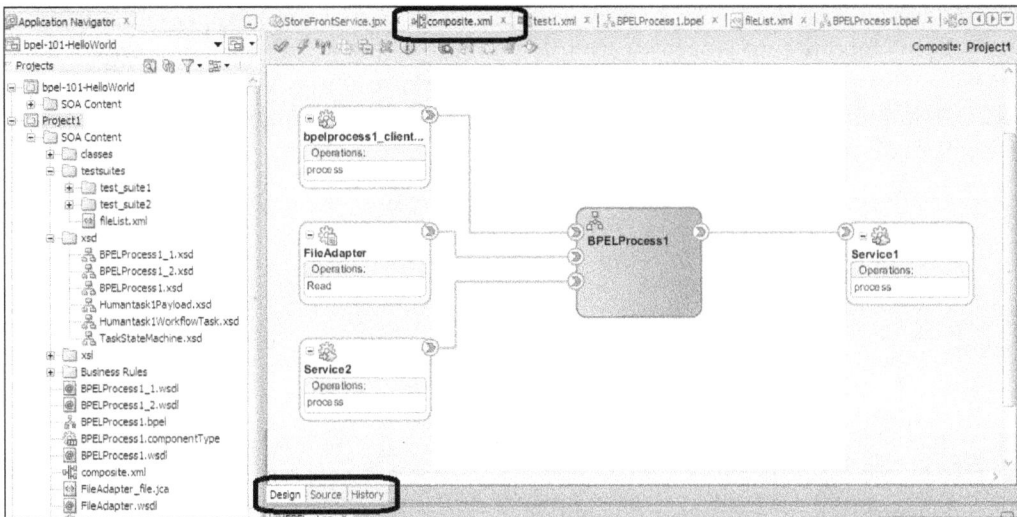

The options available for deployment are as follows:

- **JDeveloper**: JDeveloper is usually used to deploy the composite applications to develop an SOA Suite environment.

- **Oracle Enterprise Manager**: Using the **Deploy SOA Composite** wizard of the Oracle Enterprise Manager console we can deploy, un-deploy, and re-deploy a SOA composite application service archive .sar file. It supports management of different revisions of a composite application.

- **Ant Scripts**: We can use ant-sca-package scripts for packaging the service archive .sar file.

- **WebLogic Scripting Tool (WLST)**: WLST scripts can automate the manual steps one needs to take to deploy, un-deploy, and re-deploy an SOA composite application service archive .sar file using the **Deploy SOA Composite** wizard of the Oracle Enterprise Manager's console. For example, we can use the following command:

```
tar -cvpf SOABackup.tar ORACLE/Middleware/Oracle_SOA
```

The following screenshot shows how to deploy a SOA composite application using JDeveloper. Ensure that you have completed the assembly of all the components before starting deployment and SOA Suite is up and running. You can deploy an SOA Suite instance running on a local machine or on a remote server using JDeveloper.

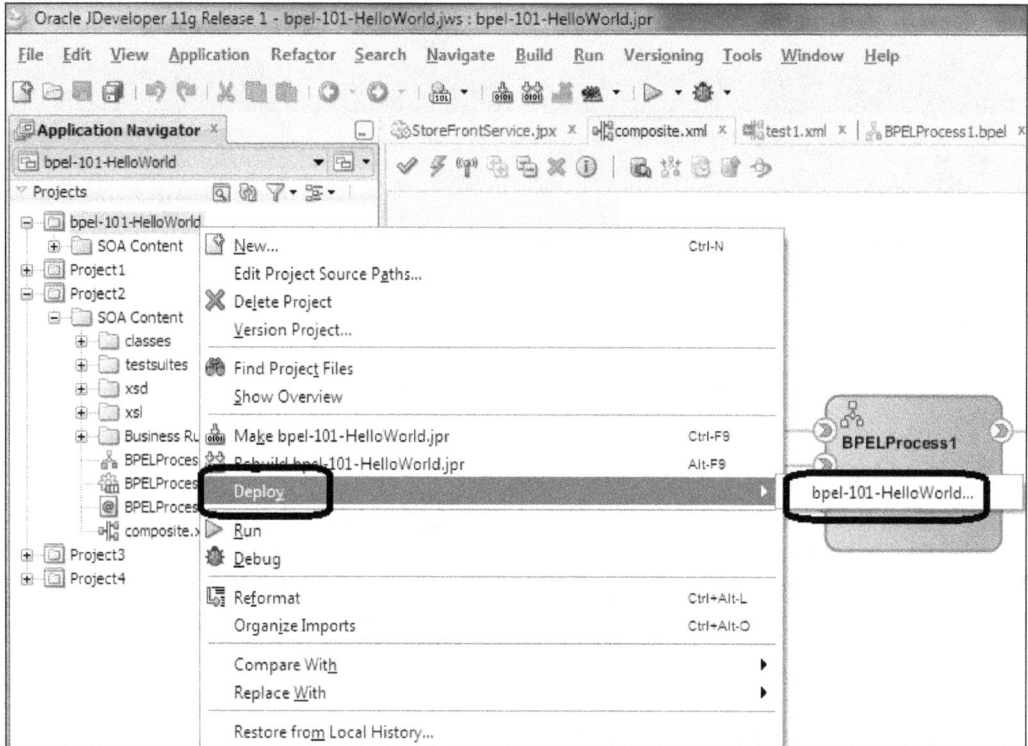

The following screenshot shows how to use the **Deploy SOA Composite** wizard of Oracle Enterprise Manager's console to deploy a SOA composite application.

Log in to Oracle Enterprise Manager's console (http: //{hostname}:{portnumber}/ em). As shown in the following screenshot, right-click on **so-infra** from the left navigation pane, select **SOA Deployment**, and then **Deploy...**.

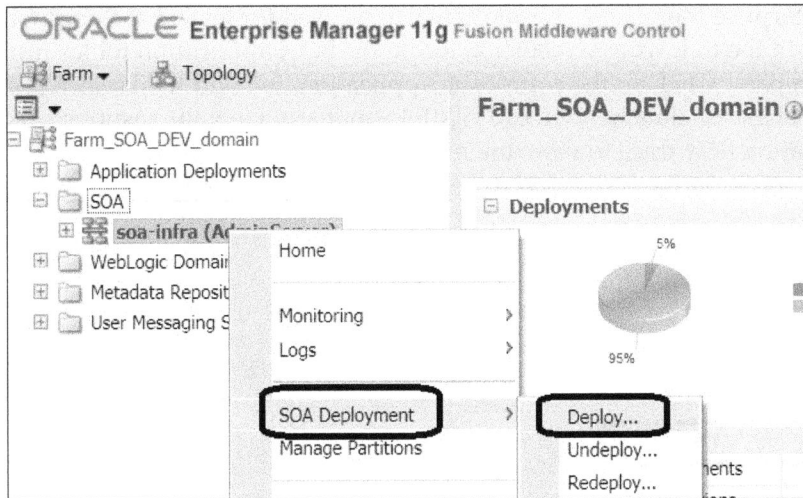

As shown in the following screenshot, select the composite application file by clicking on the **Browse...** button and then click on the **Next** button.

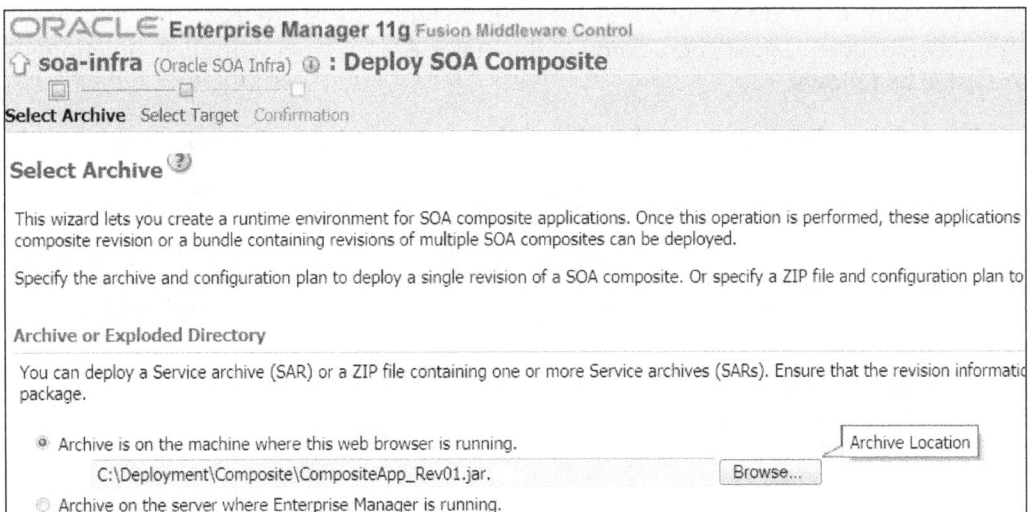

Oracle Enterprise Manager's console can also be used for testing the deployment. As shown in the following screenshot, locate the SOA application folder from the left navigation pane. Click on the composite application link and then select **Test**. On the **Test** page enter the data in XML or HTML format and view the response data. Select the application flow trace to view the message flow.

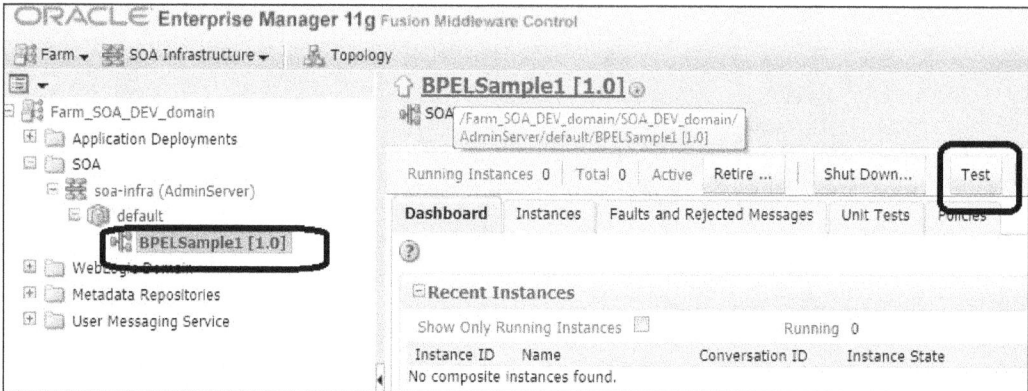

The ANT scripts for SOA composite application deployment are located in `Oracle/Middleware/Jdeveloper/bin`. Some of the major ANT scripts with their function(s) are listed as follows:

- `ant-sca-deploy.xml`: This script deploys the composite application

- `ant-sca-test.xml`: This script creates a test suite for composite application testing

- `ant-sca-compile.xml`: This script compiles the SOA composite application

- `ant-sca-package.xml`: This script packages the composite application as a `.sar` file

- `ant-sca-mgmt.xml`: This script assists us in starting, activating, and retiring SOA composite applications

Summary

In this chapter, we learned the SOA composite application architecture built using Oracle SOA Suite, Oracle Service Bus, and Oracle Registry. We also learned the development and deployment life cycle of Oracle Registry, and deployment of an SOA composite application using JDeveloper and Oracle Enterprise Manager's console. In the next chapter, we will learn the options for securing a BPEL process.

9
Securing a BPEL Process

In an enterprise environment, BPEL services usually serve either mission-critical or business-critical business processes. These BPEL services exchange sensitive information with multiple composite applications, enterprise systems, and external service providers as a service consumer or provider. That is why it is critical to ensure that only authorized users have access to BPEL services and communication is kept private. It is an industry-leading practice to implement a separate vertical layer for securing BPEL process; commonly known as the security layer. The security control's implementation needs to have defense in depth and should be capable enough to deliver the basic principles of information security to secure web services, they are as follows:

- **Confidentiality**: Data is readable to authorized systems and users only.

- **Integrity**: Data exchange between service consumers and providers is not tempered. In other words, data is not modified, unauthorized, or undetected.

- **Availability**: BPEL service(s) are available to authorized users (What can you access?) when requested and protected from denial of service attacks.

- **Authenticity**: Identity validation of consumers and providers (Who are you?).

- **Non-repudiation**: BPEL service(s) consumers can't deny submission of a request while producers can't deny receiving it.

In this chapter, we will explore the options and leading practices with network, host, application, and data layers of a system to create security controls to protect the BPEL process services deployed in a SOA Suite platform.

Securing a BPEL process

We can create composite web services by orchestrating the flow between the web services using the Oracle SOA Suite, as shown in the following diagram. Anyone can invoke a BPEL process if they know the WSDL URL; the network route is then open for them. It is required that we design and develop a solution that handles authentication, authorization, transport layer security, and protects from denial of service attacks.

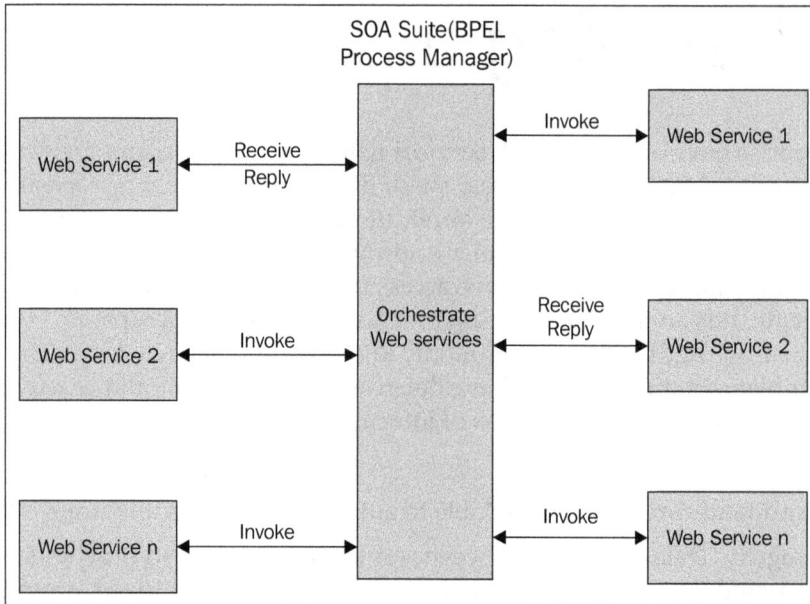

As shown in the following diagram, a client can be an SOA Suite, a J2EE container, or a third-party application. The invocation of the web service is via an SOA Suite platform. In this scenario, a client can create an authentication policy and propagate the user credential to the service provider.

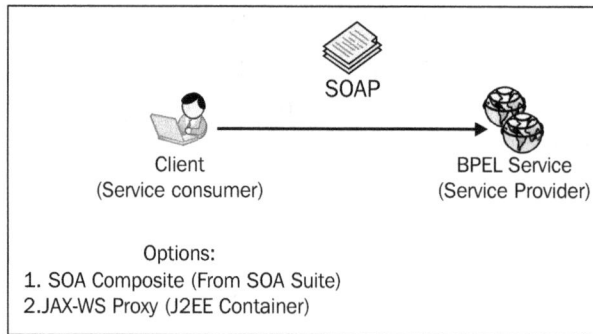

In this book, we are not covering the security for Data at Rest, which provides the data protection from the system administrators of the SOA Suite platform.

In an enterprise, the security solution for an Oracle SOA Suite is designed and deployed using some of the software and system components listed in this section. It is an industry-leading practice to select white listing over black listing design options with these components. The white listing concept is to the block everything and allow only the known good activities. On other hand, black listing concept is to generally allow all the activities and only block the known bad activities.

- Enterprise Security Gateway
- **Oracle Web Service Manager (OWSM)**
- **Security Assertion Mark-up Language (SAML)**
- WS-security headers for securing BPEL process and SOA Composite
- Oracle security products
- Network Firewall with **Intrusion Prevention System (IPS)**
- Web Application Firewall
- Data security in Transit and at Rest

Enterprise Security Gateway

Some organizations use a centralized security gateway to protect the services from an SOA platform. Some of the available options for a centralized gateway are Oracle Enterprise Gateway 11*g* and other third-party products such as Intel Expressway Service Gateway.

As shown in the following diagram, the gateway intercepts the calls between service clients and service providers, and performs authentication, authorization, and encryption. The OWSM can act as a gateway to enforce the security policies. However, some organizations can use a separate security gateway product for enforcing security in DMZ. Alternatively, the web server handles the encryption and a provider such as Oracle Access Manager and IBM Tivoli Access Manager handle the authentication and authorization.

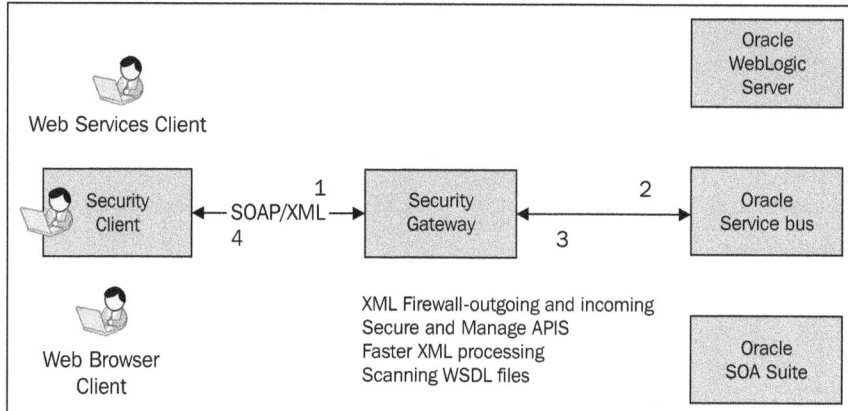

Oracle Web Service Manager (OWSM)

OWSM is for protecting web services by applying the security policies and enforcing them. It is a platform for securing and managing access to a web service. As shown in the following diagram, OWSM defines, attaches, validates, enforces, and monitors security policies for securing web services.

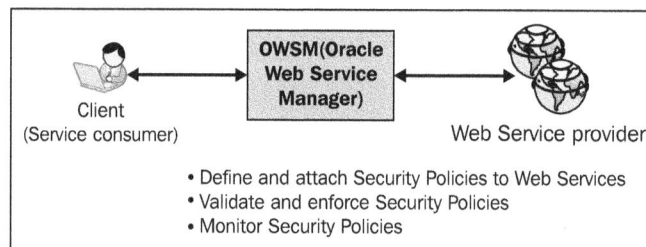

OWSM is part of the SOA Suite that doesn't require a separate install. Oracle also provides many security enforcement software products such as **Oracle Entitlement Server** and **Oracle Identity Manager**. However, OWSM satisfies the basic needs to protect most of the web service implementations. OWSM supports WS-security standards and can enforce authentication, authorization, and encryption, along with message confidentiality.

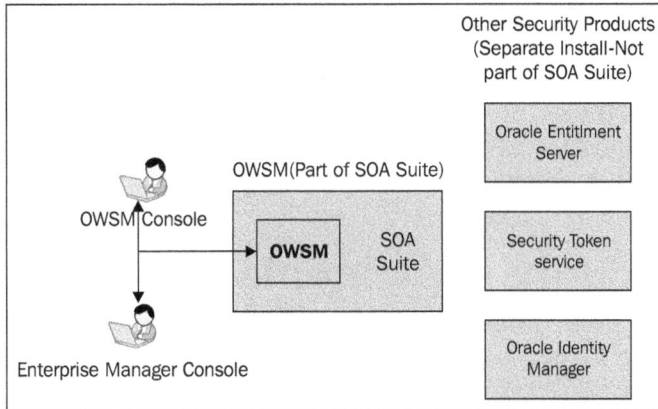

One can either use JDeveloper to attach security policies to the service endpoints or use OWSM console (part of Enterprise Manager) after deploying the composite applications in a SOA Suite platform to attach security policies to the service endpoints. We will discuss and review both these options.

The WSM-PM is an application available as part of SOA Suite, which manages the web service security policies for controlling the SAML authentications. The URL for logging in to the WSM-PM application is `http://{SOA Suite hostname}:{port Number}/wsm-pm/validator`.

All the available security policies are listed in the WSM-PM console. If the security policies are not displayed in the WSM-PM console then please verify the managed server logfiles for security policy error messages.

OWSM secures and manages access to web services using policies. Using OWSM, we can create security policies that can declaratively attach to SOAP services and clients. Usually, these policies are either **Local Policy Attachment (LPA)**, that is, defined and attached to individual web services, or **Global Policy Attachment (GPA)**, that is, defined and attached at the domain level. It is a leading practice to use GPA policies attachment wherever possible.

OWSM security implementation use cases

OWSM works as a policy interceptor and provides policy enforcement between the client and service provider. Usually, multiple policies are defined for messages and some messages may have zero policies.

A gateway can be part of the service provider, as shown in the following diagram. OWSM is part of Oracle SOA Suite and can provide policy enforcement to protect services. The OWSM agent intercepts the client messages, uses the defined policies for authorization, on success submits the request to service provider, and returns responses from service providers to the service clients.

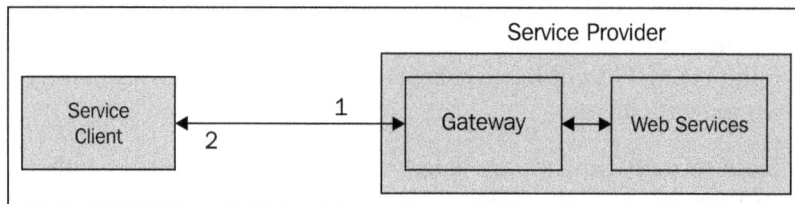

As shown in the following diagram, some of the service requests originate from the SOA Suite container, which has the capability of having OWSM agents. The client-side agent at the SOA Suite platform enforces the policies before sending the request to the service provider. The client-side agent at the SOA Suite platform also intercepts the response from the service provider before processing the response to the service clients.

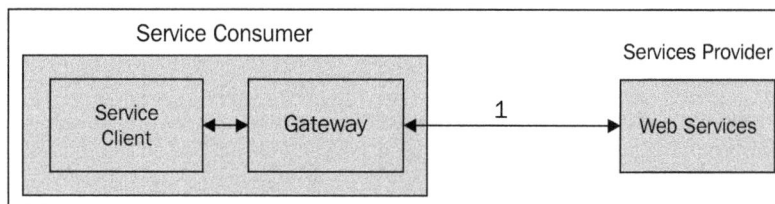

Attaching security policies using the OWSM console

To create GPAs, log in to the Enterprise Manager console (`http://{servername}:{portnumber}/em`). Right-click on the domain, select **Web Services**, and then **Policies**, as shown in the following screenshot:

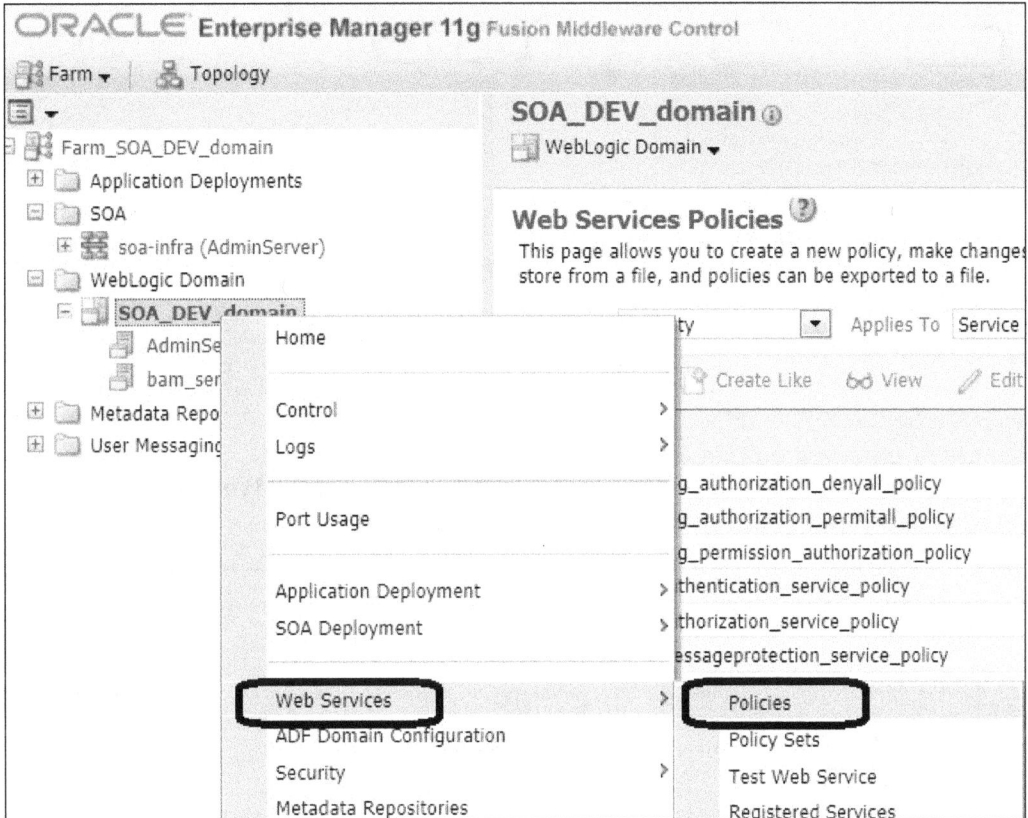

Click on **View** to get the details of the policies, as shown in the following screenshot. One can search the policies using the search function. To create a new security policy, click on the **Create** button.

The available assertion templates can be viewed by clicking the **Web Service Assertion Templates** link as shown in the following screenshot:

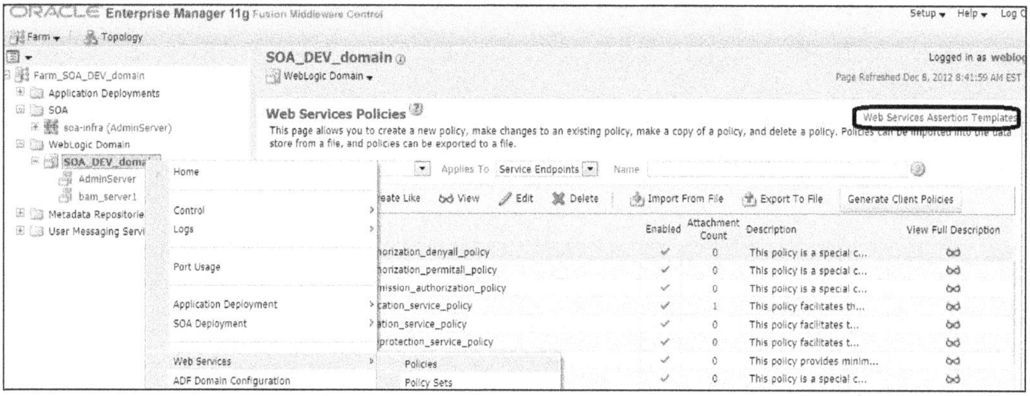

The available **Web Services Assertion Templates** can be viewed from the EM console, as shown in the following screenshot:

Attaching security policies using JDeveloper

As shown in the following screenshot, different service policies can be defined using JDeveloper:

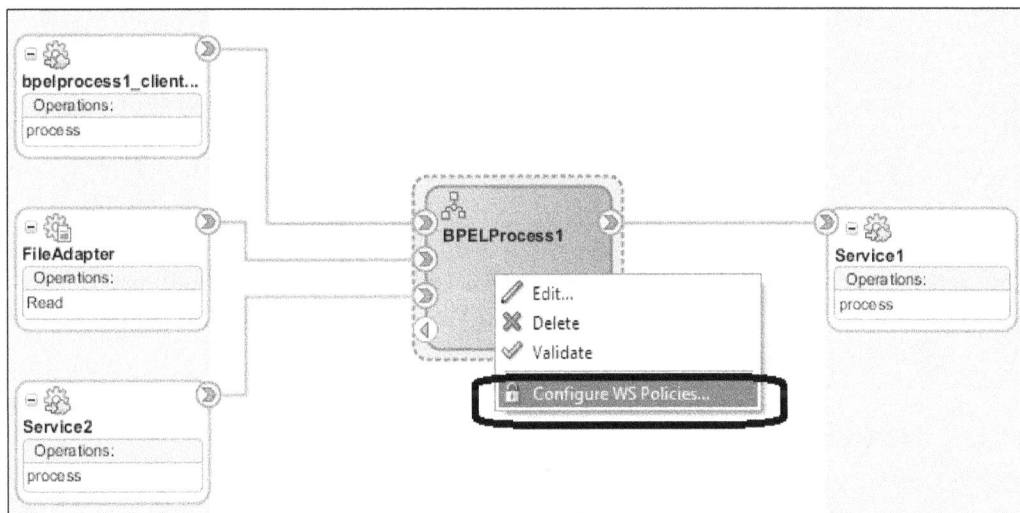

The security policies can apply to different components. Right-click on the component that requires policies on JDeveloper. You can define the security policies for call back as well. The following screenshot depicts how to configure SOA WS policies for a client:

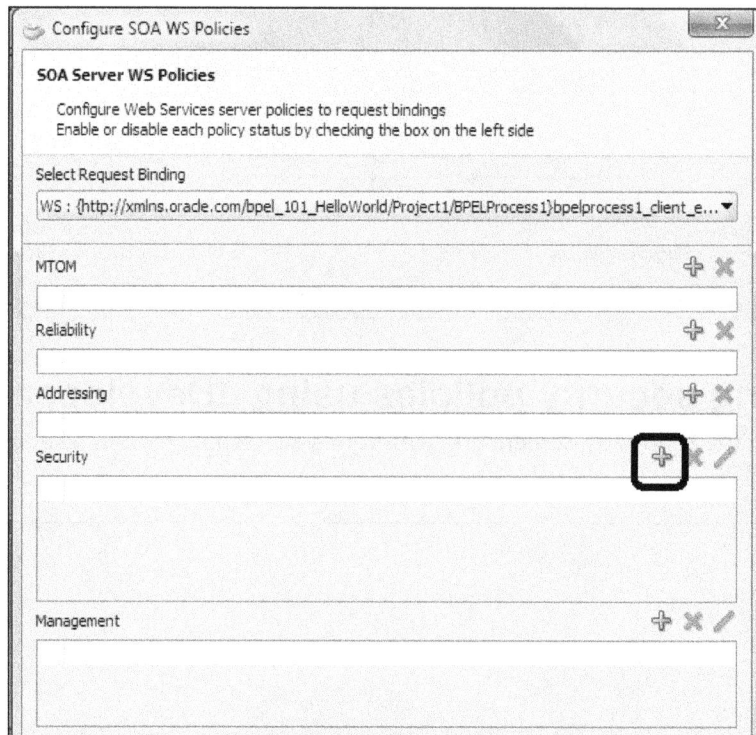

Different policy types such as **WS-ReliableMessaging**, **WS-PolicyAttachment**, **WS-Addressing**, **WS-MetadataExchange**, and **WS-SecurityPolicy** can be used along with SOA Suite.

WS-Security

OASIS manages the standards for WS-Security. WS-Security standards provide specifications about SOAP messages. For example, how to attach the signature, encryption headers, and security tokens to a message. X.509 Certificates and Kerberos tickets are used as security tokens.

As per the WS-Security standards, the username token and binary security token can be used for authenticating users. The username token can be added as part of SOAP headers. The different types of username token models available are as follows:

- Username and password
- Kerberos tickets
- SAML assertions
- PKI through X.509 certificates
- Custom token

Apart from WS-Security, some of the other OASIS standards for SOAP security are **WS-Policy, WS-Trust, WS-Privacy, WS-SecureConversation, WS-Federation,** and **WS-Authorization**.

SAML is mainly used for achieving **Single-Sign-On (SSO)**. The username token SAML provides message level authentication along with SSO. The SAML token can be used for propagating identity across multiple web services in a single transaction without transferring the username and password. It can also exchange the authorization and authentication data across security domains using tokens.

The basic concept of SAML for SSO is shown in the following diagram. If a user authenticates in one domain or website then the user doesn't need to authenticate again for other domains or websites.

For example, suppose a user logs in to a website. The website authenticates the user and creates a SAML for its partner websites. If the user tries to log in to the partner website(s), then it verifies the SAML token with the SAML provider instead of asking for the username and password again. If the SAML token verifies successfully then the user will be able to auto login to partner website(s) without re-entering the username and password. Major websites and service providers such as Google, AOL, and Yahoo have implemented SAML-based authentication for their multi-domain web assets.

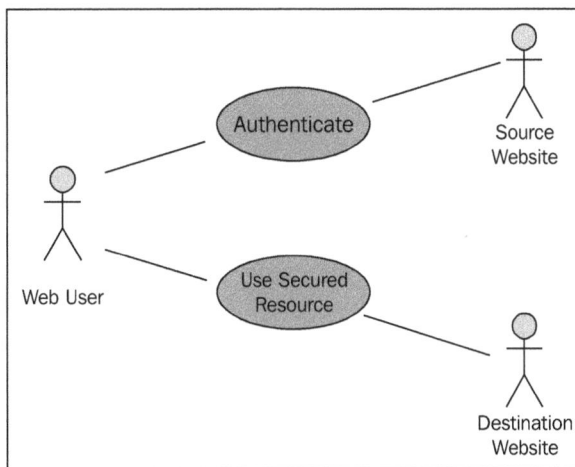

As shown in the following diagram, the initial BPEL can authenticate and authorize the service request using username tokens. The SOA Suite OWSM can attach the SAML policies and username tokens for accessing resources from external systems. The external system will validate the request based on the SAML token and then provide a response.

Usually, SAML policies such as `wss11_saml_token_client_policy` and `wss11_saml_token_service_policy` contain one or more assertions. An assertion can be authentication, authorization, or attributes. We can use JDeveloper or OWSM console for configuring the policies with BPELs.

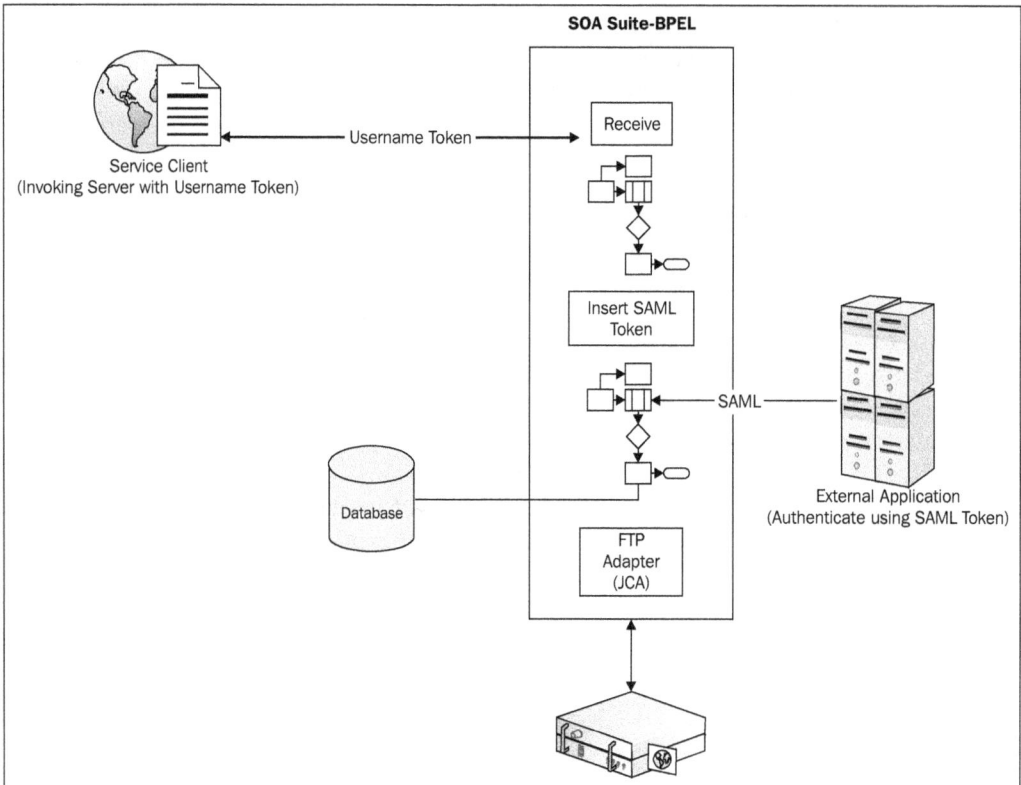

OWSM implementation – an example

The example in the following diagram explains how to configure OWSM to protect a web service using a username token:

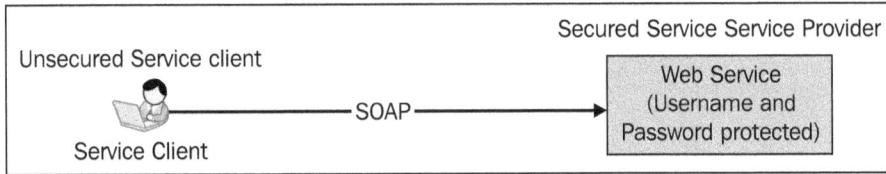

Configuring a secured service provider with username tokens

To configure a secured provider using username tokens use the following steps:

1. Right-click on **Operations** and then click on **Configure WS Policies...**, as shown in the following screenshot:

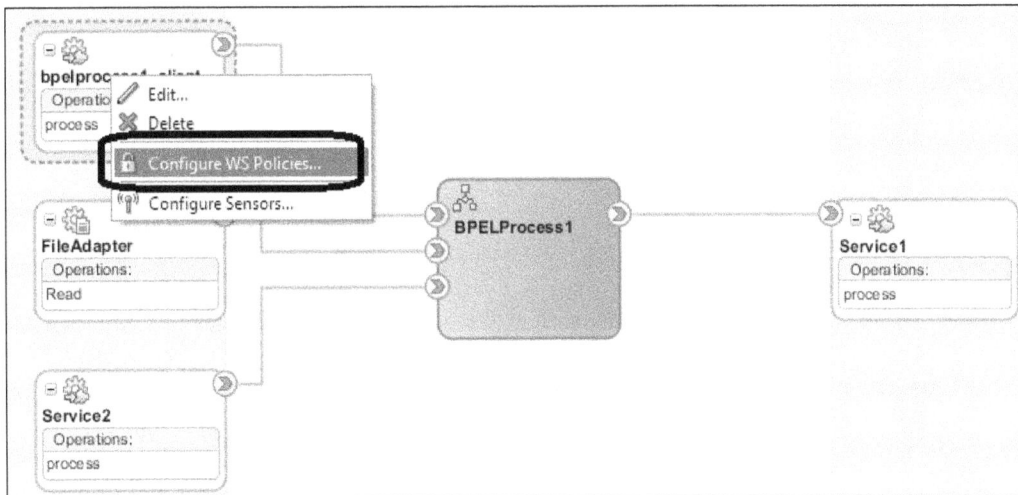

2. Click on the plus sign (+) next to **Security** and then select **oracle/wss_username_token_service_policy** from the Numbered bullet box, as shown in the following screenshot:

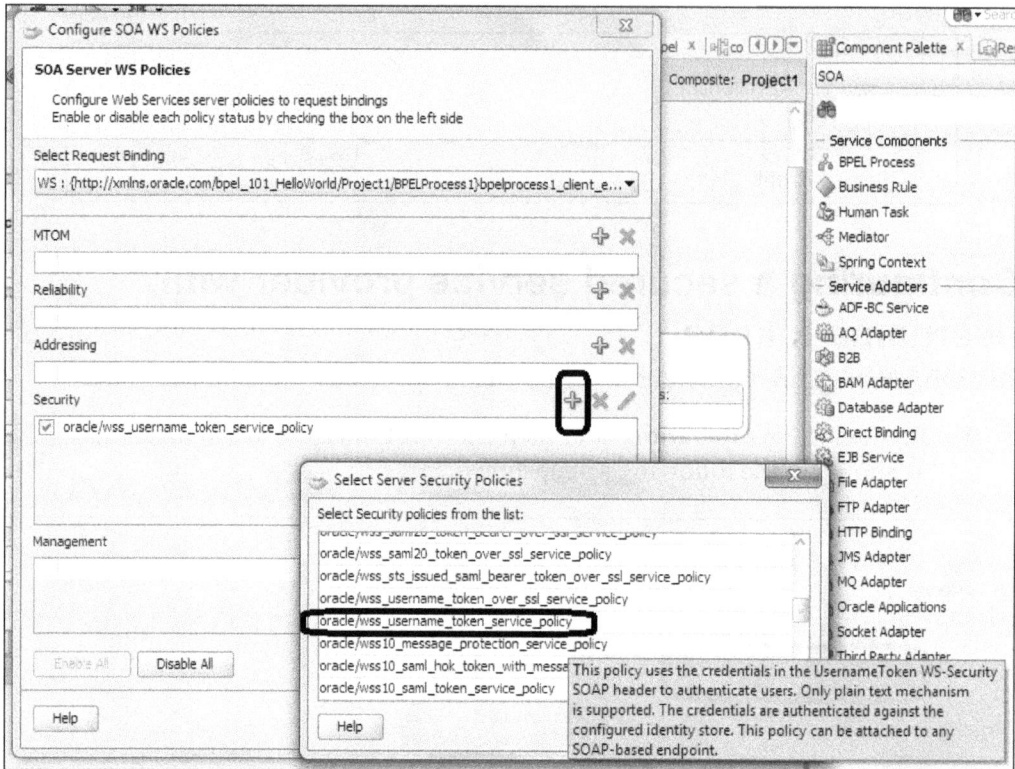

3. Deploy the composite application either using the **JDeveloper** or **Enterprise Manager** console. Any client that invokes the web service must provide a username and password as part of the SOAP header.

4. Apart from **wss_username_token_service_policy**, other major OWSM policies that are generally used are **wss11_saml_token_client policy** and **wss11_saml_token_service_policy**.

Configuring a service client for calling a secured web service

To configure a service client for calling a secured web service, you can make use of the following:

1. Select the service client from the **JDeveloper** console.

2. Right-click and select **Configure WS Policies...** and then **oracle/wss_username_token_client_policy** from the dropdown menu, as shown in the following screenshot:

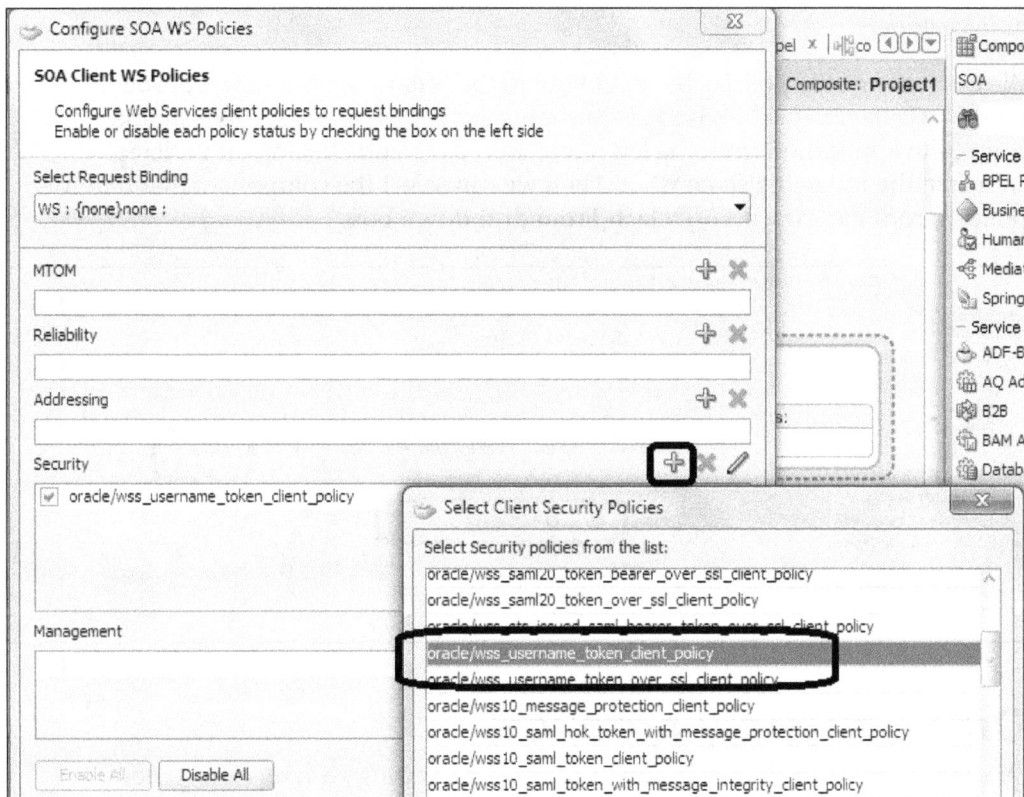

Alternatively, one can also edit the `composite.xml` source code and add the following properties to the binding to do the same. One can add the username and password as part of the properties shown in the following snippet:

```
<wsp:PolicyReference URI="oracle/wss_username_token_client_policy"
orawsp:category="security" orawsp:status="enabled"/>
<property name="oracle.webservices.auth.username" type="xs:string"
 many="false" override="may">USERNAME</property>
<property name="oracle.webservices.auth.password" type="xs:string"
              many="false" override="may">PASSWORD</property>
```

One can also do the same changes using the Enterprise Manager console instead of JDeveloper.

We can manage the policies by logging in to the Enterprise Manager console (`http://{adminserver-host}:{adminserver-port}/em`) and selecting the composite application from the left navigation pane and clicking on **Policies**, as shown in the following screenshot. Then we can select the component that requires policies from the **Attach To/Detach From** dropdown box.

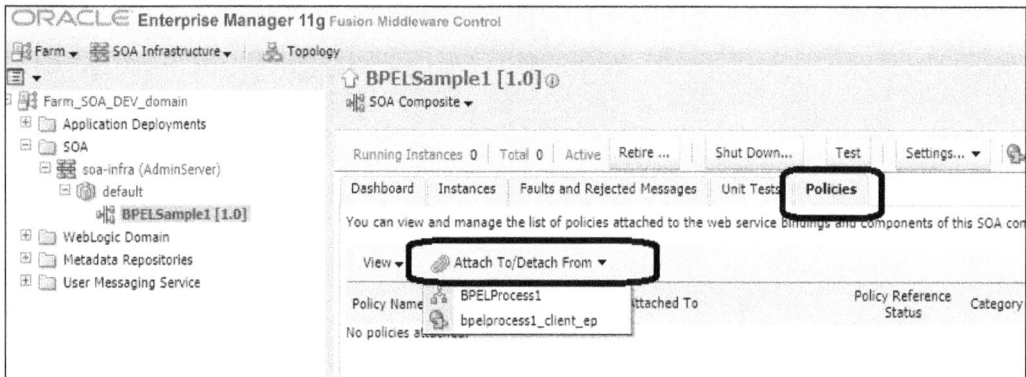

Oracle security products

Oracle provides multiple software products for securing web services. After installing Oracle SOA Suite, open the URL `http://{servername}:{port}` and then click on **Oracle Identity Management**, as shown in the following screenshot. Some of the security products have an overlap in functionalities as most of these products were acquired from different product companies.

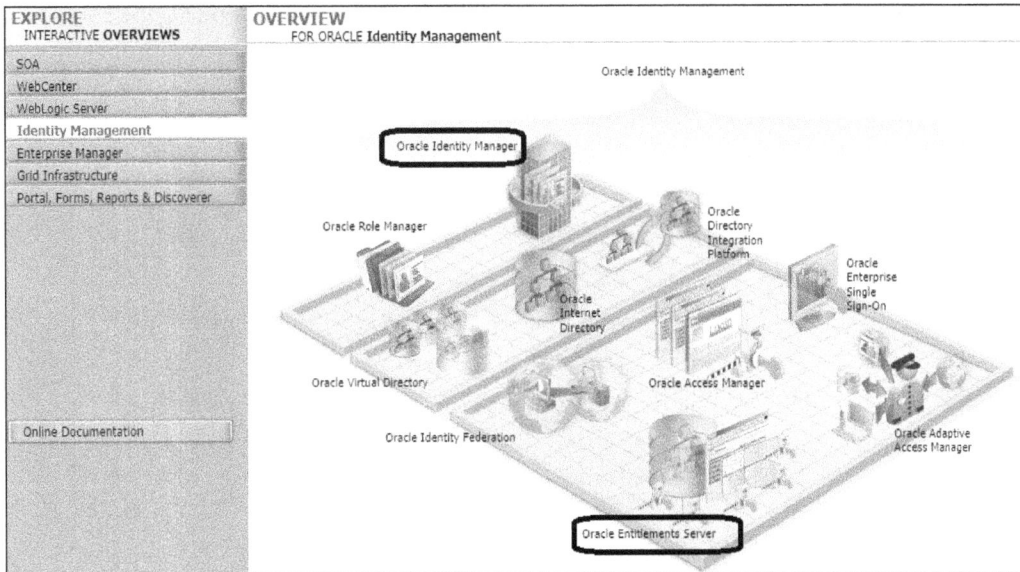

Oracle Identity Manager

Oracle Identity Manager (OIM) automates the user's access privileges and provisioning of IT resources. Oracle acquired this product from *Thor Xellerate*. OIM is a J2EE-based application and is primarily used for identity management. Oracle licenses this product based on the number of users for an enterprise that includes both internal and external users.

Oracle provides **Identity Manager Connector** for the database, Microsoft **Active Directory**, **BMC Remedy**, and others. The **Oracle Identity Manager Connector** has to be licensed to integrate and manage users for these systems.

The **Oracle Identity Manager** manages user provisioning and access privileges for the users. It has an admin console and a design console for power administrators and developers for customizing and configuring the Identity Manager.

The **Oracle Identity Manager** connects to different systems using connectors for user provisioning and providing access privileges, as shown in the following diagram:

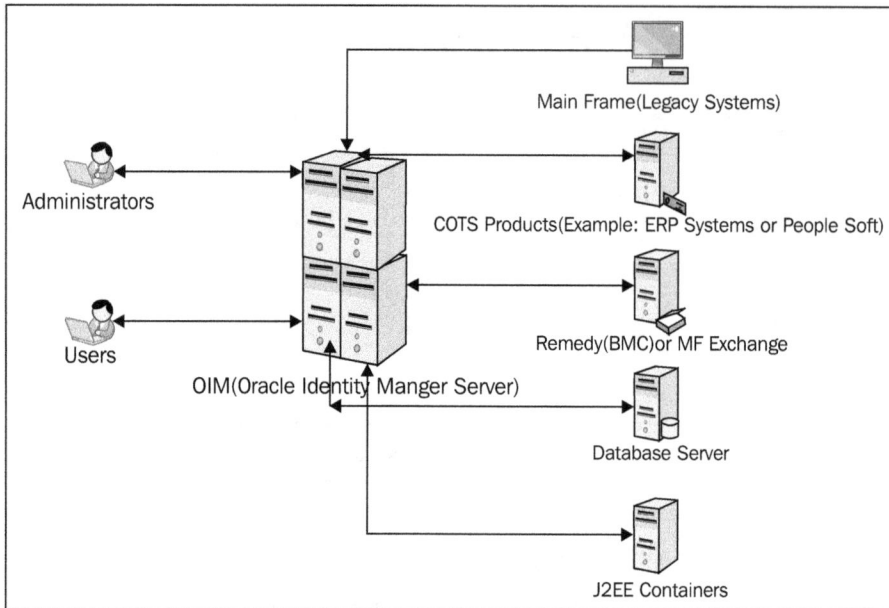

Oracle Entitlement Server

Oracle Entitlement Server (OES) is mainly used for fine-grained authorization. For example, some of the web applications have a requirement to restrict the resources based on time, such as restricting access to a certain functionality of the website between 9 AM and 5 PM. Any access after that should be denied. OES is a suitable software for this use case.

OES implements authorization based on policies and provides a centralized system for managing all the access policies, as shown in the following diagram:

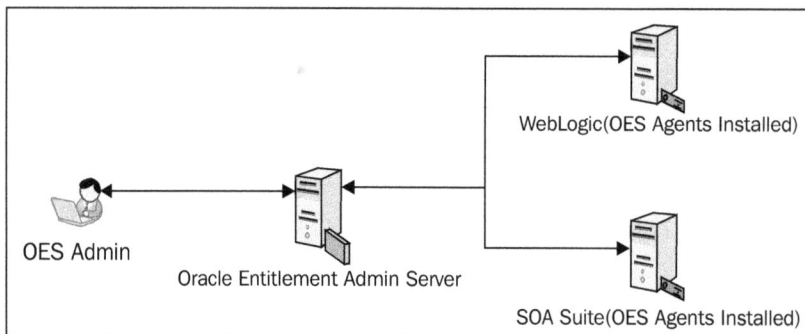

One can also protect resources using the Java permission object. The following example code snippet uses `java.io.FilePermission` for restricting access to a file:

```
Variable = new java.io.FilePermission ("File Directory path",
"write");
```

You can also protect resources based on user roles or using attributes.

Some of the other Oracle security products with brief details are as follows:

- **Oracle Access Manager (OAM) (acquired from Oblix COREid Access and Identity)**: Provides **Single-Sign-On (SSO)**, authentication, and authorization. Oracle WebGate is a web server plugin that is part of the OAM. WebGate is responsible for transferring client requests to the OAM for authentication and authorization.

- **Oracle Identity Federation (OIF) (Oblix COREid Federation)**: Enables exchanging and sharing identity information between partners.

- **Oracle Virtual Directory (OVD) (OctetString Virtual Directory Engine)**: OVD integrates the user information from different sources such as corporate databases, enterprise directory, and Microsoft Active Directory Domains and provides industry standard XML and LDAP views of user identity information.

- **Oracle Secure Token Service**: Oracle Secure Token Service creates tokens that act as a security credential for securing communication between the service client and the service provider. Secure Token Service can create the following tokens:

    ° SAML assertions
    ° Kerberos tokens (Use of Windows native authentication)
    ° Digital certificates

    The Secure Token Service is mainly based on WS-Trust standards managed by OASIS; however, it supports most of the WS_* standards. Oracle Secure Token Service can be used along with OWSM.

The following diagram shows how to protect resources deployed in WebLogic or SOA Suite using some of the Oracle security products.

The web service plugin **WebGate** will forward the client request to **Oracle Access Manager** for authentication and authorization. **Oracle Access Manager** authenticates a user based on the policy configured for **WebGate** domains. When resources are accessed from WebLogic or SOA Suite, the **Secure Token Service** client can obtain the assertion ID from the **Secure Token Service** and validates the **Secure Token** with the **Oracle Access Manager**.

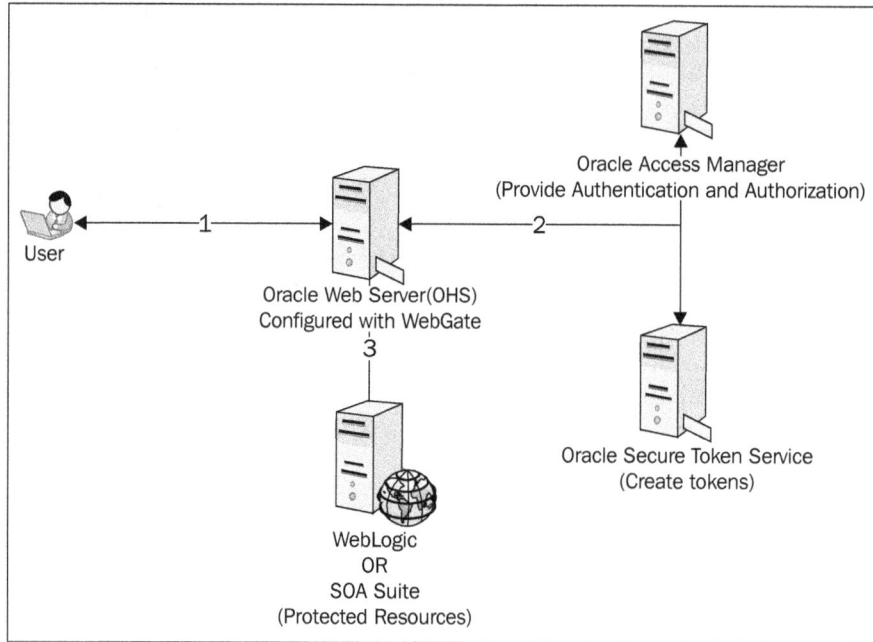

Network Firewall with Intrusion Prevention System

The traditional network firewalls allow and block traffic based on the source and destination IP addresses, also known as L4 firewall rules. In a service-oriented architecture, we are exposing services to external vendors and consuming services from external vendors. These IP addresses based on L4 firewall rules will cause functional issues whenever there is an IP address update without coordinating such changes. The modern network firewall appliances allow site domain-based firewall rules, also known as L7 firewall rules. It is an industry-leading practice to implement the L7 firewall rules for SOA composite application(s) for smooth operations and maintenance.

The leading network firewall appliances such as Cisco and Fortinet come with a built-in **Intrusion Prevention System (IPS)**, also known as a **Intrusion Detection and Prevention System (IDPS)** that monitors the network and system to identify, block, and report malicious activities. It is highly recommended to enable IPS, or introduce an inline network appliance for IPS, if you are exposing SOA services over the Internet.

Web Application Firewall

Web Application Firewall (WAF) is a hardware and software inline appliance or server plugin that monitors HTTP conversation to identify, block, and report common attacks such as **Cross-Site Scripting (XSS)**, **Cross-Site Request Forgery (CSRF)**, **Distributed Denial of Service (DDoS)**, **Buffer Overflow**, and **SQL Injection**. It is highly recommended to implement the inline WAF component for SOA composite applications. The leading vendors for WAF are Imperva, F5, and NetScaler.

Data security in Transit and at Rest

Usually HTTPS, also known as **Transport Layer Security (TLS)** and **Secure Socket Layer (SSL)** implementation, is used to protect the communication over a wire between a service client and service provider. It is a leading solution to implement a solution for Data security in Transit.

- Server authenticated SSL

  In this process, only server identity is validated by the service client using pre-established digital certificate trust for certificates issued by the public certificate authorities such as VeriSign, Thawte, GeoTrust, and many others. In this implementation, we are not restricting who can consume the services.

- Client-server authenticated SSL

  One can extend the server authenticated SSL implementation to perform a client identity validation as well to protect services. Usually, client identity certificates are issued by a private certificate authority, established by the service provider organization. In this implementation, we are restricting the users who can consume the services as establishing an HTTPS client needs to provide an identity certificate trusted by the service provider.

It is a leading practice to use a client-server authenticated SSL, also known as two-way SSL, to authenticate users of web services. The client identity certificates used for authentication are issued from a private certificate authority.

The alternate options to secure communication over wire are sTunnel (Host Layer) or IPSec (Network Layer) implementations. These are often utilized when end-to-end encryption over wire is a mandate and a software component doesn't have built-in SSL/TLS implementation.

Summary

In this chapter, we learned the various options to design and implement a security solution for securing a BPEL process. We explored the security options and industry-leading practices to implement authentication, authorization, data security in transit, and denial of service attacks for SOA composite applications. In the next chapter, we will learn the architecture options to implement high availability for business services.

10
Architecting High Availability for Business Services

Availability of business services for enterprise SOA implementations at any organization is either mission-critical or business-critical. The availability of business services for an organization can directly impact the revenue or at least the brand value. Architects must understand and define the high availability requirements for an application platform in collaboration with business. The high availability is measured by the business services uptime by the different levels of 9s such as 99.0 percent, 99.9 percent, 99.99 percent, or 99.999 percent and often referenced as availability uptime **Service Level Agreements (SLAs)**, either with business units or external customers. The high availability for an application platform providing business services has two dimensions to it; first systems architecture and second release and change management processes. In this chapter, our focus is to learn the high availability system's reference architecture(s) using the Oracle SOA Suite to implement business services with various levels of availability SLAs. The key system architecture components that assist us in achieving high availability for business services by an application platform are as follows:

- Shared services
    - Internal services: For example, Single Sign On, Enterprise Document Repository, and E-mail System.
    - External services: For example, payment gateway, credit scores look-ups, stocks buying and selling orders, and pickup and delivery orders.

- Data center(s)
    - Number of sites
    - Network
    - Power

- Load balancer(s)
    - ◦ L7/GSLB/GTM
    - ◦ L4/LSLB/LTM

- Compute resources
    - ◦ Web server(s)
    - ◦ WebLogic Application Server(s): For example, Oracle SOA Suite server
    - ◦ Database server(s)

- Storage Area Network

SOA environment

Compared to a typical web application environment, usually the SOA environment consists of many systems and/or applications. Reusing the existing applications, also known as legacy applications in a loosely coupled way to achieve the business agility/flexibility, is one of the goals of implementing SOA.

The SOA environment is highly available only when all its component systems either meet or exceed the business service's availability SLAs. We need to ensure that all the endpoint systems orchestrated by BPEL are capable of meeting the availability uptime SLAs. The SOA integration points are designed and validated to recover from the external sub systems and service outages caused by planned and unplanned maintenance windows for pre-defined durations. We should clearly articulate and identify the external sub systems and services that directly impact our service's availability uptime SLAs. The end-to-end synchronous transaction's availability is immediately impacted by a sub system's outage.

It is highly recommended that for the synchronous transactions invoked, consider implementing the retry logic until the SOA core system successfully completes the transaction. Also, for asynchronous transactions, store the critical information permanently until the SOA core system processor is able to complete the transaction successfully.

As shown in the following diagram, a user transaction may fail if one of the systems within the SOA environment is not available. Hence, it is important that we design the availability at all the components of a SOA system instead of just focusing on the BPEL/SOA Suite. The SOA BPEL system's availability is dependent on the external service's endpoints.

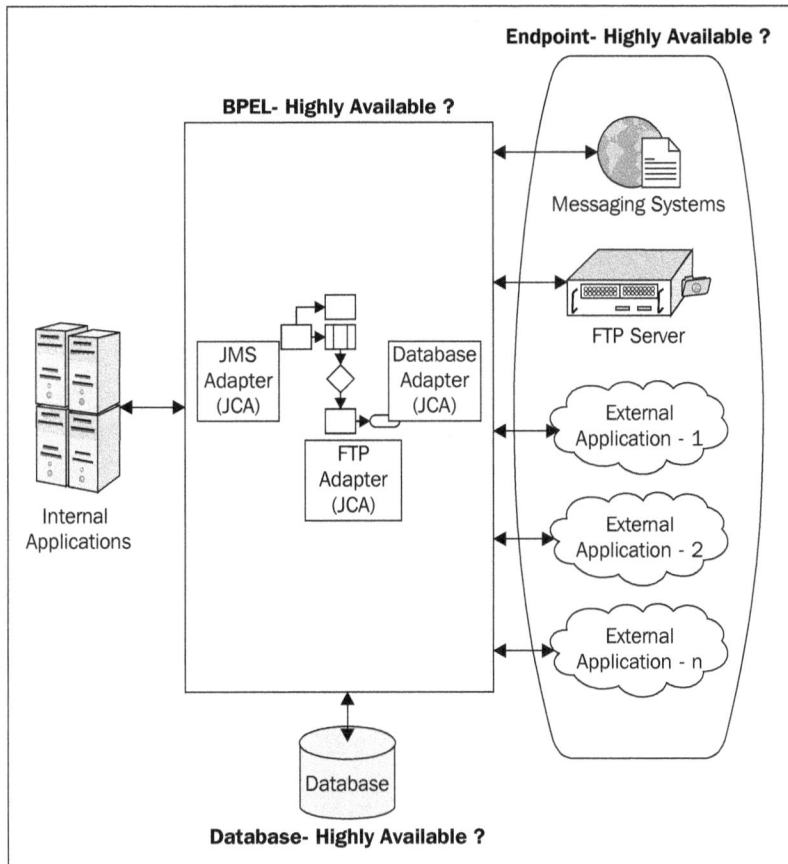

Cluster architecture

SOA Suite consists of many components and applications such as Human Workflow, BPEL Process Manager, Mediator, and Business Rules Engine. Oracle created all these components as cluster-friendly to meet the availability and scalability needs for organizations. None of the SOA Suite components are singleton services. All the web modules and EJBs within SOA Suite are stateless. State replication is not required between SOA Suite cluster nodes.

We can create BPEL composite applications and deploy in a SOA Suite cluster that has built-in features of load balancing and failover capabilities to achieve high availability and scalability needs for a business.

The following diagram shows a typical cluster environment for an SOA Suite deployment. Please note that an SOA environment always consists of many other systems. The major tiers are web, application, and database. In order to achieve the high availability-configure clustered web server(s) and application server(s), use Oracle RAC databases. In other words, build the redundant component at each tier.

- The L4 load balancers provide load balancing and failover for web servers.

- The web server proxy plugin (Apache proxy plugin or OHS plugin) provides load balancing and failover for SOA Suite application platform running within WebLogic. The other option is to use hardware load balancers such as L4 load balancers instead of web server proxy plugin.

- The multi data sources or grid link data source configured at WebLogic that is used for SOA Suite application provides load balancing and failover capabilities at the database tier.

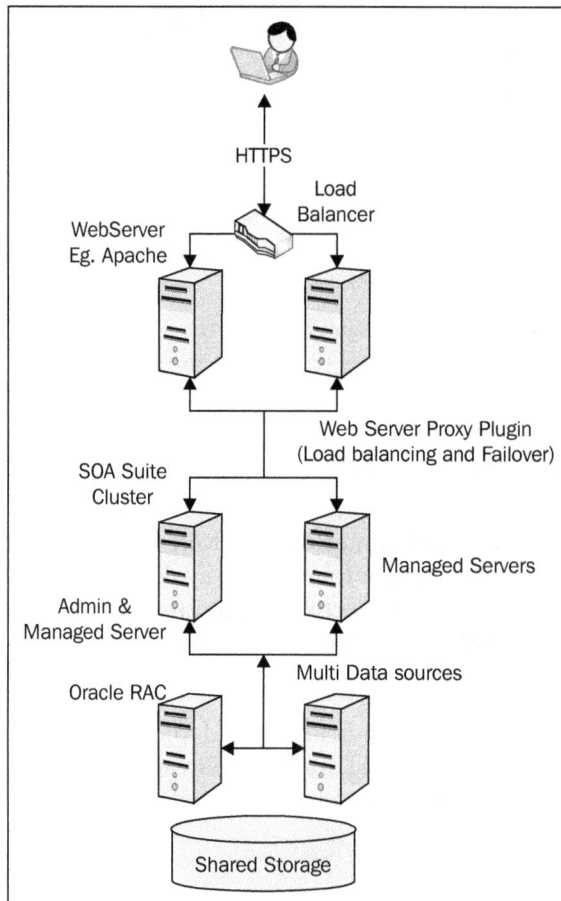

Load balancer(s)

The high availability system's architecture usually depends on load balancer appliances. These come in two types: first Layer 4/Local Server Load balancer/Local Traffic Manager (L4/LSLB/LTM), also known as local load balancers; and second Layer 7/Global Server Load Balancer (L7/GSLB/GTM), also known as global load balancers. In small implementations only local load balancers are implemented as the hot standby pair, that means, only one takes the active traffic at a given time. The multisite implementations (both physical and logical sites) also known as multi data center deployments are required to implement the combination of global load balancers and local load balancers. The global and local load balancers are the key components to achieve the availability uptime SLAs of 99.99 percent or 99.999 percent.

Compute resource(s)

In a nutshell, the Oracle SOA Suite is a standard-based J2EE application deployed on the Oracle WebLogic Server Platform. It is also important to implement redundant components for load balancing and failover options at the web, application, and database tier to meet the high availability requirements. The availability uptime SLAs of 99.9 percent or more needs each tier in compute resources to get the redundant component even for a minimal load. You may decide not to implement the redundant component at the database tier due to the cost but one needs to at least implement a standby node for database failover.

Web server(s) – clustering for scalability and availability

The hardware load balancer such as F5 or Foundry, also known as local load balancers, will provide the load balancing and failover for web servers. Different algorithms can be set for hardware load balancers.

Does the external web server always require an SOA environment? The HTTP server is included as part of WebLogic or SOA Suite container. However, configuring an external web server has the following advantages:

- **Security**: Configuring a web server in DMZ or an internet network provides an additional layer of security.
    - A web server can log all access requests in `access.log` and error messages in `error.log`, including the requests originating from IP addresses, time stamps, nature of request, and so on.

- A web server can be used for configuring application filtering and IP filtering. You can configure application filtering by configuring the proxy request by path or by MIME type. Adding a `MatchExpression` line to the `IfModule` block of `HTTP.Conf` will provide proxying by MIME type. The access control module provides IP-level restrictions. For example, allow from IP address or deny from `denial.service.attack.com`.

- **HTTPS and certificates**: Easy to configure and manage security certificates using an external web server for external requests. A web server also provides an option to secure the internal traffic from the web server to the application servers.

- **More control and cost**: A web server provides parameters for reducing connection refused errors using multiple configuration parameters such as `AcceptBackLog` and `KeepAlive`. The WebLogic server license and support cost is more expensive than generic web server(s).

You must configure a WebLogic `HttpClusterServlet` if you are planning to use WebLogic as your web server. It is not recommended if you are planning to expose the SOA services publicly over the Internet. Some of the web server(s) that one can use along with Oracle SOA Suite are listed as follows. Oracle provides separate proxy plugins for these web server(s).

- Apache HTTP Server
- Microsoft **Internet Information Server (IIS)**
- Oracle HTTP Server
- Oracle WebLogic Web Server
- Oracle iPlanet Web Server

WebLogic application server(s) and Oracle SOA Suite server(s) – clustering for scalability and availability

The web server proxy plugin will provide load balancing and failover options for SOA Suite and WebLogic clusters.

The web server proxy plugin maintains the SOA Suite or WebLogic server instance details and forwards the request to those instances based on the load balancing algorithm. Usually, the round robin or least connections load balancing is used for most of the infrastructure. The proxy plugin locates and routes the client request to the failover application server instance in case the primary instance failed for some reason. The Apache plugin is available as shared object (.so) for Linux platforms. For routing the traffic from web server to SOA Suite, configure the httpd.conf file and include the WebLogic host name and port information.

The other option is to use a layer 4 hardware load balancer for routing the traffic from web server to SOA Suite. For some infrastructure, hardware load balancing may be recommended.

You can create SOA Suite clusters during the install process and ensure that all nodes are processing requests at the same time to avoid a single point of failure.

To install the Apache proxy plugin for WebLogic 10.3.6, you should download the Apache proxy plugin as a separate ZIP file. It is available at http://edelivery.oracle.com. Extract the plugin files in your Apache server and configure httpd.conf.

Database clustering

Shared dehydration is important for SOA Suite clustering. **Oracle Real Application Clusters (Oracle RAC)** is one of the options for database clustering.

You can use Oracle Enterprise Manager Database Control for configuring Oracle RAC. Use the WebLogic console for creating the required data sources. Also, always remember to use a multi data source along with Oracle RAC and create data sources for each RAC node.

Create a JDBC multi pool using the WebLogic console and add individual data sources to the multi pool. Ensure that all the Oracle nodes receive the traffic from the SOA Suite. Use load balancing as the algorithm type while creating multi data sources.

You can shut down one of the Oracle RAC nodes to ensure that a SOA Suite failover connection for the secondary node(s) is enabled.

GridLink data source

Instead of using multi data source for configuring Oracle RAC, you can use Oracle GridLink data source for connecting WebLogic to Oracle RAC. It is supported from WebLogic Version 10.3.6 onwards. It is similar to using a proxy plugin for connecting web servers (Apache, OHS, and so on) to WebLogic; you can use an **Oracle Notification Service (ONS)** for providing load balancing and failover for Oracle Database RAC nodes.

You can use a GridLink data source for connecting WebLogic with multiple Oracle RAC systems, as shown in the following diagram:

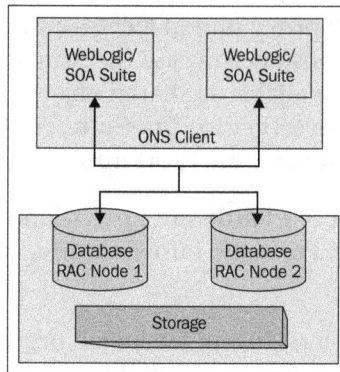

To achieve this, make use of the following steps:

1. Log in to the WebLogic console
    (`http://{adminserver-host}:{adminserver-port}/console`).

2. From the domain structure tree on the left navigation pane, expand **Services**, and click on **Data Sources**.

3. From the **Configuration** menu, select the **ONS** tab. Enable **FAN** and enter the comma-separated list of Oracle RAC node names, as shown in the following screenshot:

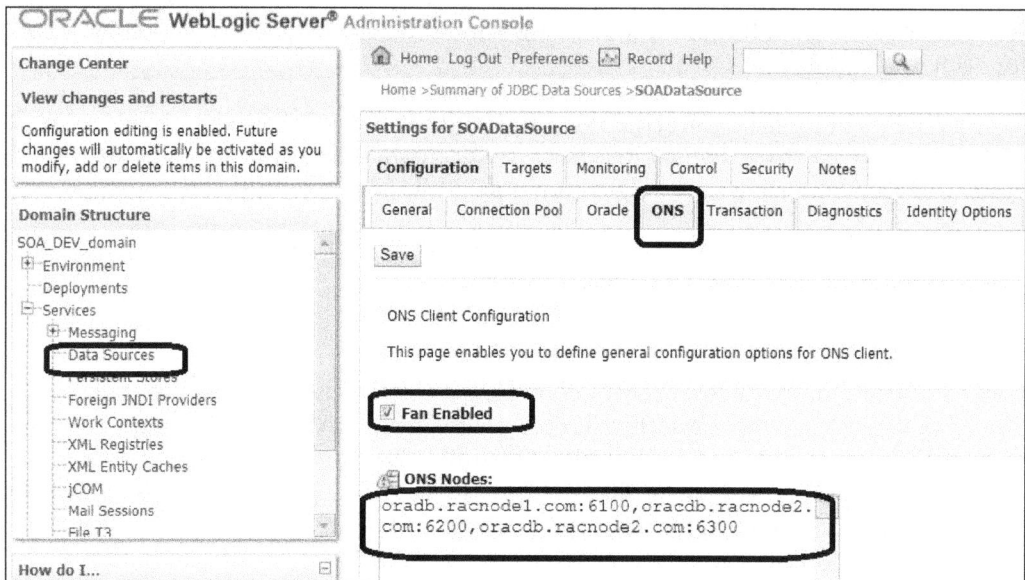

Backup and recovery strategy

It is highly recommended to implement at least two logical sites for large implementations of the business service's application platform. As we understand that high availability of business services is critical for any organization, it is recommended that you design two physical sites that provide you with built-in backup and recovery of the mission-critical business service's application platform.

You are at least required to implement an off-site backup solution for one physical site design and deployment. On other hand, if your implementation is with two sites, you may be able to live on an on-site disk-based backup solution as these sites could provide the backup for each other. Some of the implementations, irrespective of the number of physical sites, may still require implementing an off-site backup solution due to industry compliance and business policies.

As a minimum, we need to create a backup and recovery for databases, logfiles from all the servers, a web server, admin server, and a managed server. In this option, you need to fully bake the steps of recovery of databases, web server, admin and managed server, and building a web server(s) and managed server(s) from the backup copies. The backup frequency needs to be aligned with the **Recovery Point Objectives (RPO)**, and the recovery process needs to comply with the **Recovery Time Objectives (RTO)** defined by the business requirements.

In case your organization uses VMware, you can use the VMware vCenter **Site Recovery Manager (SRM)** for enabling disaster recovery.

Data center(s)

The high availability system architecture's foundation is underlying in the data center(s) used for deployment of Oracle SOA Suite components. Usually, most implementations are single, physical sites but it is highly recommended that for a medium to large deployment you create at least two logical sites within a data center to get the highest possible availability uptime for your business services. The availability uptime SLAs for 99.999 percent requires that the system's architecture be designed and deployed with at least two physical sites. If you are designing the system architecture to meet the SLAs of 99.9 percent availability uptime, you are recommended to select the data center that has the redundant network, usually from two independent sources and with at least a secondary power source from on-premise power generators. Data center(s) with two independent power sources are rare to find and are expensive to build or lease.

Deployment architecture options

As shown in the following diagram, the web server(s) and application server(s) can be installed in different hosts. The load balancing and failover capabilities are added in each layer. SOA Suite app-to-app calling is recommended to be implemented at the same endpoint as the consumer endpoint for high availability and ease of operations.

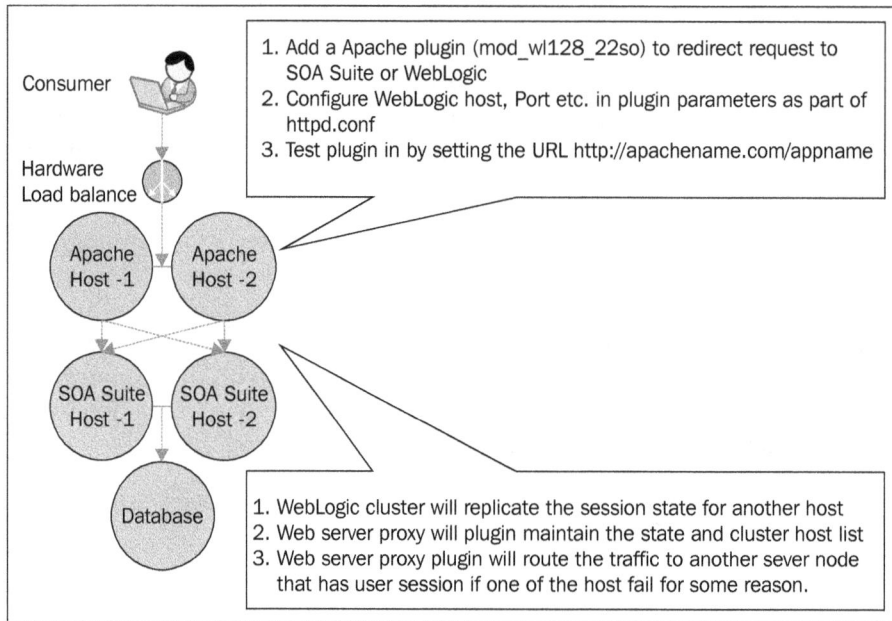

The following diagram shows other available options for configuring web server(s) and application server(s):

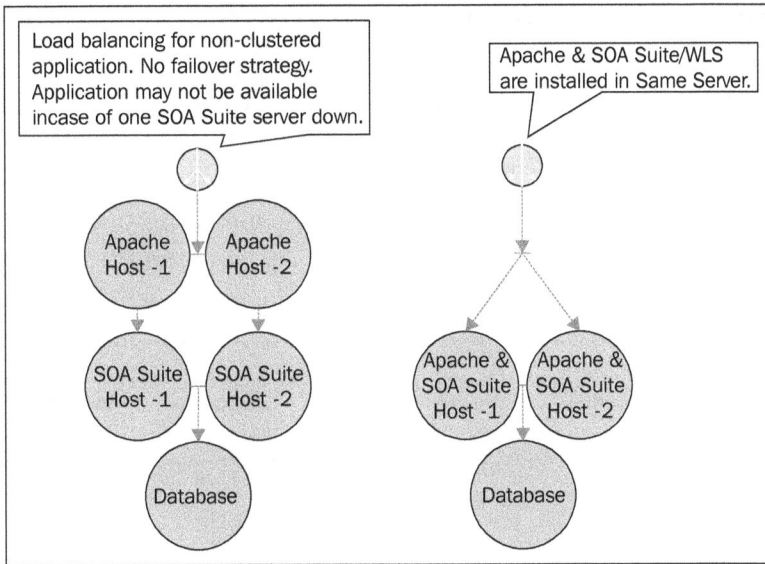

As shown in the following diagram, the other option is to use hardware load balancers between web server(s) and application server(s) for achieving load balancing and failover:

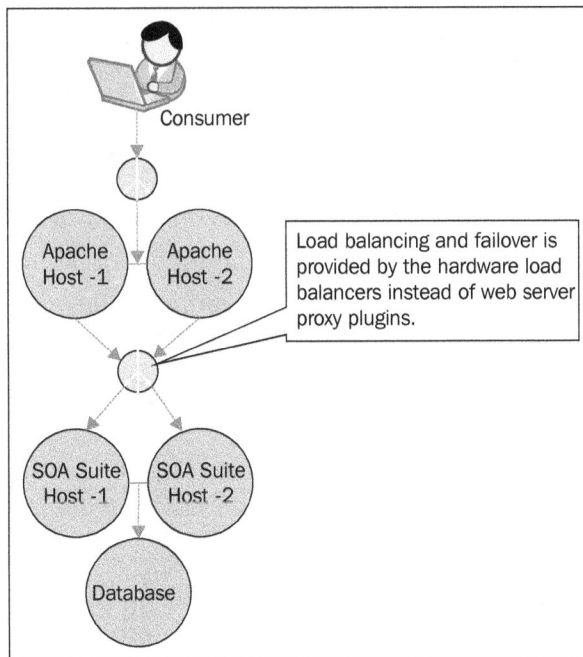

Multi data center deployment

To achieve geographically-distributed high availability, you can design multi data center deployment for an SOA environment. Ensure that all endpoint applications are available in the secondary data center, otherwise creating a geographically distributed environment is meaningless.

The L7/GSLB/GTM provides distribution of user traffic across multiple data centers and manages disaster recovery. The L4/LSLB/LTM distributes the workload across multiple web server(s) within a single data center.

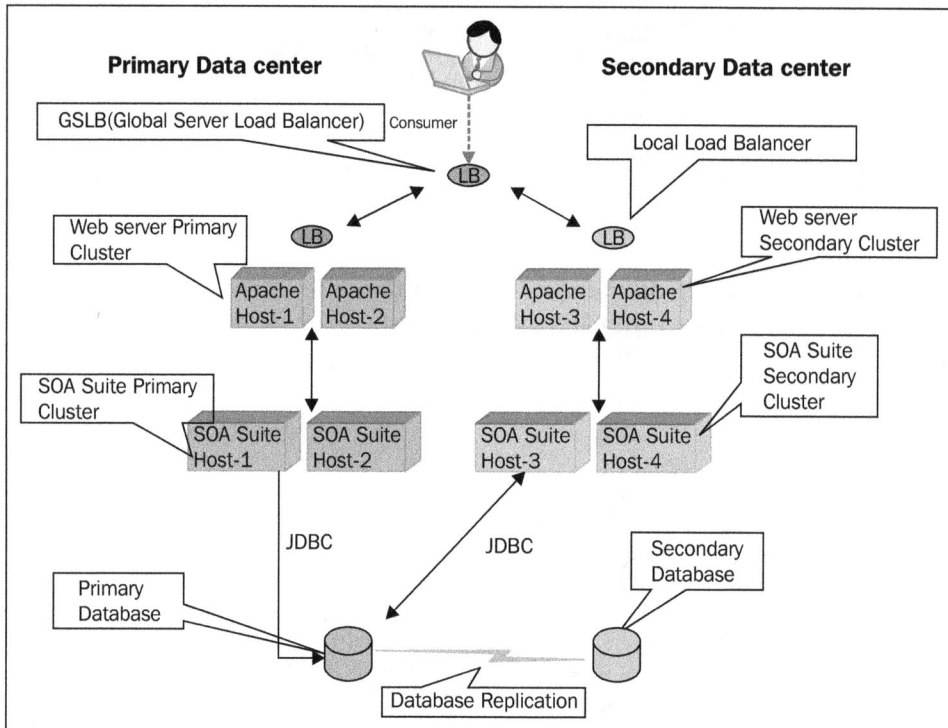

The following approaches can be used for multi data center deployment:

- Active – Active
- Active – Passive

Active – Active

This means both primary and secondary data centers will be active at the same time and user traffic will be equally distributed across data center(s). The Active – Active approach is recommended if your SOA environment cannot have any planned downtime. In this architecture, user requests will be equally distributed across multiple data center(s). Each data center configures with separate web and application layer clusters.

Achieving real-time active bi-directional data replication is one of challenges for this approach. The real-time database replication can be achieved using the Oracle Golden Gate software. The other option is to use the primary database for the traffic from primary and secondary application servers. Ensure that the latency between the secondary data center and the primary data center is less than 50 ms and you get enough bandwidth to cover the rate of change of data replication in almost real time. You can use Oracle Data Guard or storage replication such as SRDF to back up data from the primary to secondary database.

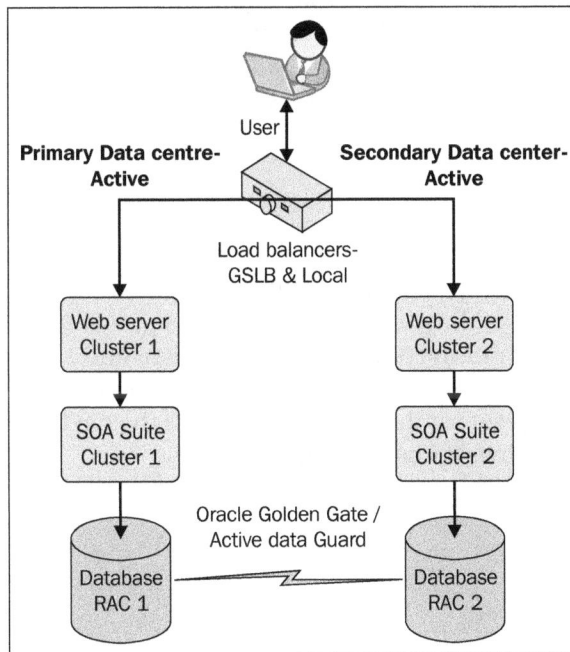

Active – Passive

In this approach, the primary data center will be active and the secondary data center will be in standby mode. The secondary data center will be active only in case of the failure of the primary data center. Most organizations use this approach for disaster recovery.

The passive data center hosts rest idly waiting for the failure of the primary data center. The switchover can be manual and automatic. Additional scripting is required for automatic failover of the user traffic to the passive data center. Storage and data has to replicate at regular intervals to achieve the failover.

The strategy for switching back from the secondary (passive) to the primary data center has to be included in the automating/manual scripting of the switchover.

Oracle Service Bus

Similar to SOA Suite or WebLogic, an **Oracle Service Bus** (**OSB**) domain can be created for a cluster to deploy for high availability. You can use a hardware load balancer or a web server proxy plugin for load balancing and failover. Some of the services within the OSB are singleton such as FTP and file proxy services.

Summary

In this chapter, we learned the system architecture options for achieving high availability for the SOA composite application's design and deployment. The key take away is that the availability uptime SLAs for an application service is equal to the lowest availability uptime of a system component and shared service(s). Therefore, each system component and shared service(s) must meet or exceed the availability uptime SLAs set for the overall system. In the next chapter, we will discuss the future of business process modeling.

11
The Future of Process Modeling

In today's competitive world, businesses cannot survive without **Information Technology (IT)** systems. Some of the most successful businesses have reliable and easy-to-use computer systems to run their core business. IT systems play a key role in their success in business operations and innovation. Therefore, IT systems should be capable of supporting business to accommodate the changes in the business processes and models.

Organizations are continuously seeking new opportunities to differentiate themselves from others offering similar services and products. This demands that the system implementation should be capable to adapt to the changing nature of the business or marketplace economically. In other words, organizations require agility and an increase in the performance of the IT systems to address the emerging competition. Process modeling with the following qualities can help us achieve this goal:

- Easy to reflect complete business process in a model
- Easy to change with the ever-changing requirements
- Understandable to the relevant stake holders of modeling process

Commercial off-the-shelf (COTS)

In the evolution of the software industry, people are looking for ways to create software systems without writing any code. Reusing the existing code is one of the strategies to reduce the complexity. In future, there may be many more COTS products available for all the business needs. Currently the COTS products are available for the areas such as payment processing, payroll processing, account management, tax calculations, employee management, education platforms, knowledge management, travel management, and employee performance management. Companies do not create systems for doing these business functions. They just utilize the appropriate COTS products.

Companies purchase COTS products for conducting certain business processes that are common in the industry. Companies select the COTS product that fits their business needs; however, they may not always find a COTS product that fits in the exact business process. Sometimes, the business adopts the general business process from the COTS product. In such a scenario, there is no need to create the application from scratch, simply start using with default configurations and templates or customize the configurations and templates to perform business function(s) for the organization.

A particular business should use a COTS product if it meets the requirements instead of creating it. However, COTS products may not be suitable for all the business functions, usually core business functions. Some companies believe that using the COTS product will reduce the business advantage as compared to their competitors.

One of the mistakes companies make is that they heavily customize the COTS product to suit their own custom business processing. Companies adopting COTS products should adopt the COTS product business process instead of trying to customize the COTS product. Heavy customization of a COTS product is not a good idea. The COTS vendors usually do not provide the source code. Any upgrade requires major changes and sometimes you may end up with extended support contracts to continue using the older versions of the COTS product due to significant upgrade costs and timelines.

In future, there will be more COTS products available to satisfy many of the business process requirements for the companies and more organizations will adopt COTS products instead of creating custom programs, One way to model and automate the business process is by using the **Business Process Management** (**BPM**) software. That can also manage and optimize the business processes across organizational divisions, systems, and applications.

The evolution of business process modeling

The BPM technology is rapidly evolving as a platform that creates business applications. Processes can now be identified, managed, measured, and aligned to business organizations and functions.

Earlier, industry leaders created their own specifications for business process management without the existence of a standard body. Some of the earlier standards for BPM and organizations responsible for creating those standards are as follows:

- **WSFL**: Web Services Flow Language (Created by IBM)
- **XLANG**: XML-based extension of Web Services Description Language (Created by Microsoft)
- **BPEL4WS**: Business Process Execution Language for web services (Created by Siebel, SAP, IBM, and Microsoft)
- **BPEL4People**: WS-BPEL extension for people (Created by IBM and SAP in 2005)
- **WS-BPEL 2.0**: Web Services Business Process Execution Language (OASIS)

The standard organization **Object Management Group (OMG)** currently manages the following specifications for BPM:

- BPMN 1.0 published in 2004
- BPMN 1.1 released in 2008
- BPMN 1.2 released in 2009
- BPMN 2.0 released in 2011

Many software vendors that create new software platforms to support the business process management are as follows:

- Oracle BPM Suite (Business Process Management)
- Oracle BPA Suite (Business Process Analysis)
- Business Process Management by IBM
- TIBCO Business Process Management
- webMethods Business Process Management by SoftwareAG
- SAP NetWeaver Business Process Management
- JBoss Business Process Management (jBPM) Suite by Redhat
- Activiti Business Process Management

Traditionally, in IT we used to create business process diagrams but now the focus is shifting and business users want to control the business process to align business processes with corporate adjectives, optimize business costing, and business flow.

The availability of a new modeling tool enables business users to create business process models without any help from the developers.

Business Process Management (BPM)

The main purpose of the BPM software is to create a system that requires complex workflow and provide flexibility to update the workflow. Some of these process scenarios are order processing, billing integration, order fulfillment, credit validation and so on. The BPM software platform is on its way to maturity.

Some of the BPM software vendors claim that businesses can make changes to the process models and reflect the changes in the production environment without engaging the IT development team. However, most of the existing BPM tools allow business users to change the process but the IT team has to be involved in the development and deployment. The future may be that a business analyst can make changes to the process and then businesses can directly make changes to the production without a detailed development and deployment process.

One of the major issues of BPM system implementation is that the software container itself gets complex such as Oracle BPM. As shown in the following diagram, the **WebLogic** server platform is a Java program deployed along with **JVM**. The **SOA Suite** is a set of web applications deployed on top of the **WebLogic** server platform. The **BPM Suite** is another set of applications deployed on top of the **SOA Suite**. The **SOA Suite** and **BPM Suite** require **Oracle Database Server Platform** as well. More programs and server platforms add more complexity and that requires high CPU and memory to execute a process. For simple processes these tools can be heavy.

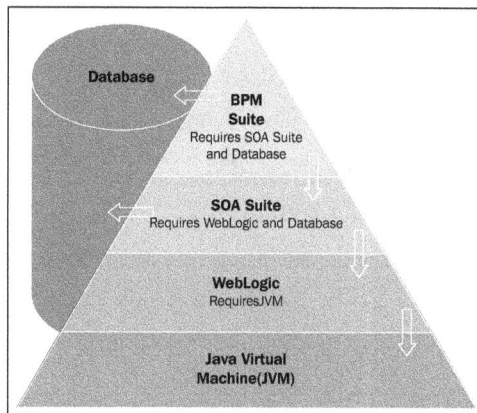

The BPMN specification has several process modeling notations for integrating processes communication and handling exceptions, and working of arrays of data. BPMN is a simple diagram with a small set of graphical elements that represent the business process.

Adaptability and efficiency matters for business processes to stay competitive and relevant in the market place. One of the key questions is how you can make it more efficient by changing it based on the business changes and implement the changes without any delay.

All business functions have several related structured activities. The end result will be a product or service. The business notations can be used for capturing the structured activities. After creating the business process models, the business notations need to be executed to achieve the results. Each process can have attributes and several processes. Combining multiple business processes creates the process for the entire organization.

The programming language for business process is **Business Process Execution Language (BPEL)** or **Business Process Model and Notation (BPMN)**. Some of the modeling tools that you can use in order to produce BPEL artifacts are as follows:

*   ARIS
*   Visio
*   BPM Composer
*   Enterprise Architect

The BPM software can be used to automate and integrate processes that span across multiple applications within and outside your organization. BPM can integrate the business partner systems as well. It bridges the gap between IT and businesses. BPM enables business users to manage and continually improve the business process by defining, measuring, and optimizing the processes. The major milestones of a BPM lifecycle are as follows:

*   Identifying key business processes
*   Designing
*   Modeling
*   Execution
*   Monitoring and reporting
*   Optimization

Oracle BPM Suite and BPA Suite

Oracle has the following two products that enable Business Process Management:

- Oracle BPM Suite (Oracle Business Process Management Suite)
- Oracle BPA Suite (Oracle Business Process Analysis Suite)

Oracle BPA Suite is for enterprise-wide modeling. BPM Suite is for the execution of BPMN. Architects and business analysts can use BPA Suite for modeling enterprise-wide architectures and processes. One can model an entire organization's strategy and business process using BPA Suite.

Both BPM Suite and BPA support BPMN modeling and notations. Apart from BPMN, BPA Suite supports modeling models such as UML and **EPC (Event-driven Process Chain** notation). EPC is one of the available modeling languages that describe business processes and workflows. BPM Suite supports only BPMN.

A comparison of BPA, BPM, and SOA Suite for reference is as follows:

SOA Suite - Oracle BPEL Process Manager	✓ BPEL Process Manager (Execute) ✓ Business Activity Monitoring (BAM) ✓ Business Rules & Mediator ✓ IDE (JDeveloper) BPEL Process Designer (Implement & Deploy)
BPA Suite - Oracle Business Process Analysis Suite	✓ Enterprise Business process modeling tool ✓ Business Process Architect ✓ Business Process Publisher ✓ Business Process Repository
BPM Suite - Oracle Business Process Manager Suite	✓ BPMN Execution Engine ✓ BPEL Execution Engine (SOA Suite) & J2EE container (WebLogic) included ✓ IDE (BPM Studio - Part of Jdeveloper) ✓ Business Process composer (Web based process modeling tool)

As shown in the following diagram, the execution engine for models created by using the BPA Suite is either BPM Suite or SOA Suite. You can use BPA suite as a simulation engine for processes. However, we must use Oracle BPM Suite for execution in run time environment. As seen in the screenshot, we are making use of the following components:

- Oracle BPA Suite/ARIS/Business Process Composer: For modeling and simulation

- BPM Suite/SOA Suite: As the execution engine

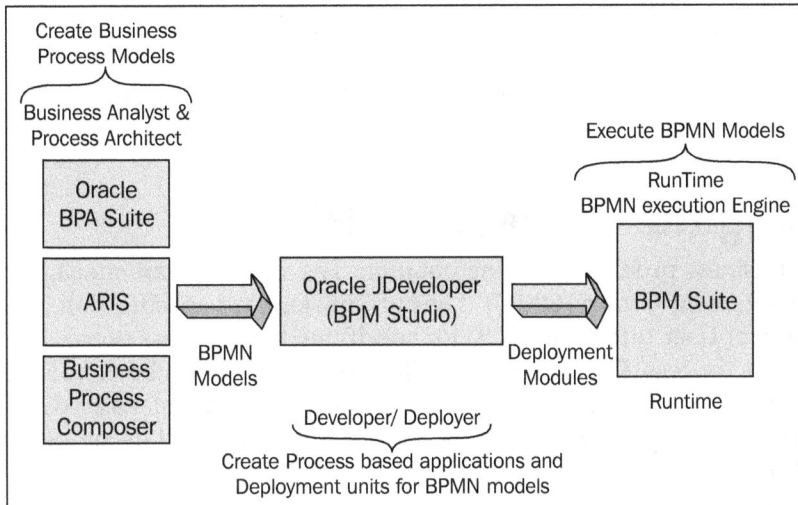

A brief description of the use cases of the components listed in the preceding diagram is as follows:

- **Oracle Business Process Composer** is a web-based tool for creating and customizing business process models

- **Oracle BPA Suite** provides comprehensive modeling, simulation of the models, and analysis of the models to support enterprise-wide business processes

- **BPM Studio** is part of **Oracle JDeveloper** that can be used for creating process-based applications based on models created using BPA Suite, ARIS or Composer.

- **BPM Suite** is a run time execution engine for BPMN

Oracle BPM Software consists of a set of programs that runs on top of Oracle SOA Suite. It manages the business process including the modeling, deployment, execution, monitoring, management, and error handling. The modeling is done using BPM Suite which is a part of JDeveloper. You can use Oracle BPA Suite or ARIS for creating models. Also, use BPM Suite for executing the BPMN models. The following table provides an idea of the container usage for implementing a BPM system:

Functional Component	Container
BPEL	SOA Suite
BPMN	BPM Suite
Models	BPA Suite or ARIS
Integrated Development Environment (IDE)	JDeveloper
JMS, EJB, JSP, and servlet	WebLogic

Modeling the process – BPMN

BPMN is a business process modeling notation. The standards are managed by **Object Management Group (OMG)**. The current standard specification is BPMN 2.0. It is a **Graphical User Interface (GUI)** for specifying the business process. You can create business process diagrams using BPMN notations. It can be Private-Internal, Abstract-Public, or Collaboration-Global. It consists of several steps associated with the organization's business process. BPMN eventually will decompose into different BPELs.

OMG BPMN 2.0 specification explains the notations of BPMN modeling. It mainly has Objects and Roles. Objects consists of Activities (Process, Tasks), Events (Start, End, Intermediate), Flow (Sequence, Message), and Gateways (Parallel, If).

BPM Studio

Oracle BPM Studio is part of Oracle JDeveloper that enables developers to create process-based applications. You need to add JDeveloper BPM studio extensions for enabling BPM. Refer to the following steps:

1. Select **Check for Updates** from the **Help** menu of JDeveloper, as shown in the following screenshot:

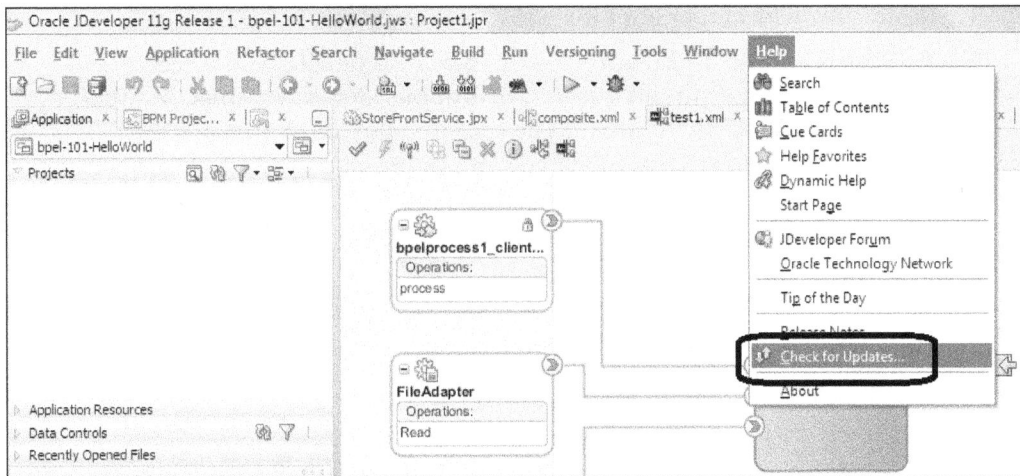

2. Select **Oracle Fusion Middleware Products** and **Official Oracle Extensions** from the initial screen. Then, select **Updates** and click on **Next**.

3. Next, select **Oracle BPM studio 11.1.1.6.0.15.53** and click on **Next**, as shown in the following screenshot:

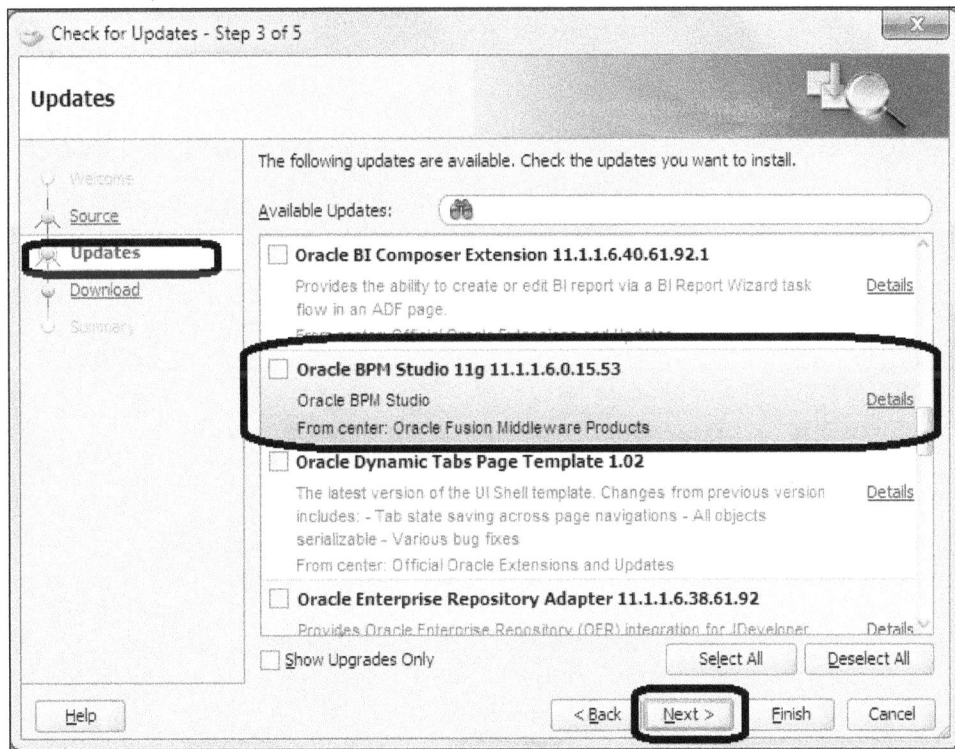

4. Restart the JDeveloper after installing these updates.

5. You can create the BPMN process by creating a new BPMN project from JDeveloper. You can select **Synchronous**, **Asynchronous**, **Manual**, or **Reusable Process** from the **Type** selection box, as shown in the following screenshot:

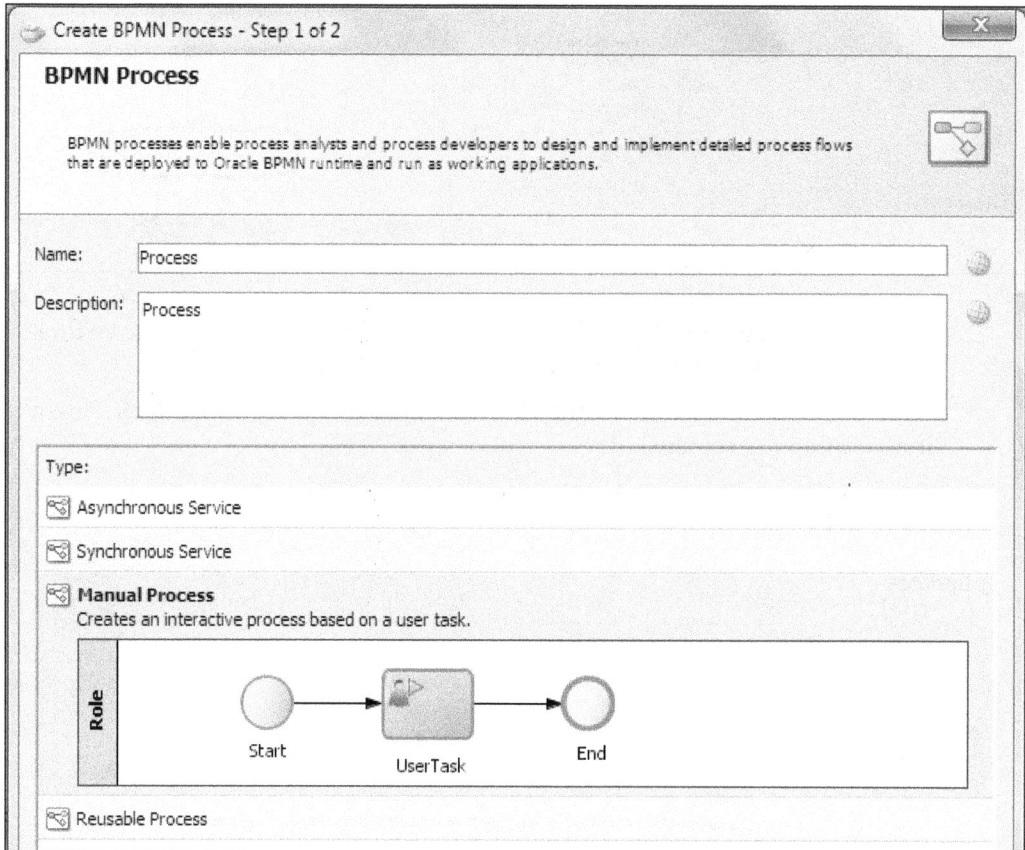

6. You can select different BPMN notations from the **Design** window, as shown in the following screenshot:

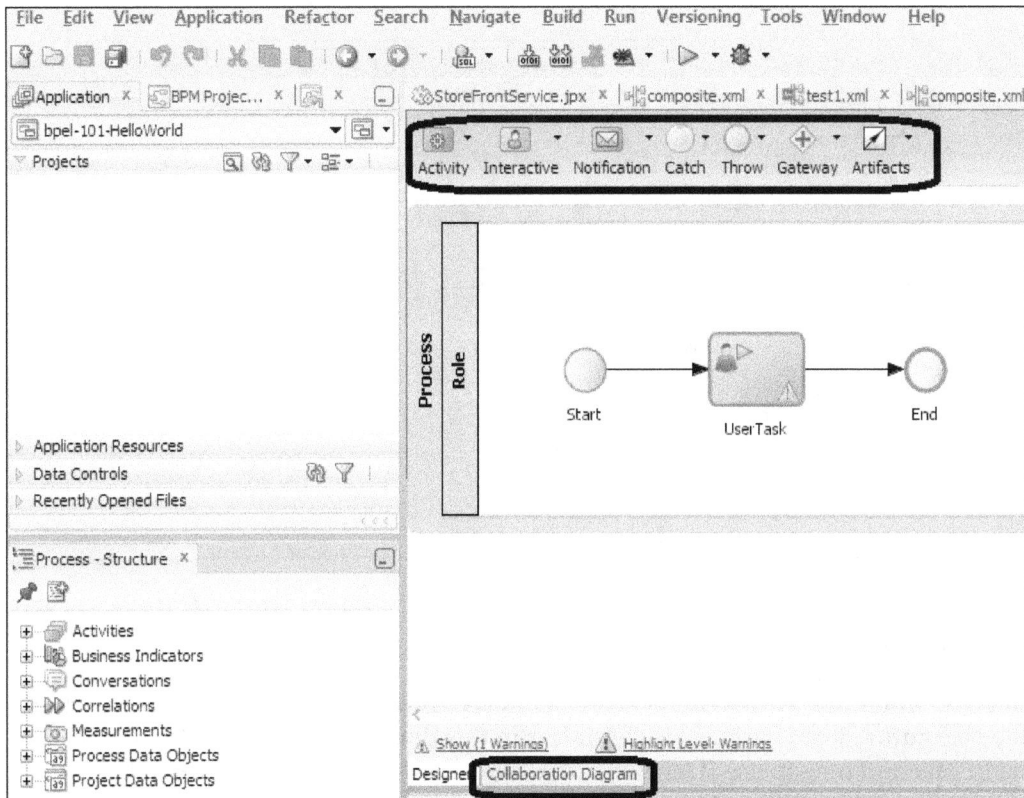

7. You can drag and drop different BPMN activities to the process editor to create a BPMN flow.

8. You can also add documentation or properties by right-clicking on BPMN notations and selecting **Properties** from the menu, as shown in the following screenshot:

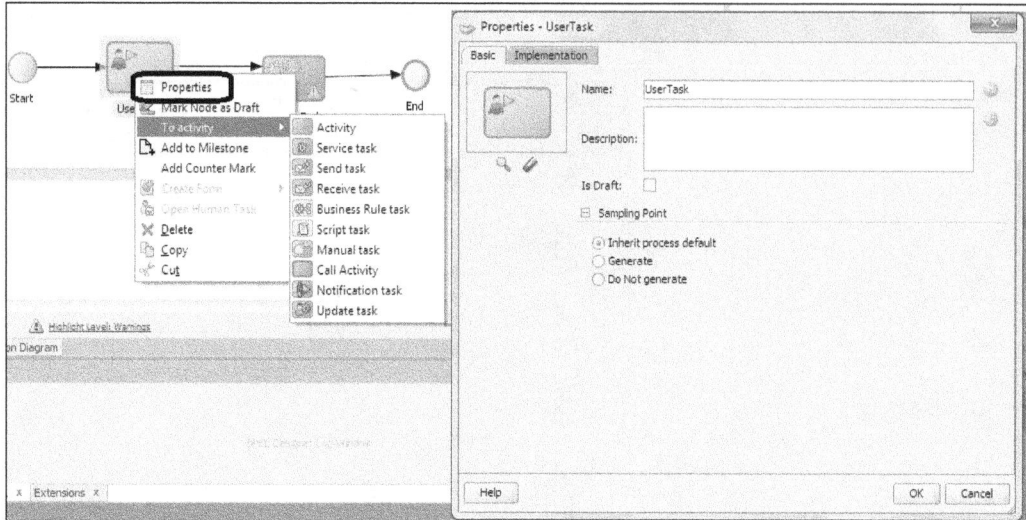

Summary

In this chapter, we learned the evolution of process modeling and what to expect in the near future from various stack holders in this domain. We also got an overview on BPMN and how to use JDeveloper to design and develop process models using BPMN. In the next chapter, we will learn the troubleshooting techniques for systems running BPEL processes.

12
Troubleshooting Techniques

Application platforms such as SOA Suite go through various issues during design, deployment, and runtime. In this chapter, our primary focus is to learn the troubleshooting techniques for commonly-found issues of a composite application deployment and runtime with the Oracle SOA Suite BPEL Process Manager. Usually, SOA composite applications runtime health depends on external service's endpoints and user activities. Therefore, runtime issues may pop up without any changes in the software and the systems managed within your organization but maybe due to the increased user activities, external updates, and/or network issues.

The following diagram shows the BPEL composite application technology stack. The troubleshooting requires knowledge in different components within the stack for resolving BPEL composite application issues.

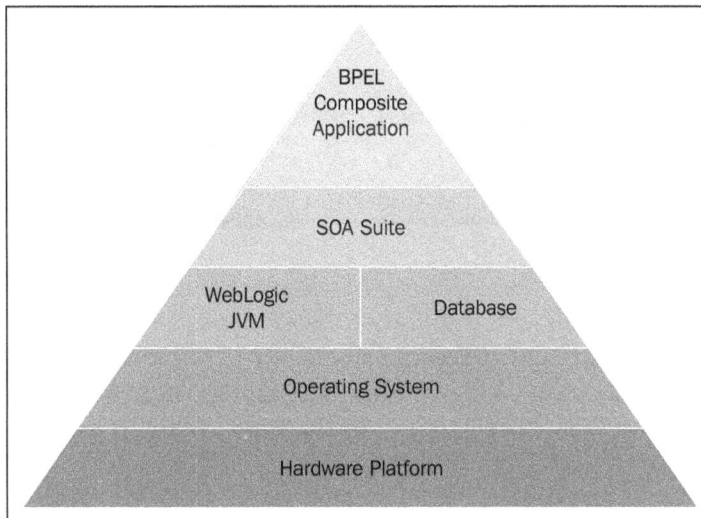

JVM issues

The Oracle SOA Suite application runs within a **Java Virtual Machine (JVM)**. Therefore, the following JVM-related issues can happen with your SOA composite application platform:

- **JVM crash**: This is a rare issue but does happen in some deployments. Please ensure that you have got the correct and Oracle SUN certified Java binaries for your server platform. Even a small mismatch can cause the JVM to crash.

- **OutofMemory errors and Memory leaks**: If the initial deployment throws OutOfMemory errors then go ahead and tune the JVM size as discussed in *Chapter 7, Performance Tuning – Systems Running BPEL Processes*. If you are randomly getting OutofMemory errors, it is most likely your allocated memory is not sufficient for the thread count configured for the application server(s). Go back to testing lab and run the load scenarios to identify memory and thread count settings. One must identify the root cause for memory leaks as this is usually due to the bad application design, third party library bugs, and/or implementation. It is a leading practice, to restart application server(s) periodically until a permanent fix is identified for the memory leak issues.

The performance of the garbage collector is very important for an application's performance. An application that spends 10 percent of its time in garbage collection can lose 75 percent of its throughput when scaled out to 32 processors.

As shown in the following screenshot, one of the common errors from JVM is `OutOfMemoryError` exception:

```
Exception in thread "main" java.lang.OutOfMemoryError: Java heap space
        at java.util.Arrays.copyOf(Unknown Source)
        at java.lang.AbstractStringBuilder.expandCapacity(Unknown Source)
        at java.lang.AbstractStringBuilder.append(Unknown Source)
        at java.lang.StringBuffer.append(Unknown Source)
        at gRapid.fetch(gRapid.java:214)
        at gRapid.main(gRapid.java:308)
```

Adjusting JVM memory parameters will resolve most of the memory issues including OutOfMemoryError exceptions. Increasing the minimum and maximum heap size along with the perm size is one of the solutions for resolving OutOfMemoryError exceptions. It is recommended that you use 80 percent of available host memory as JVM maximum memory and save the remaining for the operating system and other processes. If you are running multiple JVM(s) to run an admin server and multiple managed servers then it is recommended to create a dedicated memory share for each JVM from the 80 percent of the available host memory.

One can use a large heap size provided that it is not causing the system to "swap" pages to the disk. But it is recommended to not keep the value very high; setting up a very high heap size might lead to wasted memory and that makes full garbage collection slower and garbage collection occurs less frequently. The objective here is to utilize the largest JVM size that has the smallest window for full garbage collection for an application on a system.

The 32-bit operating system caps the conceptual heap size to around 4 GB. Individual 32-bit operating system's JVM heap size varies anywhere from 2 GB to less than 4 GB. The 64-bit heap size restriction is very high and it can be assumed that it has no restrictions for currently available server platforms. JVM parameters are a part of SOA/WebLogic startup scripts or domain environment configurations.

A sample JVM configuration is as follows:

```
-Xms4096M -Xmx4096M -XX:PermSize=1024M -XX:MaxPermSize=1024M
```

JVM Parameters		Guidelines
-XX:newSize=128m (Young Generation -Min)	High means - Less often Minor collection occur	Set -XX:NewSize to be one-fourth the size of the max heap size.
-XX:MaxNewSize=128m (Young Generation-Max)		Larger Young Generation means smaller Tenured
-Xms512m & -Xmx512m	80% of available memory	Set min heap (-Xms) equal to the max heap size (-Xmx) to minimize garbage collections.
Very High Heap Size	Full GC is slower & GC Occurs less frequently.	Setting too high can cause wasted memory. 32-bit OS cap the heap size at between 1.5 and 2.5GB. 64-bit do not have such restrictions.

JVM troubleshooting tools

Some of the JVM troubleshooting tools are as follows:

- **Logfile messages**: Gather more information from logfiles by adding additional troubleshooting parameters as part of the JVM configuration.
  - The sample JVM parameters that can be added as part of the JVM configuration is -verbose:gc, -XX:+PrintGC, -XX:+PrintGCDetails, -XX:+PrintGCTimeStamps, and -XX:+HeapDumpOnOutOfMemoryError

- ° `-XX:+PrintGC`: Provides the basic information at every garbage collection.

- ° `-XX:+PrintGCDetails`: Provides the size of live objects before and after garbage collection for the various generations, the total available space for each generation and the length of time the collection took.

- ° `-XX:+PrintGCTimeStamps`: Provides the timestamps at the start of each collection, helps you correlate garbage collection logs with other logged events.

- ° `-XX:+HeapDumpOnOutOfMemoryError`: Provides a heat dump when an out of memory error occurs for an application.

- **Java Visual VM tool**: It federates several existing tools, including `jConsole`, `jstat`, `jinfo`, `jstack`, and `jmap`. It is available from JDK 6. To start the **JVisualVM**, go to the bin directory of the JDK install and invoke the `jvisualvm` application. Please refer to *Chapter 7, Performance Tuning – Systems Running BPEL Processes*, for details.

- **Other widely used tools**: Some of the other available tools are Jprobe, Jconsole, HPROF Heap Profiler, Eclipse Memory Analyzer, IBM Heap, and Thread Analyzer.

- **JVM Utilities**: Some of the other JVM utilities are `jps`, `jmap`, `jinfo`, `jhat`, `jstack`, and so on.

  - ° `jps`: Lists all JVM processes

  - ° `jmap`: Prints heap memory usages and instance counts by classes and dumps the entire heap to a file

  - ° `jinfo`: Checks the virtual options

  - ° `jhat`: Browses a heap dump file with a web interface

  - ° `jstack`: Dumps thread stack traces and find any deadlocks

Linux troubleshooting commands

It is important to gather troubleshooting information at the operating system level to identify infrastructure issues. The operating system commands provide detailed information about SOA container behavior that can further assist us in identifying potential issues. Some of the most useful Linux commands for troubleshooting SOA Suite issues are as follows:

- `top`: This command gives you CPU and memory utilization statistics. The following command creates a text file with CPU and memory utilization:

```
$top -b -n 1 > cpuload.txt
```

As shown in the following screenshot, the `top` command provides
information about Memory and CPU utilization:

```
[singhj@soahost ~]$ top -b -n 1
top - 18:13:48 up 78 days, 21:03,  2 users,  load average: 0.03, 0.04, 0.00
Tasks:  64 total,   1 running,  63 sleeping,   0 stopped,   0 zombie
Cpu(s):  0.1%us,  0.1%sy,  0.4%ni, 99.3%id,  0.2%wa,  0.0%hi,  0.0%si,  0.0%st
Mem:   2059768k total,  1915284k used,   144484k free,   374808k buffers
Swap:  4194296k total,        0k used,  4194296k free,  1230968k cached

  PID USER      PR  NI  VIRT  RES  SHR S %CPU %MEM    TIME+  COMMAND
    1 root      15   0 10344  672  564 S  0.0  0.0  0:04.20 init
    2 root      RT  -5     0    0    0 S  0.0  0.0  0:00.00 migration/0
    3 root      34  19     0    0    0 S  0.0  0.0  0:00.21 ksoftirqd/0
    4 root      RT  -5     0    0    0 S  0.0  0.0  0:00.00 watchdog/0
    5 root      10  -5     0    0    0 S  0.0  0.0  0:01.21 events/0
    6 root      10  -5     0    0    0 S  0.0  0.0  0:01.19 khelper
   23 root      10  -5     0    0    0 S  0.0  0.0  0:00.00 kthread
   27 root      10  -5     0    0    0 S  0.0  0.0  0:00.26 kblockd/0
   28 root      20  -5     0    0    0 S  0.0  0.0  0:00.00 kacpid
  188 root      19  -5     0    0    0 S  0.0  0.0  0:00.00 cqueue/0
  191 root      19  -5     0    0    0 S  0.0  0.0  0:00.00 khubd
  193 root      10  -5     0    0    0 S  0.0  0.0  0:00.00 kseriod
```

- `ps`: This command gives a list of processes running on the machine.
  The following commands will create a text file with processor output:

  $ps -fea > processes.txt

  The command $ps -ef | grep java will list all the Java processes that
  are running.

  The command $ps -eLf | grep <Userid> | wc -l will provide the
  number of open files count by the SOA Suite container Userid.

- `strace`: The `strace` command provides debugging information about
  system calls. It is very similar to the `truss` command.

  $strace -f -p <wls pid> -o wls.strace.log

- `vmstat` {frequency in sec} {number of updates}: This command gives you
  CPU, memory, and IO stats for a virtual machine.

- `ar -r` : This command provides the system statistics including memory
  information. You can also collect the performance data to a file using the
  `sar` command.

- `mpstat` : This command provides the processor stats.

- `netstat` : This command provides the network statistics. The following commands list the incoming and outgoing network connections to a text file.

  ```
  $netstat -na > network.txt
  $netstat -nr
  $route -nee
  $ifconfig -a
  ```

- The following commands will provide information about the host's configuration within your Linux server:

  - Host network configuration

    ```
    $cat /etc/sysconfig/network
    ```

  - Host IP address and fully qualified name

    ```
    $cat /etc/hosts
    ```

  - Resolve DNS server

    ```
    $cat /etc/resolv.conf
    ```

  - `traceroute` : This command gives the network route details between the client and server taken at a given time.

  - `kill -e {pid}`: This command takes the thread dump. Replace {pid} with the JVM process ID. The thread dump is useful for analyzing the `stuckthread` error.

- `df -k`: This command gives the disk utilization in kilo bytes. Sometimes you will get file full errors as the disk space may be fully occupied due to logfiles. The file `/etc/fstab` provides additional information about the disk configuration.

- `/var/log/messages` : This command provides the system event messages and `/var/log/errors.log` provides the system errors logs

- `telnet {host} {port}`: This command helps to validate the network route and firewall is open for a client–server connection. You should always ensure that the external services are able to communicate using telnet before adding those services with BPEL.

- `lsof | wc -l`: This command provides the count of open processes. The following command will list the complete list of open files:

  ```
  $ /usr/sbin/lsof > openfiles.txt
  ```

- The following scripts provide details of LSOF commands to list the open files. Sometimes, SOA Suite container creates the open file error; the following scripts provide necessary outputs to gather troubleshooting information:

```
pids=$( ps -fea | grep java | grep -v grep | awk '{ print $2}' )
while [ 0 ]; do
for p in $pids; do
ts=$( date +%FT%H%M )
/usr/sbin/lsof -p $p > ofiles_${p}_${ts}.txt
done
sleep 300
done
```

- `hostname`: This command provides information about the hostname and server details:

```
$uname -n OR
$hostname -a -s -d -f
```

- `ethtool`: This command provides information about network interface settings. Custom changes may be required on the network interface for optimum performance for SOA Suite.

- The following commands provide the Linux version. Identifying the Linux version is important as most of the Oracle support tickets require Linux version information.

```
$cat /proc/version - Linux version information
$cat /etc/redhat-release
$lsb_release -a
$uname -mrs
```

- `sysctl - a`: This command allows you to change the kernel parameter during boot time. The `sysctl -w net.ipv4.ip_forward="1"` command will change the Linux kernel variable in `/proc/sys/kernal/sysrq`.

- `vi /etc/sysctl.conf`: This command modifies to make the changes permanent.

- The following command is used to find information from logfiles or directories:

```
$find / -type f -name '*search string*' -print
$slocate '*search string*'
Find and replace a file in linux
find ./ -name ".search string " | xargs rm -Rf


# Use either of the following commands to recursively perform a
grep from the current directory.
$find . \( -name '*' \) -print -exec grep $1 {} \;
$find . -name '*' -exec grep $1 {} \; -print
$find . -name '*' -type f -exec grep -1 $1 {} \;
```

Application issues

Always look at the logfiles for identifying the error messages. Logfiles should be observed to identify issues and error messages to identify the root cause. Use the logfile status as info for collecting more data. You must know the location of all the logfiles. You have domain, managed server, application, and container and JVM logs to help for troubleshooting.

Some of the most re-occurring issues with SOA Suite application are as follows:

- **ClassNotFoundException errors**: This can be caused by either filesystem corruption or if one fails to load the jar needed for newly-added features for your SOA composite application. In the case of filesystem corruptions, restore it from the backup or perform a green field install. On the other hand, while adding new features simply ensure that you got all the jar libraries needed with this release. Usually, if the deployment steps failed to mention all the jar files added during the design and development it gets caught while deploying in the QA and staging environments following the deployment steps document provided.

- **FileNotFoundException**: The application runtime expects a file or directory structure available to read and/or write configuration and application data files. Ensure that the file and directory structure is available for the application servers running the application and the user running the application servers have the right filesystem permissions to read and/or write files.

- **Too many open files**: The default OS settings especially for any Unix-flavored operating systems including Linux. This is a common error for a high traffic Oracle SOA application platform. Update `ulimit`, also known as file pointers setting on the system level and for the user running the application server's JVM. In our case, it is the WebLogic user. The following Linux command provides details of soft and hard file descriptor limits:

```
$ ulimit -Sn -Hn
```

  The `ulimit -Hn` command shows the hard limit and `-Sn` shows the soft limit.

  Configure the WebLogic user soft and hard file descriptor limits as follows (please use the value appropriate for your environment):

```
$ vi /etc/security/limits.conf


weblogic soft nofile 32768
weblogic hard nofile 32768
```

  Please make sure that the system-level file descriptor limit is higher than the user value. The following command provides the system-level file descriptor limit:

```
$ cat /proc/sys/fs/file-max
```

- **Stuckthread error messages**: Runtime Stuckthread must be analyzed for its root cause and you correct them as these consume the threads that are permanently not doing any work for us and impacts the system's scalability. You can take the thread dump to identify the threads that are stuck and its reason. It is a leading practice to perform periodic restart of the application server(s) as a temporary fix for freeing system's resources consumed by Stuckthread(s) in a JVM of an application server(s). It is highly recommended that you handle the Stuckthread(s) events and exceptions gracefully for better availability and scalability. In other words, one must identify and implement the permanent fix for the Stuckthread(s). Most stuck thread issues occur due to an external system holding the WebLogic thread for processing. For example, if an SOA Suite or WebLogic connects to an external database or a system for data retrieval and it did not receive a response within a certain limit and also there is no time out configured, then the WebLogic thread goes to the stuck state. Eventually, WebLogic will run out of threads.

Database issues

The database connectivity issues are either due to incorrect drivers or network connectivity. It's easy to identify using the simple telnet command test to check that your application(s) servers have allowed the network route to make the connection to the database server(s). One must perform telnet tests for all the possible client-server connections between the application and the database servers. In this scenario, all the application servers are clients and the database servers are servers for the telnet tests. It is a leading practice to perform this test for a newly deployed SOA composite application platform.

On the other hand, please pick the database driver library that works and delivers load sharing and auto recovery from failover and failback of a database server node for a database cluster with more than two server nodes. It is a leading practice to validate load sharing, failover, and failback scenarios to rollout for production runtime and perform this validation every time you are either updating the database driver or database server technology.

We often fail to establish the worst case scenarios for all the database connections needed by all the application server(s) and batch server(s). When this happens, you will notice that the application server(s) are not able to create database connections randomly. In order to avoid this, one needs to understand the maximum database connections needed from all kinds of users such as application server(s), batch server(s), and power users such as DBA, support and business analyst. JDBC connection pools must be analyzed for possible maximum sizes instead of just initial or average connections normally established to the database platform.

CPU spikes

Application server(s) running the Oracle SOA Suite can experience the CPU spikes for one of the following reason(s):

- **User activity**: The sudden peak in the user(s) requests can cause CPU spikes on the application server(s). The key is to understand the user types and their pay load and performance needs. For example, users sending individual real time transaction demands that these transactions are completed in the shortest possible time while batch and cron users won't mind waiting for the transactions to finish successfully. It is a leading practice to build separate platforms for serving real time end users and batch and cron users.

- **Request queuing**: The real spikes in the users' requests can also be caused by the CPU spikes that result in poor performance. You may plan to adjust your system architecture to avoid the queuing of users' requests by adding more application server(s).

- **Thread count**: High thread count setting in a server platform can cause CPU spikes as well. Identify an optimal setting for the thread count so that your server platform can handle it.

- **External processes**: Sometimes application batch jobs running on the application server can cause CPU spikes as well. You may have often noticed that backup, anti-virus, and logs compression task also causes the CPU spikes on the application server(s). Minimize these external tasks on the application server(s) to avoid the CPU spikes.

Load balancing issues

The load balancing solution you designed for your SOA Suite composite application must go through the functional validation for load sharing, failover, and failback.

A few facts before we worry about analyzing the load sharing issues. In the case of Active-Active load sharing between multiple sites, it is usually done through L7 load balancers; we are load balancing the users not the payload these users will bring to the application server(s). Ensure that the health checks are configured by the application server process. One should not share the service endpoints serviced by the different processes at the application server. We must validate if the health checks are working as we thought.

In some cases, you may find that the L7 load balancer is not able to perform the health checks implemented for a service endpoint. Ensure that there is a network route for the service endpoints' IP addresses and port from the L7 load balancer appliances.

If you notice that the server load sharing is not sending a fair share between servers, ensure that the least connection load sharing algorithm is used and L7 health checks are implemented for the application server health. In some cases, you may find the L4 load balancer is not able to perform the health checks implemented for a service endpoint running at the web/application server. Ensure that there is a network route for the service endpoints' IP addresses and port from the L4 load balancer appliances.

If a server or site is getting its share of users plus/minus 20 percent of the design time share, then load sharing is working fine. It is almost impossible to get the exact load sharing. For example, if there are three server(s) you may find these servers will get anywhere between 27 to 39 percent of the total users and if there are two server(s) you may find these servers will get anywhere between 40 to 60 percent of the total users.

SSL issues

We can categorize all the SSL issues into two categories; handshake failures and poor performance.

The SSL handshake failures are due to one of the following reason(s):

- **Expired certificates**: When the SSL server-side certificate is expired, you need to request the service provider to update the SSL certificate. It is a leading practice, if you are updating your SSL certificate don't use the old **Certificate Signing Request** (**CSR**) to request a new certificate. Always produce a CSR request with a new certificate key with the latest mandate on the key length. The present recommendations for SSL certificate key length is 2048.

- **Wrong site domain**: The most common mistake for site domains that are made is using `mysitedomain.com` versus `www.mysitedomain.com` and vice versa in the URL address.

- **Missing Certificate Authority (CA) in the trust store**: Install the root and intermediate CA into the trust store of SSL client application. In a client-server authentication or two-way SSL implementations we have a trust store at the server side as well.

- **Missing cipher suite**: Client and server not able to find common cipher suite to be used for encrypting the communication. This usually happens when one end is using an outdated SSL implementation. Install the missing cipher suites or update the SSL implementation.

SSL's poor performance is usually caused by not configuring an SSL cache. It is a leading practice to implement an SSL cache at web server(s) or leverage SSL offload to an L4 switch.

Network issues

Network issues are related to either the network performance or that the destination is not reachable. We need to work with the network and system engineering team to ensure that all the network interfaces are configured for full duplex to get the best possible network latency between the client and server. On the other hand, destination not reachable could be caused by the network and system firewalls or temporary network outage at either the server side or client side. The trace route command could assist you in analyzing the network issues related to the performance while a simple telnet command with trace route could help you identify the root cause for the destination not being reachable.

User activity issues

It is critical to understand the users' activities and their payload. Consider monitoring in place to produce cumulative system usage numbers and individual user system usage on a platform to quickly identify the root cause of most issues on a platform caused by the user activity. Don't produce system requirements for a peak load using average numbers that needs to be developed carefully for a business case. Sometimes, we may need to adjust the system architecture to deliver on newly developed user activity patterns. It is a leading practice to continuously update the load scenarios and validate for the system architecture deployed and identify and implement system improvements to align with user activities.

Verifying the server health

The Oracle SOA Suite BPEL Process Manager server health verification steps are as follows:

1. Verify if SOA Servers are up and running.

    Login to WebLogic administration `console http://{adminserver-host}:{adminserver-port}/console`, as shown in the following screenshot. The sever **State** must be **RUNNING** and **Health** must be **OK**, as shown in the following screenshot:

2. Ensure that the SOA-INFRA application is up and running.

   Login to the Oracle Enterprise Manager console `http://{adminserver-host}:{adminserver-port}/em` and verify if the **soa-infra** application is running or not, as shown in the following screenshot:

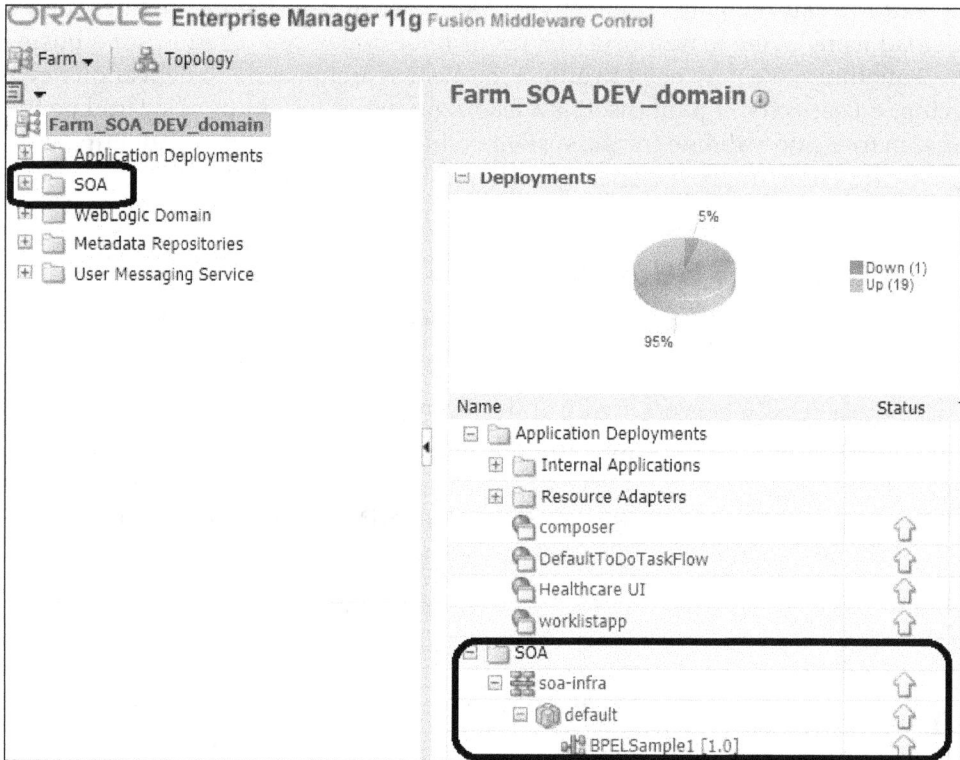

3. Please ensure that the admin server and database server are up and running. If not, please start them. Sometimes, both Admin and SOA servers are up and running, but SOA-INFRA may be down. You need to find the reason for SOA-INFRA down from the logfile.

4. One of the reasons could be that the database that hosts SOA metadata schemas may be down or you didn't start the database before starting the SOA middleware servers.

5. Check the database status by checking the data sources on the admin console (`http://{adminserver-host}:{adminserver-port}/console`). Right-click on the `WebLogic/domain/domain` directory and select **DataSource(s)**, as shown in the following screenshot. Select the **Monitoring** tab to verify the status of the data sources.

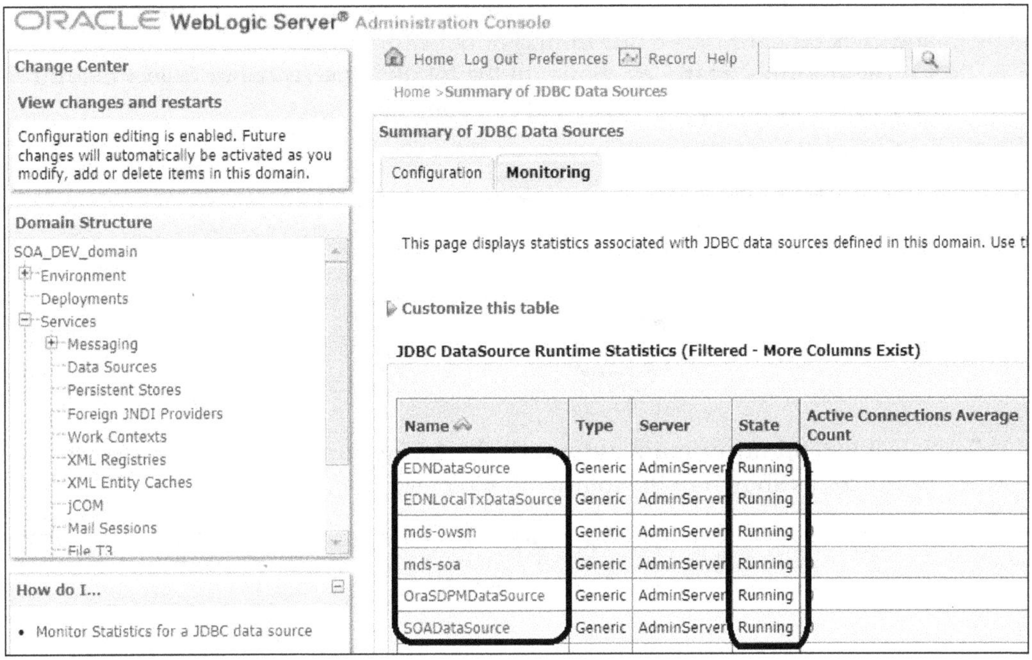

It is not possible to cover all the likely scenarios or list the possible errors here. Sometimes deleting the `tmp` folder in `/var/tmp/` and `servers/admin` from root user may help.

Extending to a domain

In some cases, you will get an error message wherein the domain has to be extended for certain functionalities. A brief description of the ways to extend the SOA domain is given as follows:

1. Go to `{ORACLE_HOME}/common/bin` or `Middleware/Weblogic/common/bin` and click on `config.sh` (for Linux) or `config.cmd` (Windows) to start the **Configuration Wizard**, as shown in the following screenshot. Select **Extend an existing WebLogic domain** and click on **Next**:

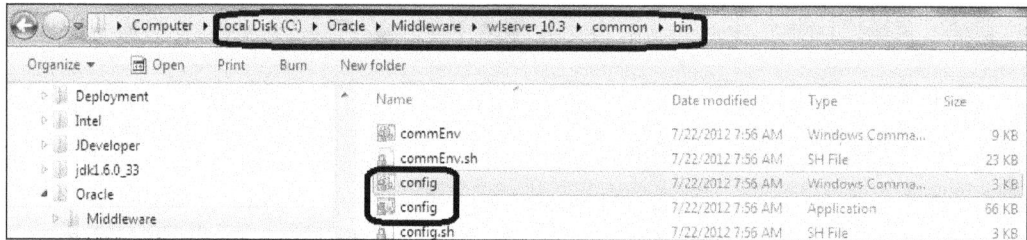

2. Select **Extend my domain automatically to support the following added products**, as shown in the following screenshot:

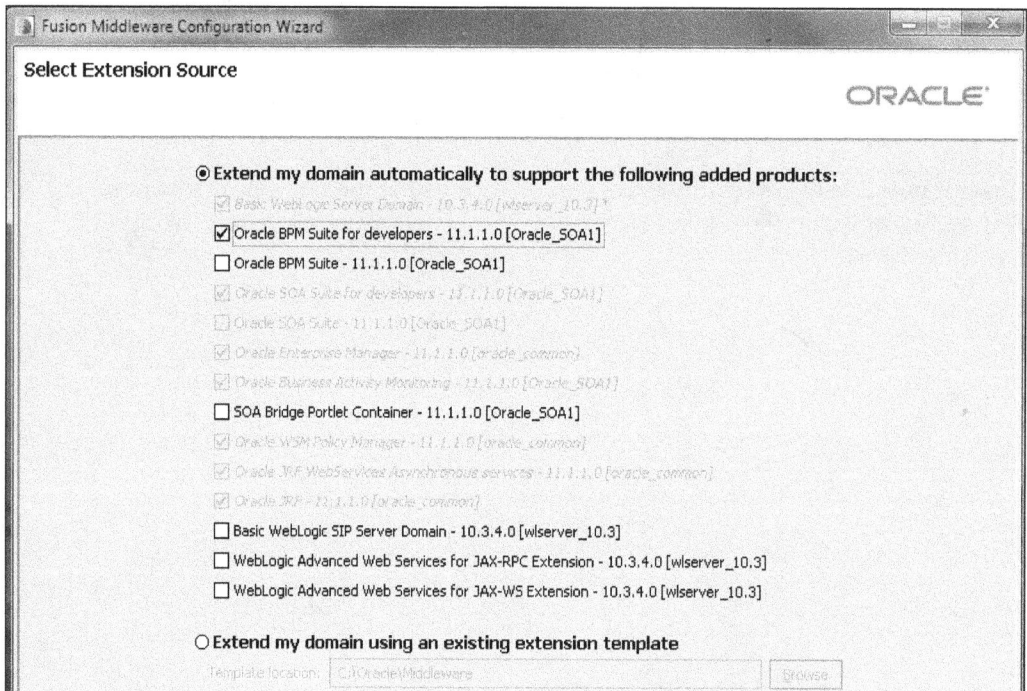

Oracle troubleshooting tools

Oracle provides several troubleshooting tools for helping you and Oracle support to solve issues within systems. You can open an SR ticket with Oracle support at `http://support.oracle.com`.

Oracle Remote Diagnostics Agent

Oracle Remote Diagnostic Agent collects diagnostic data (around 150 GB) that helps Oracle support to troubleshoot the issues. It is a set of diagnostic scripts written in Perl by Oracle that collects configuration and diagnostic data for Oracle support. It is usually installed as a part of SOA Suite install. Execute `/rda.sh` (for Linux) or `rda.cmd` (Windows) for collecting the diagnostic data. The output will be a set of HTML files that will be stored in the default directory `/rda/output`. It is a leading practice from the Oracle Support team to request the diagnostic data for your implementations.

As shown in the following screenshot, locate the `rda` executable file from your SOA directory and execute it for collecting the RDA output. You can upload the files to the Oracle support website (`http://support.oracle.com`) as part of your support ticket (SR).

WebLogic Diagnostic Framework

The purpose of the **WebLogic Diagnostic Framework (WLDF)** tool is to collect the diagnostic information from the application containers. The tool is based on configuration MBeans and is part of the WebLogic console. The tools have data creators, data collectors, data achievers, and WLDF image capture. Refer to the following steps:

1. As shown in the following screenshot, login to the WebLogic console (http://{adminserver-host}:{adminserver-port}/console) for configuring the diagnostic tool. Select **Diagnostic Modules** from the left navigation pane and click on **New**.

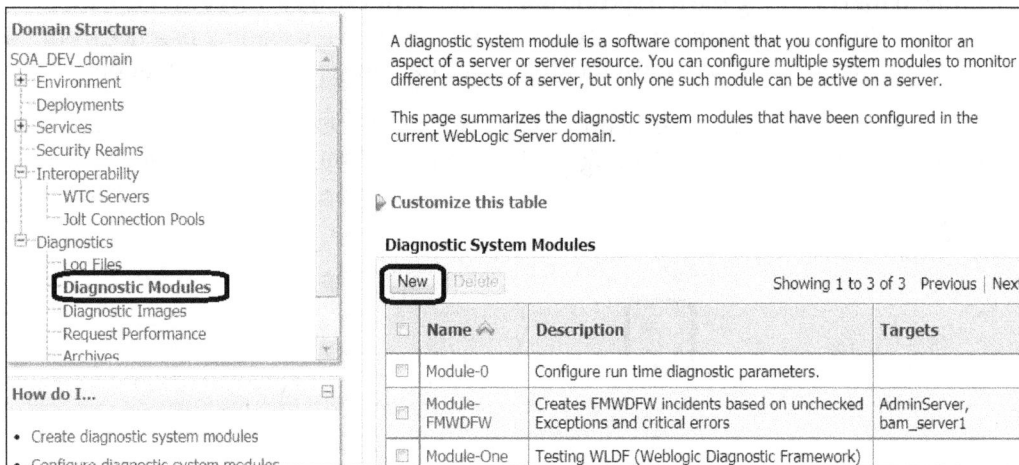

2. Select the diagnostic module, fill in the **Name** and **Description** fields, as shown in the following screenshot:

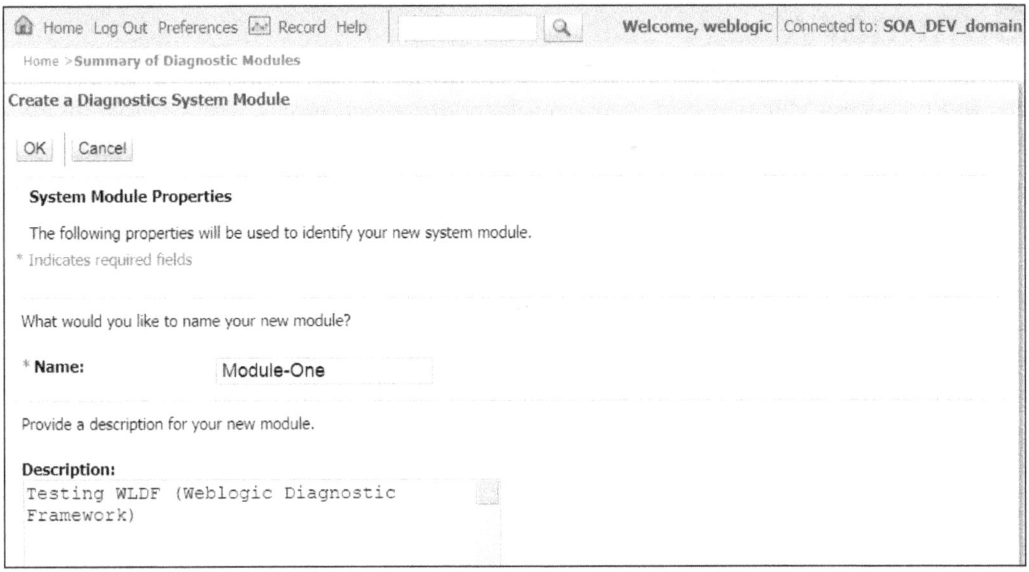

3. Create **Collected Metrics, Watches and Notifications**, and **Instrumentation** by clicking on the appropriate buttons, as shown in the following screenshot:

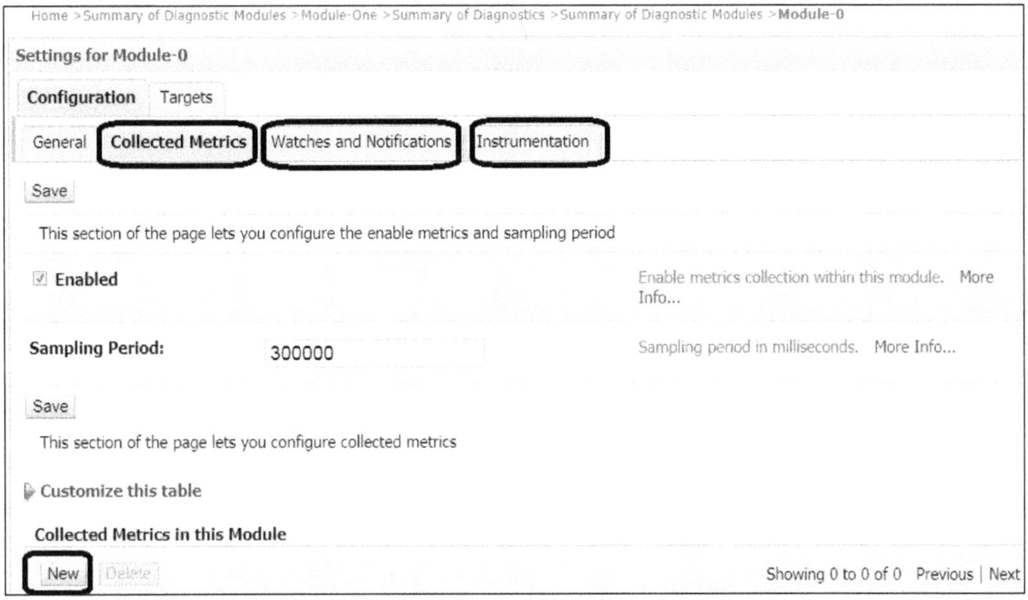

4. You need to select the appropriate MBeans to collect the data.

Summary

In this chapter, we learned the possible issues during deployment and runtime with the BPEL Process Manager and their troubleshooting techniques. The key takeaway is knowing all the possible reasons for an issue and then going through the process of elimination to identify the root cause of the issue. The art and science lies in ranking the possible reasons and selecting which one to eliminate first for an issue at hand.

This book provides you a complete handbook for technical fundamentals, hands-on tutorials, and industry-leading practices to deliver real-world enterprise SOA composite applications using Oracle SOA Suite BPEL Process Manager and JDeveloper platform. The key takeaway of this book are the industry-leading practices and the hands-on tutorials.

Index

Symbols

64-bit JVM 195
.ear (Enterprise Archive) file 59
<portType> element 88
.sar (SOA Archive) file 59
/var/log/messages command 280
-XX:+PrintGCDetails parameter 189
-XX:+PrintGC parameter 189
-XX:+PrintGCTimeStamps parameter 189
-XX:+PrintGC 278
-XX:+PrintGCDetails 278
-XX:+PrintGCTimeStamps 278

A

AcceptBacklog parameter 168
Access.log 154
Active - Active approach 261
Active - Passive approach 262
activities, BPEL
  about 62
  Invoke activity 63, 64
  Receive activity 63
  Reply activity 63
adapters
  about 77
  database adapter 79, 80
  file adapter 80
  JMS Adapter 81
  Web Service Adapter 81-83
adaptors
  Threadcount 202
Admin server log 12, 156, 157

ant-sca-compile.xml script 226
ant-sca-deploy.xml script 226
ant-sca-mgmt.xml script 226
ant-sca-package.xml script 226
ant-sca-test.xml script 226
ANT scripts
  about 223, 226
  ant-sca-compile.xml script 226
  ant-sca-deploy.xml script 226
  ant-sca-mgmt.xml script 226
  ant-sca-package.xml script 226
  ant-sca-test.xml script 226
Apache proxy plugin 252
  URL, for installing 255
application design, services-based
  about 170
  Enterprise Service Bus (ESB) 171
  service bus, use case 172, 173
  SOA Suite 171
Application Development Framework
      (ADF) 11
ar -r command 279
Assign activity 65
asynchronous BPEL processes
  about 98-100
  versus synchronous BPEL processes 71
audit level property 160, 161
Audit_Trial 203
Automatic Segment Space Management
      (ASSM) 203
Automatic Workload Repository. See AWR
AWR 203, 205

B

B2B console 12, 192, 193
backup 257
BEA 104
BEA AquaLogic Service Bus. *See* **Service Bus**
BPA Suite
  about 269
  and Oracle BPM Suite 268, 269
BPEL
  about 8, 9, 57, 87, 105, 267
  activities 58, 62, 63
  asynchronous processes 69, 70
  basic activities 64-66
  basic activities, creating 59-62
  code 9
  code, structure 58
  composite application technology stack 275
  fault and error handling activity 68
  Java code, calling from 92
  Java, invoking from 92
  process element 58
  service components 10
  services, monitoring 164-166
  structured activities 67, 68
  synchronous processes 69, 70
  syntax 9
BPEL, basic activities
  about 59-62
  Assign activity 65
  Compensate activity 66
  Empty activity 67
  Exit activity 66
  Invoke activity 65
  Receive activity 65
  RepeatUntil activity 66
  Reply activity 65
  Transform activity 65
  Wait activity 66
BPEL business processes
  deploying 47-52
  instances, managing 53, 54
  instances, testing 53, 54
  sample BPEL business processes, creating 41-47

BPEL process
  invoking, from Java 88, 89
  service, invoking from 89
BPEL Process Manager
  Oracle Database, installing 20-27
  Oracle JDeveloper, installing 14-17
  Oracle SOA Suite, installing 28-32
  SOA extensions, installing 17-19
  system components 13
BPEL Process Manager logging
  about 153
  Access.log 154
  Admin server log 156, 157
  audit level 160-164
  domain logs 154
  logging level 158-160
  managed server log 156, 157
  monitoring 164-166
BPEL Process Manager Threads 198
BPEL process, securing
  about 228, 229
  data security, at Rest 247, 248
  data security, in Transit 247, 248
  Enterprise Security Gateway 229, 230
  Network Firewall, with Intrusion Prevention System 246
  Oracle security products 242
  Oracle Web Service Manager (OWSM) 230
  Web Application Firewall (WAF) 247
BPEL, structured activites
  about 67
  flow 67
  forEach 68
  if 67
  pick 68
  scope 67
  sequence 68
  while 67
BPEL timeouts, configuring
  about 93
  EJB 's transaction timeout 96-98
  for Asynchronous BPELs 98, 100
  JTA Transaction Timeout, setting 93
  SyncMaxWaitTime parameter, changing 94, 95
  Transaction settings 96

BPEL variables 122
BPM
  about 266, 267
  BPM Suite 266
  evolution 265
  Oracle Database Server Platform 266
  SOA Suite 266
  WebLogic server platform 266
BPMN 10, 270
BPM Studio 269-273
BPM Suite. *See also* BPMN
BPM Suite
  about 266, 269
  and BPA Suite 268, 269
Bucketsets
  creating 136
Buffer Overflow 247
Business Process Execution Language. *See*
    BPEL
Business Process Execution Language for
    web services (BPEL4WS) 265
Business Process Management. *See* BPM
Business Process Model and Notation. *See*
    BPMN
Business Rule Management Systems
    (BRMS) 131
Business Rules engine
  about 131
  adding, as BPEL process part 132, 134
  bucketsets, creating 136
  creating 134
  facts, creating 135
business services 249
Business-to-Business (B2B) integration 169

C

call-and-forget service 70
Canonical Data Models 218
catch 68
CatchAll 68
Certificate Signing Request (CSR) 286
ClassNotFoundException errors 282
client
  and web services, interaction 104
client-server authenticated SSL 247

cluster environment 252
Commercial off-the-shelf. *See* COTS
Compensate activity 66
Composer 12, 194
composite.xml file 222
ConcurrentThreshold 202
correlation
  about 74
  manual correlation 74
  set 74
correlation set
  about 75
  associating 76
COTS 264
CPU spikes, SOA Suite
  about 284
  external processes 285
  request queuing 284
  thread count 285
  user activity 284
Create, Read, Update, and Delete (CRUD)
    data 78
Cross-Site Request Forgery (CSRF) 247
Cross-Site Scripting (XSS) 247
custom XPath functions
  about 116
  class 118
  creating 117
  JAR file, creating 119
  JDeveloper registering with 119
  SOA Suite, registering with 118, 119

D

Database. *See* Oracle Database
database adapter 79, 80
database, issues 284
database sessions 195
Data center(s)
  about 257
  application server(s), configuring 258, 259
  deployment architecture, options 258
  multi data center deployment 260
  web server(s), configuring 258, 259
decoupling 78
DefaultToDo 12, 194

Dehydration 149
Dehydration Store
  about 149, 203
  purging, options 150, 151
df -k command 280
discovery registry option 212
Distributed Denial of Service (DDoS) 247
DNS 211
domain, extending
  about 290
  Oracle Remote Diagnostics Agent 291
  Oracle troubleshooting, tools 291
  WebLogic Diagnostic Framework (WLDF)
    292, 293
domain logs 154
Domain Name Server. *See* DNS
Dynamic Monitoring Service (DMS) 12, 192

E

EDA 177
EJB 's transaction timeout 96, 97, 98
EM
  SOA composites, testing from 140, 141
EM Console 199
Empty activity 67
Enterprise Manager (EM) 12, 191
Enterprise Security Gateway 229, 230
Enterprise Service Bus (ESB) 171
EPC 268
ethtool command 281
Event-Driven Architecture. *See* EDA
event-driven interaction 178, 179
Event-driven Process Chain. *See* EPC
Exit activity 66
external processes 285

F

F5 253
facts
  creating 135
fault and error handling activity, BPEL
  about 68
  catch 68

CatchAll 68
  throw 69
file adapter 80
file descriptors 201
FileNotFoundException 282
first Layer 4/Local Server Load balancer/
    Local Traffic first Layer 4/Local Server
    Load balancer/Local Traffic Manager
    (L4/LSLB/LTM) 253
flow 67
flow activity, orchestration 109-111
forEach 68
Foundry 253

G

Garbage collection. *See* GC
garbage collector 276
GC
  about 184
  algorithm, selecting 187
  JVisualVM 188, 189
  Major Garbage Collection (majorGC) 185
  Minor Garbage Collection (minorGC) 185
  permanent generation 186
  tool 188
  tuning 186, 187
GC algorithm, selecting
  about 187
  heap size, selecting 188
  NewSize, selecting 187
global load balancers 253
Global Policy Attachment (GPA) 232
Global Server Load Balancer (GSLB) 200
Global Traffic Manager (GTM) 200
Global Transaction Timeout parameters. *See*
    JTA Transaction Timeout
Graphical User Interface (GUI) 270
GridLink data source
  used, for connecting WebLogic with
    multiple Oracle RAC systems 256
GSLB configuration 200
GTM configuration 200

H

heap size
 selecting 188
hostname command 281
HTTPS 247
Human Task
 about 126, 179, 180
 BPEL process part 128-131
 components, used for implementing human
  workflow 84, 85
 creating 127
 standalone Human Task 127
 worklist application 126, 127
human workflow
 implementing, with Human Task
  components 84, 85

I

if 67
inbound messages
 emulating 146
Information Technology. See IT
Init.Ora 203
installation
 Oracle Database 20-27
 Oracle JDeveloper 14-17
 SOA extensions 18, 19
 SOA Suite 28-32
instances
 viewing, on JDeveloper 143
integration technologies
 history 8
interaction design patterns
 about 174
 asynchronous request and response 175
 one-way message 177
 single request and mandatory response 176
 single request and multiple responses 176
 single request and optional response 176
 synchronous request and response 174
intermediate registry option 212

Intrusion Detection and Prevention System
  (IDPS)
Intrusion Prevention System (IPS) 247
Invoke activity 63-65
IP addresses 246
IT 263
IXPathFunction interface 118

J

J2EE components 11
J2EE Connector Architecture. See JCA
Java
 BPEL process, invoking from 88, 89
 code, calling from BPEL 92
 invoking, from BPEL 92
Java Virtual Machine. See JVM
Java Visual VM tool 278
JCA 77
JCA adaptors
 ConcurrentThreshold 202
 MaxRaiseSize 202
 Threadcount 202
JDeveloper
 about 223
 design page 108
 instances, viewing 143
 installing 14-17
 messages, viewing 143
 SOA composites, testing from 142
 used, for attaching security policies
  235, 236
JDeveloper IDE 10
jhat 278
jinfo 278
jmap 278
Jmap (-histo:live pid) parameter 189
JMS Adapter 81
JMS modules 199
jps 278
jstack 278
JTA Transaction Timeout
 setting 93

JVisualVM 188, 189, 278
JVM
  about 184
  troubleshooting, tools 277
JVM, issues
  about 276
  JVM crash 276
  Linux troubleshooting commands 278-281
  OutofMemory errors and Memory leaks
    276
JVM troubleshooting, tools
  Java Visual VM tool 278
  JVM utilities 278
  Logfile messages 277
JVM, utilities
  jhat 278
  jinfo 278
  jmap 278
  jps 278
  jstack 278

L

L4 firewall rules 246
L4 load balancers 200, 201, 252
L4 (Transport Layer) 200
L7 load balancers 200
Launch Flow Trace button 141
legacy application 250
Linux, troubleshooting commands
  ar -r command 279
  df -k command 280
  ethtool command 281
  hostname command 281
  lsof | wc -l command 280
  mpstat command 279
  netstat command 280
  ps command 279
  strace command 279
  sysctl - a command 281
  telnet {host} {port} command 280
  top command 278
  /var/log/messages command 280
  vi /etc/sysctl.conf command 281
  vmstat command 279

load balancers
  about 200
  issues 285
  local load balancers 253
Local Policy Attachment (LPA) 232
Local Server Load Balancer (LSLB). *See* L4
  (Transport Layer)
Local Traffic Manager (LTM) 200
Logfile messages
  -XX:+PrintGC 278
  -XX:+PrintGCDetails 278
  -XX:+PrintGCTimeStamps 278
  about 277
logging level 158, 159
logging levels 198
LSLB configuration 201
lsnrctl status command 153
lsof | wc -l command 280
LTM configuration 201

M

Major Garbage Collection (majorGC) 185
managed server log 156, 157
management layer 208
MaxRaiseSize 202
MBean browser 167, 168
MDS (Metadata service) 26
mediator routing rules 197
mediator worker threads 197
Memory leaks 276
Memory_Target 203
Message Oriented Middleware (MOM)
  78, 81
messages
  viewing, on JDeveloper 143
MessagingService endpoint 12, 194
MessagingServices preferences 12, 194
Minor Garbage Collection (minorGC) 185
Model View Controller (MVC) framework
  11
mpstat command 279
multi data center deployment
  about 260
  Active - Active approach 261
  Active - Passive approach 262

N

netstat command 280
Network Firewall
  with Intrusion Prevention System (IPS) 246
network, issues 286
NewSize
  selecting 187
nonBlockingInvoke property 112

O

OAM. *See* Oracle Access Manager (Oblix
    COREid Access and Identity)
OASIS 221, 237
OASIS Web Services Business Process
    Execution Language. *See* WSBPEL
Object Management Group (OMG) 265, 270
OES 244
OHS plugin 252
OIM 243
operating system
  about 201
  adaptors 202
  file descriptors 201
ORA BAM 26
Oracle Access Manager (Oblix COREid
    Access and Identity) 245
Oracle BPA Suite. *See* BPA Suite
Oracle BPEL Process Manager
  about 74
  web applications, for troubleshooting issues
    151-153
Oracle BPM Studio. *See* BPM Studio
Oracle BPM Suite. *See* BPM Suite
Oracle Business Process Analysis Suite. *See*
    BPA Suite
Oracle Business Process Composer 269
Oracle Business Process Management Suite.
    See BPM Suite
Oracle Database
  installing 20-27
Oracle Database Server Platform 266
Oracle Enterprise Manager 223
Oracle Enterprise Service Bus (OSB) 170

Oracle Entitlement Server. *See* OES
Oracle Identity Federation (Oblix COREid
    Federation) 245
Oracle Identity Manager. *See* OIM
Oracle Identity Manager Connector 243
Oracle JDeveloper. *See* JDeveloper
Oracle Notification Service (ONS) 255
Oracle RAC
  about 255
  and WebLogic connecting, GridLink data
    source used 256
Oracle Real Application Clusters.
    See Oracle RAC
Oracle Registry 211
Oracle Remote Diagnostics Agent 291
Oracle Repository
  about 212
  discovery registry option 212
  intermediate registry option 212
  lifecycle model 212
  publishing registry option 212
  stanalone registry option 212
Oracle Secure Token Service 245
Oracle security products
  about 242
  OES 244, 245
  OIM 243
  Oracle Access Manager (Oblix COREid
    Access and Identity) 245
  Oracle Identity Federation (Oblix COREid
    Federation) 245
  Oracle Secure Token Service 245
  Oracle Virtual Directory (OctetString
    Virtual Directory Engine) 245
Oracle Service Bus. *See* Service Bus
Oracle Service Registry. *See* Service
    Registry
Oracle SOA Suite. *See* SOA Suite
Oracle SOA Suite server(s) 255
Oracle Virtual Directory (OctetString
    Virtual Directory Engine) 245
Oracle Web Service Manager. *See* OWSM
ORA SDPM 26
orchestration
  about 106-108

approach 107
custom XPath functions 116
custom XPath functions, creating 117
flow activity 109, 110, 111
process orchestration 106
scope activity 119-122
switch activity 112-115
while activity 112-115
order processing 57
Organization for the Advancement of Structured Information Standards. *See* OASIS
outbound messages
emulating 147, 148
OutofMemory errors 276
OWSM
about 230
implementation, example 239
secured service provider configuring, username tokens used 239, 240
security implementation, use cases 232
used, for attaching security policies 233, 234
WS-Security 236

P

Partner Link 90, 91
Payload validation and audit level 196
performance tuning
about 183
high-level plan 183
permanent generation 186
pick 68
process element 58
process orchestration 106
property aliases 76, 77
ps command 279
publishing registry option 212

R

Receive activity 63, 65
recovery 257
Recovery Point Objectives (RPO) 257
Recovery Time Objectives (RTO) 257

RepeatUntil activity 66
Reply activity 63, 65
replyOutput 71
Repository Creation Utility (RCU) 20
Request-driven interaction 178

S

SAML 237
SCA 221
scope 67
scope activity, orchestration 119-122
second Layer 7/Global Server second Layer 7/Global Server Load Balancer (L7/ GSLB/GTM) 253
secured service provider
configuring, username tokens used 239, 240
secured web service
calling, service client configured for 241, 242
Secure Socket Layer. *See* SLS
Secure Token Service 246
Security Assertion Mark-up Language. *See* SAML
security policies, OWSM
attaching, JDeveloper used 235, 236
attaching, OWSM console used 233, 234
sequence 68
server authenticated SSL 247
Service Bus
about 218, 219
functionalities 219, 220
use case 172, 173
using, for application 172
service client
configured, for calling secured web service 241, 242
Service Component Architecture (SCA) 218
Service Level Agreements (SLAs) 184, 249
Service Oriented Architecture. *See* SOA
Service Registry
installing, steps for 213
services, consuming 216, 217
services, publishing 214, 215

services
  architecture, guidelines 169, 170
  design, guidelines 169, 170
  invoking, from BPEL process 89
  Partner Link 90, 91
simple object access protocol (SOAP)
    71, 105
Single-Sign-On (SSO) 237
Site Recovery Manager (SRM) 257
SLS 247
SOA 106, 170, 177, 210
SOA composite application
  about 207
  architecture 208, 210
  components 11
SOA composite application instance state
  197
SOA composites
  testing, from EM 140, 141
  testing, from JDeveloper 142
SOA deployment
  packaging model 222
SOA environment 250
SOA extensions
  installing 17-19
SOA Infra 12, 26, 190
SOA Infrastructure. *See* SOA Infra
SOA MBeans 194
SOA Suite
  about 10, 184, 190, 202, 218, 266
  components 184
  B2B console 192, 193
  components 219
  CPU spikes 284
  domain, creating 32-37, 40
  Dynamic Monitoring Service (DMS) 192
  enterprise manager console 191
  GUIs 194
  installing 28-32
  management applications and services 12
  service components 11
  SOA infra application 190
  SOA MBeans 194
  tuning 195, 196
  WebLogic console 190

SOA Suite application, issues
  ClassNotFoundException errors 282
  FileNotFoundException 282
  Stuckthread error messages 283
  too many open files 283
SOA Suite deployment
  about 221
  Ant Scripts 223
  composite.xml file 222
  JDeveloper 223
  Oracle Enterprise Manager 223
  packaging model 222
  WebLogic Scripting Tool (WLST) 223
SOA Suite, tuning
  64-bit JVM 195
  BPEL Process Manager Threads 198
  database sessions 195
  EM Console 199
  JMS modules 199
  logging levels 198
  mediator routing rules 197
  mediator worker threads 197
  Payload validation and audit level 196
  SOA composite application instance state
    197
  transaction timeouts 195
SQL Injection 247
SSL, issues
  about 286
  certificates, expired 286
  cipher suite, missing 286
  Missing Certificate Authority (CA), in trust
    source 286
  site domain, wrong 286
stanalone registry option 212
standalone Human Task 127
strace command 279
Stuckthread error messages 283
Sun HotSpot JVM 184
switch activity, orchestration 112-115
synchronous BPEL processes
  timeout value, selecting 72, 73
  versus asynchronous BPEL processes 71
SyncMaxWaitTime parameter
  changing 94, 95
sysctl - a command 281

T

telnet {host} {port} command 280
test suite
  creating 144, 145
  inbound messages, emulating 146
  outbound messages, emulating 147, 148
  test, initiating 146
Test Web Service button 140
thread count 285
throw 69
timeout property 72, 73
TLS 247
top command 278
transaction setting 96
transaction timeouts 195
Transform activity 65
Transport Layer Security. *See* TLS
troubleshooting
  techniques 275
TTL (Time to Live) 200

U

UDDI 211
Unique Identifier (UID) 71
Universal Description, Discovery,
    and Integration. *See* UDDI
user activity 284
user activity, issues
  about 287
  server health, verifying 287-289
username tokens
  used, for configuring secured service
    provider 239, 240

V

Validate, Enrich, Transform, Routing, and
    Operate. *See* VETRO
variables, BPEL
  WSDL message type (Message Type)
    122-124
  XML schema element (Element) 122, 125
  XML schema type (Type) 122, 123

VETRO 218
vi /etc/sysctl.conf command 281
vmstat command 279

W

WAF 247
Wait activity 66
Web Application Firewall. *See* WAF
web applications
  history 7
WebGate 246
WebLogic application server(s) 255
WebLogic console 190
WebLogic Diagnostic Framework. *See*
    WLDF
WebLogic domains
  extending 159, 160
WebLogic Scripting Tool (WLST) 167, 223
WebLogic server platform 266
web server proxy plugin 252
Web server(s)
  external webserver configuration,
    advantages 253, 254
Web Service Adapter 81-83
Web Service Description Language (WSDL)
    87, 88
web services
  and client, interaction 104
Web Services Business Process Execution
    Language. *See* WSBPEL
Web Services Business Process Execution
    Language (WS-BPEL 2.0) 265
Web Services Description Language
    (WSDL) 57, 103
Web Services Flow Language (WSFL)
    104, 265
Web Services Inspection Language (WSIL)
    12, 194
Web Services Manager (WSM) 12, 194
Welcome Page 12
while 67
while activity, orchestration 112-115
WLDF 292, 293
Worklist 12, 126, 127, 194

WS-Addressing 74, 236
WS-Authorization 237
WSBPEL 10
WS-BPEL extension for people
	(BPEL4People) 265
WSDL 170
WSDL message type (Message Type)
	122-124
WSDL standard 103
WSDL XML document
	elements 103
WS-Federation 237
WS-MetadataExchange 236
WSM-PM 231
WS-Policy 237

WS-PolicyAttachment 236
WS-Privacy 237
WS-ReliableMessaging 236
WS-SecureConversation 237
WS-Security 236
WS-SecurityPolicy 236
WS-Trust 237

X

XLANG workflow standard 104
XML-based extension of Web Services
	Description Language (XLANG) 265
XML schema element (Element) 122, 125
XML schema type (Type) 122, 123
Xpath Expression Builder 115

[PACKT] enterprise

PUBLISHING

professional expertise distilled

Thank you for buying
Oracle SOA BPEL Process Manager 11gR1 –
A Hands-on Tutorial

About Packt Publishing

Packt, pronounced 'packed', published its first book "Mastering phpMyAdmin for Effective MySQL Management" in April 2004 and subsequently continued to specialize in publishing highly focused books on specific technologies and solutions.

Our books and publications share the experiences of your fellow IT professionals in adapting and customizing today's systems, applications, and frameworks. Our solution based books give you the knowledge and power to customize the software and technologies you're using to get the job done. Packt books are more specific and less general than the IT books you have seen in the past. Our unique business model allows us to bring you more focused information, giving you more of what you need to know, and less of what you don't.

Packt is a modern, yet unique publishing company, which focuses on producing quality, cutting-edge books for communities of developers, administrators, and newbies alike. For more information, please visit our website: www.packtpub.com.

About Packt Enterprise

In 2010, Packt launched two new brands, Packt Enterprise and Packt Open Source, in order to continue its focus on specialization. This book is part of the Packt Enterprise brand, home to books published on enterprise software – software created by major vendors, including (but not limited to) IBM, Microsoft and Oracle, often for use in other corporations. Its titles will offer information relevant to a range of users of this software, including administrators, developers, architects, and end users.

Writing for Packt

We welcome all inquiries from people who are interested in authoring. Book proposals should be sent to author@packtpub.com. If your book idea is still at an early stage and you would like to discuss it first before writing a formal book proposal, contact us; one of our commissioning editors will get in touch with you.

We're not just looking for published authors; if you have strong technical skills but no writing experience, our experienced editors can help you develop a writing career, or simply get some additional reward for your expertise.

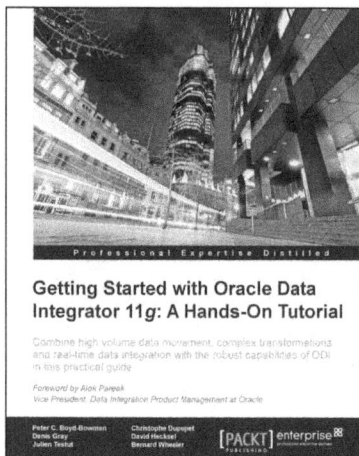

Getting Started with Oracle Data Integrator 11g: A Hands-On Tutorial

ISBN: 978-1-84968-068-4   Paperback: 384 pages

Combine high volume data movement, complex transformations and real-life data integration with the robust capabilities of ODI in this practical guide

1. Discover the comprehensive and sophisticated orchestration of data integration tasks made possible with ODI, including monitoring and error-management

2. Get to grips with the product architecture and building data integration processes with technologies including Oracle, Microsoft SQL Server and XML files

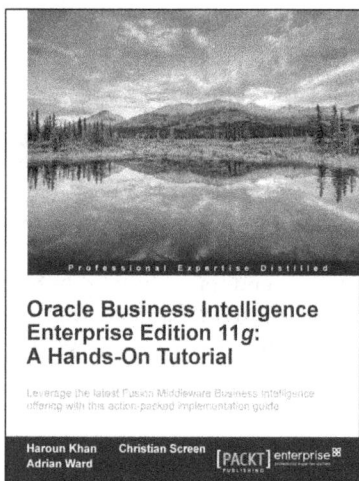

Oracle Business Intelligence Enterprise Edition 11g: A Hands-On Tutorial

ISBN: 978-1-84968-566-5   Paperback: 620 pages

Leverage the latest Fusion Middleware Business Intelligence offering with this action-packed implementation guide

1. Get to grips with the OBIEE 11g suite for analyzing and reporting on your business data

2. Immerse yourself in BI upgrading techniques, using Agents and the Action Framework and much more

3. A practical, from the coalface tutorial, bursting with step by step instructions and real world case studies to help you implement the suite's powerful analytic capabilities

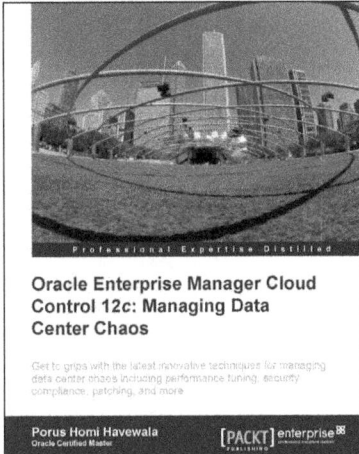

Oracle Enterprise Manager Cloud Control 12c: Managing Data Center Chaos

ISBN: 978-1-84968-478-1   Paperback: 394 pages

Get to grips with the latest innovative techniques for managing data center chaos including performance tuning, security compliance, patching, and more

1. Learn about the tremendous capabilities of the latest powerhouse version of Oracle Enterprise Manager 12c Cloud Control

2. Take a deep dive into crucial topics including Provisioning and Patch Automation, Performance Management and Exadata Database Machine Management

3. Take advantage of the author's experience as an Oracle Certified Master in this real world guide including enterprise examples and case studies

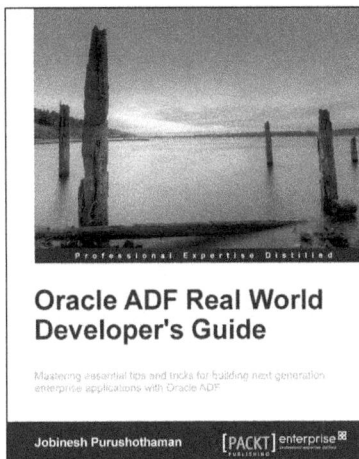

Oracle ADF Real World Developer's Guide

ISBN: 978-1-84968-482-8   Paperback: 590 pages

Mastering essential tips and tricks for building next generation enterprise applications with Oracle ADF

1. Full of illustrations, diagrams, and tips with clear step-by-step instructions and real-time examples

2. Get to know the visual and declarative programming model offered by ADF

3. In depth coverage of ADF business components and ADF binding layer

Please check **www.PacktPub.com** for information on our titles

www.ingramcontent.com/pod-product-compliance
Lightning Source LLC
Chambersburg PA
CBHW080924220326

41598CB00034B/5672